Unesco: education thesaurus

Fourth revised edition

A list of terms
for indexing and retrieving
documents and data
in the field of education —
with French and Spanish equivalents

Ministry of Education, Ontario
Information Centre, 13th Floor,
Mowat Block, Queen's Park,
Toronto, Ont. M7A 1L2

IBEdata Unesco 1984

Published in 1984 by
the United Nations Educational,
Scientific and Cultural Organization
7 Place de Fontenoy, 75700 Paris (France)

ISBN 92-3-102061-7

Printed in Switzerland by Presses Centrales S.A., Lausanne

© Unesco 1984

Preface

This new edition of the *Unesco:IBE education thesaurus* has undergone a major revision as a result of the experience gained by the Documentation Centre of the IBE, as well as that of other national and international institutions which have shared with us their suggestions prompted by using the thesaurus for indexing.

A large number of changes have been introduced in order to improve the relevance of descriptors and more than 200 new descriptors have been added to broaden the number of terms in certain fields, particularly for educational research. The supplementary list of descriptors used specifically in the field of adult education has also been revised. However, some descriptors from the adult education list which are frequently used elsewhere have been incorporated into the main list.

As in the past, the IBE is extremely interested to receive the reactions of users of the *Thesaurus* since it is only through this kind of feedback that it is possible to introduce appropriate modifications. We would therefore be very grateful if you could send your comments to the following address: International Bureau of Education, Documentation and Information Unit, P.O. Box 199, 1211 Geneva 20, Switzerland.

This *Thesaurus* forms one of the IBE's data bases entitled IBETERM and is stored on computer using the CDS/ISIS programme developed by the Unesco Library, Archives and Documentation Services, which also provided the photocomposition programme used to prepare the final text.

The designations employed and the presentation of the material in this publication do not imply the expression of any opinion whatsoever on the part of the Unesco secretariat concerning the legal status of any country, territory, city or area, or of its authorities, or concerning the delimitations of its frontiers or boundaries.

Contents

Introduction *p. v*

I. General headings for fields and facets *p. 1*

II. Alphabetical array of descriptors and identifiers *p. 5*

III. Alphabetical array of adult education descriptors *p. 203*

IV. Facetted array of descriptors and identifiers *p. 216*

V. Rotated list of descriptors *p. 258*

Introduction

The *Unesco:IBE education thesaurus* is an international list of descriptors for the indexing and retrieval of documents and data in the field of education. It forms a tool for those working in Unesco programmes or in other international activities requiring a systematic approach to educational documentation and data. In particular, it is the terminology used in the development of the data bases of the International Bureau of Education (IBE) which are being built up by a decentralized process with the participation of a growing number of centres and institutions in Member States of Unesco.

The *Thesaurus* may also have an interest for national specialists - either because they wish to make use of IBE products or because they intend to develop national systems of information retrieval based on a thesaurus. In the latter case, a word of caution is needed: national needs and conditions, terminology and language, are the foundation of a programme. The present international list will need considerable adaptation, and all those working on the construction of a national thesaurus of education are invited to correspond with the IBE to exchange experiences and to seek economy and efficiency in their efforts (see address at end of Introduction).

To understand and use the *Unesco:IBE education thesaurus* one needs to be familiar with the way it is designed. These introductory notes explain the underlying principles and the contents of the *Thesaurus* with the intention of increasing its usefulness.

The Thesaurus as an international list

Basically, the *Thesaurus* is a list of terms selected for international use in indexing and retrieving educational information. The file of these terms is stored in a computer memory and is used to generate photo-composed text for books such as the present one.

The terms are stored in English, French and Spanish forms, these being the three languages that are currently used for preparing input to the IBE data bases. The computer programme assumes a one-to-one relationship between terms in the three languages; somewhat an over-simplification of actual usage. To cite a case: in English the terms 'safety' and 'security' represent concepts that are clearly needed in educational indexing; in French or Spanish a single word, *sécurité* or *seguridad*, would suffice to cover the two concepts but, to maintain the one-to-one rule, the French list has to adopt *sécurité* in the first case, *sentiment de sécurité* in the second, and Spanish follows suit. Much more complex situations occur with the basic terms for education and educational establishments, giving rise to a series of tripartite negotiations.

From these remarks, it will be clear that the *Thesaurus* is in no sense a tool for translators. Even at the grammatical level, the English list places common nouns consistently in the plural, whereas the editors of the other two language lists have preferred the singular.

To define the *Thesaurus* in negative terms, by exclusion, the point should be made that (like others of its kind) it is neither a dictionary nor a classification scheme. Dictionaries and glossaries record standard usage of words and terms, and so they have to be rooted in national practice. A first systematic step towards preparing multilingual glossaries of education has been taken by the IBE with the publication of the *Terminology of special education,* followed by a *Terminology of adult education, Terminology of technical and vocational education, Terminology of science and technologie education* et *Glossary of educational technology terms.* This is a distinctly different approach from a thesaurus. Again, librarians have at their disposal a range of classification schemes for cataloguing and holding their materials. A thesaurus makes possible an additional device, that of indexing by keywords, but it does not attempt to align itself with any existing scheme of classification.

To conclude, then, this thesaurus should be seen as a list of English-French-Spanish terms used for indexing at the international level. It is an authorized list in which the choice of terms and the meanings ascribed to them have something of an arbitrary character, since usage in any particular country cannot be taken as a standard or a final court of appeal. The authority of the thesaurus derives from international programmes in education, exemplified by Unesco and other international organizations and by the professional work of comparative educators.

Relationships

As national centres for educational information develop systems for handling documentation and data by computer, they have perforce to create thesauri - in the national language - for use by educators in the country. The first of these to emerge was the ERIC system in the United States, the thesaurus being used to index the abstracts prepared for the *Research in education* file and, later, the *Current index to journals of education.* Since then, a number of countries in Europe and in Latin America have set about preparing thesauri. Developments are reported from several countries where the volume of literature justifies machine treatment or where (as in Scandinavia) several neighbouring countries can pool their resources.

Activity and interest in the countries of Western Europe led the Council of Europe to set up its EUDISED projet in 1969 (European Documentation and Information System for Education); and in 1972-73 preparatory work was carried out on the *EUDISED thesaurus,* issued in 1974. This regional project represents a concordance between descriptor lists made up independently in France, the Federal Republic of Germany and the United Kingdom. The EUDISED list now exists in Danish, Dutch, English, French, German, Greek, Italian, Portuguese and Spanish. The *EUDISED thesaurus* has been used since 1975 to prepare experimental multinational bibliographies in three areas: research and development; educational periodicals; and audiovisual aids.

There are obvious differences in the approaches used by the Council of Europe and the IBE: the former starts from equality among several national languages, in the expectation that indexing may be done economically both for national and for international purposes; the IBE list takes the 'international' languages - English, French and Spanish - and attempts to provide a culture-free set of terms for international exchange purposes.

No doubt progress in the creation of data bases - and in the extent of computer memory that can be used for education - will bring with it some form of reconciliation between these two approaches. In particular, the IBE has an interest in attempting to make a concordance with each national thesaurus as it emerges. This amounts to a term-by-term scrutiny so that relationships may be established, and so that every term in a national thesaurus may be 'translated' into an IBE term. Such devices will permit computerized indexes to be fed into a single data base.

Coverage

The *Unesco:IBE education thesaurus* attempts to cover the field of 'education and training' with a sufficient number of terms to index documents that are considered to have international interest. Like all thesauri, this one contains built-in biases. Since international programmes involve governments and are directed to operational projects, the international descriptor list will tend to be richer in terms from the policy/administration/organization sectors, poorer in terms from the research/learning/instruction sectors. National thesauri may be biased in the other direction.

This distinction is of course simply the result of defining different target groups of users for an information system. The original ERIC system was addressed to a wide audience but, by definition, was restricted to research reports. Since then the categories of document have been expanded, with an effect on the selection of terms for the *ERIC thesaurus*. Again, the *EUDISED thesaurus* began from an academic and research base but, as products were created experimentally, they were supposed to interest policy makers and administrators as well as research workers and practising teachers.

In other words, it seems inevitable that any information system in education must broaden its coverage (of documents) to meet the needs of the widest possible group of users.

This has certainly been the case with the *Unesco:IBE education thesaurus* and the associated data bases of the IBE. Any definition of an 'international' user group which restricts the sense of 'education and training' soon runs into the problem of distinguishing the general from the specialized. Thus, international programmes are concerned with educational policies, plans and programmes, but they also involve architects, curriculum specialists and educators dealing with handicapped children, to name but three groups each of which has need of specialized terms (or gives particular meanings to general terms). Hence the thesaurus is obliged to sample all aspects of the education system. But within the limits imposed on the thesaurus as a whole, it is impossible to accommodate the entire range of specialized terminology. Hence the thesaurus must be conceived as a core list on which specialized lists can be based.

The IBE has entered a special list of terms relating to adult education in the computer file. At the same time, all the terms in the thesaurus which may be of use to adult educators (roughly half the total) have been identified. This device will permit the printing of a special adult education list with photocopies provided to interested centres. Adult education indexers and documentalists will then be invited to use a two-tiered method of indexing, at both general and specialized levels. By such a means, other educators not specialized in adult education will be able to benefit from the analytical work of the specialists.

This arrangement has made it possible to keep this education thesaurus at a reasonable size, while building up sets of more specialized lists in what may be termed 'nesting' thesauri.

Fields

The descriptors in the thesaurus are placed in seven broad groups which are termed fields. But it should be noted that the fields overlap and inter-penetrate each other and cannot be sharply defined or delimited. Perhaps a diagram may make these aspects clearer (see Figure 1). Use of the thesaurus requires an understanding of the approach followed in this first stage of classification.

FIGURE 1. The relationship of fields

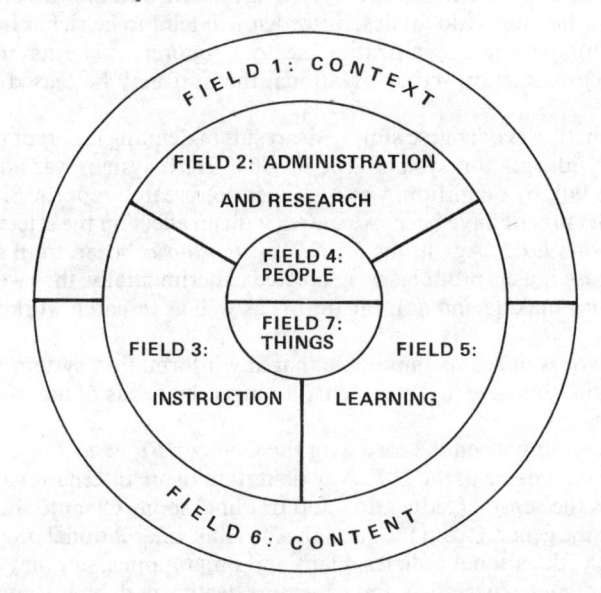

```
         FIELD 1: CONTEXT
      FIELD 2: ADMINISTRATION
           AND RESEARCH
              FIELD 4:
              PEOPLE
              FIELD 7:
   FIELD 3:   THINGS    FIELD 5:
   INSTRUCTION          LEARNING
         FIELD 6: CONTENT
```

The description of education in an international or comparative setting starts from the context in which the system or process of education is placed. One can then identify the framework of the education system, by reference to administrative or research processes. Next in line comes the instructional process - the organization of education. This leads to the group of terms relating to people. The reciprocal process to instruction is that of growing and learning, which forms a fifth group. The content of education, with curricular expressions of it, makes the next group. And finally, there are the terms used for things. An eighth field providing identifiers of place and time lies outside this context and is described in detail under the sub-heading 'Identifiers'.

From this cursory view, a more detailed account of these seven fields may be developed.

Field 1: Context. Education is essentially determined by the society in which it is located. This context can be described in terms of political, social, cultural or economic situations in each country. The main concepts are 'goals' and 'policies'. International practices require the inclusion of some specific terms, but do not form a separate part. Finally, a section of broad educational terms must be added.

Field 2: Administration and research. This field covers the principles of educational administration and planning, and the processes involved (agents, functions, relationships). The field should be responsive to the needs of indexing official regulations, as well as descriptions and studies of administrative organization and planning. The decision has been taken to place educational research, at least in regard to the basic descriptors for research procedures, in this second field.

Field 3: Teaching. The organization of the system of education is to be understood broadly to cover formal schooling and the different aspects of less formal education and training. The field includes terms for indexing the institutions concerned, their organization and the development of curricula. The centre of the field is occupied by teaching and training methods, counselling and certification. While it extends to various instructional programmes, the field stops short of the content of education which is consigned to the sixth field.

Field 4: People. In a sense a projection of the fields around it, this set of terms is designed to hold descriptors for classes of people when these are the subject matter of a document being indexed. To avoid indefinite expansion, the list concentrates on students and teachers.

Field 5: Growing and learning. The focus here is on individual development. The terms for growth lead on to biological and psychological ways of looking at learning, child development and maturation. Inevitably, reference is needed also to the process of socialization and thus to the relationships into which the individual enters.

Field 6: Content. Clearly the content of education is as wide as human knowledge and activity; the nature of the thesaurus must be recalled in order to provide certain limits. In the first part are placed those terms which are needed for indexing the subject-matter of education in the formal setting - essentially primary and secondary schools. For the content of higher education and adult education the choice has to be more limited. Then, in the second part, come curricular terms.

Field 7: Things. As with some of the earlier fields, the focus is on the objects and equipment used in education.

Facets

While the fields described above provide a general approach to the construction and development of the thesaurus, they are too broad to serve as working tools. The terms of each field are therefore placed in facets, i.e. small groups of terms which cover related concepts. This classification device is intended to aid indexers and searchers, and it should make the task of revising the thesaurus easier. While a certain logical or systematic order is following in presenting facets, it is desirable that the facets themselves remain flexible, so that sub-divisions may be created or fused as the need arises.

Part I of the thesaurus is a list of the eight fields (numbered respectively from 100 to 800), with the facets of each. The subject-headings provided for facets must be regarded as approximate; the full definition of each group being the sum total of the concepts covered by the terms it contains. The second and third digits give a ready serial numbering of the facets.

As a rule of thumb, facets within a given field are mutually exclusive. Upon analysis of the concept, or of the meaning of a term, there should be no doubt about its placement. It may be observed, however, that the same clarity does not hold between facets in different fields. The political content of 'legislation' occurs in field 1, and the term recurs in field 2, where educational legislation is an aspect of administration and control. The various connotations of 'health' will be found in several fields.

Descriptors

The main element of the thesaurus is the descriptor, i.e. the term or terms used for indexing and searching. To facilitate usage, each descriptor is accompanied by additional information. A short explanation of the structure may be helpful at this point.

Part II of the thesaurus is a complete list of the descriptors in alphabetical order. As stated earlier, the thesaurus exists in three parallel versions — English, French and Spanish; for the English version, each descriptor is followed immediately by its French and Spanish equivalents.

Next follow cross-references. In order to take account of synonyms or near-synonyms currently used, the thesaurus follows the USE and UF (= used for) device. Common terms which the indexer or searcher may first think of, but which have not been chosen for use in this thesaurus, are also listed. The statement: 'USE' — serves to send the user to the accepted thesaurus term. An example is the term 'elementary schools', which is followed by: 'USE primary schools'. Reciprocally, at 'primary schools' the thesaurus will show: 'UF elementary schools'. Because English, French and Spanish usage varies here, the cross-referencing is unique for each language.

The SN (scope note) is the next element. As a rule SNs are given in a thesaurus only to avoid ambiguities. But in an international list of terms, with more arbitrary decisions, the SN has a larger role: it serves to explain the scope of a term as well as to delimit it. These notes are not dictionary definitions so much as brief descriptions of the sense or senses in which terms should be used.

In cases where a descriptor is felt to be too general, the SN will show an asterisk. This is a danger signal meaning: 'Use a more precise term if you can'. Where the indexer cannot find a suitable descriptor, he will of course revert to the general term despite the asterisk. But, as records accumulate, the device will permit the IBE to identify how often, and on what occasions, the general terms have been used.

Finally come the hierarchic relationships: BT (broader terms), NT (narrower terms) and RT (related terms). The BT—NT relationships are set out with a practical purpose in mind — to make the user's task easier. Hence, not all relationships between concepts covered by the thesaurus are treated to the same extent of detail.

In particular, when descriptors are alphabetically close together, it is assumed that the user will establish relationships of his own accord.

The RT relationship is to a great extent covered by the serial number of the facet in which the term is placed. Then, if necessary, descriptors in other facets or even other fields may be listed. Because of the lack of mutual exclusiveness between fields, the RT reference may give two facet numbers, in which case the first is the more important.

Part III is a list of descriptors concerning adult education presented in alphabetical order. This list was prepared by specialists of adult education. The contents do not form part of the main thesaurus, but were considered essential for indexing documents in that discipline. Descriptors in this list also appear in the faceted display (Part IV) preceded by the capital letter 'A'.

The fourth part of the thesaurus simply sets out all terms by facet in English. Since the main alphabetical display gives the full information on each descriptor, there is no need to repeat scope notes, references and so on.

The fifth display is a rotated list of descriptors, printed in the form of key-words out of context. By this arrangement, each of the essential words in a descriptor-term is placed in alphabetical order so as to bring together the various occurrences of a given word, whether it be at the beginning, middle or end of a descriptor.

Identifiers

In addition to descriptors, the thesaurus also contains identifiers. They are placed in field 8, and will be found set out alphabetically in the second display as well as arranged by group at the end of the faceted display (Part IV).

Identifiers (in the 800 series) are for the most part proper nouns — the names of places, institutions, functions — but some are given in adjectival form. Identifiers are self-evident terms which do not need the cross-referencing or structured approach used with descriptors. They are constants rather than variables. Scope notes are used only to explain acronyms.

Experience has shown the need to avoid undisciplined growth in the terminology. Accordingly, some effort has been made to display the identifiers in coherent groups. Geographical locations (continents, regions, countres) form the first set; then come a few terms for time (or historical location); finally there are the names of organizations and institutions (United Nations agencies, sections of Unesco, other intergovernmental bodies, international non-governmental organizations, national bodies, etc.).

Terminological choices

In constructing an international list of terms, a number of choices must be made — on the selection of terms, on the meanings that are to be attached to them. While reasonable care should be taken to respect national usage, the thesaurus must be based on some arbitrary choices: the selection of one term from a number of synonyms; or else, the parallel use of several near-synonyms. What is important is to ensure consistency and to enable users fully to understand the meaning ascribed to each term.

To facilitate use of the thesaurus, some of the basic decisions underlying the list are given below. These remarks apply only to the English language version.

Education. The thesaurus is about 'education', a term which is too broad to be of any use in indexing and has to be qualified in many ways. A distinction is made between formal (i.e. institutionalized) education and training, informal education (individual, not organized) and non-formal education (organized but not completely institutionalized). The thesaurus is richest in respect of terms for formal education, but the present edition reflects a serious effort to meet the needs of adult education.

Levels and forms of education are expressed in the following way: pre-primary, primary, secondary, higher and adult education. Various concepts arising from considerations of unified schooling and continuing education cut across these levels.

Goals, aims and objectives. These three words, each qualified by 'educational', are retained as central concepts. *Goals* are seen as societal, expressing the values of a particular country, setting directions for the education system as a whole. *Aims* are more limited. They apply to some part of the education system and are usually expressed by the people directly concerned with the system. *Objectives* are taken to cover the intended or expected results of the process of education and training. Although common English usage does not make such sharp distinctions, there do appear to be three successive concepts for which the three terms may well be used. As such, they form the basis of the first three fields of the thesaurus.

Democratization of education. A whole set of closely related terms exist, many of them near-synonyms. The terms retained for the thesaurus may perhaps be best shown diagramatically as in Figure 2.

FIGURE 2. The relationship of synonyms for 'democratization of education'.

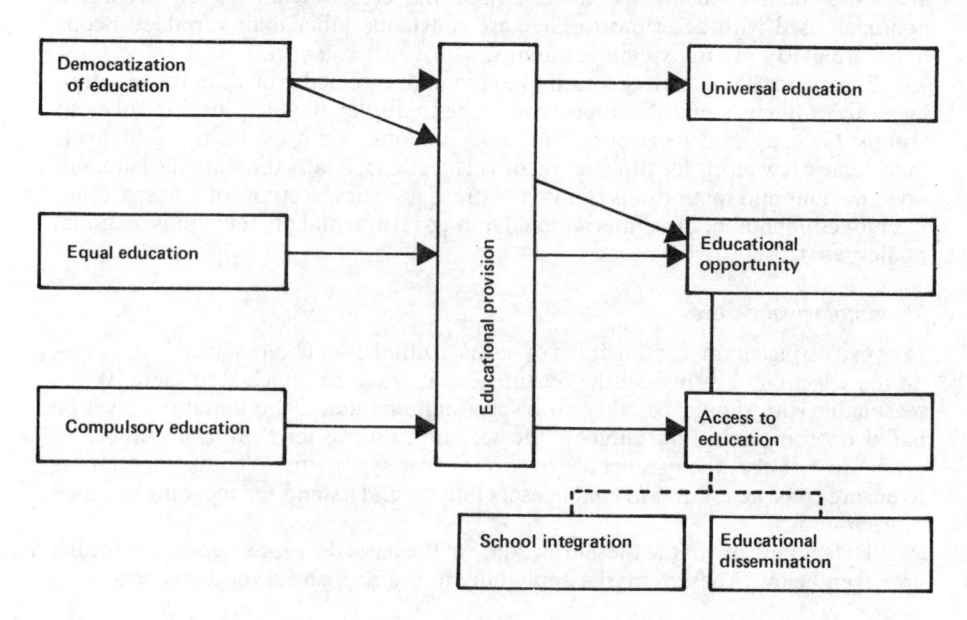

The selection of terms, as well as their connotations, tend to reflect a policy, or an administrative rather than an individual standpoint. Thus, 'universal education' is taken as the achievement in the system of the individual right to education; just as 'equal education' is used for the term 'equality of opportunity'.

Geographical range of agencies and organizations. The three terms 'agencies', 'organizations' and 'institutions' are given distinct meanings: the first is applied to official or governmental bodies; 'organization' refers to voluntary or non-governmental bodies; and 'institution' is taken in the sociological sense (e.g. church, family) as well as in the applied sense of a given centre for education or research. At the geographical level, the retained terms are: 'international', 'regional' (covering several countries), 'national', 'provincial' ('national regional' is used for cases where a region is treated as part of a country), 'local' and 'community'.

Teaching, instruction and training. Again common usage tends to confuse these terms, and the thesaurus does not at present distinguish between them, i.e. usage rather than philology is followed. The term 'instruction' (and its adjective) has been preferred as a more general concept, embracing both teaching and training.

Schools, colleges and universities. The word 'school', qualified in many ways, is used generally for educational institutions below the higher level, and 'college' is given a similar role at the higher level. Only exceptionally does the thesaurus give 'university'.

Pupils and students. Despite distinctions in national usage, the preferred term in the thesaurus is 'students', which is taken to cover all age-groups of learners.

Guidance and counselling. Commonly linked, the two terms are distinguished in the thesaurus. Guidance is given a more general, administrative significance (as in 'guidance aims', 'guidance services'), whereas counselling relates to the act or processes. The former concept is thus placed in field 2 and the latter in field 3.

Programmes. This all-purpose word is applied to many distinct concepts. No attempt has been made in the thesaurus to sort these out by adopting separate terms. In a general view:

FIELD 1: Plan of activities at the broadest contextual level, for example:
    international programmes
    regional programmes
    government programmes
    community programmes

FIELD 2: Similar plan of activities, but with the connotation of educational administration, along with the component term 'projects', for example:

    educational programmes
    provincial programmes
    construction programmes
    exchange programmes
    school meal programmes

FIELD 3: Organized plans of teaching and learning activities where the emphasis is on the process, along with the term 'curriculum', for example:

>   instructional programmes
>   adult education programmes
>   college programmes
>   youth programmes

FIELD 6: Organized plans of teaching and learning activities where content predominates, for example:

>   language programmes
>   reading programmes
>   science programmes
>   work experience programmes

FIELD 7: The word is also used for products used in the teaching-learning process, so that some terms are placed here:

>   audiovisual programmes
>   computer programmes

Linguistic choices

The English version of the thesaurus is composed largely of common nouns. Whenever possible, these are used in the plural form; the singular is reserved for specific processes, properties or conditions. According to this distinction, a number of doublets occur: culture/cultures; language/languages; and so on, for the purpose of describing distinct concepts.

Multi-word terms are used, however, whenever single-word terms are too general for indexing or search purposes. The introduction of adjectives to qualify and make the single-word term more precise is a characteristic feature of thesaurus construction. For technical reasons hyphens are avoided and a certain unfamiliar appearance may result. At times the components are joined, as in 'nonformal'; at others they are left apart, as in 'out of school'.

Another type of multi-word term consists of the binding of two existing words (e.g. 'teachers' and 'students') to represent a different concept ('student teachers'). Bound terms of this nature should cause no difficulty.

In a few cases, parenthetical qualifiers are placed after terms. These qualifiers are a means of fixing the sense of a term when several quite different concepts are usually covered by the term, i.e. it is a homograph. An example is: 'degrees (titles)'.

The English participle, with the value of a noun, is a special case. The Barhydt-Schmidt Thesaurus (see Bibliography) has an interesting facet - No. 2, Activities - which places the emphasis on verbal forms. The *Unesco:IBE education thesaurus* is based on nouns in the belief that it is not practicable to dwell on formal grammatical differences when indexing. However, the present participle lies ready to hand, serving as a noun for the description of an activity or process. In the thesaurus a number of terms are given in this form: 'budgeting' and 'budgets' appear as a doublet, for example.

In orthography, the thesaurus adopts British English usage, with the *Oxford English dictionary* as a final authority. This rule is designed to ensure conformity with Unesco editorial practice.

With the exception of the scope notes, punctuation is reduced to a minimum; no apostrophes or hyphens are employed. Parentheses occur in the few cases where qualifiers are felt to be indispensable.

Use and revision of the thesaurus

As a rule, users of the thesaurus will start from the alphabetical list of descriptors; having located suitable terms for the purpose in hand - indexing or searching - they will then use the RT facet number and turn to the group of related terms in the faceted display to see whether additional or better terms can be found. Additional help, either at the start of a search for a term or during the checking process, may be obtained from the rotated list in the final display.

It is essential that indexers employ the most precise term they can find, and use general terms sparingly.

There is need to bear in mind also the possibility of indexing with specificity by linking descriptors (100 to 700) and identifiers (800). In a sense the distinction made in the thesaurus between descriptors and identifiers rests on a linguistic basis. Descriptors cover concepts in education and provide common or abstract nouns for describing such concepts; to varying degrees these nouns become more specific by the addition of objectives or participles. On the other hand, identifiers are constants rather than variables. In many cases an identifier term will be used to index the content of a document in much the same way as a descriptor term. However, identifiers can also take an adjectival as well as a nominal quality. Some examples may demonstrate the point.

(a) The first group of identifiers covers geographical location. Over 200 terms are set out as names of continents, regions and countries. Any of these can be linked to the descriptor 'national language' (or 'history' or 'geography'), thereby obviating the need for additional descriptors. Thus 'national language' and 'national literature' are given in field 6, 'Japan' in the identifiers, but the terms 'Japanese' or 'Japanese language' or 'Japanese literature' are not needed since the concepts can be covered by consecutive co-ordination - 'national language of Japan' - and so on.

(b) The second set of identifiers, much smaller, provides for time-location. Again, in a noun sense a period - 'Middle ages' - may be used alone, but more often the terms will be placed alongside a descriptor.

As stated at the outset, the *Unesco:IBE education thesaurus* has been designed to serve in the data bases built up by the IBE. These are currently stored at the International Computing Centre in Geneva. The main file, coded 'IBEDOC', consists of documents indexed according to the CDS/ISIS programme developed by Unesco. The bibliographical reference is followed by relevant descriptors which may or may not be accompanied by an abstract, depending on the function of the document added to IBEDOC.

In building up the IBEDOC file, the IBE works closely with other Unesco units and interested international institutions. At present, two other centres regularly prepare inputs; the Unesco Institute for Education, Hamburg (literature on lifelong education; and the Université Laval, Canada (educational technology). The Unesco regional offices for education also participate.

The IBE is also developing other data bases to hold information on centres and institutions. These files are still of modest size; but they too hold records which are indexed by means of the thesaurus.

It is important that users bear in mind the fact that the development of a thesaurus is a continuous and organic process. Once issued and put into operation, the list must change to reflect changes in the concepts and vocabulary of the field it is designed to cover. This is a process in which all users participate. Interested centres are invited to correspond with the IBE (Case postale 199, 1211 Geneva 20, Switzerland) on any aspect of the thesaurus and its use. Possible transactions are:
— comments on the thesaurus, with proposals for strengthening it as a tool for indexing and retrieving information;
— indication of work on a national thesaurus, in which case provision by the IBE of the magnetic tape record of the thesaurus might be a useful service;
— desire to use the IBE data bases, where centres have access to a computer, in which case the IBE could make available the magnetic tape record of IBE-DOC.

BIBLIOGRAPHY

Bakewell, K.G.B. The Unesco: IBE education thesaurus (second edition); a description and assessment. *Education libraries bulletin* (London), vol. 19, Summer 1976, p. 9-19.

Barhydt, G.C.; Schmidt, C.T. *Information retrieval thesaurus of education terms.* Cleveland, Ohio, Press of Case Western Reserve University, 1968, 133 p.

Conseil de l'Europe. Centre de documentation pour l'éducation en Europe. *Thesaurus EUDISED multilingue pour le traitement de l'information en éducation.* La Haye/Paris, Mouton, 1973. 381 p. (Also in Dutch, English, German, Spanish)

Iljon, A. *Concordance et compatibilité de deux thesauri en pédagogie: le thesaurus monolingue allemand du DOPAED (Thesaurus Pädagogik) et le thesaurus multilingue EUDISED.* Berlin, Pädagogisches Zentrum, 1974. 218 p.

International Labour Office. *ILO Thesaurus/Thesaurus BIT/Tesauro OIT.* Geneva, 1978. 223 p.

Instituto Colombiano para el Fomento de la Educación Superior. Centro de Documentación. *Thesaurus Colombiano de Educación.* Versión preliminar. Bogotá, el Instituto, 1977. 316 p.

Macrothesaurus: a basic list of economic and social development terms. Paris, Organisation for Economic Co-operation and Development, 1972. 225 p. (Also in French).

Macrothesaurus for information processing in the field of economic and social development. New English edition. Paris, OECD, 1978. 438 p.

Educational Resources Information Center. *Thesaurus of ERIC descriptors.* 9th ed. Phoenix, Arizona, Oryx Press, 1982. 569 p.

UNISIST. *Guidelines for the establishment and development of monolingual thesauri.* Revised version. Paris, Unesco, 1973. 37 p.

I. General headings for fields and facets

FIELD 1: CONTEXT

100 ABSTRACT IDEAS
101 POLICIES
102 POLITICAL STRUCTURE
103 CENTRAL AGENCIES
104 INTERMEDIATE, LOCAL AGENCIES
105 AGENCY ROLE, RELATIONSHIP
106 AID
107 SERVICES
108 PLANNING
109 PROGRAMMES
110 ORGANIZATIONS
120 SOCIETY
121 DIVISIONS
122 COMMUNITY
123 ETHNIC DISTRIBUTION
124 DEMOGRAPHY
125 INSTITUTIONS
126 FAMILY
130 CULTURE
131 LANGUAGE
140 RESEARCH AND TECHNOLOGY
145 COMMUNICATIONS
150 ECONOMY
151 DEVELOPMENT
152 FINANCIAL
153 LABOUR
154 EMPLOYMENT
155 OCCUPATIONS
160 HEALTH
161 DISEASES
170 LEGAL TERMS
180 BROAD EDUCATIONAL CONCEPTS
181 NARROWER EDUCATIONAL CONCEPTS
182 EDUCATIONAL POLICIES
183 EDUCATION BY TYPE
184 EDUCATION BY FORM
185 LEVELS OF EDUCATION
186 EDUCATION BY GROUP, LOCALITY
187 EDUCATION BY AGENTS
188 EDUCATION BY IDEOLOGY

FIELD 2: ADMINISTRATION

200 ADMINISTRATIVE POLICIES
201 MANAGEMENT
202 RECORD KEEPING
203 SURVEYS
204 INFORMATION DISSEMINATION
205 EDUCATIONAL PLANNING
206 STUDENT ACCOUNTING
207 TEACHER ACCOUNTING
208 SCHOOL ACCOUNTING
210 SUPERVISION
211 GUIDANCE
212 TEACHER EVALUATION
213 CURRICULUM EVALUATION
220 PERSONNEL ADMINISTRATION
221 RECRUITMENT
222 TENURE
223 TEACHER EMPLOYMENT
230 LEGISLATION
231 RESPONSIBILITY
232 STANDARDS
233 SANCTIONS
240 REVENUE
241 EXPENDITURE
242 SALARIES
243 ACCOUNTING AND BUDGETING
250 PHYSICAL FACILITIES PLANNING
251 FACILITIES MANAGEMENT
252 FACILITIES DESIGN
253 CONSTRUCTION PROGRAMMES

260 SCHOOL SYSTEMS
261 ADMINISTRATIVE ORGANIZATION
262 ROLES AND RELATIONSHIPS
263 LOCAL RELATIONSHIPS
264 SCHOOL DISTRICTS
265 SCHOOL ADMINISTRATION
266 STUDENT PROGRESS
267 DISCIPLINE
270 SCHOOL SERVICES
271 EDUCATIONAL PROGRAMMES
272 SPECIFIC PROGRAMMES AND PROJECTS
280 FIELD OF RESEARCH
281 PROBLEMS
282 TYPE OF RESEARCH
283 RESEARCH METHODOLOGY
284 DATA
285 VARIABLES

FIELD 3: TEACHING

300 EDUCATIONAL OBJECTIVES
301 SCHOOLS — BY LEVEL
302 SCHOOLS — BY ADMINISTRATION
303 SCHOOLS — BY ORGANIZING PRINCIPLE
304 SCHOOLS — SPECIAL
305 SCHOOLS — EXPERIMENTAL
306 SCHOOLS — BY CURRICULUM
307 COLLEGES
310 OTHER INSTITUTIONS
311 CENTRES
312 RESEARCH CENTRES
313 CLINICS
320 INSTRUCTIONAL PROGRAMMES
321 ADULT PROGRAMMES
322 SPECIAL PROGRAMMES
330 CURRICULUM
331 CURRICULUM DEVELOPMENT
332 CURRICULUM TYPE
333 COURSES
334 SHORT COURSES
335 INDIVIDUAL STUDY
340 SCHOOL ORGANIZATION
341 GROUPING
342 GRADE ORGANIZATION
343 CLASSES
344 SCHOOL CALENDARS
350 TEACHING
351 TRAINING
352 INSTRUCTION
355 EDUCATIONAL METHODS
356 CLASSROOM TECHNIQUES
357 ACTIVITIES
360 EDUCATIONAL MEDIA
361 PROGRAMMED INSTRUCTION
370 COUNSELLING
371 COUNSELLING — SPECIFIC GROUPS
372 IDENTIFICATION
373 THERAPY
374 SPECIAL METHODS
380 EDUCATIONAL ENVIRONMENT
381 EXTRACURRICULAR
382 EXTENSION EDUCATION
390 CERTIFICATION
391 TESTING
392 TESTS — GENERAL
393 EDUCATIONAL TESTS
394 PSYCHOLOGICAL TESTS

FIELD 4: PEOPLE

400 STAGES OF MAN
401 FAMILIES
402 DISADVANTAGED
403 HANDICAPPED
410 STUDENTS
411 SCHOOL STUDENTS
412 NONFORMAL STUDENTS
413 COLLEGE STUDENTS
414 LANGUAGE OF STUDENTS
415 ACHIEVERS
416 ABILITY OF STUDENTS
420 EDUCATIONAL PERSONNEL
421 TEACHERS
422 COLLEGE TEACHERS
423 SCHOOL PERSONNEL
424 INSTRUCTIONAL STAFF
425 SUBJECT TEACHERS
426 METHODS TEACHERS
430 CONSULTANTS
431 COUNSELLORS

432 THERAPISTS
433 HEALTH PERSONNEL
440 LEADERS
441 PERSONNEL
442 COMMITTEES
443 GROUPS
450 WORKERS COLLECTIVELY
451 CLASSES OF WORKERS
452 TECHNICIANS
460 LAW AND ORDER PROFESSIONS
461 ARTS AND PHYSICAL PROFESSIONS
462 SOCIAL PROFESSIONS
463 SCIENTIFIC PROFESSIONS
470 MIGRANTS
475 RELIGIOUS GROUPS

FIELD 5: LEARNING

500 AGE
501 SEX
502 GROWTH PATTERNS
503 PHYSIOLOGY
510 PERCEPTION
511 RESPONSE
512 LEARNING
513 LEARNING PROCESSES
514 STAGES OF LEARNING
520 ABILITY
521 THOUGHT PROCESSES
522 ABSTRACT REASONING
530 PERSONALITY DEVELOPMENT
531 MATURATION
532 SPEECH
533 BASIC SKILLS
534 SKILL DEVELOPMENT
535 ACHIEVEMENT
536 INDIVIDUAL NEEDS
537 LEARNING ACTIVITIES
540 AFFECTION
541 INTERESTS
542 HABITS
550 ENVIRONMENTAL INFLUENCES
551 ADJUSTMENT
552 ATTITUDES
553 RELATIONSHIP

554 GROUP MEMBERSHIP
555 SELF CONCEPT
560 BEHAVIOUR
561 INDIVIDUAL CHARACTERISTICS
562 EXPERIENCE
563 CAREERS
570 STATES OF HANDICAP
571 HANDICAPS
572 EMOTIONAL DISTURBANCE

FIELD 6: CONTENT

600 LIBERAL ARTS
610 FINE ARTS
615 LITERATURE
616 LITERARY GENRES
620 LANGUAGE ARTS
621 LINGUISTICS
622 GRAMMAR
625 LANGUAGE FAMILIES
626 LANGUAGES
627 LANGUAGES IN TIME
630 SCIENCES
631 MATHEMATICS
632 BIOLOGICAL SCIENCES
633 PHYSICAL SCIENCES
640 SOCIAL SCIENCES
641 HISTORY
642 BEHAVIOURAL SCIENCES
645 TECHNOLOGY
646 AGRONOMY
647 ENGINEERING
650 PROFESSIONAL
651 HEALTH
660 READING INSTRUCTION
661 READING METHODS
662 LANGUAGE INSTRUCTION
663 LANGUAGE METHODS
670 SCIENCE INSTRUCTION
671 SCIENCE METHODS
672 VOCATIONAL INSTRUCTION
673 VOCATIONAL METHODS
680 SOCIAL STUDIES
681 PROFESSIONAL EDUCATION
682 MORAL EDUCATION
683 HEALTH EDUCATION
684 AESTHETIC EDUCATION

690 TEACHER EDUCATION
691 EDUCATION COURSES

FIELD 7: THINGS

700 RESOURCES
710 CAPITAL ASSETS
711 EDUCATIONAL SPACES
712 ANCILLARY SPACES
720 PUBLICATIONS
721 DOCUMENTS
722 BOOKS
723 RECORDS
724 GUIDES
725 INSTRUCTIONAL MATERIALS
730 AUDIOVISUAL AIDS
731 AUDIOVISUAL EQUIPMENT
732 AUDIOVISUAL PROGRAMMES
733 EXHIBITS
734 SPECIAL AIDS
740 SUPPLIES
741 CLASSROOM MATERIALS
742 SCHOOL SHOPS
743 MOTOR VEHICLES
750 AGRICULTURAL SUPPLIES
751 MEDICAL SUPPLIES
760 COMPUTERS

FIELD 8: IDENTIFIERS OF PLACE AND TIME

800 CONTINENTS
801 REGIONS AND SUBREGIONS
802 AFRICA — COUNTRIES AND TERRITORIES
803 AMERICA — COUNTRIES AND TERRITORIES
804 ASIA — COUNTRIES AND TERRITORIES
805 EUROPE — COUNTRIES AND TERRITORIES
806 OCEANIA — COUNTRIES AND TERRITORIES
807 ARAB COUNTRIES
808 ATLANTIC OCEAN TERRITORIES
809 INDIAN OCEAN TERRITORIES
840 TIME LOCATION
850 UN INTERNATIONAL AGENCIES
851 UNESCO ASSOCIATED UNITS
852 OTHER INTERGOVERNMENTAL AGENCIES
853 NON GOVERNMENTAL ORGANIZATIONS
860 NATIONAL AGENCIES
880 FORM TERMS FOR DOCUMENTS

II. Alphabetical array of descriptors and identifiers

ABILITY
CAPACITE
CAPACIDAD
NT COGNITIVE ABILITY
    CREATIVE ABILITY
    INTELLIGENCE
    LANGUAGE ABILITY
    PSYCHOMOTOR SKILLS
    READING ABILITY
RT 520

ABILITY GROUPING
GROUPEMENT PAR APTITUDES
AGRUPAMIENTO POR APTITUDES
UF STREAMING
BT GROUPING PROCEDURES
RT 341

ABLE STUDENTS
BON ELEVE
ALUMNO CAPAZ
SN Relating to ability to perform at some specified level
RT 416

ABSTRACT REASONING
RAISONNEMENT ABSTRAIT
RAZONAMIENTO ABSTRACTO
UF INTELLECTUALIZATION
BT THOUGHT PROCESSES
RT 522

ABSTRACTING
ELABORATION DE RESUMES ANALYTIQUES
ELABORACION DE RESUMENES ANALITICOS
RT 202

ABSTRACTS
RESUME ANALYTIQUE
RESUMEN ANALITICO
RT 880

ABYSSINIA

May 1984

USE **ETHIOPIA**

ACADEMIC FREEDOM
LIBERTES ACADEMIQUES
LIBERTAD ACADEMICA
RT 180

ACADEMIC STANDARDS
NORME ACADEMIQUE
REQUISITOS ACADEMICOS
SN Criteria established by an educational institution to determine levels of student achievement
RT 391

ACCELERATED COURSES
COURS ACCELERE
CURSO ACELERADO
BT COURSES
RT 333

ACCELERATED PROGRAMMES
PROGRAMME ACCELERE
PROGRAMA ACELERADO
BT INSTRUCTIONAL PROGRAMMES
RT 320

ACCELERATION
SCOLARITE ACCELEREE
ESCOLARIDAD ACELERADA
SN The process of progressing through the school grades at a rate faster than that of the average child
RT 266

ACCESS TO EDUCATION
ACCES A L'EDUCATION
ACCESO A LA EDUCACION
BT EDUCATIONAL OPPORTUNITIES
RT 181

ACCIDENT PREVENTION
PREVENTION DES ACCIDENTS
PREVENCION DE ACCIDENTES
RT 673

ACCIDENTS
ACCIDENT
ACCIDENTE
RT 265

ACCOUNTABILITY
RESPONSABILITE
   CONTRACTUELLE
RESPONSABILIDAD
   CONTRACTUAL
RT 231

ACCOUNTANTS
COMPTABLE
CONTADOR
RT 460

ACCOUNTING
COMPTABILITE
CONTABILIDAD
NT SCHOOL ACCOUNTING
RT 243

ACCREDITATION (INSTITUTIONS)
AGREMENT (INSTITUTIONS)
ACREDITACION (INSTITUCIONES)
RT 210

ACCULTURATION
ACCULTURATION
ACULTURACION
SN Absorption into any group of certain features of the culture
RT 130

ACHIEVEMENT NEED
BESOIN DE REUSSITE
NECESIDAD DE EXITO
SN Psychological factor providing impetus to excel
BT PSYCHOLOGICAL NEEDS
RT 536

ACHIEVEMENT RATING
CLASSIFICATION DES
   PERFORMANCES
ESCALA DE RENDIMIENTO
SN Both the process of comparing achieved performance and the ranking assigned
RT 391

ACHIEVEMENT TESTS
TEST DE RENDEMENT
PRUEBA DE CONOCIMIENTOS
BT EDUCATIONAL TESTS
RT 393

ACOUSTICS
ACOUSTIQUE
ACUSTICA
SN Refers to noise control and sound correction in educational spaces
RT 252

ACTION PROGRAMMES (COMMUNITY)
PROGRAMME D'ACTION
   (COLLECTIVITE)
PROGRAMA DE ACCION
   (COMUNIDAD)
SN Improvement sponsored by community
BT COMMUNITY PROGRAMMES
RT 282

ACTION RESEARCH
RECHERCHE–ACTION
INVESTIGACION POR LA ACCION
RT 282

ACTIVE SCHOOLS
ECOLE ACTIVE
ESCUELA ACTIVA
RT 184

ACTIVITIES
ACTIVITE
ACTIVIDAD
NT EXTRACURRICULAR
   ACTIVITIES
   GROUP ACTIVITIES
   HEALTH ACTIVITIES

INTEGRATED ACTIVITIES
OUT OF SCHOOL ACTIVITIES
RECREATIONAL ACTIVITIES
SCHOOL ACTIVITIES
RT 357

ACTIVITY LEARNING
APPRENTISSAGE PAR L'ACTION
APRENDIZAJE MEDIANTE LA
   PRACTICA
SN Learning by doing
BT LEARNING
RT 512

ACTIVITY METHODS
METHODE ACTIVE
METODO ACTIVO
BT TEACHING METHODS
RT 355

ADJUSTMENT
ADAPTATION
ADAPTACION
SN To environment
NT EMOTIONAL ADJUSTMENT
    SOCIAL ADJUSTMENT
    STUDENT ADJUSTMENT
    VOCATIONAL ADJUSTMENT
RT 551

ADJUSTMENT PROBLEMS
PROBLEME D'ADAPTATION
PROBLEMA DE ADAPTACION
RT 551

ADMINISTRATION
ADMINISTRATION
ADMINISTRACION
NT EDUCATIONAL
    ADMINISTRATION
RT 200

ADMINISTRATIVE ORGANIZATION
ORGANISATION ADMINISTRATIVE
ORGANIZACION ADMINISTRATIVA
SN Structure and functioning of
    agencies concerned with education,
    term may be used also for a
    single agency or part of it, as
    long as main concept is that of
    organization
RT 261
    EDUCATIONAL
    ADMINISTRATION

ADMINISTRATIVE POLICIES
POLITIQUE ADMINISTRATIVE
POLITICA ADMINISTRATIVA
RT 200

ADMINISTRATIVE PRINCIPLES
PRINCIPE ADMINISTRATIF
PRINCIPIO ADMINISTRATIVO
RT 200

ADMINISTRATIVE PROBLEMS
PROBLEME ADMINISTRATIF
PROBLEMA ADMINISTRATIVO
RT 281

ADMINISTRATIVE WORKERS
EMPLOYE D'ADMINISTRATION
EMPLEADO ADMINISTRATIVO
BT EMPLOYEES
RT 451

ADMINISTRATOR RESPONSIBILITY
RESPONSABILITE DE
   L'ADMINISTRATEUR
RESPONSABILIDAD DEL
   ADMINISTRADOR
BT RESPONSIBILITY
RT 231
    ADMINISTRATOR ROLE

ADMINISTRATOR ROLE
ROLE DE L'ADMINISTRATEUR
PAPEL DEL ADMINISTRADOR
RT 262
    ADMINISTRATOR
    RESPONSIBILITY

ADMINISTRATOR SELECTION
SELECTION DES
    ADMINISTRATEURS
SELECCION DE
    ADMINISTRADORES
RT 223

ADMISSION
ADMISSION
ADMISION
RT 266

ADMISSION REQUIREMENTS
CONDITION D'ADMISSION
REQUISITOS DE INGRESO
SN Conditions (examination certificates, proof of skills, etc.) of entrance to courses of study, further study, training, etc.
RT 232

ADOLESCENCE
ADOLESCENCE
ADOLESCENCIA
RT 500

ADOLESCENTS
ADOLESCENT
ADOLESCENTE
SN In approximately 13–18 year age group
RT 400

ADOPTED CHILDREN
ENFANT ADOPTE
NIÑO ADOPTADO
BT CHILDREN
RT 401

ADOPTION OF INNOVATIONS
ADOPTION D'INNOVATIONS
ADOPCION DE INNOVACIONES
SN In general policy sense
BT EDUCATIONAL INNOVATIONS
NT REPLICATION OF INNOVATIONS
RT 200

ADULT CHARACTERISTICS
CARACTERISTIQUE DE L'ADULTE
CARACTERISTICAS DEL ADULTO
RT 561

ADULT COUNSELLING
ORIENTATION DES ADULTES
ASESORIA DE ADULTOS
BT COUNSELLING
RT 371

ADULT EDUCATION
EDUCATION DES ADULTES
EDUCACION DE ADULTOS
RT 186

ADULT EDUCATION CENTRES
CENTRE D'EDUCATION D'ADULTES
CENTRO DE EDUCACION DE ADULTOS
May 1984
SN Covers institutions providing general as well as vocational education for people who have left school
NT STUDY CENTRES
RT 311

ADULT EDUCATION PROGRAMMES
PROGRAMME D'EDUCATION DES ADULTES
PROGRAMA DE EDUCACION DE ADULTOS
RT 321

ADULT EDUCATION SYSTEMS
SYSTEME D'EDUCATION DES ADULTES
SISTEMA DE EDUCACION DE ADULTOS
RT 260

ADULT EDUCATORS
EDUCATEUR D'ADULTES
EDUCADOR DE ADULTOS
SN When specifically adjectival, as in adult educator role or shortage, use "teacher role", etc.
BT TEACHERS
RT 421

ADULT LEADERS
ANIMATEUR DE GROUPE
 D'ADULTES
ANIMADOR DE GRUPO DE
 ADULTOS
SN In context of adult education
RT 440

ADULT LEARNING
APPRENTISSAGE A L'AGE ADULTE
APRENDIZAJE DE ADULTOS
BT LEARNING
RT 514

ADULT READING PROGRAMMES
PROGRAMME DE LECTURE POUR
 ADULTES
PROGRAMA DE LECTURA PARA
 ADULTOS
BT READING PROGRAMMES
RT 660

ADULT STUDENTS
ELEVE ADULTE
ALUMNO ADULTO
RT 412

ADULTS
ADULTE
ADULTO
NT ILLITERATE ADULTS
 MEN
 WOMEN
RT 400

ADVANCED STUDENTS
ELEVE EN AVANCE
ALUMNO ADELANTADO
RT 416

ADVISORY COMMITTEES
COMITE CONSULTATIF
COMITE CONSULTIVO
BT COMMITTEES
RT 442

AESTHETIC EDUCATION
EDUCATION ESTHETIQUE
EDUCACION ESTETICA
                                May 1984
RT 684

AFARS AND ISSAS
                                May 1984
USE **DJIBOUTI**

AFFECTIVE BEHAVIOUR
COMPORTEMENT AFFECTIF
COMPORTAMIENTO AFECTIVO
BT BEHAVIOUR
NT AGGRESSION
RT 540

AFFECTIVE OBJECTIVES
OBJECTIF AFFECTIF
OBJETIVO AFECTIVO
BT EDUCATIONAL OBJECTIVES
RT 300

AFFECTIVITY
AFFECTIVITE
AFECTIVIDAD
BT PSYCHOLOGICAL NEEDS
RT 540

AFFILIATED SCHOOLS
ECOLE ANNEXE
ESCUELA AFILIADA
SN Schools providing experiences for
 student teachers or teacher interns,
 although not integral parts of
 teacher education institutions
RT 305

AFGHANISTAN
AFGHANISTAN
AFGANISTAN
BT MIDDLE EAST

AFRICA
AFRIQUE
AFRICA
NT AFRICA SOUTH OF THE
  SAHARA
 ENGLISH SPEAKING AFRICA
 FRENCH SPEAKING AFRICA

AFRICA SOUTH OF THE SAHARA

NORTH AFRICA

AFRICA SOUTH OF THE SAHARA
AFRIQUE AU SUD DU SAHARA
AFRICA AL SUR DEL SAHARA
BT   AFRICA
NT   CENTRAL AFRICA
     EAST AFRICA
     SOUTHERN AFRICA
     WEST AFRICA

AFRICAN LANGUAGES
LANGUES AFRICAINES
LENGUAS AFRICANAS
RT   625

AFRO ASIATIC LANGUAGES
LANGUES AFRO-ASIATIQUES
LENGUAS AFROASIATICAS
RT   625

AFTER SCHOOL ACTIVITIES
USE **EXTRACURRICULAR
     ACTIVITIES**

AGE
AGE
EDAD
SN   Includes physiological and mental aging processes
RT   500

AGE DIFFERENCES
DIFFERENCE D'AGE
DIFERENCIA DE EDAD
BT   INDIVIDUAL DIFFERENCES
RT   500

AGE GROUPS
GROUPE D'AGE
GRUPO DE EDAD
BT   GROUPS
RT   443

AGENCIES
ORGANISME OFFICIEL
ORGANISMO OFICIAL
SN   Official bodies or distinct parts of government structure
NT   CENTRAL EDUCATIONAL
     AGENCIES
     COMMUNITY AGENCIES
       (PUBLIC)
     INTERNATIONAL AGENCIES
     PROVINCIAL AGENCIES
     REGIONAL AGENCIES
     SOCIAL AGENCIES
     WELFARE AGENCIES
     YOUTH AGENCIES
RT   103

AGENCY ROLE
ROLE DES ORGANISMES
  OFFICIELS
PAPEL DE LOS ORGANISMOS
  OFICIALES
RT   105

AGGRESSION
AGRESSION
AGRESION
BT   AFFECTIVE BEHAVIOUR
RT   540

AGRARIAN REFORM
REFORME AGRAIRE
REFORMA AGRARIA
UF   LAND REFORM
     RURAL RESETTLEMENT
RT   151

AGREEMENTS
ACCORD
ACUERDO
SN   Arrangements for regulating an educational question concluded between the authorities within a country, with international agencies, or between two or more countries
RT   170

AGRICULTURAL COLLEGES
ECOLE SUPERIEURE
  D'AGRICULTURE
ESCUELA SUPERIOR DE
  AGRONOMIA
BT   COLLEGES
RT   307

ALGEBRA

AGRICULTURAL DEVELOPMENT
DEVELOPPEMENT AGRICOLE
DESARROLLO AGRICOLA
BT   DEVELOPMENT
RT   151

AGRICULTURAL EDUCATION
ENSEIGNEMENT AGRICOLE
ENSEÑANZA AGRICOLA
BT   VOCATIONAL EDUCATION
RT   672

AGRICULTURAL ENGINEERING
GENIE AGRICOLE
INGENIERIA AGRONOMICA
RT   646

AGRICULTURAL EXTENSION
USE **RURAL EXTENSION**

AGRICULTURAL OCCUPATIONS
METIER AGRICOLE
OCUPACION AGRICOLA
BT   OCCUPATIONS
RT   155

AGRICULTURAL PRODUCTION
PRODUCTION AGRICOLE
PRODUCCION AGRICOLA
RT   150

AGRICULTURAL SUPPLIES
FOURNITURE AGRICOLE
SUMINISTROS AGRICOLAS
BT   SUPPLIES
RT   750

AGRICULTURAL TECHNICIANS
TECHNICIEN AGRICOLE
TECNICO AGRICOLA
BT   TECHNICIANS
RT   452

AGRICULTURAL TRAINING
FORMATION AGRICOLE
FORMACION AGRICOLA
RT   673

AGRICULTURAL WORKERS
TRAVAILLEUR AGRICOLE
TRABAJADOR AGRICOLA
BT   WORKERS
RT   451

AGRICULTURE
AGRICULTURE
AGRICULTURA
NT   AGRONOMY
       ANIMAL SCIENCE
RT   646

AGRONOMY
AGRONOMIE
AGRONOMIA
SN   Application of principles of
       biological and earth sciences to
       culture and production of
       agricultural plants
BT   AGRICULTURE
RT   646

ALBANIA
ALBANIE
ALBANIA
BT   EASTERN EUROPE

ALCOHOL EDUCATION
EDUCATION ANTI-ALCOOLIQUE
EDUCACION ANTIALCOHOLICA
RT   683

ALECSO
ALECSO
ALECSO
SN   Arab League Educational, Cultural
       and Scientific Organization

ALGEBRA
ALGEBRE
ALGEBRA
BT   MATHEMATICS
RT   631

May 1984

ALGEBRAIC CONCEPTS

ALGEBRAIC CONCEPTS
CONCEPT ALGEBRIQUE
CONCEPTO ALGEBRAICO
BT   MATHEMATICAL CONCEPTS
RT   631

ALGERIA
ALGERIE
ARGELIA
BT   ARAB COUNTRIES
      MEDITERRANEAN
        COUNTRIES
      NORTH AFRICA

ALLOCATION PER STUDENT
ALLOCATION PAR ELEVE
ASIGNACION POR ALUMNO
RT   243

ALPHABETS
ALPHABET
ALFABETO
RT   620

ALTERNATIVE EDUCATION
EDUCATION ALTERNATIVE
EDUCACION ALTERNATIVA
May 1984
SN   Educational programmes that are offered as alternatives within or without the formal educational system
RT   184
      271

AMERICA
AMERIQUE
AMERICA
NT   LATIN AMERICA
      NORTH AMERICA

AMERICAN INDIAN LANGUAGES
LANGUES INDO–AMERICAINES
LENGUAS INDOAMERICANAS
RT   625

AMERICAN SAMOA
SAMOA AMERICAINES
SAMOA AMERICANA
May 1984
BT   POLYNESIA

AMETROPIA
AMETROPIE
AMETROPIA
SN   Covering all ocular refractive errors
RT   570

ANALYSIS OF VARIANCE
USE **STATISTICAL ANALYSIS**

ANALYTICAL METHOD
USE **GLOBAL METHOD**

ANATOMY
ANATOMIE
ANATOMIA
BT   BIOLOGY
RT   632

ANCIENT TIME
ANTIQUITE
ANTIGUEDAD
May 1984
RT   840

ANCILLARY SERVICES
ECONOMAT
ECONOMATO
BT   SCHOOL SERVICES
RT   270

ANCILLARY SPACES
ESPACES AUXILIAIRES
DEPENDENCIAS
RT   712

ANDORRA
ANDORRE
ANDORRA
BT   WESTERN EUROPE

ANGOLA
ANGOLA
ANGOLA
BT   SOUTHERN AFRICA

ANIMAL SCIENCE
ZOOTECHNIE
ZOOTECNIA
BT   AGRICULTURE
RT   646

ANNOTATED BIBLIOGRAPHY
BIBLIOGRAPHIE ANNOTEE
BIBLIOGRAFIA ANOTADA
                                                    May 1984
BT   BIBLIOGRAPHY
RT   880

ANTARCTIC REGIONS
REGIONS ANTARCTIQUES
REGIONES ANTARTICAS
                                                    May 1984
BT   POLAR REGIONS
RT   ARCTIC REGIONS
     SOUTH POLE

ANTHOLOGIES
ANTHOLOGIE
ANTOLOGIA
RT   722

ANTHROPOLOGY
ANTHROPOLOGIE
ANTROPOLOGIA
BT   SOCIAL SCIENCES
RT   640

ANTI SOCIAL BEHAVIOUR
COMPORTEMENT ANTISOCIAL
COMPORTAMIENTO ANTISOCIAL
BT   BEHAVIOUR
RT   572

ANTIGUA AND BARBUDA
ANTIGUA ET BARBUDA
ANTIGUA Y BARBUDA
                                                    May 1984
BT   CARIBBEAN

ANXIETY
ANXIETE
ANSIEDAD
BT   PSYCHOLOGICAL PATTERNS
RT   540

APPLIED MATHEMATICS
MATHEMATIQUES APPLIQUEES
MATEMATICA APLICADA
BT   MATHEMATICS
RT   631

APPLIED RESEARCH
RECHERCHE APPLIQUEE
INVESTIGACION APLICADA
                                                    May 1984
RT   282

APPRENTICESHIP
APPRENTISSAGE (METIERS)
APRENDIZAJE (OFICIOS)
RT   351

APTITUDE
APTITUDE
APTITUD
NT   VOCATIONAL APTITUDES
RT   520

APTITUDE TESTS
TEST D'APTITUDES
PRUEBA DE APTITUD
BT   EDUCATIONAL TESTS
RT   393

ARAB COUNTRIES
PAYS ARABES
PAISES ARABES
UF   ARAB STATES
NT   ALGERIA
     BAHRAIN
     EGYPT
     IRAQ
     JORDAN
     KUWAIT
     LEBANON
     LIBYAN ARAB JAMAHIRIYA
     MOROCCO
     QATAR
     SAUDI ARABIA

ARAB REPUBLIC OF EGYPT
  SUDAN
  SYRIAN AR
  TUNISIA
  UNITED ARAB EMIRATES
  DEMOCRATIC YEMEN
  YEMEN
RT MEDITERRANEAN
   COUNTRIES
  MIDDLE EAST

ARAB REPUBLIC OF EGYPT
USE **EGYPT**

ARAB STATES
USE **ARAB COUNTRIES**

ARABIC
LANGUE ARABE
LENGUA ARABE
RT 626

ARBITRATION
USE **DISPUTE SETTLEMENT**

ARCHITECTS
ARCHITECTE
ARQUITECTO
RT 461

ARCHITECTURAL CONCEPTS
PRINCIPES ARCHITECTURAUX
CONCEPTOS ARQUITECTONICOS
RT 252

ARCHITECTURAL DRAWINGS
PLAN (ARCHITECTURE)
DIBUJO ARQUITECTONICO
RT 252

ARCHITECTURE
ARCHITECTURE
ARQUITECTURA
RT 650
  BUILDINGS
  EDUCATIONAL SPACES

ARCTIC REGIONS
REGIONS ARCTIQUES
REGIONES ARTICAS
        May 1984
BT POLAR REGIONS
RT ANTARCTIC REGIONS
  GREENLAND
  NORTH POLE

AREA ANALYSIS
ANALYSE DES SURFACES
ANALISIS DE SUPERFICIES
SN Refers to the area of buildings
RT 252

AREA STUDIES
ETUDE REGIONALE
  INTERDISCIPLINAIRE
ESTUDIO REGIONAL
  INTERDISCIPLINARIO
SN Study of political or geographical area including history, geography, language and general culture
RT 680

ARGENTINA
ARGENTINE
ARGENTINA
BT SOUTH AMERICA

ARITHMETIC
ARITHMETIQUE
ARITMETICA
BT MATHEMATICS
RT 631

ARITHMETICAL CONCEPTS
CONCEPT ARITHMETIQUE
CONCEPTO ARITMETICO
        May 1984
RT 631

ARMED FORCES EDUCATION
ENSEIGNEMENT DANS LES
  FORCES ARMEES
ENSEÑANZA EN LAS FUERZAS
  ARMADAS
SN Provided to people while in the armed forces
RT 186

ARMENIAN SSR
RSS D'ARMENIE
RSS DE ARMENIA
May 1984
BT   USSR

ART
ART
ARTE
NT   COMMERCIAL ART
RT   610

ART APPRECIATION
INITIATION ARTISTIQUE
INICIACION ARTISTICA
RT   684

ART EDUCATION
EDUCATION ARTISTIQUE
EDUCACION ARTISTICA
RT   684

ART TEACHERS
PROFESSEUR D'ART
PROFESOR DE ARTE
RT   425

ARTICULATION
ARTICULATION
ARTICULACION
SN   Between levels of education or types of school
BT   TRANSFER POLICY
RT   205

ARTICULATION (SPEECH)
ARTICULATION (PAROLE)
ARTICULACION (HABLA)
BT   SPEECH
RT   532

ARTISTS
ARTISTE
ARTISTA
RT   461

ASSOCIATIVE LEARNING

ASCENSION ISLAND
ILE DE L'ASCENSION
ISLA DE ASCENSION
May 1984
BT   ATLANTIC OCEAN TERRITORIES

ASFEC
ASFEC
ASFEC
SN   Regional Centre for Functional Literacy in Rural Areas for the Arab States

ASIA
ASIE
ASIA
NT   FAR EAST
      MIDDLE EAST
      SOUTH ASIA
      SOUTH EAST ASIA

ASPIRATION
ASPIRATION
ASPIRACION
SN   Desire to accomplish what one sets out to do
RT   541

ASSIGNMENTS
TACHE
TAREA
NT   TEACHING ASSIGNMENTS
RT   356

ASSOCIATED SCHOOLS (UNESCO)
ECOLE ASSOCIEE (UNESCO)
ESCUELA ASOCIADA (UNESCO)
RT   305

ASSOCIATIVE LEARNING
APPRENTISSAGE ASSOCIATIF
APRENDIZAJE ASOCIATIVO
BT   LEARNING
RT   512

ASTRONOMY
ASTRONOMIE
ASTRONOMIA
BT SCIENCES
RT 633

ATHEISTIC EDUCATION
EDUCATION ATHEE
EDUCACION ATEA
RT 188

ATHLETES
ATHLETE
ATLETA
RT 461

ATHLETIC ACTIVITIES
ACTIVITE SPORTIVE
ACTIVIDAD DEPORTIVA
UF SPORTS
BT PHYSICAL ACTIVITIES
RT 357

ATHLETIC EQUIPMENT
EQUIPEMENT SPORTIF
EQUIPO DEPORTIVO
BT EQUIPMENT
RT 740

ATHLETICS
ATHLETISME
ATLETISMO
RT 651

ATLANTIC OCEAN TERRITORIES
TERRITOIRES DE L'OCEAN
  ATLANTIQUE
TERRITORIOS DEL OCEANO
  ATLANTICO
                          May 1984
NT ASCENSION ISLAND
   AZORES
   BOUVET ISLAND
   CANARY ISLANDS
   CAPE VERDE
   FALKLAND ISLANDS
   ICELAND
   MADEIRA
   SAINT HELENA

ATLASES
ATLAS
ATLAS
RT 722

ATTENDANCE
FREQUENTATION
ASISTENCIA
NT ATTENDANCE RATE
RT 266

ATTENDANCE OFFICERS
CONTROLEUR DE L'OBLIGATION
   SCOLAIRE
INSPECTOR DE ASISTENCIA
   ESCOLAR
RT 420

ATTENDANCE RATE
TAUX DE FREQUENTATION
TASA DE ASISTENCIA
BT ATTENDANCE
RT 206

ATTENDANCE RECORDS
REGISTRE DE PRESENCE
REGISTRO DE ASISTENCIA
BT RECORDS (FORMS)
RT 723

ATTENTION
ATTENTION
ATENCION
RT 535

ATTENTION SPAN
DUREE DE L'ATTENTION
DURACION DE LA ATENCION
RT 535

ATTITUDES
ATTITUDE
ACTITUD
NT CHILDHOOD ATTITUDES
   CLASS ATTITUDES
   FAMILY ATTITUDES
   SCHOOL ATTITUDES
   SOCIAL ATTITUDES
   STUDENT ATTITUDES
   TEACHER ATTITUDES

WORK ATTITUDES
RT 552

AUDIENCES
AUDITOIRE
AUDITORIO
NT LISTENING GROUPS
RT 442

AUDIOVISUAL AIDS
AUXILIAIRE AUDIOVISUEL
AUXILIARES AUDIOVISUALES
SN Includes all single medium and multimedia instructional aids; where emphasis on content use audiovisual programmes
RT 730
　　INSTRUCTIONAL MATERIALS
　　AUDIOVISUAL INSTRUCTION

AUDIOVISUAL COMMUNICATION
COMMUNICATION AUDIOVISUELLE
COMUNICACION AUDIOVISUAL
RT 360

AUDIOVISUAL EQUIPMENT
EQUIPEMENT AUDIOVISUEL
EQUIPO AUDIOVISUAL
SN Covers purely audio or visual items
BT EQUIPMENT
NT TAPE RECORDERS
RT 731

AUDIOVISUAL INSTRUCTION
ENSEIGNEMENT AUDIOVISUEL
ENSEÑANZA AUDIOVISUAL
RT 360
　　AUDIOVISUAL AIDS

AUDIOVISUAL PROGRAMMES
PROGRAMME AUDIOVISUEL
PROGRAMA AUDIOVISUAL
SN The records in printed or other form of the content of a programme
RT 732

AUDIOVISUAL TESTS
TEST AUDIOVISUEL
PRUEBA AUDIOVISUAL
　　　　　　　　　　　　May 1984
BT PHYSICAL EXAMINATIONS
RT 393

AUDITION (PHYSIOLOGY)
AUDITION (PHYSIOLOGIE)
AUDICION (FISIOLOGIA)
UF HEARING
RT 503

AUDITORY PERCEPTION
PERCEPTION AUDITIVE
PERCEPCION AUDITIVA
BT PERCEPTION
RT 510

AURAL STIMULI
STIMULUS AUDITIF
ESTIMULO AUDITIVO
BT STIMULI
RT 510

AUSTRALASIA
AUSTRALASIE
AUSTRALASIA
　　　　　　　　　　　　May 1984
NT AUSTRALIA
　　NEW ZEALAND

AUSTRALIA
AUSTRALIE
AUSTRALIA
BT AUSTRALASIA
NT LORD HOWE ISLAND
　　NORFOLK ISLAND
　　TASMANIA

AUSTRIA
AUTRICHE
AUSTRIA
BT WESTERN EUROPE

AUTHORS
AUTEUR
AUTOR
RT 461

AUTISM

AUTISM
AUTISME
AUTISMO
RT 572

AUTOMATIC PROMOTION
USE **PROMOTION POLICIES**

AUTOMATION
AUTOMATION
AUTOMATIZACION
RT 140
    CYBERNETICS

AVERAGE STUDENTS
ELEVE MOYEN
ALUMNO MEDIO
RT 416

AVIATION TECHNOLOGY
AERONAUTIQUE
AERONAUTICA
BT TECHNOLOGY
RT 645

AZORES
ACORES
AZORES
BT ATLANTIC OCEAN
    TERRITORIES
    WESTERN EUROPE

BACHELORS DEGREES
DIPLOME UNIVERSITAIRE (1ER CYCLE)
DIPLOMA DE BACHILLER
SN First university degree
BT DEGREES (TITLES)
RT 390

BAHAMAS
BAHAMAS
BAHAMAS
BT CARIBBEAN

BAHRAIN
BAHREIN
BAHREIN
BT ARAB COUNTRIES
    GULF STATES

BANGLADESH
BANGLADESH
BANGLADESH
BT SOUTH ASIA

BANKS ISLANDS
ILES DE BANKS
ISLAS DE BANKS
May 1984
BT MELANESIA

BARBADOS
BARBADE
BARBADOS
BT CARIBBEAN

BASIC EDUCATION
EDUCATION DE BASE
EDUCACION BASICA
SN For children and adults
RT 183

BASIC RESEARCH
May 1984
USE **FUNDAMENTAL RESEARCH**

BASIC SCHOOLS
ECOLE D'ENSEIGNEMENT DE BASE
ESCUELA DE EDUCACION BASICA
SN Institutions combining primary and part of secondary level
RT 301

BASIC SKILLS
COMPETENCE FONDAMENTALE
HABILIDADES BASICAS
BT SKILLS
RT 533

BASIC TRAINING
FORMATION DE BASE
FORMACION BASICA
SN Specially organized training, given outside of production activities of an undertaking, and aimed at imparting the basic knowledge and skill required for a given group of occupations
BT TRAINING

RT 351

BEGINNING READING
INITIATION A LA LECTURE
INICIACION EN LA LECTURA
RT 660

BEGINNING TEACHERS
MAITRE DEBUTANT
DOCENTE PRINCIPIANTE
RT 424

BEHAVIOUR
COMPORTEMENT
COMPORTAMIENTO
NT AFFECTIVE BEHAVIOUR
 ANTI SOCIAL BEHAVIOUR
 CONFORMITY
 GROUP BEHAVIOUR
 INFANT BEHAVIOUR
 LEADERSHIP
 STUDENT BEHAVIOUR
 TEACHER BEHAVIOUR
RT 560

BEHAVIOUR CHANGE
CHANGEMENT DE
 COMPORTEMENT
CAMBIO DE CONDUCTA
SN Complete or partial alteration in the observable activity or response of a person as a result of a learning experience
RT 560

BEHAVIOUR DEVELOPMENT
DEVELOPPEMENT DU
 COMPORTEMENT
EVOLUCION DEL
 COMPORTAMIENTO
NT HABIT FORMATION
RT 530

BEHAVIOUR PROBLEMS
PROBLEME DE COMPORTEMENT
PROBLEMAS DE
 COMPORTAMIENTO
RT 281

BEHAVIOUR THEORIES
THEORIE DU COMPORTEMENT
TEORIA DEL COMPORTAMIENTO
BT THEORIES
RT 560

BEHAVIOURAL COUNSELLING
CONSEILS SUR LE
 COMPORTEMENT
CONSEJOS SOBRE EL
 COMPORTAMIENTO
SN Designed to assist the integration of the individual in his environment
BT COUNSELLING
RT 370

BEHAVIOURAL OBJECTIVES
OBJECTIF DU COMPORTEMENT
OBJETIVO RELATIVO AL
 COMPORTAMIENTO
SN Objectives indicating desired changes in behaviour resulting from learning
BT EDUCATIONAL OBJECTIVES
RT 300

BEHAVIOURAL SCIENCE RESEARCH
RECHERCHE SUR LE
 COMPORTEMENT
INVESTIGACION DEL
 COMPORTAMIENTO
RT 280

BEHAVIOURAL SCIENCES
SCIENCES DU COMPORTEMENT
CIENCIAS DEL
 COMPORTAMIENTO
BT SCIENCES
NT PSYCHOLOGY
 SOCIOLOGY
RT 642

BELGIUM
BELGIQUE
BELGICA
BT WESTERN EUROPE

BELIZE

BELIZE
BELIZE
BELIZE
May 1984
UF BRITISH HONDURAS
BT CENTRAL AMERICA

BENIN
BENIN
BENIN
UF DAHOMEY
BT WEST AFRICA
RT FRENCH SPEAKING AFRICA

BERMUDA
BERMUDES
BERMUDAS
BT CENTRAL AMERICA
   LATIN AMERICA
   NORTH AMERICA
RT CARIBBEAN

BHUTAN
BHOUTAN
BHUTAN
BT HIMALAYAN STATES

BIAS
PREJUGE
PREDISPOSICION
RT 552

BIBLIOGRAPHY
BIBLIOGRAPHIE
BIBLIOGRAFIA
NT ANNOTATED BIBLIOGRAPHY
RT 880

BICULTURALISM
BICULTURALISME
BICULTURALISMO
RT 130
   BILINGUAL EDUCATION

BILATERAL AID
AIDE BILATERALE
AYUDA BILATERAL
SN Support by one country to another
RT 106

BILINGUAL EDUCATION
ENSEIGNEMENT BILINGUE
EDUCACION BILINGUE
SN Encouragement of bilingualism through the teaching of regular courses in both the national language and a second language
RT 183
   BICULTURALISM

BILINGUAL STUDENTS
ELEVE BILINGUE
ALUMNO BILINGUE
RT 414

BILINGUAL TEACHERS
ENSEIGNANT BILINGUE
PROFESOR BILINGUE
RT 426

BILINGUALISM
BILINGUISME
BILINGUISMO
RT 131

BIOGRAPHIES
BIOGRAPHIE
BIOGRAFIA
RT 616

BIOLOGY
BIOLOGIE
BIOLOGIA
BT SCIENCES
NT ANATOMY
   BOTANY
   ECOLOGY
   GENETICS
   HEREDITY
   PHYSIOLOGY
   ZOOLOGY
RT 632

BIRTH ORDER
RANG DE NAISSANCE
ORDEN DE NACIMIENTO
RT 500

BLACKBOARDS
USE **CHALKBOARDS**

BLIND
AVEUGLE
CIEGO
SN Children or adults
RT 403

BLIND EDUCATION
EDUCATION DES AVEUGLES
EDUCACION DE CIEGOS
BT SPECIAL EDUCATION
RT 322

BLOCK RELEASE
CONGES D'ETUDES GROUPES
LICENCIA DE ESTUDIOS
    PROLONGADA
BT RELEASED TIME
RT 222

BLOCK TIMETABLES
USE **FLEXIBLE TIMETABLING**

BOARDERS
INTERNE
INTERNO
                              May 1984
RT 410

BOARDING FACILITIES
PENSION
PENSION
NT STUDENT HOUSING
RT 712

BOARDING SCHOOLS
INTERNAT
ESCUELA CON INTERNADO
RT 303

BOARDS OF EDUCATION
USE **GOVERNING BOARDS**

BOARDS OF TRUSTEES
USE **GOVERNING BOARDS**

BODY HEIGHT
TAILLE
ESTATURA
UF HEIGHT
RT 502

BODY WEIGHT
POIDS
PESO
UF WEIGHT
RT 502

BOLIVIA
BOLIVIE
BOLIVIA
BT SOUTH AMERICA

BOND ISSUES
EMISSION D'OBLIGATIONS
EMISION DE TITULOS
RT 240

BOOKMOBILES
BIBLIOBUS
BIBLIOTECA AMBULANTE
RT 743

BOOKS
LIVRE
LIBRO
NT CHILDRENS BOOKS
    TEXTBOOK
RT 722

BORNEO
                              May 1984
USE **INDONESIA**

BORSTALS
                              May 1984
USE **CORRECTIONAL
    INSTITUTIONS**

BOTANY
BOTANIQUE
BOTANICA
BT BIOLOGY
RT 632

BOTSWANA

BOTSWANA
BOTSWANA
BOTSWANA
BT SOUTHERN AFRICA
RT ENGLISH SPEAKING AFRICA

BOUVET ISLAND
ILE BOUVET
ISLA BOUVET
May 1984
BT ATLANTIC OCEAN
    TERRITORIES

BRAILLE
BRAILLE
BRAILLE
RT 374

BRAIN DRAIN
EXODE DES CERVEAUX
EXODO DE INTELECTUALES
RT 124

BRANCHING PROGRAMMES
PROGRAMME RAMIFIE
PROGRAMA RAMIFICADO
RT 361

BRAZIL
BRESIL
BRASIL
BT SOUTH AMERICA

BREDA
BREDA
BREDA
SN Regional Office for Education in
    Africa

BRIDGE CLASSES
USE **TRANSFER CLASSES**

BRITISH EASTERN CARIBBEAN
    GROUP
May 1984
USE **CARIBBEAN**

BRITISH HONDURAS
May 1984
USE **BELIZE**

BRUNEI
BRUNEI
BRUNEI
BT MALAYSIA

BUDDHISTS
BOUDDHISTE
BUDISTA
RT 475

BUDGETING
PREPARATION DU BUDGET
ELABORACION DEL PRESUPUESTO
BT MANAGEMENT
RT 243

BUDGETS
BUDGET
PRESUPUESTO
RT 243

BUILDING DESIGN
CONCEPTION DES BATIMENTS
DISEÑO DE EDIFICIOS
SN Includes plans and component
    elements
RT 252

BUILDING ELEMENTS
ELEMENT DE CONSTRUCTION
ELEMENTOS DE CONSTRUCCION
RT 253

BUILDING ENGINEERING
INGENIERIE DU BATIMENT
INGENIERIA DE CONSTRUCCION
RT 252

BUILDING EVALUATION
EVALUATION DES BATIMENTS
EVALUACION DE LOS EDIFICIOS
RT 251

BUILDING FINANCE
FINANCEMENT DE LA
 CONSTRUCTION
FINANCIAMIENTO DE LA
 CONSTRUCCION
RT 251

BUILDING IMPROVEMENT
AMELIORATION DES BATIMENTS
MEJORAMIENTO DE LOS
 EDIFICIOS
SN Includes renovation
RT 253

BUILDING MATERIALS
MATERIAUX DE CONSTRUCTION
MATERIALES DE CONSTRUCCION
RT 253
 CONSTRUCTION
  PROGRAMMES

BUILDING PROGRAMMES
USE **CONSTRUCTION**
 PROGRAMMES

BUILDING TRADES
ENTREPRISE DE CONSTRUCTION
EMPRESA DE CONSTRUCCION
RT 155
 DRAFTSMEN

BUILDING USE
UTILISATION DES BATIMENTS
UTILIZACION DE LOS EDIFICIOS
RT 251

BUILDINGS
BATIMENT
EDIFICIO
RT 710
 ARCHITECTURE
 EDUCATIONAL SPACES

BULGARIA
BULGARIE
BULGARIA
BT EASTERN EUROPE

BURMA
BIRMANIE
BIRMANIA
BT SOUTH EAST ASIA

BURUNDI
BURUNDI
BURUNDI
BT CENTRAL AFRICA
  EAST AFRICA
RT FRENCH SPEAKING AFRICA

BUSINESS
USE **COMMERCE**

BUSINESS SUBJECTS
DISCIPLINES COMMERCIALES
ESTUDIOS COMERCIALES
SN Study programme relating to office
 occupations
RT 673

BYELORUSSIAN SSR
RSS DE BIELORUSSIE
RSS DE BIELORRUSIA
BT USSR

CALCULATION
CALCUL
CALCULO
SN The act or process of computing
 or estimating through the use of
 numbers and/or other
 mathematical symbols
RT 631

CALISTHENICS
GYMNASTIQUE
CALISTENIA
RT 651

CAMBODIA
USE **DEMOCRATIC KAMPUCHEA**

CAMEROON UR
CAMEROUN (REPUBLIQUE UNIE)
CAMERUN (REPUBLICA UNIDA)
BT CENTRAL AFRICA
  WEST AFRICA
RT FRENCH SPEAKING AFRICA

CANADA
CANADA
CANADA
BT   NORTH AMERICA

CANARY ISLANDS
ILES CANARIES
ISLAS CANARIAS
BT   ATLANTIC OCEAN
         TERRITORIES
      WESTERN EUROPE
RT   NORTH AFRICA
      WEST AFRICA

CANTON AND ENDERBY ISLANDS
ILES CANTON ET ENDERBY
ISLAS CANTON Y ENDERBY
                                    May 1984
UF   ENDERBY ISLANDS
BT   MICRONESIA

CAPE VERDE
CAP–VERT
CABO VERDE
BT   ATLANTIC OCEAN
         TERRITORIES

CAPITAL
CAPITAL
CAPITAL
RT   150

CAPITAL ASSETS
BIENS CAPITAUX
BIENES INMUEBLES
UF   PROPERTY
      REAL ESTATE
RT   710

CAPITAL COSTS
USE **CAPITAL OUTLAY (FOR FIXED ASSETS)**

CAPITAL OUTLAY (FOR FIXED ASSETS)
DEPENSE D'EQUIPEMENT
GASTOS DE EQUIPAMIENTO
UF   CAPITAL COSTS
BT   EXPENDITURES
RT   241

CARDIOVASCULAR SYSTEM
SYSTEME CARDIOVASCULAIRE
SISTEMA CARDIOVASCULAR
RT   502

CAREER CHOICE
CHOIX D'UNE CARRIERE
ELECCION DE CARRERA
BT   VOCATIONAL DEVELOPMENT
RT   563

CAREER COUNSELLING
CONSULTATION SUR LA
      CARRIERE
ASESORAMIENTO SOBRE LA
      CARRERA
BT   COUNSELLING
NT   OCCUPATIONAL
         INFORMATION
      REHABILITATION
         COUNSELLING
RT   370

CAREER EDUCATION
PREPARATION A LA VIE ACTIVE
PREPARACION PARA LA VIDA
      ACTIVA
SN   Educational programme that gives all students informed guidance, counselling and instruction to prepare them to enter a career field
RT   183

CAREER PLANNING
PLANIFICATION DE LA CARRIERE
PLANIFICACION DE LA CARRERA
RT   563

CAREERS
CARRIERE
CARRERA
RT   563
      VOCATIONAL GUIDANCE

CARIBBEAN
CARAIBES
CARIBE
UF   BRITISH EASTERN
         CARIBBEAN GROUP

CENSUS DATA

    GREATER ANTILLES
    LEEWARD ISLANDS
    LESSER ANTILLES
    WEST INDIES
    WINDWARD ISLANDS
BT LATIN AMERICA
NT ANTIGUA AND BARBUDA
    BAHAMAS
    BARBADOS
    CAYMAN ISLANDS
    CUBA
    DOMINICA
    DOMINICAN REPUBLIC
    GRENADA
    GUADELOUPE
    HAITI
    JAMAICA
    MARTINIQUE
    MONTSERRAT
    NETHERLANDS ANTILLES
    PUERTO RICO
    SAINT BARTHELEMY
    SAINT KITTS-NEVIS-
      ANGUILLA
    SAINT LUCIA
    SAINT MARTIN
    SAINT VINCENT
    TRINIDAD AND TOBAGO
    TURKS AND CAICOS ISLANDS
    VIRGIN ISLANDS (UK)
    VIRGIN ISLANDS (USA)
RT BERMUDA
    CENTRAL AMERICA

CAROLINE ISLANDS
ARCHIPEL DES CAROLINES
ISLAS CAROLINAS
May 1984
BT MICRONESIA

CASE STUDIES
ETUDE DE CAS
ESTUDIO DE CASOS
RT 282

CATALOGUE
CATALOGUE
CATALOGO
RT 880

CATALOGUING
CATALOGAGE
CATALOGACION
RT 202

CATCHMENT AREA
ZONE DE RECRUTEMENT
ZONA DE MATRICULA
UF SCHOOL ZONING
SN Geographical area from which an educational institution draws its students
RT 264

CATHOLIC SCHOOLS
USE **PRIVATE SCHOOLS**

CATHOLICS
CATHOLIQUE
CATOLICO
RT 475

CAUCASIAN LANGUAGES
LANGUES CAUCASIENNES
LENGUAS CAUCASICAS
RT 625

CAYMAN ISLANDS
ILES CAYMAN
ISLAS CAIMAN
BT CARIBBEAN

CELC
CELC
CELC
SN Commonwealth Education Liaison Committee

CELEBES
USE **INDONESIA**

CENSUS DATA
DONNEE DU RECENSEMENT
DATOS DEL CENSO
RT 124

May 1984

25

CENTRAL AFRICA

CENTRAL AFRICA
AFRIQUE CENTRALE
AFRICA CENTRAL
BT   AFRICA SOUTH OF THE
       SAHARA
NT   BURUNDI
     CAMEROON UR
     CENTRAL AFRICAN
       REPUBLIC
     CHAD
     CONGO
     EQUATORIAL GUINEA
     GABON
     RWANDA
     SAO TOME AND PRINCIPE
     ZAIRE

CENTRAL AFRICAN REPUBLIC
REPUBLIQUE CENTRAFICAINE
REPUBLICA CENTROAFRICANA
May 1984
BT   CENTRAL AFRICA
RT   FRENCH SPEAKING AFRICA

CENTRAL AMERICA
AMERIQUE CENTRALE
AMERICA CENTRAL
BT   LATIN AMERICA
NT   BELIZE
     BERMUDA
     COSTA RICA
     EL SALVADOR
     GUATEMALA
     HONDURAS
     NICARAGUA
     PANAMA
     PANAMA CANAL ZONE
RT   CARIBBEAN
     MEXICO

CENTRAL AND WESTERN ASIA
May 1984
USE **MIDDLE EAST**

**CENTRAL EDUCATIONAL
  AGENCIES**
ORGANISME CENTRAL DE
  L'EDUCATION
ORGANISMO CENTRAL DE
  EDUCACION

UF   MINISTRIES OF EDUCATION
BT   AGENCIES
RT   261

CENTRAL GOVERNMENT
GOUVERNEMENT CENTRAL
GOBIERNO CENTRAL
UF   FEDERAL GOVERNMENT
BT   GOVERNMENT
RT   103

CENTRAL GOVERNMENT AID
AIDE DU GOUVERNEMENT
  CENTRAL
AYUDA DEL GOBIERNO CENTRAL
UF   STATE AID
NT   STATE AID TO PROVINCES
RT   106

CENTRAL GOVERNMENT LAWS
LEGISLATION DU
  GOUVERNEMENT CENTRAL
LEGISLACION DEL GOBIERNO
  CENTRAL
BT   LAWS
RT   170

**CENTRAL PROVINCIAL
  RELATIONSHIP**
RELATIONS ETAT–PROVINCE
RELACION ESTADO–PROVINCIA
BT   RELATIONSHIP
RT   105

CENTRALIZATION
CENTRALISATION
CENTRALIZACION
RT   200

CENTRES OF INTEREST
CENTRE D'INTERET
CENTRO DE INTERES
SN   Ideas, principles or themes around
     which curriculum may be built,
     usually derived from the
     environment
RT   331

26

CERTIFICATION
ATTRIBUTION DE DIPLOMES
OTORGAMIENTO DE DIPLOMA
SN   Award of educational certificate
NT   TEACHER CERTIFICATION
RT   390

CEYLON
USE **SRI LANKA**

CHAD
TCHAD
CHAD
BT   CENTRAL AFRICA
RT   FRENCH SPEAKING AFRICA

CHALKBOARDS
TABLEAU NOIR
PIZARRON
UF   BLACKBOARDS
RT   741

CHANGE AGENTS
AGENT NOVATEUR
AGENTE DEL CAMBIO
SN   In context of innovations
RT   440

CHANGING ATTITUDES
CHANGEMENT D'ATTITUDE
CAMBIO DE ACTITUD
RT   552

CHANNEL ISLANDS
ILES ANGLO–NORMANDES
ISLAS ANGLONORMANDAS
                                     May 1984
BT   WESTERN EUROPE

CHARTS
GRAPHIQUE
GRAFICO
SN   Graphic displays with emphasis on quantitative aspects, e.g. a statistical series
RT   733

CHEMISTRY
CHIMIE
QUIMICA
BT   SCIENCES
RT   633

CHILD CARE
SOINS A L'ENFANT
CUIDADO DEL NIÑO
RT   126

CHILD CARE CENTRES
CRECHE
GUARDERIA INFANTIL
RT   311

CHILD CARE WORKERS
PUERICULTRICE
PUERICULTORA
RT   430

CHILD DEVELOPMENT
DEVELOPPEMENT DE L'ENFANT
DESARROLLO DEL NIÑO
RT   530

CHILD DEVELOPMENT SPECIALISTS
SPECIALISTE DU DEVELOPPEMENT DE L'ENFANT
ESPECIALISTA EN DESARROLLO DEL NIÑO
BT   SPECIALISTS
RT   430

CHILD LABOUR
TRAVAIL DES MINEURS
TRABAJO DE MENORES
RT   153

CHILD LANGUAGE
LANGAGE DE L'ENFANT
LENGUAJE INFANTIL
RT   532

CHILD PSYCHOLOGY
PSYCHOLOGIE DE L'ENFANT
PSICOLOGIA DEL NIÑO
BT   PSYCHOLOGY
RT   642

CHILD REARING

CHILD REARING
USE **UPBRINGING**

CHILD RESPONSIBILITY
RESPONSABILITE DE L'ENFANT
RESPONSABILIDAD DEL NIÑO
BT   RESPONSIBILITY
RT   231

CHILD WELFARE
PROTECTION DE L'ENFANCE
BIENESTAR DE LA INFANCIA
BT   WELFARE
RT   100

CHILDHOOD
ENFANCE
INFANCIA
NT   EARLY CHILDHOOD
RT   500

CHILDHOOD ATTITUDES
ATTITUDE DE L'ENFANT
ACTITUD DEL NIÑO
BT   ATTITUDES
RT   552

CHILDHOOD NEEDS
BESOINS DE L'ENFANT
NECESIDADES DEL NIÑO
BT   INDIVIDUAL NEEDS
RT   536

CHILDREN
ENFANT
NIÑO
NT   ADOPTED CHILDREN
      MINORITY GROUP CHILDREN
RT   400

CHILDRENS BOOKS
LIVRE POUR ENFANTS
LIBRO PARA NIÑOS
BT   BOOKS
RT   722

CHILDRENS GAMES
JEU DE L'ENFANT
JUEGO INFANTIL
BT   PLAY
RT   537

CHILE
CHILI
CHILE
BT   SOUTH AMERICA

CHINA
CHINE
CHINA
UF   PEOPLES REPUBLIC OF
      CHINA
BT   FAR EAST

CHINESE
LANGUE CHINOISE
LENGUA CHINA
RT   626

CHRISTIAN EDUCATION
EDUCATION CHRETIENNE
EDUCACION CRISTIANA
                              May 1984
RT   188

CHRISTMAS ISLAND
ILE CHRISTMAS
ISLA CHRISTMAS
                              May 1984
BT   INDIAN OCEAN TERRITORIES

CHRISTMAS ISLAND (LINE
   ISLANDS)
                              May 1984
USE **LINE ISLANDS**

CHURCHES
USE **RELIGIOUS INSTITUTIONS**

CIECC
CIECC
CIECC
SN   Inter-American Council for
      Education, Science and Culture

CINEMA
CINEMA
CINE
SN Film as art form
RT 610

CIRCULATION
CIRCULATION
CIRCULACION
SN For movement of students within educational spaces
RT 251

CITIES
USE **MUNICIPALITIES**

CITIZEN PARTICIPATION
PARTICIPATION DU CITOYEN
PARTICIPACION DEL CIUDADANO
SN In processes of policy making and government
RT 105
    CITIZENSHIP

CITIZEN ROLE
ROLE DU CITOYEN
PAPEL DEL CIUDADANO
RT 105
    CITIZENSHIP

CITIZENSHIP
CITOYENNETE
CIUDADANIA
RT 101
    CITIZEN PARTICIPATION
    CITIZEN ROLE
    CIVICS

CITY GOVERNMENT
AUTORITES MUNICIPALES
GOBIERNO MUNICIPAL
BT GOVERNMENT
RT 104
    MUNICIPALITIES

CIVICS
INSTRUCTION CIVIQUE
EDUCACION CIVICA
RT 640
    CITIZENSHIP

CIVIL ENGINEERING
GENIE CIVIL
INGENIERIA CIVIL
BT ENGINEERING
RT 647

CIVIL LIBERTIES
USE **HUMAN RIGHTS**

CIVIL RIGHTS
DROIT CIVIQUE
DERECHOS CIVICOS
RT 170
    HUMAN RIGHTS

CIVIL SERVANTS
FONCTIONNAIRE
FUNCIONARIO PUBLICO
SN In executive positions
RT 460

CLADES
CLADES
CLADES
SN Latin American Social and Economic Documentation Centre

CLASS ACTIVITIES
ACTIVITE DE LA CLASSE
ACTIVIDAD DE LA CLASE
BT SCHOOL ACTIVITIES
RT 357

CLASS ATTITUDES
ATTITUDE DE CLASSE
ACTITUD DE LA CLASE
SN Relates to social class
BT ATTITUDES
RT 552

CLASS MANAGEMENT
CONDUITE DE LA CLASSE
CONDUCCION DE LA CLASE
RT 691

CLASS SIZE
DIMENSION DE LA CLASSE
TAMAÑO DE LA CLASE
RT 343

CLASSES
CLASSE
CLASE
SN Groups of students
NT LITERACY CLASSES
　　NONGRADED CLASSES
　　SPECIAL CLASSES
　　TRANSFER CLASSES
RT 343

CLASSICAL LANGUAGES
LANGUES CLASSIQUES
LENGUAS CLASICAS
BT LANGUAGES
RT 627

CLASSIFICATION
CLASSIFICATION
CLASIFICACION
RT 202

CLASSROOM ARRANGEMENT
AGENCEMENT DE LA SALLE DE CLASSE
ARREGLO DEL AULA
RT 356

CLASSROOM COMMUNICATION
COMMUNICATION EN CLASSE
COMUNICACION EN LA CLASE
RT 355

CLASSROOM ENVIRONMENT
ENVIRONNEMENT DE LA CLASSE
AMBIENTE DE LA CLASE
BT EDUCATIONAL ENVIRONMENT
RT 380

CLASSROOM MATERIALS
MATERIEL DE LA CLASSE
MATERIAL DE LA CLASE
RT 741

CLASSROOM PARTICIPATION
PARTICIPATION DE LA CLASSE
PARTICIPACION DE LA CLASE
BT PARTICIPATION
RT 356

CLASSROOM RESEARCH
RECHERCHE PEDAGOGIQUE APPLIQUEE
INVESTIGACION EN EL AULA
BT EDUCATIONAL RESEARCH
RT 280

CLASSROOM TECHNIQUES
TECHNIQUE DE LA CLASSE
TECNICA DIDACTICA
BT TEACHING TECHNIQUES
RT 356

CLASSROOMS
SALLE DE CLASSE
AULA
NT SPECIAL CLASSROOMS
RT 711

CLEARINGHOUSES
USE **INFORMATION CENTRES**

CLERICAL OCCUPATIONS
EMPLOI DE BUREAU
EMPLEO DE OFICINA
BT OCCUPATIONS
RT 155

CLERICAL WORKERS
EMPLOYE DE BUREAU
EMPLEADO DE OFICINA
BT EMPLOYEES
RT 451

CLIMATIC FACTORS
FACTEUR CLIMATIQUE
FACTOR CLIMATICO
RT 285

CLINICAL DIAGNOSIS
DIAGNOSTIC CLINIQUE
DIAGNOSTICO CLINICO
SN Identification of conditions requiring treatment
RT 372

CLINICS
CLINIQUE
CLINICA
RT   313

CLOSED CIRCUIT TELEVISION
TELEVISION EN CIRCUIT FERME
TELEVISION EN CIRCUITO
   CERRADO
BT   INSTRUCTIONAL TELEVISION
RT   360

CLOTHING
HABILLEMENT
VESTUARIO
RT   740

CLUBS
CLUB
CLUB
NT   YOUTH CLUBS
RT   381

COACHING TEACHERS
REPETITEUR
PASANTE
RT   425

CODED SPEECH
MESSAGE CODE
LENGUAJE EN CODIGO
SN   Representation of high frequency
      sounds in low frequency range
BT   SPEECH
RT   374

CODIFICATION
CODIFICATION
CODIFICACION
SN   Of laws
RT   230

COEDUCATION
COEDUCATION
COEDUCACION
RT   186

COEDUCATIONAL SCHOOLS
ECOLE MIXTE
ESCUELA MIXTA
RT   303

COGNITIVE ABILITY
APTITUDE COGNITIVE
APTITUD COGNOSCITIVA
BT   ABILITY
RT   520

COGNITIVE DEVELOPMENT
DEVELOPPEMENT COGNITIF
DESARROLLO COGNOSCITIVO
BT   MENTAL DEVELOPMENT
RT   530

COGNITIVE OBJECTIVES
OBJECTIF COGNITIF
OBJETIVO COGNOSCITIVO
BT   EDUCATIONAL OBJECTIVES
RT   300

COGNITIVE PROCESSES
PROCESSUS COGNITIF
PROCESO COGNOSCITIVO
NT   MEMORIZING
RT   521

COLLECTIVE AGREEMENTS
CONVENTION COLLECTIVE
CONVENIO COLECTIVO
SN   Includes negotiation as well as
      results of agreement between
      employers and employees
RT   153

COLLECTIVE SETTLEMENTS
GROUPE COLLECTIVISTE
GRUPO COMUNITARIO
SN   Communities practising common
      ownership and cooperative living
RT   122

COLLECTIVISM
COLLECTIVISME
COLECTIVISMO
RT   101

COLLEGE ADMINISTRATION

COLLEGE ADMINISTRATION
ADMINISTRATION DE
  L'ENSEIGNEMENT SUPERIEUR
ADMINISTRACION DE LA
  ENSEÑANZA SUPERIOR
BT EDUCATIONAL
      ADMINISTRATION
RT 265

COLLEGE CURRICULUM
CURRICULUM UNIVERSITAIRE
CURRICULO DE LA ENSEÑANZA
  SUPERIOR
NT GRADUATE STUDY
      UNDERGRADUATE STUDY
RT 330

COLLEGE DEANS
DOYEN
DECANO
RT 422

**COLLEGE ENTRANCE
  EXAMINATIONS**
EXAMEN D'ENTREE
  (ENSEIGNEMENT SUPERIEUR)
EXAMEN DE INGRESO
  (ENSEÑANZA SUPERIOR)
BT ENTRANCE EXAMINATIONS
RT 392

COLLEGE FACULTY
USE **COLLEGE TEACHERS**

COLLEGE GRADUATES
DIPLOME D'UNIVERSITE (1ER
  CYCLE)
GRADUADO UNIVERSITARIO
BT GRADUATES
RT 413

COLLEGE INSTRUCTION
ENSEIGNEMENT UNIVERSITAIRE
ENSEÑANZA UNIVERSITARIA
RT 352

COLLEGE LIBRARIES
BIBLIOTHEQUE UNIVERSITAIRE
BIBLIOTECA UNIVERSITARIA
BT LIBRARIES
RT 310

COLLEGE LOCATION
REPARTITION ETABLISSEMENTS
  SUPERIEURS
UBICACION DE INSTITUTOS
  SUPERIORES
SN Includes choice of location for
    new institutions
RT 208

COLLEGE MAJORS
MATIERE PRINCIPALE
  (ENSEIGNEMENT SUPERIEUR)
MATERIA PRINCIPAL
  (ENSEÑANZA SUPERIOR)
RT 333

COLLEGE MINORS
MATIERE SECONDAIRE
  (ENSEIGNEMENT SUPERIEUR)
MATERIA SECUNDARIA
  (ENSEÑANZA SUPERIOR)
RT 333

COLLEGE PLACEMENT
VENTILATION DES ETUDIANTS
DISTRIBUCION DE LOS
  ESTUDIANTES
SN Applies to orientation of students
    to a particular college or within
    college to particular studies
RT 266

COLLEGE PLANNING
PLANIFICATION UNIVERSITAIRE
PLANIFICACION DE LA
  ENSEÑANZA SUPERIOR
SN In both programme and
    architectural senses, applies to all
    higher education
    institutions. Administrative planning
    at higher education institutions
BT EDUCATIONAL PLANNING
RT 205

COLLEGE PREPARATION
PREPARATION A
  L'ENSEIGNEMENT SUPERIEUR
PREPARACION PARA LA
  ENSEÑANZA SUPERIOR
RT 330

COLLEGE PROGRAMMES
PROGRAMME D'ETUDES
  SUPERIEURES
PROGRAMA DE ESTUDIOS
  SUPERIORES
NT DOCTORAL PROGRAMMES
  SPECIAL DEGREE
    PROGRAMMES
RT 320

COLLEGE ROLE
ROLE DE L'UNIVERSITE
PAPEL DE LA UNIVERSIDAD
SN Functions expected of or carried
  out by the college in society
RT 187

COLLEGE SCHOOL COOPERATION
COOPERATION UNIVERSITE–
  ECOLE
COOPERACION UNIVERSIDAD–
  ESCUELA
RT 265

COLLEGE STUDENTS
ETUDIANT
ESTUDIANTE
UF UNDERGRADUATES
RT 413

COLLEGE SUPERVISORS
DIRECTEUR DE STAGE
SUPERVISOR DE PRACTICAS
  DOCENTES
SN Staff members of a college who
  observe student teachers
RT 426

COLLEGE TEACHERS
ENSEIGNANT DU SUPERIEUR
PROFESOR DE ENSEÑANZA
  SUPERIOR
UF COLLEGE FACULTY

BT TEACHERS
NT LECTURERS
  PROFESSORS
RT 422

COLLEGES
ETABLISSEMENT
  D'ENSEIGNEMENT SUPERIEUR
ESTABLECIMIENTO DE
  ENSEÑANZA SUPERIOR
SN Basic term for institution of
  higher education
NT AGRICULTURAL COLLEGES
  JUNIOR COLLEGES
  OPEN COLLEGES
  PRIVATE COLLEGES
  PUBLIC COLLEGES
  RESIDENTIAL COLLEGES
  TEACHERS COLLEGES
  TECHNICAL COLLEGES
  UNIVERSITIES
RT 187

COLOMBIA
COLOMBIE
COLOMBIA
BT SOUTH AMERICA

COLOMBO PLAN
PLAN DE COLOMBO
PLAN DE COLOMBO

COLONIALISM
COLONIALISME
COLONIALISMO
RT 101

COMECON
COMECON
COMECON
SN Council for Mutual Economic
  Assistance

COMMERCE
COMMERCE
COMERCIO
UF BUSINESS
RT 150

COMMERCIAL ART
ART PUBLICITAIRE
ARTE PUBLICITARIO
BT ART
RT 610

COMMERCIAL EDUCATION
ENSEIGNEMENT COMMERCIAL
ENSEÑANZA COMERCIAL
BT VOCATIONAL EDUCATION
RT 672

COMMERCIAL WORKERS
EMPLOYE DE COMMERCE
EMPLEADO DE COMERCIO
BT EMPLOYEES
RT 451

COMMISSION REPORT
RAPPORT DE COMMISSION
INFORME DE COMISION
RT 880

COMMITTEES
COMITE
COMITE
NT ADVISORY COMMITTEES
RT 442

COMMON CORE
TRONC COMMUN
TRONCO COMUN
SN Portion of total course common and obligatory for all students, generally expressed in terms of grade organization
RT 342

COMMONWEALTH
COMMONWEALTH
COMUNIDAD BRITANICA DE NACIONES
RT 801

COMMONWEALTH SECRETARIAT
SECRETARIAT DU COMMONWEALTH
SECRETARIA DE LA CBN

COMMUNICABLE DISEASES
MALADIE TRANSMISSIBLE
ENFERMEDAD TRASMISIBLE
UF CONTAGIOUS DISEASES
BT DISEASES
RT 161

COMMUNICATION
COMMUNICATION
COMUNICACION
SN Process of imparting, receiving information. When stress on two-way process, use interaction process
NT COMMUNICATION PROBLEMS
   VERBAL COMMUNICATION
RT 204

COMMUNICATION PROBLEMS
PROBLEME DE COMMUNICATION
PROBLEMAS DE LA COMUNICACION
BT COMMUNICATION
RT 204

COMMUNICATION SKILLS
APTITUDE A COMMUNIQUER
APTITUD PARA LA COMUNICACION
BT SKILLS
RT 533

COMMUNICATIONS
MOYEN DE COMMUNICATION
MEDIOS DE COMUNICACION
RT 145

COMMUNICATIONS SATELLITES
SATELLITE DE COMMUNICATION
SATELITE DE COMUNICACION
RT 731

COMMUNIST EDUCATION
EDUCATION COMMUNISTE
EDUCACION COMUNISTA
May 1984
RT 188

COMMUNITY
COMMUNAUTE
COMUNIDAD
RT 102
         COMMUNITY ROLE

COMMUNITY AGENCIES (PUBLIC)
ORGANISME COMMUNAUTAIRE
ORGANISMO LOCAL
BT AGENCIES
RT 104

COMMUNITY CHARACTERISTICS
CARACTERISTIQUE DE LA
   COMMUNAUTE
CARACTERISTICAS DE LA
   COLLECTIVIDAD
RT 285

COMMUNITY COLLEGES
USE **JUNIOR COLLEGES**

COMMUNITY CONTROL
CONTROLE PAR LA
   COMMUNAUTE
CONTROL POR LA COMUNIDAD
SN Relates to powers vested in
     communities
RT 102

COMMUNITY DEVELOPMENT
DEVELOPPEMENT
   COMMUNAUTAIRE
DESARROLLO COMUNITARIO
SN Educational processes and
     activities in a community which
     embody the principle of self help
BT DEVELOPMENT
RT 151

COMMUNITY EDUCATION
EDUCATION COMMUNAUTAIRE
EDUCACION COMUNITARIA
UF SOCIAL EDUCATION
SN Enabling process through which
     children and adults receive a sense
     of identification with their
     community, become sensitive to its
     shortcomings and develop methods
     of participation in those activities

needed for the solution of social
problems
RT 186

COMMUNITY INFLUENCE
INFLUENCE DE LA
   COMMUNAUTE
INFLUENCIA DE LA COMUNIDAD
RT 122

COMMUNITY LEADERS
ANIMATEUR DE COMMUNAUTE
ANIMADOR DE LA COMUNIDAD
RT 440

COMMUNITY ORGANIZATIONS
ORGANISATION
   COMMUNAUTAIRE
ORGANIZACION DE LA
   COMUNIDAD
BT ORGANIZATIONS
RT 110
         COMMUNITY PROGRAMMES

COMMUNITY PARTICIPATION
PARTICIPATION DE LA
   COMMUNAUTE
PARTICIPACION DE LA
   COMUNIDAD
                                      May 1984
BT PARTICIPATION
RT COMMUNITY ROLE
     122

COMMUNITY PLANNING
PLANIFICATION
   COMMUNAUTAIRE
PLANIFICACION COMUNITARIA
BT PLANNING
RT 108

COMMUNITY PROBLEMS
PROBLEME COMMUNAUTAIRE
PROBLEMAS DE LA COMUNIDAD
RT 122

COMMUNITY PROGRAMMES
PROGRAMME COMMUNAUTAIRE
PROGRAMA COMUNITARIO
BT   PROGRAMMES
NT   ACTION PROGRAMMES
      (COMMUNITY)
RT   109
      COMMUNITY
      ORGANIZATIONS

COMMUNITY RESOURCES
RESSOURCES COMMUNAUTAIRES
RECURSOS DE LA COMUNIDAD
BT   RESOURCES
RT   700

COMMUNITY ROLE
ROLE DE LA COMMUNAUTE
PAPEL DE LA COMUNIDAD
RT   105
      COMMUNITY
      COMMUNITY PARTICIPATION

COMMUNITY SCHOOLS
ECOLE COMMUNAUTAIRE
ESCUELA DE LA COMUNIDAD
RT   302

COMMUNITY SERVICES
SERVICES COMMUNAUTAIRES
SERVICIOS COMUNITARIOS
BT   SERVICES
RT   107
      SCHOOL SERVICES

COMMUNITY STUDY
ETUDE COMMUNAUTAIRE
ESTUDIO SOBRE LA COMUNIDAD
RT   680

COMOROS
COMORES
COMORAS
BT   INDIAN OCEAN TERRITORIES
RT   FRENCH SPEAKING AFRICA

COMPARATIVE ANALYSIS
ANALYSE COMPARATIVE
ANALISIS COMPARATIVO
RT   282

COMPARATIVE EDUCATION
EDUCATION COMPAREE
EDUCACION COMPARADA
SN   Study of the comparison of
      current educational theory in
      practice in different countries
RT   640

COMPENSATORY EDUCATION
EDUCATION COMPENSATOIRE
EDUCACION COMPENSATORIA
SN   For deprived or disadvantaged
      students
RT   186

**COMPENSATORY EDUCATION
PROGRAMMES**
PROGRAMME D'EDUCATION
    COMPENSATOIRE
PROGRAMA DE EDUCACION
    COMPENSATORIA
BT   EDUCATIONAL PROGRAMMES
RT   271

COMPETENCY–BASED EDUCATION
ENSEIGNEMENT BASE SUR LES
    PERFORMANCES
ENSEÑANZA CENTRADA EN EL
    RENDIMIENTO
May 1984
RT   352

COMPETITIVE SELECTION
SELECTION COMPETITIVE
SELECCION COMPETITIVA
BT   SELECTION
RT   266

COMPLEMENTARY EDUCATION
EDUCATION COMPLEMENTAIRE
EDUCACION COMPLEMENTARIA
RT   184

COMPLEXITY LEVEL
NIVEAU DE COMPLEXITE
NIVEL DE COMPLEJIDAD
RT 522

COMPOSITION (LITERARY)
REDACTION
REDACCION
RT 620

COMPREHENSION
COMPREHENSION
COMPRENSION
BT INTELLIGENCE
RT 521

COMPREHENSIVE SCHOOLS
ECOLE POLYVALENTE
ESCUELA POLIVALENTE
RT 306

COMPREHENSIVE SECONDARY SCHOOLS
ECOLE SECONDAIRE POLYVALENTE
ESCUELA SECUNDARIA POLIVALENTE
BT SECONDARY SCHOOLS
RT 306

COMPULSORY EDUCATION
SCOLARITE OBLIGATOIRE
ESCOLARIDAD OBLIGATORIA
RT 180
    EDUCATIONAL LEGISLATION

COMPUTER ASSISTED INSTRUCTION
ENSEIGNEMENT ASSISTE PAR ORDINATEUR
ENSEÑANZA MEDIANTE COMPUTADORA
RT 361

COMPUTER LANGUAGES
LANGAGE D'ORDINATEUR
LENGUAJE DE COMPUTACION
RT 760

COMPUTER PROGRAMMES
PROGRAMME D'ORDINATEUR
PROGRAMA DE COMPUTACION
RT 760

COMPUTER SCIENCES
INFORMATIQUE
INFORMATICA
RT 630

COMPUTERS
ORDINATEUR
COMPUTADORA
RT 760

CONCEPT FORMATION
FORMATION DE CONCEPT
FORMACION DE CONCEPTOS
BT LEARNING PROCESSES
RT 513

CONCEPT TEACHING
ENSEIGNEMENT CONCEPTUEL
ENSEÑANZA CONCEPTUAL
BT TEACHING
RT 350

CONCEPTUAL SCHEMES
SCHEME CONCEPTUEL
ESQUEMA CONCEPTUAL
RT 522

CONDITIONED RESPONSE
REFLEXE CONDITIONNE
REFLEJO CONDICIONADO
RT 511

CONESCAL
CONESCAL
CONESCAL
SN Regional School Building Centre for Latin America and the Caribbean

CONFERENCE REPORT
RAPPORT DE CONFERENCE
INFORME DE CONFERENCIA
RT 880

CONFERENCES

CONFERENCES
CONFERENCE
CONFERENCIA
RT 204

CONFLICT
CONFLIT
CONFLICTO
RT 572

CONFLICT RESOLUTION
RESOLUTION DE CONFLIT
SOLUCION DE CONFLICTOS
RT 572

CONFORMITY
CONFORMITE
CONFORMISMO
BT BEHAVIOUR
RT 554

CONGO
CONGO
CONGO
UF CONGO (BRAZZA)
BT CENTRAL AFRICA
RT FRENCH SPEAKING AFRICA

CONGO (BRAZZA)
USE **CONGO**

CONGO DR
                    May 1984
USE **ZAIRE**

CONGO (KINSHASA)
USE **ZAIRE**

CONNECTED DISCOURSE
DISCOURS
DISCURSO
RT 620

CONSERVATION EDUCATION
USE **ENVIRONMENTAL EDUCATION**

CONSOLIDATION OF SCHOOLS
REGROUPEMENT SCOLAIRE
REAGRUPAMIENTO ESCOLAR
RT 264

CONSORTIA
CONSORTIUM
CONSORCIO
RT 261

CONSTRUCTION COSTS
COUT DE CONSTRUCTION
COSTOS DE CONSTRUCCION
BT COSTS
RT 251

CONSTRUCTION EQUIPMENT
EQUIPEMENT DE CONSTRUCTION
EQUIPOS DE CONSTRUCCION
RT 253

CONSTRUCTION INDUSTRY
INDUSTRIE DU BATIMENT
INDUSTRIA DE LA
    CONSTRUCCION
BT INDUSTRY
RT 150

CONSTRUCTION PRACTICES
PRATIQUE DE LA CONSTRUCTION
PRACTICAS DE LA
    CONSTRUCCION
RT 253

CONSTRUCTION PROCEDURES
PROCEDE DE CONSTRUCTION
PROCEDIMIENTOS DE
    CONSTRUCCION
RT 253

CONSTRUCTION PROGRAMMES
PROGRAMME DE CONSTRUCTION
PROGRAMA DE CONSTRUCCION
UF BUILDING PROGRAMMES
RT 253
       BUILDING MATERIALS

CONSULTANTS
CONSULTANT
CONSULTOR
SN Professionals who take part in specified educational programmes for limited time or on part-time basis
NT INTERNATIONAL EDUCATION CONSULTANTS
MEDICAL CONSULTANTS
READING CONSULTANTS
SCIENCE CONSULTANTS
RT 430

CONSUMER EDUCATION
EDUCATION DU CONSOMMATEUR
EDUCACION DEL CONSUMIDOR
SN Study of intelligent and effective methods of buying and using goods and services
RT ECONOMICS
186

CONTAGIOUS DISEASES
USE **COMMUNICABLE DISEASES**

CONTENT ANALYSIS
ANALYSE DE CONTENU
ANALISIS DEL CONTENIDO
RT 331

CONTINUATION EDUCATION
ECOLE DE LA DEUXIEME CHANCE
ENSEÑANZA DE SEGUNDA OPORTUNIDAD
SN Programmes for those who have not had the opportunity, or who have dropped out, to enable them to complete their formal education
RT 184

CONTINUATION STUDENTS
ELEVE DE L'ENSEIGNEMENT COMPLEMENTAIRE
ALUMNO DE EDUCACION DE SEGUNDA OPORTUNIDAD
SN Students, having rejected conventional schooling, are provided with special continuation educational programmes
RT 412

CONTINUING EDUCATION
USE **LIFELONG EDUCATION**

CONTINUOUS ASSESSMENT
EVALUATION CONTINUE
EVALUACION CONTINUA
RT 391

CONTINUOUS LEARNING
USE **LIFELONG EDUCATION**

CONTINUOUS PROGRESS PLAN
PLAN INDIVIDUEL DE PROGRESSION
PLAN DE PROGRESO INDIVIDUAL
UF FLEXIBLE PROGRESSION
SN Arrangement of curriculum and grouping procedures so as to permit students to progress at individual rates through school
RT 331
NONGRADED CURRICULUM

CONTRACTS
CONTRAT
CONTRATO
RT 241

CONTRASTIVE LINGUISTICS
LINGUISTIQUE COMPARATIVE
LINGUISTICA COMPARADA
BT LINGUISTICS
RT 621

CONTROL GROUPS
GROUPE TEMOIN
GRUPO DE CONTROL
RT 283

CONVENTIONAL INSTRUCTION
ENSEIGNEMENT CONVENTIONNEL
ENSEÑANZA CONVENCIONAL
BT INSTRUCTION
RT 352

CONVERSATIONAL LANGUAGE COURSES
COURS DE CONVERSATION
CURSO DE CONVERSACION
RT 663

COOK ISLANDS
ILES COOK
ISLAS DE COOK
May 1984
BT POLYNESIA

COOPERATIVE EDUCATION
USE **WORK EXPERIENCE PROGRAMMES**

COOPERATIVES
COOPERATIVE
COOPERATIVA
SN Economic enterprise wholly owned by its users
RT 150

COORDINATION
COORDINATION
COORDINACION
SN Bringing different undertakings into functional relationship
NT EDUCATIONAL COORDINATION
PROGRAMME COORDINATION
RT 102

COPYRIGHTS
DROIT D'AUTEUR
DERECHOS DE AUTOR
RT 170

CORE COURSES
COURS COMMUN
CURSO COMUN
BT COURSES
RT 333

CORE CURRICULUM
PROGRAMME COMMUN
PROGRAMA OBLIGATORIO COMUN
RT 330

CORRECTIONAL EDUCATION
EDUCATION SURVEILLEE
EDUCACION CORRECCIONAL
RT 186

CORRECTIONAL INSTITUTIONS
ETABLISSEMENT D'EDUCATION SURVEILLEE
INSTITUCION CORRECCIONAL
May 1984
UF BORSTALS
RT 170

CORRECTIONAL SCHOOLS
CENTRE D'EDUCATION SURVEILLEE
ESCUELA CORRECCIONAL
May 1984
RT 304

CORRECTIVE READING
LECTURE CORRECTIVE
LECTURA CORRECTIVA
SN Reading instruction for retarded readers within a regular class
RT 660

CORRELATION
CORRELATION
CORRELACION
RT 283

CORRESPONDENCE COURSES
COURS PAR CORRESPONDANCE
CURSO POR CORRESPONDENCIA
BT COURSES
RT 333

CORRESPONDENCE SCHOOLS
ECOLE PAR CORRESPONDANCE
ESCUELA POR CORRESPONDENCIA
RT 303

CORRESPONDENCE TUITION
ENSEIGNEMENT PAR CORRESPONDANCE
ENSEÑANZA POR CORRESPONDENCIA
SN Method of instruction with teacher

COURSE EVALUATION

student interaction by mail
RT 335

COST EFFECTIVENESS
RAPPORT COUT/EFFICACITE
RELACION COSTO–RENDIMIENTO
RT 243

COST REDUCTION
REDUCTION DES COUTS
REDUCCION DE LOS COSTOS
BT COSTS
RT 243

COSTA RICA
COSTA RICA
COSTA RICA
BT CENTRAL AMERICA

COSTS
COUT
COSTO
NT CONSTRUCTION COSTS
    COST REDUCTION
    ESTIMATED COSTS
    PROGRAMME COSTS
    UNIT COSTS
RT 241

COUNCIL OF EUROPE
CONSEIL DE L'EUROPE
CONSEJO DE EUROPA

COUNSELLING
CONSULTATION D'ORIENTATION
ASESORAMIENTO
NT ADULT COUNSELLING
    BEHAVIOURAL COUNSELLING
    CAREER COUNSELLING
    EDUCATIONAL COUNSELLING
    FAMILY COUNSELLING
    GROUP COUNSELLING
    INDIVIDUAL COUNSELLING
RT 370
    GUIDANCE

COUNSELLING CENTRES
CENTRE D'ORIENTATION
CENTRO DE ORIENTACION
RT 311

COUNSELLING OBJECTIVES
OBJECTIF DE L'ORIENTATION
OBJETIVO DEL ASESORAMIENTO
BT EDUCATIONAL OBJECTIVES
RT 370

COUNSELLOR FUNCTIONS
ROLE DU CONSEILLER
    D'ORIENTATION
FUNCION DEL CONSEJERO
RT 370

COUNSELLOR QUALIFICATIONS
QUALIFICATION DU CONSEILLER
    D'ORIENTATION
CALIFICACION DEL CONSEJERO
BT QUALIFICATIONS
RT 223

COUNSELLOR TRAINING
FORMATION DES CONSEILLERS
    D'ORIENTATION
FORMACION DE CONSEJEROS
RT 681

COUNSELLORS
CONSEILLER D'ORIENTATION
CONSEJERO
NT EMPLOYMENT COUNSELLORS
    PRIMARY SCHOOL
        COUNSELLORS
    SECONDARY SCHOOL
        COUNSELLORS
RT 431

COURSE DURATION
DUREE DU COURS
DURACION DEL CURSO
RT 333

COURSE EVALUATION
EVALUATION DU COURS
EVALUACION DEL CURSO
RT 333

COURSE OBJECTIVES

COURSE OBJECTIVES
OBJECTIF DU COURS
OBJETIVO DEL CURSO
BT   EDUCATIONAL OBJECTIVES
RT   300

COURSE ORGANIZATION
ORGANISATION DU COURS
ORGANIZACION DEL CURSO
RT   333

COURSES
COURS
CURSO
NT   ACCELERATED COURSES
     CORE COURSES
     CORRESPONDENCE COURSES
     CREDIT COURSES
     ELECTIVE COURSES
     EVENING COURSES
     INSERVICE COURSES
     NONCREDIT COURSES
     OPTIONAL COURSES
     ORIENTATION COURSES
     REMEDIAL COURSES
     SANDWICH COURSES
     SHORT COURSES
RT   333

COURT LITIGATION
LITIGE JURIDIQUE
JURISDICCION
RT   170

COURTS
TRIBUNAL
TRIBUNAL
RT   170

CREATIVE ABILITY
APTITUDE CREATRICE
APTITUD CREADORA
BT   ABILITY
RT   520

CREATIVE DEVELOPMENT
DEVELOPPEMENT DE LA
  CREATIVITE
DESARROLLO DE LA
  CREATIVIDAD

RT   530

CREATIVE TEACHING
ENSEIGNEMENT VISANT LA
  CREATIVITE
ENSEÑANZA BASADA EN LA
  CREATIVIDAD
BT   TEACHING
RT   350

CREATIVE THINKING
PENSEE CREATRICE
PENSAMIENTO CREADOR
BT   THOUGHT PROCESSES
RT   521

CREATIVITY
CREATIVITE
CREATIVIDAD
RT   522

CRECHES
USE **PRESCHOOL CENTRES**

CREDENTIALS
TITRE DE REFERENCE
CREDENCIAL
SN   Apply to certification of
     individuals
RT   232

CREDIT COURSES
COURS PAR UNITES
  CAPITALISABLES
CURSO CON UNIDADES DE
  VALOR
BT   COURSES
RT   333

CREDIT SYSTEM
SYSTEME DE CREDITS
SISTEMA DE UNIDADES DE
  VALOR
BT   DEGREE REQUIREMENTS
RT   390

CREFAL
CREFAL
CREFAL
SN Regional Centre for Functional Literacy in Rural Areas for Latin America

CREOLES
LANGUES CREOLES
LENGUAS CRIOLLAS
SN Languages developing from a pidgin and having native speakers
RT 625

CRIPPLES
INFIRME
INVALIDO
RT 403

CRITERIA
CRITERE
CRITERIO
SN Judgements serving as the basis for quantitative or qualitative comparison
NT EVALUATION CRITERIA
    RESEARCH CRITERIA
RT 283

CRITERION REFERENCED TESTS
TEST A REFERENCE CRITERIELLE
EVALUACION DE UN PROCESO EXPERIMENTAL
RT 392

CRITICAL PATH METHOD
USE **NETWORK ANALYSIS**

CRITICAL THINKING
PENSEE CRITIQUE
PENSAMIENTO CRITICO
BT THOUGHT PROCESSES
RT 521

CROSS AGE TEACHING
ENSEIGNEMENT MUTUEL INTER-NIVEAUX
ENSEÑANZA POR ALUMNOS MAYORES
SN Utilization of older students from higher grade levels to provide increased help and attention for younger students at lower grade levels
BT TEACHING
RT 350

CROSS CULTURAL STUDIES
ETUDE TRANSCULTURELLE
ESTUDIO INTERCULTURAL
RT 282

CSME
CSME
CSME
SN World Confederation of Teachers

CUBA
CUBA
CUBA
BT CARIBBEAN

CULTURAL ACTIVITIES
ACTIVITE CULTURELLE
ACTIVIDAD CULTURAL
RT 537

CULTURAL BACKGROUND
MILIEU CULTUREL
MEDIO CULTURAL
SN The cumulative intellectual, artistic, and social heritage and experience of an individual or group
RT 130

CULTURAL CENTRES
CENTRE CULTUREL
CENTRO CULTURAL
RT 310

CULTURAL DISADVANTAGEMENT
HANDICAP CULTUREL
DESVENTAJA CULTURAL
RT 130

CULTURAL ENVIRONMENT
ENVIRONNEMENT CULTUREL
AMBIENTE CULTURAL
BT ENVIRONMENT
NT HOME ENVIRONMENT

CULTURAL EXCHANGE

       SOCIAL ENVIRONMENT
RT   550

CULTURAL EXCHANGE
ECHANGE CULTUREL
INTERCAMBIO CULTURAL
RT   130

CULTURAL FACTORS
FACTEUR CULTUREL
FACTOR CULTURAL
RT   285

CULTURAL INTERRELATIONSHIPS
INTERRELATION CULTURELLE
INTERRELACION CULTURAL
RT   130

CULTURAL ISOLATION
ISOLEMENT CULTUREL
AISLAMIENTO CULTURAL
RT   130

CULTURAL POLICIES
POLITIQUE CULTURELLE
POLITICA CULTURAL
BT   POLICIES
RT   130
       EDUCATIONAL POLICIES

CULTURAL TRAITS
ASPECT CULTUREL
ASPECTO CULTURAL
RT   561

CULTURALLY DISADVANTAGED
DEFAVORISE CULTUREL
DESFAVORECIDO CULTURAL
RT   402

CULTURE
CULTURE
CULTURA
SN General context and content but not referring to specific forms which are indexed under "cultures"
NT URBAN CULTURE
RT   130
       CULTURES

CULTURES
CIVILISATION
CIVILIZACION
RT   600
       CULTURE

CURIOSITY
CURIOSITE
CURIOSIDAD
BT INDIVIDUAL
       CHARACTERISTICS
RT   561

CURRICULUM
CURRICULUM
CURRICULO
RT   330
       INSTRUCTIONAL
       PROGRAMMES

CURRICULUM DEVELOPMENT
DEVELOPPEMENT DU
   CURRICULUM
ELABORACION DEL CURRICULO
SN Systematic process of building curriculum for a particular stage of education or institution, involves setting out aims, content, methods, evaluation procedure
RT   331
       LEARNING NEEDS

CURRICULUM EVALUATION
EVALUATION DU CURRICULUM
EVALUACION DEL CURRICULO
BT EVALUATION
RT   213

CURRICULUM GUIDES
PROGRAMME DES COURS
  (FASCICULES)
GUIA DE ESTUDIOS
BT GUIDES
RT   724

CURRICULUM PLANNING
PLANIFICATION DU CURRICULUM
PLANIFICACION DEL CURRICULO
BT EDUCATIONAL PLANNING
RT   213

CURRICULUM PROBLEMS
PROBLEME DE CURRICULUM
PROBLEMAS CURRICULARES
RT 281

CURRICULUM RESEARCH
RECHERCHE SUR LE
    CURRICULUM
INVESTIGACION CURRICULAR
BT EDUCATIONAL RESEARCH
RT 280

CURRICULUM STUDY CENTRES
CENTRE D'ETUDES SUR LE
    CURRICULUM
CENTRO DE ESTUDIOS DEL
    CURRICULO
RT 312

CYBERNETICS
CYBERNETIQUE
CIBERNETICA
RT 650
        AUTOMATION

CYPRUS
CHYPRE
CHIPRE
BT MEDITERRANEAN
        COUNTRIES
        MIDDLE EAST
        WESTERN EUROPE

CZECHOSLOVAKIA
TCHECOSLOVAQUIE
CHECOSLOVAQUIA
BT EASTERN EUROPE

DAHOMEY
USE **BENIN**

DANCE
DANSE
DANZA
RT 610

DATA ANALYSIS
ANALYSE DES DONNEES
ANALISIS DE DATOS
RT 284

DATA BASE
BASE DE DONNEES
BASE DE DATOS
SN Of a research study
RT 283

DATA COLLECTION
COLLECTE DES DONNEES
RECOPILACION DE DATOS
RT 203

DATA PROCESSING
TRAITEMENT DES DONNEES
PROCESAMIENTO DE DATOS
BT INFORMATION PROCESSING
NT TIME SHARING
RT 284

DAY CARE SERVICES
SERVICES DE GARDERIE
    D'ENFANTS
SERVICIO DE GUARDERIA
    INFANTIL
RT 270

DAY RELEASE
CONGE D'ETUDES
    HEBDOMADAIRE
LICENCIA DE ESTUDIOS POR DIA
BT RELEASED TIME
RT 222

DAY SCHOOLS
EXTERNAT
EXTERNADO
RT 303

DAY STUDENTS
ELEVE EXTERNE
ALUMNO EXTERNO
RT 410

DEAF

DEAF
SOURD
SORDO
SN Children or adults
RT 403

DEAF EDUCATION
EDUCATION DES SOURDS
EDUCACION DE SORDOS
BT SPECIAL EDUCATION
RT 322

DEATH
MORT
MUERTE
RT 500

DECENTRALIZATION
DECENTRALISATION
DESCENTRALIZACION
RT 200

DECISION MAKING
PRISE DE DECISION
TOMA DE DECISION
RT 201

DEDUCTIVE METHODS
METHODE DEDUCTIVE
METODO DEDUCTIVO
BT TEACHING METHODS
RT 355

DEFICIT (FACILITIES)
DEFICIT (INSTALLATIONS)
DEFICIT (INSTALACIONES)
BT EDUCATIONAL NEEDS
RT 250

DEGREE REQUIREMENTS
CONDITION D'OBTENTION DU
  DIPLOME
REQUISITO PARA LA OBTENCION
  DEL TITULO
NT CREDIT SYSTEM
RT 390

DEGREES (TITLES)
GRADE UNIVERSITAIRE
GRADO (TITULO)
NT BACHELORS DEGREES
   DOCTORAL DEGREES
   MASTERS DEGREES
   SPECIALIST IN EDUCATION
     DEGREES
RT 390

DELINQUENCY
DELINQUANCE
DELINCUENCIA
RT 572

DELINQUENCY CAUSES
CAUSE DE DELINQUANCE
CAUSAS DE DELINCUENCIA
RT 285

DELINQUENCY PREVENTION
PREVENTION DE LA
  DELINQUANCE
PREVENCION DE LA
  DELINCUENCIA
RT 281

DELINQUENTS
DELINQUANT
DELINCUENTE
RT 403

DEMOCRACY
DEMOCRATIE
DEMOCRACIA
RT 101

DEMOCRATIC KAMPUCHEA
KAMPUCHEA DEMOCRATIQUE
KAMPUCHEA DEMOCRATICA
UF CAMBODIA
   KHMER REPUBLIC

DEMOCRATIC YEMEN
YEMEN DEMOCRATIQUE
YEMEN DEMOCRATICO
UF SOUTHERN YEMEN
BT ARAB COUNTRIES
   MIDDLE EAST

DEMOCRATIZATION OF EDUCATION
DEMOCRATISATION DE L'EDUCATION
DEMOCRATIZACION DE LA EDUCACION
SN Policy of ensuring equality of educational opportunity in order to achieve universal education
NT EDUCATIONAL OPPORTUNITIES
    EQUAL EDUCATION
RT 180

DEMOGRAPHY
DEMOGRAPHIE
DEMOGRAFIA
BT SOCIAL SCIENCES
RT 640

DEMONSTRATION PROJECTS
PROJET MODELE
PROYECTO MODELO
BT PROJECTS
RT 272

DEMONSTRATIONS (EDUCATIONAL)
DEMONSTRATION PEDAGOGIQUE
DEMOSTRACION PEDAGOGICA
RT 671

DENMARK
DANEMARK
DINAMARCA
BT SCANDINAVIA
    WESTERN EUROPE

DENOMINATIONAL SCHOOLS
USE **PRIVATE SCHOOLS**

DENTAL HEALTH
HYGIENE DENTAIRE
SALUD DENTAL
BT PHYSICAL HEALTH
RT 502

DENTISTRY
ART DENTAIRE
ODONTOLOGIA
RT 651

DEPARTMENTAL TEACHING PLANS
PLAN DE REPARTITION DES MATIERES
PLAN DE ESTUDIOS POR DEPARTAMENTOS
SN Plan under which each teacher teaches one subject or one group of closely related subjects
RT 340

DEPARTMENTS (SCHOOL)
SECTION (ECOLE)
DEPARTAMENTO (ESCUELA)
BT SCHOOL ORGANIZATION
RT 340

DEPRESSED AREAS (ECONOMIC)
ZONE DESERITEE
ZONA DESFAVORECIDA
UF SLUMS
RT 151

DEPRIVED GROUPS
USE **DISADVANTAGED GROUPS**

DESCRIPTIVE LINGUISTICS
LINGUISTIQUE DESCRIPTIVE
LINGUISTICA DESCRIPTIVA
BT LINGUISTICS
RT 621

DESIGN PROCEDURE
MODE DE CONCEPTION
CONCEPCION DEL DISEÑO
RT 252

DEVELOPED COUNTRIES
PAYS DEVELOPPE
PAISES DESARROLLADOS
SN States which are technologically advanced and have relatively high living standards
RT 101

DEVELOPING COUNTRIES
PAYS EN DEVELOPPEMENT
PAISES EN DESARROLLO
RT   101

DEVELOPMENT
DEVELOPPEMENT
DESARROLLO
NT   AGRICULTURAL
         DEVELOPMENT
     COMMUNITY DEVELOPMENT
     ECONOMIC DEVELOPMENT
     EDUCATIONAL
         DEVELOPMENT
     HUMAN RESOURCES
         DEVELOPMENT
     MANPOWER DEVELOPMENT
     RURAL DEVELOPMENT
     SOCIAL DEVELOPMENT
RT   151

DEVELOPMENT EDUCATION
EDUCATION POUR LE
    DEVELOPPEMENT
EDUCACION PARA EL
    DESARROLLO
RT   682

DEVELOPMENT STUDIES
ETUDES DU DEVELOPPEMENT
ESTUDIOS SOBRE DESARROLLO
                                        MAY 1984
RT   640

DEVELOPMENTAL PSYCHOLOGY
PSYCHOLOGIE GENETIQUE
PSICOLOGIA EVOLUTIVA
BT   PSYCHOLOGY
RT   642

DIAGNOSTIC TEACHING
CLASSE D'OBSERVATION
CLASE DE OBSERVACION
BT   TEACHING
RT   350

DIAGNOSTIC TESTS
TEST DE DIAGNOSTIC
PRUEBA DE DIAGNOSTICO
RT   392

DIAGRAMS
DIAGRAMME
DIAGRAMA
UF   ORGANIGRAMS
SN   Graphic displays showing
     structures and relationships, e.g. of
     a school system, of a ministry
RT   733

DIALECTS
DIALECTE
DIALECTO
RT   625

DICTION
DICTION
DICCION
BT   SPEECH
RT   532

DICTIONARY
DICTIONNAIRE
DICCIONARIO
                                        MAY 1984
RT   880

DIDACTICS
USE **PRINCIPLES OF TEACHING**

DIFFERENTIATED STAFFS
PERSONNEL DIFFERENCIE
PERSONAL DIFERENCIADO
SN   Staffs utilizing various levels of
     professional and semi-professional
     personnel
BT   TEACHING PERSONNEL
RT   424

DIFFUSION
PROPAGATION
DIFUSION
RT   204

DYSPLAY BOARDS

DIPLOMAS
DIPLOME
DIPLOMA
SN   Certificate of higher education with less weight than a degree
RT   390

DIRECTORY
REPERTOIRE
REPERTORIO
RT   880

DISADVANTAGED GROUPS
GROUPE DEFAVORISE
GRUPO DESFAVORECIDO
UF   DEPRIVED GROUPS
BT   GROUPS
RT   443

DISADVANTAGED SCHOOLS
ECOLE DEFAVORISEE
ESCUELA DESFAVORECIDA
SN   With majority of students considered to come from disadvantaged background
RT   304

DISARMAMENT EDUCATION
EDUCATION POUR LE DESARMEMENT
EDUCACION PARA EL DESARME
                                                MAY 1984
RT   682

DISCIPLINE
DISCIPLINE
DISCIPLINA
SN   Considered as a factor in school administration
RT   267

DISCIPLINE POLICY
SYSTEME DISCIPLINAIRE
SISTEMA DISCIPLINARIO
RT   231

DISCIPLINE PROBLEMS
PROBLEME DISCIPLINAIRE
PROBLEMA DISCIPLINARIO
RT   281

DISCOVERY LEARNING
APPRENTISSAGE PAR LA DECOUVERTE
APRENDIZAJE MEDIANTE EL DESCUBRIMIENTO
BT   LEARNING
RT   512

DISCUSSION GROUPS
GROUPE DE DISCUSSION
GRUPO DE DISCUSION
RT   343

DISCUSSION (TEACHING TECHNIQUE)
DISCUSSION (TECHNIQUE PEDAGOGIQUE)
DISCUSION
NT   GROUP DISCUSSION
RT   356

DISEASE CONTROL
PREVENTION DE LA MALADIE
PREVENCION DE LA ENFERMEDAD
RT   161

DISEASE RATE
TAUX DE MORBIDITE
TASA DE MORBILIDAD
RT   161

DISEASES
MALADIE
ENFERMEDAD
NT   COMMUNICABLE DISEASES
     PSYCHOSOMATIC DISEASES
RT   161

DISPLAY BOARDS
PRESENTOIR
TABLERO
RT   741

49

DISPUTE SETTLEMENT
REGLEMENT DE CONFLIT
SOLUCION DE CONFLICTOS
UF   ARBITRATION
RT   233

DISQUALIFICATION
DISQUALIFICATION
DESCALIFICACION
SN   Barred from professional activity
RT   233

DISTANCE
DISTANCE
DISTANCIA
SN   Considered as a factor in school administration
RT   264

DISTANCE EDUCATION
TELE-ENSEIGNEMENT
ENSEÑANZA A DISTANCIA
SN   Systematic use of techniques like radio, correspondence, television, to reach off-campus students. More restrictive than open learning systems
RT   355
      EDUCATIONAL MEDIA

DISTRIBUTIVE EDUCATION
ENSEIGNEMENT DES TECHNIQUES DE VENTE
ENSEÑANZA DE TECNICAS DE COMERCIALIZACION
SN   Studies relating to the marketing occupations
BT   VOCATIONAL EDUCATION
RT   672

DJIBOUTI
DJIBOUTI
DJIBOUTI
May 1984
UF   AFARS AND ISSAS
BT   EAST AFRICA
RT   FRENCH SPEAKING AFRICA

DOCTORAL DEGREES
DOCTORAT
GRADO DE DOCTOR
BT   DEGREES (TITLES)
RT   390

DOCTORAL PROGRAMMES
PROGRAMME DE DOCTORAT
PROGRAMA DE DOCTORADO
BT   COLLEGE PROGRAMMES
RT   320

DOCTORAL THESES
THESE DE DOCTORAT
TESIS DE DOCTORADO
RT   721

DOCUMENTALISTS
DOCUMENTALISTE
DOCUMENTALISTA
RT   462

DOCUMENTATION
DOCUMENTATION
DOCUMENTACION
SN   Document generation, processing, and use
NT   EDUCATIONAL DOCUMENTATION
RT   202

DOCUMENTATION CENTRES
CENTRE DE DOCUMENTATION
CENTRO DE DOCUMENTACION
RT   310

DOCUMENTS
DOCUMENT
DOCUMENTO
RT   721

DOMINICA
DOMINIQUE
DOMINICA
May 1984
BT   CARIBBEAN

EARLY CHILDHOOD EDUCATION

DOMINICAN REPUBLIC
REPUBLIQUE DOMINICAINE
REPUBLICA DOMINICANA
BT   CARIBBEAN

DOUBLE SHIFT SCHOOLS
ECOLE A MI-TEMPS
ESCUELA DE MEDIA JORNADA
RT   303

DOWNS SYNDROME
SYNDROME DE DOWN
SINDROME DE DOWN
UF   MONGOLISM
RT   570

DRAFTSMEN
DESSINATEUR
DIBUJANTE TECNICO
BT   TECHNICIANS
RT   452
        BUILDING TRADES

DRAMA
DRAME
DRAMA
RT   616

DRAMA WORKSHOPS
ATELIER D'ART DRAMATIQUE
TALLER DE ARTE DRAMATICO
RT   381

DRAVIDIAN LANGUAGES
LANGUES DRAVIDIENNES
LENGUAS DRAVIDICAS
RT   625

DROPOUT PROGRAMMES
PROGRAMME DE RECUPERATION
PROGRAMA DE RECUPERACION
RT   320

DROPOUT RATE
TAUX D'ABANDON EN COURS
   D'ETUDES
TASA DE DESERCION ESCOLAR
RT   206

DROPOUTS
ELEVE ABANDONNANT LA
   SCOLARITE
ALUMNO DESERTOR
RT   411

DROPPING OUT
ABANDON EN COURS D'ETUDES
DESERCION
SN   Premature leaving before
       completing a cycle or course of
       education already begun
RT   266

DRUG ABUSE
TOXICOMANIE
TOXICOMANIA
RT   572

DRUG EDUCATION
EDUCATION ANTIDROGUE
EDUCACION ANTIDROGADICCION
RT   683

DUAL ENROLMENT
DOUBLE INSCRIPTION
MATRICULA DOBLE
SN   Enrolment of students in two
       schools at the same time
BT   ENROLMENT
RT   206

DYSLEXIA
DYSLEXIE
DISLEXIA
BT   LANGUAGE HANDICAPS
RT   570

EARLY CHILDHOOD
PREMIERE ENFANCE
PRIMERA INFANCIA
BT   CHILDHOOD
RT   500

EARLY CHILDHOOD EDUCATION
EDUCATION DE LA PREMIERE
   ENFANCE
EDUCACION DE LA PRIMERA
   INFANCIA
UF   INFANT EDUCATION

EARTH SCIENCES

SN Relates to period of infancy, i.e. to about three years of age
RT 186

EARTH SCIENCES
SCIENCES DE LA TERRE
CIENCIAS DE LA TIERRA
BT SCIENCES
RT 633

EAST AFRICA
AFRIQUE ORIENTALE
AFRICA ORIENTAL
BT AFRICA SOUTH OF THE SAHARA
NT DJIBOUTI
 BURUNDI
 ETHIOPIA
 KENYA
 MADAGASCAR
 MALAWI
 MOZAMBIQUE
 ZIMBABWE
 RWANDA
 SOMALIA
 TANZANIA UR
 UGANDA
 ZAMBIA
RT INDIAN OCEAN TERRITORIES

EAST ASIA
May 1984
USE **FAR EAST**

EAST GERMANY
May 1984
USE **GERMAN DR**

EASTER ISLAND
ILES DE PAQUES
ISLA DE PASCUA
May 1984
BT POLYNESIA

EASTERN EUROPE
EUROPE ORIENTALE
EUROPA ORIENTAL
BT EUROPE
NT ALBANIA
 BULGARIA
 CZECHOSLOVAKIA
 GERMAN DR
 HUNGARY
 POLAND
 ROMANIA
 USSR
 YUGOSLAVIA

EASTERN HEMISPHERE
HEMISPHERE ORIENTAL
HEMISFERIO ORIENTAL
May 1984
RT WESTERN HEMISPHERE

ECA
CEA
CEPA
SN Economic Commission for Africa

ECE
CEE (ONU)
CEPE
SN Economic Commission for Europe

ECLA
CEPAL
CEPAL
SN Economic Commission for Latin America

ECOLOGY
ECOLOGIE
ECOLOGIA
BT BIOLOGY
RT 632

ECONOMIC BACKGROUND
USE **SOCIOECONOMIC BACKGROUND**

ECONOMIC CLIMATE
CONJONCTURE ECONOMIQUE
COYUNTURA ECONOMICA
SN Covers economic conditions
RT 150

EDUCATIONAL ADMINISTRATION

ECONOMIC DEVELOPMENT
DEVELOPPEMENT ECONOMIQUE
DESARROLLO ECONOMICO
BT DEVELOPMENT
RT 151

ECONOMIC FACTORS
FACTEUR ECONOMIQUE
FACTOR ECONOMICO
RT 285

ECONOMIC POLICIES
POLITIQUE ECONOMIQUE
POLITICA ECONOMICA
BT POLICIES
RT 150

ECONOMIC PROGRESS
PROGRES ECONOMIQUE
PROGRESO ECONOMICO
RT 150

ECONOMIC RESEARCH
RECHERCHE ECONOMIQUE
INVESTIGACION ECONOMICA
RT 280

ECONOMIC STATUS
STATUT ECONOMIQUE
CONDICION ECONOMICA
BT STATUS
RT 121

ECONOMICS
SCIENCE ECONOMIQUE
CIENCIAS ECONOMICAS
BT SOCIAL SCIENCES
NT EDUCATIONAL ECONOMICS
RT 640
    CONSUMER EDUCATION

ECOSOC
ECOSOC
ECOSOC
SN Economic and Social Council

ECUADOR
EQUATEUR
ECUADOR
BT SOUTH AMERICA
RT GALAPAGOS ISLANDS

ECWA
ECWA
ECWA
SN Economic Commission for Western Asia

EDUCATED UNEMPLOYMENT
CHOMAGE DES DIPLOMES
DESOCUPACION DE LOS
    GRADUADOS
BT UNEMPLOYMENT
RT 154

EDUCATION
EDUCATION
EDUCACION
SN Process by which a person develops abilities, attitudes and other forms of behaviour considered to have value in the society in which he lives; when education is informal it virtually equals growth; when it occurs in a selected and controlled environment it may be either formal or non-formal
RT 180

EDUCATION COURSES
COURS DE PEDAGOGIE
CURSO DE PEDAGOGIA
RT 691

EDUCATION WORK RELATIONSHIP
RELATION TRAVAIL-EDUCATION
RELACION EDUCACION-TRABAJO
RT 182

EDUCATIONAL ADMINISTRATION
ADMINISTRATION DE L'EDUCATION
ADMINISTRACION DE LA EDUCACION
SN Relating to part or all of

EDUCATIONAL ADMINISTRATORS

    educational system
BT ADMINISTRATION
NT COLLEGE ADMINISTRATION
     SCHOOL ADMINISTRATION
RT 200
     ADMINISTRATIVE
       ORGANIZATION

EDUCATIONAL ADMINISTRATORS
ADMINISTRATEUR DE
  L'EDUCATION
ADMINISTRADOR DE LA
  EDUCACION
BT EDUCATIONAL PERSONNEL
NT SUPERINTENDENTS
RT 420

EDUCATIONAL AIMS
BUT EDUCATIF
META EDUCACIONAL
SN Express the direction given to all or part of the system of education by educators and thus formulate educational goals at a greater level of specificity
RT 200
     EDUCATIONAL GOALS
     EDUCATIONAL OBJECTIVES

EDUCATIONAL ANTHROPOLOGY
ANTHROPOLOGIE DE
  L'EDUCATION
ANTROPOLOGIA DE LA
  EDUCACION
RT 642

EDUCATIONAL BACKGROUND
ACQUIS EDUCATIF
NIVEL EDUCACIONAL
RT 221

EDUCATIONAL BENEFITS
AVANTAGE EDUCATIF
BENEFICIO EDUCACIONAL
SN Individual benefits obtained from acquisition of advanced education
RT 181

EDUCATIONAL CERTIFICATES
CERTIFICAT DE FIN D'ETUDES
CERTIFICADO DE ESTUDIOS
SN Named award granted on completion of a specified course of education
NT PRIMARY SCHOOL
     CERTIFICATES
     SECONDARY SCHOOL
       CERTIFICATES
     VOCATIONAL SCHOOL
       CERTIFICATES
RT 390

EDUCATIONAL COMPLEXES
COMPLEXE SCOLAIRE
COMPLEJOS EDUCACIONALES
SN A set of educational services placed together to provide for the needs of a wide age range of students
RT 187

EDUCATIONAL COORDINATION
COORDINATION
  EDUCATIONNELLE
COORDINACION EDUCACIONAL
SN Of different agencies and organizations concerned with education
BT COORDINATION
RT 200

EDUCATIONAL COUNSELLING
CONSULTATION EDUCATIVE
CONSEJERIA EDUCACIONAL
BT COUNSELLING
RT 370

EDUCATIONAL DEMAND
DEMANDE D'EDUCATION
DEMANDA DE EDUCACION
SN Consumer demand for education
RT 181

EDUCATIONAL DEVELOPMENT
DEVELOPPEMENT DE
  L'EDUCATION
DESARROLLO DE LA EDUCACION
SN Developmental change of one or

more characteristics of the educational systems variables in a positive direction in terms of some valued criterion
BT DEVELOPMENT
RT 182

EDUCATIONAL DEVELOPMENT TRENDS
TENDANCE DU DEVELOPPEMENT EDUCATIF
TENDENCIAS DEL DESARROLLO DE LA EDUCACION
RT 182

EDUCATIONAL DIAGNOSIS
DIAGNOSTIC PEDAGOGIQUE
DIAGNOSTICO EDUCACIONAL
SN Identification of the nature or level of student ability or skill
RT 391

EDUCATIONAL DISADVANTAGEMENT
HANDICAP EDUCATIF
MARGINACION EDUCACIONAL
RT 181

EDUCATIONAL DISCRIMINATION
DISCRIMINATION EN EDUCATION
DISCRIMINACION EDUCACIONAL
RT 181

EDUCATIONAL DOCUMENTATION
DOCUMENTATION SUR L'EDUCATION
DOCUMENTACION SOBRE EDUCACION
BT DOCUMENTATION
RT 202

EDUCATIONAL ECONOMICS
ECONOMIE DE L'EDUCATION
ECONOMIA DE LA EDUCACION
BT ECONOMICS
RT 640

EDUCATIONAL ENVIRONMENT
MILIEU EDUCATIF
AMBIENTE EDUCACIONAL
BT ENVIRONMENT
NT CLASSROOM ENVIRONMENT
RT 380

EDUCATIONAL EQUIPMENT
EQUIPEMENT EDUCATIF
EQUIPO EDUCACIONAL
BT EQUIPMENT
RT 740

EDUCATIONAL EXPECTATIONS
ASPIRATIONS EDUCATIVES
EXPECTATIVAS EDUCACIONALES
RT 541

EDUCATIONAL EXPERIENCE
EXPERIENCE EDUCATIVE
EXPERIENCIA EDUCACIONAL
BT EXPERIENCE
RT 562

EDUCATIONAL EXPERIMENTS
EXPERIMENTATION PEDAGOGIQUE
EXPERIMENTO EDUCACIONAL
RT 282

EDUCATIONAL FACILITIES
INSTALLATION SCOLAIRE
INSTALACIONES EDUCACIONALES
NT RECREATIONAL FACILITIES
   RELOCATABLE FACILITIES
   SPORTS FACILITIES
RT 710

EDUCATIONAL FINANCE
FINANCEMENT DE L'EDUCATION
FINANCIAMIENTO DE LA EDUCACION
RT 243
   152

EDUCATIONAL FUTUROLOGY
FUTUROLOGIE DE L'EDUCATION
FUTUROLOGIA DE LA EDUCACION

May 1984

EDUCATIONAL GAMES

SN The aspect of futurology which has as its object to foresee the future development of education
RT 100

EDUCATIONAL GAMES
JEU EDUCATIF
JUEGO EDUCATIVO
BT PLAY
RT 356

EDUCATIONAL GOALS
FINALITE DE L'EDUCATION
FINALIDADES DE LA EDUCACION
SN The ends set explicitly or implicitly by a society for the educational system it maintains; expressed at times in broad political, cultural and economic terms (e.g. citizenship, democracy, group unity), at times referring specifically to formal education (e.g. access to education, equal education)
RT 180
    EDUCATIONAL AIMS
    EDUCATIONAL OBJECTIVES

EDUCATIONAL GUIDANCE
ORIENTATION SCOLAIRE
ORIENTACION EDUCACIONAL
BT GUIDANCE
RT 211

EDUCATIONAL HISTORY
HISTOIRE DE L'EDUCATION
HISTORIA DE LA EDUCACION
BT HISTORY
RT 641

EDUCATIONAL IMPROVEMENT
AMELIORATION DE L'EDUCATION
MEJORAMIENTO DE LA EDUCACION
RT 182

EDUCATIONAL INFORMATION
INFORMATION SUR L'EDUCATION
INFORMACION SOBRE EDUCACION
RT 200

EDUCATIONAL INFRASTRUCTURE
INFRASTRUCTURE DE L'EDUCATION
INFRAESTRUCTURA EDUCACIONAL
UF EDUCATIONAL PROVISION
SN Entire range of human resources and facilities made available for formal and non-formal education
RT 181

EDUCATIONAL INNOVATIONS
INNOVATION EDUCATIVE
INNOVACION EDUCACIONAL
SN Changes in objectives, content or methods initiated as a rule in experimental situations
BT INNOVATION
NT ADOPTION OF INNOVATIONS
RT 200

EDUCATIONAL INSTITUTIONS
INSTITUTION EDUCATIVE
INSTITUCION EDUCACIONAL
RT 125

EDUCATIONAL INTEREST
INTERET EDUCATIF
INTERES EDUCACIONAL
SN Interest in continuing one's education
RT 541

EDUCATIONAL LEAVE
CONGE D'ETUDES
LICENCIA DE PERFECCIONAMIENTO
UF STUDY LEAVE
RT 222

EDUCATIONAL PERSONNEL

EDUCATIONAL LEGISLATION
LEGISLATION DE L'EDUCATION
LEGISLACION DE LA EDUCACION
BT LAWS
NT SCHOOL ATTENDANCE LAWS
RT 230
      COMPULSORY EDUCATION

EDUCATIONAL MEDIA
MOYEN D'ENSEIGNEMENT
MEDIOS DE ENSEÑANZA
SN Application of all modern means of communication for educational purposes
RT 360
      DISTANCE EDUCATION

EDUCATIONAL METHODS
METHODE EDUCATIVE
METODO EDUCACIONAL
NT SELF INSTRUCTIONAL METHODS
      TEACHING METHODS
RT 355

EDUCATIONAL MISSIONS
MISSION D'EXPERT EN EDUCATION
MISION DE EXPERTOS EN EDUCACION
SN Specialist groups providing a country with technical assistance under international programmes
BT TECHNICAL ASSISTANCE
NT INTERNATIONAL EXPERTS
RT 205

EDUCATIONAL NEEDS
BESOIN EDUCATIONNEL
NECESIDADES EDUCACIONALES
SN Broadly at level of system
BT NEEDS
NT DEFICIT (FACILITIES)
RT 181

EDUCATIONAL OBJECTIVES
OBJECTIF EDUCATIF
OBJETIVO EDUCACIONAL
SN Intended or expected results of the educational process

NT AFFECTIVE OBJECTIVES
      BEHAVIOURAL OBJECTIVES
      COGNITIVE OBJECTIVES
      COUNSELLING OBJECTIVES
      COURSE OBJECTIVES
      PSYCHOMOTOR OBJECTIVES
      TRAINING OBJECTIVES
RT 300
      EDUCATIONAL AIMS
      EDUCATIONAL GOALS

EDUCATIONAL OPPORTUNITIES
CHANCE D'EDUCATION
OPORTUNIDAD EDUCACIONAL
BT DEMOCRATIZATION OF EDUCATION
      OPPORTUNITIES
NT ACCESS TO EDUCATION
RT 180
      YOUTH OPPORTUNITIES

EDUCATIONAL ORGANIZATION
ORGANISATION DE L'EDUCATION
ORGANIZACION DE LA EDUCACION
UF EDUCATIONAL STRUCTURE
      EDUCATIONAL SYSTEM
      NATIONAL EDUCATIONAL SYSTEM
SN Arrangement into an organic whole of the interdependent institutions and programmes providing formal or non-formal education
NT SCHOOL SYSTEMS
RT 260

EDUCATIONAL OUTPUT
RENDEMENT DE L'EDUCATION
RENDIMIENTO DE LA EDUCACION
May 1984
SN At level of the educational systems
RT 181

EDUCATIONAL PERSONNEL
PERSONNEL DE L'EDUCATION
PERSONAL DE EDUCACION
NT EDUCATIONAL ADMINISTRATORS

EDUCATIONAL PHILOSOPHY

      INSPECTORS
      SUPERVISORS
      TEACHERS
      TRAINERS
RT   420

EDUCATIONAL PHILOSOPHY
PHILOSOPHIE DE L'EDUCATION
FILOSOFIA DE LA EDUCACION
RT   180

EDUCATIONAL PLANNING
PLANIFICATION DE L'EDUCATION
PLANIFICACION DE LA
   EDUCACION
BT   PLANNING
NT   COLLEGE PLANNING
      CURRICULUM PLANNING
      PROGRAMME PLANNING
      SCHOOL PLANNING
RT   205

EDUCATIONAL POLICIES
POLITIQUE D'EDUCATION
POLITICA EDUCACIONAL
SN Official statements of goals to which the system of education is directed
BT   POLICIES
RT   182
      CULTURAL POLICIES
      SOCIAL POLICIES

EDUCATIONAL POLICY TRENDS
TENDANCE DE LA POLITIQUE
   EDUCATIVE
TENDENCIAS DE POLITICA
   EDUCACIONAL
RT   182

EDUCATIONAL PRACTICE
PRATIQUE EDUCATIVE
PRAXIS EDUCATIVA
RT   182

EDUCATIONAL PRINCIPLES
USE **PRINCIPLES OF TEACHING**

EDUCATIONAL PRIORITIES
PRIORITE DE L'EDUCATION
PRIORIDADES EDUCACIONALES
SN At the level of education systems
RT   182

EDUCATIONAL PROBLEMS
PROBLEME EDUCATIF
PROBLEMA EDUCACIONAL
SN At level of the educational system
RT   182
      281

EDUCATIONAL PROGRAMMES
PROGRAMME D'EDUCATION
PROGRAMA DE EDUCACION
SN Series of planned activities, with administrative connotation, relating to development of institutions, what goes on in them and budget provisions; to be distinguished from "instructional programmes"
BT   PROGRAMMES
NT   COMPENSATORY EDUCATION
      PROGRAMMES
      EXCHANGE PROGRAMMES
      GUIDANCE PROGRAMMES
      LITERACY CAMPAIGNS
RT   271

EDUCATIONAL PROVISION
USE **EDUCATIONAL INFRASTRUCTURE**

EDUCATIONAL PSYCHOLOGY
PSYCHOLOGIE DE L'EDUCATION
PSICOLOGIA DE LA EDUCACION
BT   PSYCHOLOGY
RT   642

EDUCATIONAL QUALITY
QUALITE DE L'EDUCATION
CALIDAD DE LA EDUCACION
UF   RELEVANCE (EDUCATION)
RT   181

EDUCATIONAL RADIO
RADIO EDUCATIVE
RADIO EDUCATIVA
BT RADIO
RT 360

EDUCATIONAL READINGS
RENCONTRES PEDAGOGIQUES
JORNADAS PEDAGOGICAS
May 1984
SN Special form of educational experience exchange presenting progressive educational experience at teachers' meetings
BT TEACHER IMPROVEMENT
RT 690

EDUCATIONAL REFORM
REFORME DE L'EDUCATION
REFORMA DE LA EDUCACION
SN Change planned or in process of implementation relating to major part of national system of education
RT 200

EDUCATIONAL RESEARCH
RECHERCHE EN EDUCATION
INVESTIGACION EDUCACIONAL
NT CLASSROOM RESEARCH
    CURRICULUM RESEARCH
    EXCEPTIONAL CHILD
       RESEARCH
    READING RESEARCH
RT 280

EDUCATIONAL RESEARCHERS
CHERCHEUR EN EDUCATION
INVESTIGADOR EN EDUCACION
BT RESEARCHERS
RT 430

EDUCATIONAL RESOURCES
RESSOURCE DE L'EDUCATION
RECURSOS EDUCACIONALES
BT RESOURCES
RT 700

EDUCATIONAL SCIENCES
SCIENCES DE L'EDUCATION
CIENCIAS DE LA EDUCACION
May 1984
RT 640

EDUCATIONAL SEMINARS
SEMINAIRE PEDAGOGIQUE
SEMINARIO EDUCACIONAL
BT SEMINARS
RT 204

EDUCATIONAL SOCIOLOGY
SOCIOLOGIE DE L'EDUCATION
SOCIOLOGIA DE LA EDUCACION
BT SOCIOLOGY
RT 642

EDUCATIONAL SPACES
ESPACE EDUCATIF
ESPACIOS EDUCACIONALES
RT 711
    ARCHITECTURE
    BUILDINGS

EDUCATIONAL SPECIFICATIONS
SPECIFICATION PEDAGOGIQUE
ESPECIFICACIONES
   EDUCACIONALES
SN Detailed, precise expert presentation of a plan or proposal for educational facilities including equipment, classrooms, laboratories, curriculum, etc.
BT SPECIFICATIONS
RT 232

EDUCATIONAL STATISTICS
STATISTIQUES DE L'EDUCATION
ESTADISTICAS EDUCACIONALES
May 1984
BT STATISTICAL DATA
NT SCHOOL STATISTICS
RT 284

EDUCATIONAL STRATEGIES
STRATEGIE DE L'EDUCATION
ESTRATEGIAS DE LA EDUCACION
SN Conversion of policy goals into operational terms, including some

EDUCATIONAL STRUCTURE

indication of alternative paths to reach these goals
RT 182

EDUCATIONAL STRUCTURE
USE **EDUCATIONAL ORGANIZATION**

EDUCATIONAL SYSTEM
USE **EDUCATIONAL ORGANIZATION**

EDUCATIONAL TECHNOLOGY
TECHNOLOGIE DE L'EDUCATION
TECNOLOGIA EDUCACIONAL
SN Theory and application of educational media in systematic way
RT 360

EDUCATIONAL TELEVISION
TELEVISION EDUCATIVE
TELEVISION EDUCATIVA
BT TELEVISION
NT INSTRUCTIONAL TELEVISION
RT 360

EDUCATIONAL TESTING
ADMINISTRATION DE TEST SCOLAIRE
SOMETER A PRUEBAS EDUCACIONALES
BT TESTING
RT 391

EDUCATIONAL TESTS
TEST SCOLAIRE
PRUEBA ESCOLAR
NT ACHIEVEMENT TESTS
   APTITUDE TESTS
   INTEREST TESTS
   LANGUAGE TESTS
   PERFORMANCE TESTS
   READING TESTS
   SCIENCE TESTS
   VERBAL TESTS
RT 392

EDUCATIONAL THEORIES
THEORIE DE L'EDUCATION
TEORIA DE LA EDUCACION
BT THEORIES
RT 180

EDUCATIONAL WASTAGE
DEPERDITION SCOLAIRE
MALOGRO ESCOLAR
SN Effects of the associated problems of repetition and dropping out
RT 205

EDUCATIONALLY DISADVANTAGED
DEFAVORISE SUR LE PLAN EDUCATIF
DESFAVORECIDO EDUCACIONAL
RT 402

EDUCATIONALLY RETARDED
USE **SLOW LEARNERS**

EEC
CEE
CEE
SN European Economic Community

EGYPT
EGYPTE
EGIPTO
UF ARAB REPUBLIC OF EGYPT
BT ARAB COUNTRIES
   MEDITERRANEAN COUNTRIES
   NORTH AFRICA
RT ENGLISH SPEAKING AFRICA

EIDETIC IMAGES
IMAGE EIDETIQUE
IMAGEN EIDETICA
RT 511

EIGHTEENTH CENTURY
DIX-HUITIEME SIECLE
SIGLO DIECIOCHO

EMOTIONAL DEVELOPMENT

EIRE
                May 1984
USE **IRELAND**

EL SALVADOR
EL SALVADOR
EL SALVADOR
UF   SALVADOR
BT   CENTRAL AMERICA

ELDERLY PEOPLE
PERSONNE AGEE
ANCIANO
SN   Beyond customary age of retirement
RT   400

ELECTIONS
USE **VOTING**

ELECTIVE COURSES
COURS A OPTION
CURSO ELECTIVO
SN   Any of a number of courses from which student has to select
BT   COURSES
RT   333

ELECTRICIANS
ELECTRICIEN
ELECTRICISTA
RT   452

ELECTRICITY
ELECTRICITE
ELECTRICIDAD
RT   633

ELECTROMECHANICAL TECHNOLOGY
ELECTROMECANIQUE
ELECTROMECANICA
BT   TECHNOLOGY
RT   645

ELECTRONIC TECHNICIANS
ELECTRONICIEN
TECNICO ELECTRONICO
BT   TECHNICIANS
RT   452

ELECTRONICS
ELECTRONIQUE
ELECTRONICA
RT   633

ELEMENTARY EDUCATION
USE **PRIMARY EDUCATION**

ELEMENTARY SCHOOLS
USE **PRIMARY SCHOOLS**

ELEMENTARY SCIENCE
SCIENCES ELEMENTAIRES
CIENCIAS ELEMENTALES
RT   670

ELITIST EDUCATION
EDUCATION ELITISTE
EDUCACION ELITISTA
RT   180

ELLICE ISLANDS
                May 1984
USE **KIRIBATI**

EMERGENCY PROGRAMMES
PROGRAMME D'URGENCE
PROGRAMA DE EMERGENCIA
RT   271

EMIGRATION
EMIGRATION
EMIGRACION
RT   124

EMOTIONAL ADJUSTMENT
ADAPTATION EMOTIONNELLE
ADAPTACION EMOCIONAL
BT   ADJUSTMENT
RT   551

EMOTIONAL DEVELOPMENT
DEVELOPPEMENT EMOTIONNEL
DESARROLLO EMOCIONAL
RT   530

EMOTIONAL DISTURBANCE

EMOTIONAL DISTURBANCE
TROUBLE CARACTERIEL
TRASTORNO AFECTIVO
RT 572

EMOTIONAL EXPERIENCE
EXPERIENCE EMOTIONNELLE
EXPERIENCIA EMOCIONAL
BT EXPERIENCE
RT 562

EMOTIONAL PROBLEMS
PROBLEME EMOTIONNEL
PROBLEMA EMOCIONAL
RT 540

EMOTIONALLY DISTURBED
CARACTERIEL
AFECTIVAMENTE INADAPTADO
SN Children or adults
BT HANDICAPPED
RT 403

EMPIRICAL RESEARCH
RECHERCHE EMPIRIQUE
INVESTIGACION EMPIRICA
                      May 1984
RT 282

EMPLOYEES
EMPLOYE
EMPLEADO
NT ADMINISTRATIVE WORKERS
    CLERICAL WORKERS
    COMMERCIAL WORKERS
    SERVICE WORKERS
RT 450

EMPLOYER EMPLOYEE
  RELATIONSHIP
USE **LABOUR RELATIONS**

EMPLOYERS
EMPLOYEUR
EMPLEADOR
RT 450

EMPLOYMENT
EMPLOI
EMPLEO
SN Remunerative work either for an employer or in self–employment
NT SEASONAL EMPLOYMENT
    SHELTERED EMPLOYMENT
    TEACHER EMPLOYMENT
RT 154

EMPLOYMENT COUNSELLORS
ORIENTEUR PROFESSIONNEL
CONSEJERO OCUPACIONAL
BT COUNSELLORS
RT 431

EMPLOYMENT EXPERIENCE
EXPERIENCE PROFESSIONNELLE
EXPERIENCIA PROFESIONAL
RT 221

EMPLOYMENT OPPORTUNITIES
POSSIBILITE D'EMPLOI
OPORTUNIDAD DE EMPLEO
BT OPPORTUNITIES
RT 154
    EQUAL OPPORTUNITIES
      (JOBS)

EMPLOYMENT PROGRAMMES
PROGRAMME D'EMPLOI
PROGRAMA DE EMPLEO
BT PROGRAMMES
RT 154

EMPLOYMENT QUALIFICATIONS
QUALIFICATION
  PROFESSIONNELLE
CALIFICACION PROFESIONAL
RT 390

EMPLOYMENT SERVICES
SERVICES DE L'EMPLOI
SERVICIOS DE EMPLEO
BT SERVICES
RT 154

ENROLMENT

EMPLOYMENT STATISTICS
STATISTIQUES DE L'EMPLOI
ESTADISTICAS SOBRE EMPLEO
RT 154

EMPLOYMENT STRATEGIES
STRATEGIE DE L'EMPLOI
ESTRATEGIA DEL EMPLEO
RT 154

ENCYCLOPAEDIA
ENCYCLOPEDIE
ENCICLOPEDIA
May 1984
RT 880

ENDERBY ISLANDS
May 1984
USE **CANTON AND ENDERBY ISLANDS**

ENGINEERING
INGENIERIE
INGENIERIA
NT CIVIL ENGINEERING
RT 647

ENGINEERING EDUCATION
FORMATION DES INGENIEURS
FORMACION DE INGENIEROS
RT 681

ENGINEERING TECHNICIANS
TECHNICIEN EN INGENIERIE
TECNICO EN INGENIERIA
BT TECHNICIANS
RT 452

ENGINEERING TECHNOLOGY
TECHNOLOGIE DE L'INGENIERIE
TECNOLOGIA DE LA INGENIERIA
BT TECHNOLOGY
RT 645

ENGINEERS
INGENIEUR
INGENIERO
RT 463

ENGINES
MACHINE
MAQUINA
RT 742

ENGLAND
USE **UK**

ENGLISH
LANGUE ANGLAISE
LENGUA INGLESA
RT 626

ENGLISH SPEAKING AFRICA
AFRIQUE ANGLOPHONE
AFRICA ANGLOFONA
BT AFRICA
RT BOTSWANA
   EGYPT
   GAMBIA
   GHANA
   KENYA
   LESOTHO
   LIBERIA
   MALAWI
   MAURITIUS
   NAMIBIA
   NIGERIA
   ZIMBABWE
   SIERRA LEONE
   SOUTH AFRICA (REPUBLIC)
   SAINT HELENA
   SUDAN
   SWAZILAND

ENRICHMENT PROGRAMMES
PROGRAMME DE RENFORCEMENT
PROGRAMA DE REFUERZO
BT INSTRUCTIONAL PROGRAMMES
RT 320

ENROLMENT
EFFECTIF
MATRICULA
NT DUAL ENROLMENT
   ENROLMENT RATIO
RT 266

ENROLMENT INFLUENCES
INFLUENCE SUR LE
  RECRUTEMENT
INFLUENCIA EN LA MATRICULA
SN Factors affecting enrolment
RT 285

ENROLMENT PROJECTIONS
PROJECTION DES EFFECTIFS
PROYECCIONES DE LA
  MATRICULA
RT 206

ENROLMENT RATIO
TAUX D'INSCRIPTION
TASA DE MATRICULA
SN Enrolment as percentage of
    relevant age group
BT ENROLMENT
RT 206

ENROLMENT TRENDS
EVOLUTION DES EFFECTIFS
EVOLUCION DE LA MATRICULA
RT 206

ENSEIGNEMENT UNIVERSITAIRE
  EXTRA MUROS
USE **EDUCATION PERI–
  UNIVERSITAIRE**

ENTRANCE EXAMINATIONS
EXAMEN D'ENTREE
EXAMEN DE INGRESO
NT COLLEGE ENTRANCE
    EXAMINATIONS
RT 392

ENVIRONMENT
ENVIRONNEMENT
AMBIENTE
NT CULTURAL ENVIRONMENT
    EDUCATIONAL
      ENVIRONMENT
    PHYSICAL ENVIRONMENT
    WORK ENVIRONMENT
RT 140

ENVIRONMENTAL EDUCATION
EDUCATION RELATIVE A
  L'ENVIRONNEMENT
EDUCACION AMBIENTAL
UF CONSERVATION EDUCATION
RT 683

ENVIRONMENTAL INFLUENCES
INFLUENCE DE
  L'ENVIRONNEMENT
INFLUENCIA DEL AMBIENTE
RT 550

EQUAL EDUCATION
EGALITE DEVANT L'EDUCATION
IGUALDAD DE EDUCACION
UF EQUALITY OF EDUCATIONAL
      OPPORTUNITY
    NONDISCRIMINATORY
      EDUCATION
SN Ensuring opportunities regardless
    of race, colour, creed, sex, ability
    or background
BT DEMOCRATIZATION OF
    EDUCATION
RT 180

EQUAL OPPORTUNITIES (JOBS)
EGALITE DEVANT L'EMPLOI
IGUALDAD DE OPORTUNIDAD
  (TRABAJO)
BT OPPORTUNITIES
RT 153
    EMPLOYMENT
      OPPORTUNITIES
    YOUTH OPPORTUNITIES

EQUALITY OF EDUCATIONAL
  OPPORTUNITY
USE **EQUAL EDUCATION**

EQUALIZATION AID
SUBVENTION COMPENSATOIRE
SUBVENCION COMPENSATORIA
SN Funds made available to
    compensate for varying financial
    resources in different parts of a
    country or between different
    institutions so as to achieve a
    common minimal level of

ETHNIC DISTRIBUTION

provision
BT STATE AID TO PROVINCES
RT 152

EQUATORIAL GUINEA
GUINEE EQUATORIALE
GUINEA ECUATORIAL
UF SPANISH GUINEA
BT CENTRAL AFRICA

EQUIPMENT
EQUIPEMENT
EQUIPO
NT ATHLETIC EQUIPMENT
　AUDIOVISUAL EQUIPMENT
　EDUCATIONAL EQUIPMENT
　LABORATORY EQUIPMENT
　LIBRARY EQUIPMENT
　MECHANICAL EQUIPMENT
　SCIENCE EQUIPMENT
RT 740

EQUIPMENT STANDARDS
NORME D'EQUIPEMENT
NORMAS DE EQUIPAMIENTO
BT STANDARDS
RT 232

EQUIVALENCES
EQUIVALENCE
EQUIVALENCIA
SN Of degrees or certificates
RT 232

ERGONOMICS
ERGONOMIE
ERGONOMIA
SN Includes all factors affecting human performances within a space
RT 252

ESCAP
CESAP
CESPAP
SN Economic and Social Commission for Asia and Pacific

ESSAY TESTS
EPREUVE D'ESSAI
PRUEBA DE ENSAYO
RT 392

ESSAYS
ESSAI
ENSAYO
RT 616

ESTIMATED COSTS
COUT ESTIMATIF
COSTO ESTIMADO
BT COSTS
RT 243

ESTONIAN SSR
RSS D'ESTONIE
RSS DE ESTONIA
BT USSR

May 1984

ETHICAL INSTRUCTION
ENSEIGNEMENT DE LA MORALE
ENSEÑANZA DE LA MORAL
RT 682

ETHICS
ETHIQUE
ETICA
RT 600

ETHIOPIA
ETHIOPIE
ETIOPIA
UF ABYSSINIA
BT EAST AFRICA

ETHNIC CONFLICT
CONFLIT RACIAL
CONFLICTO ETNICO
RT 123

ETHNIC DISTRIBUTION
REPARTITION ETHNIQUE
DISTRIBUCION ETNICA
RT 123

ETHNIC GROUPS
GROUPE ETHNIQUE
GRUPO ETNICO
SN Includes general concept and references to specific groups not otherwise classified
BT GROUPS
RT 443

ETHNIC ORIGINS
ORIGINE ETHNIQUE
ORIGEN ETNICO
RT 550

ETIOLOGY
ETIOLOGIE
ETIOLOGIA
RT 285

ETYMOLOGY
ETYMOLOGIE
ETIMOLOGIA
RT 622

EUROPE
EUROPE
EUROPA
NT EASTERN EUROPE
    WESTERN EUROPE
RT MEDITERRANEAN COUNTRIES

EUROPEAN COMMUNITIES
COMMUNAUTES EUROPEENNES
COMUNIDADES EUROPEAS

EVALUATION
EVALUATION
EVALUACION
NT CURRICULUM EVALUATION
    MATERIALS EVALUATION
    PERSONNEL EVALUATION
    PROGRAMME EVALUATION
RT 210
    283

EVALUATION CRITERIA
CRITERE D'EVALUATION
CRITERIO DE EVALUACION
BT CRITERIA
RT 210

EVALUATION METHODS
METHODE D'EVALUATION
METODO DE EVALUACION
RT 210
    283

EVENING COURSES
COURS DU SOIR
CURSO NOCTURNO
SN Whether formal or non-formal, at any level
BT COURSES
RT 307

EVENING SCHOOLS
ECOLE DU SOIR
ESCUELA NOCTURNA
RT 303

EVENING STUDENTS
ELEVE DES COURS DU SOIR
ALUMNO DE CURSO NOCTURNO
RT 410

EXAMINATIONS
EXAMEN
EXAMEN
UF TESTS
RT 392

EXAMINERS
EXAMINATEUR
EXAMINADOR
RT 420

EXCEPTIONAL CHILD EDUCATION
EDUCATION DES ATYPIQUES
EDUCACION DE NIÑOS ATIPICOS
RT 322

EXCEPTIONAL CHILD RESEARCH
RECHERCHE SUR LES ENFANTS ATYPIQUES
INVESTIGACION SOBRE NIÑOS ATIPICOS
BT   EDUCATIONAL RESEARCH
RT   280

EXCEPTIONAL STUDENTS
ELEVE ATYPIQUE
ALUMNO ATIPICO
SN   Covers atypical students of any kind
NT   GIFTED STUDENTS
     HANDICAPPED STUDENTS
RT   416

EXCHANGE PROGRAMMES
PROGRAMME D'ECHANGE
PROGRAMA DE INTERCAMBIO
SN   Providing systematically for the exchange of students or teachers between institutions
BT   EDUCATIONAL PROGRAMMES
RT   271

EXERCISE (PHYSIOLOGY)
EXERCICE PHYSIQUE
EJERCICIO FISICO
BT   PHYSICAL ACTIVITIES
RT   503

EXHIBITION AREAS
AIRE D'EXPOSITION
AREA DE EXPOSICION
RT   711

EXHIBITS
MATERIEL D'EXPOSITION
MATERIAL DE EXPOSICION
RT   733

EXPENDITURE PER STUDENT
DEPENSE PAR ELEVE
GASTO POR ALUMNO
BT   EXPENDITURES
RT   243

EXPENDITURES
DEPENSE
GASTO
NT   CAPITAL OUTLAY (FOR FIXED ASSETS)
     EXPENDITURE PER STUDENT
     OPERATING EXPENSES
RT   241

EXPERIENCE
EXPERIENCE
EXPERIENCIA
NT   EDUCATIONAL EXPERIENCE
     EMOTIONAL EXPERIENCE
     SENSORY EXPERIENCE
     SOCIAL EXPERIENCE
     WORK EXPERIENCE
RT   562
     221

EXPERIMENTAL CURRICULUM
CURRICULUM EXPERIMENTAL
CURRICULO EXPERIMENTAL
RT   332

EXPERIMENTAL EDUCATION
PEDAGOGIE EXPERIMENTALE
PEDAGOGIA EXPERIMENTAL
RT   280

EXPERIMENTAL GROUPS
GROUPE EXPERIMENTAL
GRUPO EXPERIMENTAL
RT   283

EXPERIMENTAL PSYCHOLOGY
PSYCHOLOGIE EXPERIMENTALE
PSICOLOGIA EXPERIMENTAL
BT   PSYCHOLOGY
RT   642

EXPERIMENTAL RESEARCH
RECHERCHE EXPERIMENTALE
INVESTIGACION EXPERIMENTAL
                                        May 1984
RT   282

EXPERIMENTAL SCHOOLS
ECOLE EXPERIMENTALE
ESCUELA EXPERIMENTAL
RT 305

EXPERIMENTAL TEACHING
ENSEIGNEMENT EXPERIMENTAL
ENSEÑANZA EXPERIMENTAL
RT 282

EXPERIMENTS
EXPERIENCES
EXPERIMENTO
NT LABORATORY EXPERIMENTS
   SCIENCE EXPERIMENTS
RT 671

EXPERTS
USE **INTERNATIONAL EXPERTS**

EXPULSION
EXPULSION
EXPULSION
RT 267

EXTENDED DAY SCHOOLS
ECOLE A JOURNEE PROLONGEE
ESCUELA DE JORNADA
   PROLONGADA
SN Where time spent at school is extended to allow for custodial care while parents are absent from home
RT 303

EXTENDED SCHOOL YEAR
ANNEE SCOLAIRE PROLONGEE
AÑO ESCOLAR PROLONGADO
RT 344

EXTENSION AGENTS
VULGARISATEUR
AGENTE DE EXTENSION
   CULTURAL
RT 440

EXTENSION EDUCATION
EDUCATION PERISCOLAIRE
EXTENSION CULTURAL
SN Instructional activities of educational institutions directed to clientele outside immediate student body
NT LIBRARY EXTENSION
   RURAL EXTENSION
   UNIVERSITY EXTENSION
   URBAN EXTENSION
RT 382

EXTERNAL CANDIDATES
CANDIDAT LIBRE
ESTUDIANTE LIBRE
May 1984
RT 412

EXTINCTION (PSYCHOLOGY)
EXTINCTION (PSYCHOLOGIE)
EXTINCION (PSICOLOGIA)
SN Progressive reduction in conditioned response after prolonged repetition of the eliciting stimulus without reinforcement
RT 511

EXTRA MURAL EDUCATION
USE **UNIVERSITY EXTENSION**

EXTRACURRICULAR ACTIVITIES
ACTIVITE HORS PROGRAMME
ACTIVIDAD FUERA DE
   PROGRAMA
May 1984
UF AFTER SCHOOL ACTIVITIES
BT ACTIVITIES
RT 357

EYE MOVEMENTS
MOUVEMENT OCULAIRE
MOVIMIENTO OCULAR
RT 503

FAMILY EDUCATION

FABLES
FABLE
FABULA
RT 616

FACILITIES DESIGN
CONCEPTION DES
 INSTALLATIONS
DISEÑO DE EDIFICIOS Y EQUIPOS
RT 252

FACILITIES MANAGEMENT
GESTION DES INSTALLATIONS
ADMINISTRACION DE EDIFICIOS
 Y EQUIPOS
RT 251

FACILITIES PLANNING
PLANIFICATION DES
 INSTALLATIONS
PLANIFICACION DE LAS
 INSTALACIONES
RT 650

FACILITY GUIDELINES
MODE D'UTILISATION
 (INSTALLATIONS)
NORMAS SOBRE INSTALACIONES
SN Written guidelines, specifications, standards, or criteria used in assessing physical facility requirements
RT 232

FACILITY REQUIREMENTS
BESOIN EN INSTALLATIONS
NECESIDAD DE EDIFICIOS Y
 EQUIPOS
SN Any aspect of the physical plant determined necessary to accommodate various functions
RT 250

FACTOR ANALYSIS
USE **STATISTICAL ANALYSIS**

FACULTY
USE **TEACHING PERSONNEL**

FAEROE ISLANDS
ILES FEROE
ISLAS FEROE
BT SCANDINAVIA
    WESTERN EUROPE

FAILURE
ECHEC
FRACASO
RT 267
    PROMOTION POLICIES

FAILURE FACTORS
FACTEUR D'ECHEC
FACTOR DE FRACASO
RT 285

FALKLAND ISLANDS
ILES MALOUINES
ISLAS MALVINAS
BT ATLANTIC OCEAN
    TERRITORIES
RT SOUTH AMERICA

FAMILY ATTITUDES
ATTITUDE DE LA FAMILLE
ACTITUD DE LA FAMILIA
BT ATTITUDES
RT 552

FAMILY BACKGROUND
MILIEU FAMILIAL
MEDIO FAMILIAR
BT SOCIAL BACKGROUND
RT 126

FAMILY COUNSELLING
CONSULTATION FAMILIALE
CONSEJERIA FAMILIAR
BT COUNSELLING
RT 371

FAMILY EDUCATION
EDUCATION FAMILIALE
EDUCACION FAMILIAR
SN Education within and by the family

FAMILY INFLUENCE

RT 186

FAMILY INFLUENCE
INFLUENCE FAMILIALE
INFLUENCIA FAMILIAR
RT 550
    PARENT ROLE

FAMILY LIFE EDUCATION
USE **POPULATION EDUCATION**

FAMILY MOBILITY
MOBILITE DE LA FAMILLE
MOVILIDAD DE LA FAMILIA
BT MOBILITY
RT 124

FAMILY PLANNING
PLANNING FAMILIAL
PLANIFICACION FAMILIAR
BT SOCIAL PLANNING
RT 126

FAMILY PROBLEMS
PROBLEME FAMILIAL
PROBLEMA FAMILIAR
RT 281

FAMILY PROJECTS
PROJET CONCERNANT LA
   FAMILLE
PROYECTO FAMILIAR
BT PROJECTS
RT 272

FAMILY RELATIONSHIP
RELATIONS FAMILIALES
RELACIONES FAMILIARES
BT INTERPERSONAL
     RELATIONSHIP
     RELATIONSHIP
NT PARENT CHILD
     RELATIONSHIP
     PARENT STUDENT
     RELATIONSHIP
RT 553

FAMILY ROLE
ROLE DE LA FAMILLE
PAPEL DE LA FAMILIA
RT 126

FAMILY SCHOOL RELATIONSHIP
RELATIONS ECOLE–FAMILLE
RELACION FAMILIA–ESCUELA
BT RELATIONSHIP
RT 380

FAMILY (SOCIOLOGICAL UNIT)
FAMILLE (UNITE SOCIOLOGIQUE)
FAMILIA (UNIDAD SOCIOLOGICA)
NT FOSTER FAMILY
     RURAL FAMILY
RT 126

FAMILY STRUCTURE
STRUCTURE DE LA FAMILLE
ESTRUCTURA FAMILIAR
RT 126

FAO
OAA
FAO
SN Food and Agricultural
     Organization

FAR EAST
EXTREME–ORIENT
LEJANO ORIENTE
UF EAST ASIA
BT ASIA
NT CHINA
     HONG KONG
     JAPAN
     KOREA DPR
     KOREA R
     MACAO
     MONGOLIA
     TAIWAN

FARMERS
FERMIER
AGRICULTOR
SN Covers agricultural personnel
RT 451

FATHERS
PERE
PADRE
BT   PARENTS
RT   401

FATIGUE
FATIGUE
FATIGA
RT   503

FEAR
PEUR
MIEDO
BT   PSYCHOLOGICAL PATTERNS
RT   540

FEASIBILITY STUDIES
ETUDE DE FAISABILITE
ESTUDIO DE FACTIBILIDAD
RT   282

FED
FED
FED
SN   European Development Fund

FEDERAL GOVERNMENT
USE **CENTRAL GOVERNMENT**

FEDERATIVE STRUCTURE
STRUCTURE FEDERALE
ESTRUCTURA FEDERAL
RT   102

FEEDBACK
INFORMATION EN RETOUR
RETROINFORMACION
BT   INFORMATION SYSTEMS
     LEARNING PROCESSES
RT   204

FEES
DROIT D'INSCRIPTION
DERECHO DE MATRICULA
RT   240
     FREE EDUCATION

FELLOWSHIPS
BOURSE DE RECHERCHE
BECA DE INVESTIGACION
SN   Reserve for post-graduate level,
     adult education and international
     programmes
BT   GRANTS
RT   242

FEMALE
SEXE FEMININ
SEXO FEMENINO
RT   501

FICTION
FICTION
FICCION
RT   616

FID
FID
FID
SN   International Federation for
     Documentation

FIELD EXPERIENCE PROGRAMMES
PROGRAMME D'EXPERIENCE SUR
    LE TERRAIN
PROGRAMA DE EXPERIENCIAS
    EN EL TERRENO
RT   671

FIELD RESEARCH
RECHERCHE SUR LE TERRAIN
INVESTIGACION EN EL TERRENO
May 1984
RT   282

FIELD STUDIES
ETUDE SUR LE TERRAIN
ESTUDIO EN EL TERRENO
RT   282
     INTERVIEWS

FIGURATIVE LANGUAGE
RHETORIQUE
RETORICA
RT   620

FIJI ISLANDS
ILES FIDJI
ISLAS FIDJI
BT   MELANESIA

FILING
CLASSEMENT
ARCHIVO
RT   202

FILM PROJECTORS
PROJECTEUR DE FILM
PROYECTOR
BT   PROJECTION EQUIPMENT
RT   731

FILMS
FILM
PELICULA
BT   MASS MEDIA
NT   INSTRUCTIONAL FILMS
     SINGLE CONCEPT FILMS
     SOUND FILMS
RT   730

FILMSTRIPS
FILM FIXE
PELICULA FIJA
RT   730

FINANCIAL NEEDS
BESOIN FINANCIER
NECESIDAD FINANCIERA
BT   NEEDS
RT   152

FINANCIAL POLICY
POLITIQUE FINANCIERE
POLITICA FINANCIERA
RT   152

FINANCIAL SERVICES
SERVICES FINANCIERS
SERVICIOS FINANCIEROS
BT   SERVICES
RT   150

FINANCIAL SUPPORT
AIDE FINANCIERE
AYUDA FINANCIERA
NT   PRIVATE FINANCIAL
     SUPPORT
RT   240

FINE ARTS
BEAUX–ARTS
BELLAS ARTES
RT   610

FINES (PENALTIES)
AMENDE
MULTA
RT   233

FINISHES
FINITION
TERMINACION
RT   253

FINLAND
FINLANDE
FINLANDIA
BT   SCANDINAVIA
     WESTERN EUROPE

FIRST AID
PREMIERS SECOURS
PRIMEROS AUXILIOS
RT   683

FISCAL MANAGEMENT
GESTION FISCALE
POTESTAD FISCAL
SN   Ability of government to manage
     public funds
RT   152

FISE
FISE
FISE
SN   World Federation of Teachers'
     Unions

FOSTER FAMILY

FISHERIES
PECHERIE
PESQUERIA
RT 750

FLEXIBLE PROGRESSION
USE **CONTINUOUS PROGRESS PLAN**

FLEXIBLE SCHEDULES
USE **FLEXIBLE TIMETABLING**

FLEXIBLE TIMETABLING
HORAIRE FLEXIBLE
HORARIO FLEXIBLE
UF BLOCK TIMETABLES
     FLEXIBLE SCHEDULES
BT TIMETABLES
RT 340

FOLLOWUP STUDIES
ETUDE COMPLEMENTAIRE
ESTUDIO DE SEGUIMIENTO
RT 282

FOOD
ALIMENTATION
ALIMENTACION
RT 160

FOOD SERVICES
SERVICES ALIMENTAIRES
SERVICIO DE ALIMENTACION
BT SERVICES
RT 160

FOREIGN POLICY
POLITIQUE ETRANGERE
POLITICA EXTERIOR
RT 102

FOREIGN STUDENT ADVISERS
CONSEILLER POUR ETUDIANTS
    ETRANGERS
CONSEJEROS PARA ESTUDIANTES
    EXTRANJEROS
RT 431

FOREIGN STUDENTS
ETUDIANT ETRANGER
ESTUDIANTE EXTRANJERO
RT 413

FOREIGN WORKERS
TRAVAILLEUR ETRANGER
TRABAJADOR EXTRANJERO
UF MIGRANT WORKERS
BT WORKERS
RT 470

FORESTRY
SYLVICULTURE
SILVICULTURA
RT 646

FORM CLASSES (LANGUAGES)
CATEGORIE GRAMMATICALE
CATEGORIA GRAMATICAL
RT 622

FORMAL EDUCATION
USE **SCHOOL SYSTEMS**

FORMATIVE EVALUATION
EVALUATION OPERATIONNELLE
EVALUACION OPERACIONAL
BT PROGRAMME EVALUATION
RT 205

FORMER TEACHERS
ANCIEN ENSEIGNANT
EX DOCENTE
SN Teachers who have left the profession
RT 424

FORMOSA   *May 1984*
USE **TAIWAN**

FOSTER FAMILY
FAMILLE ADOPTIVE
FAMILIA ADOPTIVA
BT FAMILY (SOCIOLOGICAL
     UNIT)
RT 126

73

FOSTER HOMES
FOYER D'ADOPTION
HOGAR DE ADOPCION
SN Private homes provided by other than natural parents, with or without adoption
RT 126

FOUNDATION PROGRAMMES
PROGRAMME DES FONDATIONS
PROGRAMA DE LAS FUNDACIONES
SN Activities of private and public foundations concerned with education
BT PROGRAMMES
RT 109

FRANCE
FRANCE
FRANCIA
BT MEDITERRANEAN COUNTRIES
   WESTERN EUROPE

FREE EDUCATION
ENSEIGNEMENT GRATUIT
ENSEÑANZA GRATUITA
SN Non fee–paying
RT 180
   FEES

FREEDOM OF SPEECH
LIBERTE D'EXPRESSION
LIBERTAD DE EXPRESION
BT HUMAN RIGHTS
RT 100

FRENCH
LANGUE FRANCAISE
LENGUA FRANCESA
RT 626

FRENCH GUIANA
GUYANE FRANCAISE
GUAYANA FRANCESA
UF GUIANA
BT SOUTH AMERICA

FRENCH POLYNESIA
POLYNESIE FRANCAISE
POLINESIA FRANCESA
UF MARQUESA ISLANDS
BT POLYNESIA
NT SOCIETY ISLANDS
   TUAMOTU ISLANDS
   TUBUAI ISLANDS

FRENCH SPEAKING AFRICA
AFRIQUE FRANCOPHONE
AFRICA FRANCOFONA
BT AFRICA
RT DJIBOUTI
   BENIN
   BURUNDI
   CAMEROON UR
   CENTRAL AFRICAN REPUBLIC
   CHAD
   CONGO
   GABON
   GUINEA
   IVORY COAST
   MADAGASCAR
   MALI
   MAURITANIA
   NIGER
   RWANDA
   SENEGAL
   TOGO
   UPPER VOLTA
   ZAIRE
   COMOROS

FRIENDLY ISLANDS
USE **TONGA**

FULL TIME TRAINING
FORMATION A PLEIN TEMPS
FORMACION A TIEMPO COMPLETO
BT VOCATIONAL TRAINING
RT 351

May 1984

FUNCTIONAL LITERACY
ALPHABETISATION
  FONCTIONNELLE
ALFABETIZACION FUNCIONAL
SN General concept of relating
  literacy to improved living
  conditions
BT LITERACY
RT 180

**FUNCTIONAL LITERACY
  PROGRAMMES**
PROGRAMME
  D'ALPHABETISATION
  FONCTIONNELLE
PROGRAMA DE ALFABETIZACION
  FUNCIONAL
RT 321

FUNCTIONAL LITERACY PROJECTS
PROJET D'ALPHABETISATION
  FONCTIONNELLE
PROYECTO DE ALFABETIZACION
  FUNCIONAL
RT 321

FUNCTIONAL READING
LECTURE FONCTIONNELLE
LECTURA FUNCIONAL
BT READING PROCESSES
RT 521

FUNDAMENTAL CONCEPTS
CONCEPT FONDAMENTAL
CONCEPTO FUNDAMENTAL
NT GENERALIZATION
RT 522

FUNDAMENTAL RESEARCH
RECHERCHE FONDAMENTALE
INVESTIGACION FUNDAMENTAL
                                    May 1984
UF BASIC RESEARCH
RT 282

FUNDS IN TRUST
FONDS EN FIDEICOMMIS
FONDOS EN FIDEICOMISO
SN Used internationally in situation
  where a government or foundation
  provides funds to an agency for a
  specified purpose
RT 240

FURNITURE
MOBILIER
MOBILIARIO
RT 741

FURNITURE DESIGN
CONCEPTION DE MOBILIER
DISEÑO DEL MOBILIARIO
RT 252

FURNITURE INDUSTRY
INDUSTRIE DU MEUBLE
INDUSTRIA DEL MUEBLE
BT INDUSTRY
RT 150

FURTHER TRAINING
PERFECTIONNEMENT
PERFECCIONAMIENTO
BT TRAINING
RT 351

FUTUNA ISLANDS
                                    May 1984
USE **WALLIS AND FUTUNA
  ISLANDS**

FUTURE
FUTUR
FUTURO

GABON
GABON
GABON
BT CENTRAL AFRICA
RT FRENCH SPEAKING AFRICA

GALAPAGOS ISLANDS
ILES GALAPAGOS
ISLAS GALAPAGOS
                                    May 1984
BT SOUTH AMERICA
RT ECUADOR

GAMBIA

GAMBIA
GAMBIE
GAMBIA
BT   WEST AFRICA
　　　ENGLISH SPEAKING AFRICA

GENERAL ASSEMBLY
ASSEMBLEE GENERALE
ASAMBLEA GENERAL

GENERAL EDUCATION
ENSEIGNEMENT GENERAL
ENSEÑANZA GENERAL
SN   Education which, in its choice of subject–matter, does not envisage any kind of specialization with a view to preparing students for work in a particular sector
RT   183

GENERAL SCIENCE
SCIENCES GENERALES
CIENCIAS GENERALES
RT   670

GENERAL SECONDARY SCHOOLS
ECOLE SECONDAIRE
　D'ENSEIGNEMENT GENERAL
ESCUELA SECUNDARIA GENERAL
BT   SECONDARY SCHOOLS
RT   306

GENERAL TECHNICAL
　EDUCATION
USE **POLYTECHNICAL EDUCATION**

GENERALIZATION
GENERALISATION
GENERALIZACION
BT   FUNDAMENTAL CONCEPTS
RT   522

GENERATIVE GRAMMAR
GRAMMAIRE GENERATIVE
GRAMATICA GENERATIVA
BT   GRAMMAR
RT   622

GENETICS
GENETIQUE
GENETICA
BT   BIOLOGY
RT   632

GEOGRAPHIC CONCEPTS
CONCEPT GEOGRAPHIQUE
CONCEPTO GEOGRAFICO
RT   640

GEOGRAPHIC DISTRIBUTION
REPARTITION GEOGRAPHIQUE
DISTRIBUCION GEOGRAFICA
SN   Of population
RT   124

GEOGRAPHIC REGIONS
REGION GEOGRAPHIQUE
REGION GEOGRAFICA
SN   Divisions of national territory for purposes of government and administration
RT   102

GEOGRAPHY
GEOGRAPHIE
GEOGRAFIA
BT   SOCIAL SCIENCES
RT   640

GEOGRAPHY INSTRUCTION
ENSEIGNEMENT DE LA
　GEOGRAPHIE
ENSEÑANZA DE LA GEOGRAFIA
RT   680

GEOGRAPHY TEACHERS
PROFESSEUR DE GEOGRAPHIE
PROFESOR DE GEOGRAFIA
May 1984
RT   425

GEOLOGY
GEOLOGIE
GEOLOGIA
RT   633

GEOMETRIC CONCEPTS
CONCEPT GEOMETRIQUE
CONCEPTO GEOMETRICO
BT   MATHEMATICAL CONCEPTS
RT   631

GEOMETRY
GEOMETRIE
GEOMETRIA
                                    May 1984
BT   MATHEMATICS
RT   631

GEORGIAN SSR
RSS DE GEORGIE
RSS DE GEORGIA
                                    May 1984
BT   USSR

GERMAN
LANGUE ALLEMANDE
LENGUA ALEMANA
RT   626

GERMAN DR
REPUBLIQUE DEMOCRATIQUE
   ALLEMANDE
REPUBLICA DEMOCRATICA
   ALEMANA
UF   EAST GERMANY
BT   EASTERN EUROPE

GERMANIC LANGUAGES
LANGUES GERMANIQUES
LENGUAS GERMANICAS
RT   625

GERMANY FR
ALLEMAGNE (REPUBLIQUE
   FEDERALE)
ALEMANIA (REPUBLICA FEDERAL)
UF   WEST GERMANY
BT   WESTERN EUROPE

GHANA
GHANA
GHANA
BT   WEST AFRICA
RT   ENGLISH SPEAKING AFRICA

GIBRALTAR
GIBRALTAR
GIBRALTAR
BT   WESTERN EUROPE

GIFTED STUDENTS
ELEVE DOUE
ALUMNO SUPERDOTADO
BT   EXCEPTIONAL STUDENTS
RT   416

GIFTED TEACHERS
MAITRE DOUE
MAESTRO TALENTOSO
RT   424

GILBERT AND ELLICE ISLANDS
                                    May 1984
USE **KIRIBATI**

GIRLS ENROLMENT
SCOLARISATION DES FILLES
ESCOLARIDAD DE LAS JOVENES
                                    May 1984
RT   186

GLOBAL METHOD
METHODE GLOBALE
METODO GLOBAL
UF   ANALYTICAL METHOD
RT   661

GLOSSARY
GLOSSAIRE
GLOSARIO
UF   TERMINOLOGY
     THESAURUS
RT   880

GOAL ORIENTATION
POURSUITE D'UNE FINALITE
ORIENTACION HACIA UNA
   FINALIDAD
SN   Psychological disposition toward
     achieving one's objectives
RT   541

GOVERNING BOARDS

GOVERNING BOARDS
CONSEIL D'ADMINISTRATION
CONSEJO DE ADMINISTRACION
UF   BOARDS OF EDUCATION
      BOARDS OF TRUSTEES
SN   Group charged with the responsibility for some degree of control over managing the affairs of public or private institutions
RT   261

GOVERNMENT
GOUVERNEMENT
GOBIERNO
NT   CENTRAL GOVERNMENT
      CITY GOVERNMENT
      LOCAL GOVERNMENT
      PROVINCIAL GOVERNMENT
RT   102

GOVERNMENT PROGRAMMES
PROGRAMME GOUVERNEMENTAL
PROGRAMA GUBERNAMENTAL
BT   NATIONAL PROGRAMMES
RT   109

GOVERNMENT PUBLICATIONS
PUBLICATION OFFICIELLE
PUBLICACION OFICIAL
BT   PUBLICATIONS
RT   720

GOVERNMENT ROLE
ROLE DU GOUVERNEMENT
PAPEL DEL GOBIERNO
RT   105

GOVERNMENTAL STRUCTURE
STRUCTURE GOUVERNEMENTALE
ESTRUCTURA GUBERNAMENTAL
RT   103

GRADE ORGANIZATION
ORGANISATION PAR CLASSES
ORGANIZACION POR GRADOS
SN   Pattern of grades making up a school course
RT   342

GRADE REPETITION
REDOUBLEMENT
REPETICION
RT   267
      REPETITION RATE

GRADES (PROGRAMME DIVISIONS)
CLASSE (DIVISION DU PROGRAMME)
GRADOS (DIVISIONES DEL CICLO ESCOLAR)
UF   INSTRUCTIONAL PROGRAMME DIVISIONS
NT   INTERMEDIATE GRADES
      KINDERGARTEN
      PRIMARY GRADES
      SECONDARY GRADES
RT   342

GRADING
CLASSEMENT DES ELEVES
CLASIFICACION DE LOS ALUMNOS
UF   STUDENT PLACEMENT
RT   391

GRADUATE STUDY
ETUDES UNIVERSITAIRES (2E & 3E CYCLES)
ESTUDIOS DE POSTGRADO
BT   COLLEGE CURRICULUM
RT   330

GRADUATES
DIPLOME
GRADUADO
NT   COLLEGE GRADUATES
      SECONDARY SCHOOL GRADUATES
RT   410

GRADUATION
OBTENTION D'UN DIPLOME
GRADUACION
RT   390

GRAMMAR
GRAMMAIRE
GRAMATICA
NT GENERATIVE GRAMMAR
   STRUCTURAL GRAMMAR
   TRADITIONAL GRAMMAR
RT 622

GRANTS
BOURSE
BECA
SN Funds made available to individuals for study or research purposes
NT FELLOWSHIPS
   SCHOLARSHIPS
   TRAINING ALLOWANCES
RT 241

GRAPHIC ARTS
ARTS GRAPHIQUES
ARTES GRAFICAS
RT 610

GREATER ANTILLES
May 1984
USE **CARIBBEAN**

GREECE
GRECE
GRECIA
BT MEDITERRANEAN
   COUNTRIES
   WESTERN EUROPE

GREENLAND
GROENLAND
GROENLANDIA
BT SCANDINAVIA
   NORTH AMERICA
RT ARCTIC REGIONS

GRENADA
GRENADE
GRANADA
BT CARIBBEAN

GROUP ACTIVITIES
ACTIVITE DE GROUPE
ACTIVIDAD EN GRUPO
BT ACTIVITIES
RT 357

GROUP BEHAVIOUR
COMPORTEMENT DE GROUPE
CONDUCTA DEL GRUPO
BT BEHAVIOUR
RT 560

GROUP COUNSELLING
CONSULTATION DE GROUPE
ASESORAMIENTO DE GRUPO
BT COUNSELLING
RT 371

GROUP DISCUSSION
DISCUSSION DE GROUPE
DISCUSION EN GRUPO
SN Method of learning through interaction in peer groups
BT DISCUSSION (TEACHING TECHNIQUE)
RT 356

GROUP DYNAMICS
DYNAMIQUE DE GROUPE
DINAMICA DE GRUPO
RT 355

GROUP INSTRUCTION
ENSEIGNEMENT DE GROUPE
ENSEÑANZA EN GRUPO
UF GROUP TRAINING
BT INSTRUCTION
NT LARGE GROUP INSTRUCTION
RT 352

GROUP MEMBERSHIP
APPARTENANCE AU GROUPE
MIEMBRO DE UN GRUPO
RT 554

GROUP NORMS
NORME DE GROUPE
NORMA DEL GRUPO
RT 284

GROUP STRUCTURE

GROUP STRUCTURE
STRUCTURE DU GROUPE
ESTRUCTURA DEL GRUPO
RT 122

GROUP TRAINING
USE **GROUP INSTRUCTION**

GROUP TRAINING CENTRES
ATELIER CENTRAL DE
  FORMATION
UNIDAD CENTRAL DE
  CAPACITACION
SN Central facility providing workshops for a number of educational establishments
RT 311

GROUP UNITY
COHESION DU GROUPE
SOLIDARIDAD DEL GRUPO
SN Cohesiveness of groups of people, families, tribes and nations
RT 122

GROUPING (INSTRUCTIONAL PURPOSES)
CONSTITUTION DE GROUPES
  D'ETUDES
CONSTITUCION DE GRUPOS DE
  ESTUDIO
UF STUDENT GROUPING
RT 341

GROUPING PROCEDURES
MODALITE DE GROUPEMENT
MODALIDAD DE AGRUPAMIENTO
NT ABILITY GROUPING
   HETEROGENEOUS GROUPING
   HOMOGENEOUS GROUPING
RT 341

GROUPS
GROUPE
GRUPO
NT AGE GROUPS
   DISADVANTAGED GROUPS
   ETHNIC GROUPS
   LOW INCOME GROUPS
   MINORITY GROUPS
   PEER GROUPS
   RELIGIOUS CULTURAL
     GROUPS
   SELF DIRECTED GROUPS
RT 443

GROWTH PATTERNS
TYPE DE CROISSANCE
MODELOS DE DESARROLLO
RT 502

GUADELOUPE
GUADELOUPE
GUADALUPE
BT CARIBBEAN

GUAM
GUAM
GUAM
 May 1984
BT MARIANA ISLANDS

GUATEMALA
GUATEMALA
GUATEMALA
BT CENTRAL AMERICA

GUIANA
 May 1984
USE **FRENCH GUIANA**

GUIDANCE
ORIENTATION
ORIENTACION
SN A basic component of education comprising services provided to orientate the individual in his educational progress and career choice
NT EDUCATIONAL GUIDANCE
RT 211
   COUNSELLING

GUIDANCE AIMS
BUT DE L'ORIENTATION
OBJETIVO DE LA ORIENTACION
RT 211

GUIDANCE FUNCTIONS
FONCTION D'ORIENTATION
FUNCION DE ORIENTACION
RT 211

GUIDANCE PERSONNEL
PERSONNEL DE L'ORIENTATION
PERSONAL DE ORIENTACION
RT 431

GUIDANCE PROGRAMMES
PROGRAMME D'ORIENTATION
PROGRAMA DE ORIENTACION
BT EDUCATIONAL PROGRAMMES
RT 271

GUIDANCE SERVICES
SERVICES D'ORIENTATION
SERVICIO DE ORIENTACION
RT 270

GUIDANCE THEORIES
THEORIE DE L'ORIENTATION
TEORIA DE LA ORIENTACION
BT THEORIES
RT 211

GUIDES
GUIDE
GUIA
NT CURRICULUM GUIDES
    STUDY GUIDE
    TEACHING GUIDE
RT 724

GUINEA
GUINEE
GUINEA
BT WEST AFRICA
RT FRENCH SPEAKING AFRICA

GUINEA-BISSAU
GUINEE-BISSAU
GUINEA-BISSAU
BT WEST AFRICA

GULF STATES
ETATS DU GOLFE
ESTADOS DEL GOLFO
May 1984
BT MIDDLE EAST
    ARAB COUNTRIES
NT BAHRAIN
    KUWAIT
    QATAR
    UNITED ARAB EMIRATES

GUYANA
GUYANE
GUAYANA
BT SOUTH AMERICA

HABIT FORMATION
FORMATION DES HABITUDES
FORMACION DE HABITOS
BT BEHAVIOUR DEVELOPMENT
RT 542

HAITI
HAITI
HAITI
BT CARIBBEAN

HAND TOOLS
OUTIL
HERRAMIENTA
RT 742

HANDICAP DETECTION
DEPISTAGE DES HANDICAPS
DETECCION DE DEFICIENCIAS
RT 372

HANDICAPPED
HANDICAPE
DEFICIENTE
SN Persons with physical, mental or emotional handicaps
NT EMOTIONALLY DISTURBED
    HOMEBOUND PERSONS
    HOSPITALIZED PERSONS
    NEUROTICS
    PHYSICALLY HANDICAPPED
    PSYCHOTICS
    RETARDED CHILDREN
RT 403

HANDICAPPED STUDENTS
ELEVE HANDICAPE
ALUMNO DEFICIENTE
SN Handicapped persons in the school situation
BT EXCEPTIONAL STUDENTS
RT 411

HANDICAPS
HANDICAP
DEFICIENCIA
NT LANGUAGE HANDICAPS
   MENTAL HANDICAPS
   MULTIPLE HANDICAPS
   NEUROLOGICAL HANDICAPS
   PERCEPTUAL DISORDERS
   PHYSICAL HANDICAPS
   SPEECH HANDICAPS
   VISUAL HANDICAPS
RT 571

HANDICRAFTS
ARTISANAT
ARTESANIA
RT 610

HANDWRITING
ECRITURE MANUSCRITE
ESCRITURA MANUSCRITA
RT 620

HANDWRITING DEVELOPMENT
AMELIORATION EN ECRITURE
MEJORAMIENTO DE LA ESCRITURA
UF HANDWRITING IMPROVEMENT
RT 534

HANDWRITING IMPROVEMENT
USE **HANDWRITING DEVELOPMENT**

HANDWRITING INSTRUCTION
ENSEIGNEMENT DE L'ECRITURE
ENSEÑANZA DE LA ESCRITURA
RT 663

HARD OF HEARING
MALENTENDANT
DURO DE OIDO
SN Children or adults
RT 403

HAWAII
HAWAI
HAWAI
May 1984
BT POLYNESIA
   USA

HEADS OF DEPARTMENT (SCHOOL)
CHEF DE DEPARTEMENT SCOLAIRE
JEFE DE DEPARTAMENTO
May 1984
RT 423

HEADS OF HOUSEHOLDS
CHEF DE FAMILLE
JEFE DE FAMILIA
RT 401

HEALTH
SANTE
SALUD
NT MENTAL HEALTH
   PHYSICAL HEALTH
   PUBLIC HEALTH
RT 160
   HYGIENE

HEALTH ACTIVITIES
ACTIVITE SANITAIRE
ACTIVIDAD PARA LA SALUD
BT ACTIVITIES
RT 357

HEALTH EDUCATION
EDUCATION SANITAIRE
EDUCACION PARA LA SALUD
RT 683

HEALTH NEEDS
BESOIN SANITAIRE
NECESIDADES PARA LA SALUD
BT NEEDS
RT 160

HEALTH PERSONNEL
PERSONNEL DE LA SANTE
PERSONAL DE SANIDAD
RT 433

HEALTH PROGRAMMES
PROGRAMME SANITAIRE
PROGRAMA DE SANIDAD
BT PROGRAMMES
NT IMMUNIZATION
    PROGRAMMES
RT 160

HEALTH SERVICES
SERVICES DE SANTE
SERVICIOS DE SANIDAD
BT SERVICES
NT MEDICAL SERVICES
    SCHOOL HEALTH SERVICES
RT 107

HEARING
USE **AUDITION (PHYSIOLOGY)**

HEARING AIDS
PROTHESE AUDITIVE
AUDIFONO
RT 734

HEARING THERAPISTS
AUDIOLOGISTE
AUDIOLOGO
BT THERAPISTS
RT 432

HEARING THERAPY
TRAITEMENT DES TROUBLES
    AUDITIFS
TERAPIA DEL SISTEMA AUDITIVO
BT THERAPY
RT 373

HEIGHT
USE **BODY HEIGHT**

HEREDITY
HEREDITE
HERENCIA
BT BIOLOGY
RT 502

HETEROGENEOUS GROUPING
GROUPEMENT HETEROGENE
AGRUPAMIENTO HETEROGENEO
BT GROUPING PROCEDURES
RT 341

HIGH ACHIEVERS
TRES BON ELEVE
ALUMNO DESTACADO
RT 415

HIGH SCHOOLS
USE **SECONDARY SCHOOLS**

HIGHER EDUCATION
ENSEIGNEMENT SUPERIEUR
ENSEÑANZA SUPERIOR
UF POST SECONDARY
     EDUCATION
   TERTIARY EDUCATION
SN Stage following secondary
   education regardless of course
   duration or certificates awarded;
   preferred term for institutions is
   "colleges"
RT 185

HIMALAYAN STATES
ETATS HIMALAYENS
ESTADOS DEL HIMALAYA
                              May 1984
BT SOUTH ASIA
NT BHUTAN
   NEPAL
   SIKKIM

HISTORY
HISTOIRE
HISTORIA
SN Used by itself or linked to
   geographical identifier

HISTORY INSTRUCTION
BT   SOCIAL SCIENCES
NT   EDUCATIONAL HISTORY
     MODERN HISTORY
     NATIONAL HISTORY
     WORLD HISTORY
RT   641

HISTORY INSTRUCTION
ENSEIGNEMENT DE L'HISTOIRE
ENSEÑANZA DE LA HISTORIA
RT   680

HISTORY TEACHERS
PROFESSEUR D'HISTOIRE
PROFESOR DE HISTORIA
                              May 1984
RT   425

HOLLAND
                              May 1984
USE **NETHERLANDS**

HOLY SEE
SAINT–SIEGE
SANTA SEDE
UF   PAPAL STATE
     VATICAN CITY
BT   WESTERN EUROPE
RT   ITALY

HOME ECONOMICS
ECONOMIE DOMESTIQUE
ECONOMIA DOMESTICA
RT   640

HOME ECONOMICS EDUCATION
ENSEIGNEMENT MENAGER
ENSEÑANZA DE ECONOMIA
     DOMESTICA
RT   683

HOME ECONOMICS TEACHERS
PROFESSEUR D'ECONOMIE
     DOMESTIQUE
PROFESOR DE ECONOMIA
     DOMESTICA
RT   425

HOME ENVIRONMENT
ENVIRONNEMENT FAMILIAL
AMBIENTE FAMILIAR
BT   CULTURAL ENVIRONMENT
RT   550

HOME INSTRUCTION
ENSEIGNEMENT A DOMICILE
ENSEÑANZA A DOMICILIO
RT   352

HOME STUDY
ETUDES A DOMICILE
ESTUDIOS A DOMICILIO
RT   335

HOMEBOUND PERSONS
PERSONNE RETENUE A LA
     MAISON
PERSONA CONFINADA
SN   Physically or mentally disabled
     persons confined to their homes
BT   HANDICAPPED
RT   403

HOMEWORK
DEVOIRS A DOMICILE
TAREA ESCOLAR A DOMICILIO
RT   356

HOMOGENEOUS GROUPING
GROUPEMENT HOMOGENE
AGRUPAMIENTO HOMOGENEO
BT   GROUPING PROCEDURES
RT   341

HONDURAS
HONDURAS
HONDURAS
BT   CENTRAL AMERICA

HONG KONG
HONG KONG
HONG KONG
BT   FAR EAST

HORTICULTURE
HORTICULTURE
HORTICULTURA
RT 646

HOSPITAL SCHOOLS
ECOLE EN MILIEU HOSPITALIER
ESCUELA EN HOSPITAL
RT 304

HOSPITALIZED PERSONS
PERSONNE HOSPITALISEE
PERSONA HOSPITALIZADA
BT HANDICAPPED
RT 403

HOSPITALS
HOPITAL
HOSPITAL
RT 313

HOUSEWIVES
FEMME AU FOYER
AMA DE CASA
RT 451

HOUSING
LOGEMENT
VIVIENDA
NT STAFF HOUSING
RT 126

HUMAN BODY
CORPS HUMAIN
CUERPO HUMANO
RT 502

HUMAN CAPITAL
USE **HUMAN RESOURCES**

HUMAN DIGNITY
DIGNITE HUMAINE
DIGNIDAD HUMANA
RT 100

HUMAN ENGINEERING
TECHNOLOGIE DU
  COMPORTEMENT HUMAIN
TECNICA APLICADA A LA
  COMODIDAD OPERATIVA

SN Activity or science of designing, building or equipping environments or mechanical devices to anthropometric, physiological or psychological requirements of human operators
RT 140

HUMAN RELATIONS
RELATIONS HUMAINES
RELACIONES HUMANAS
RT 122

HUMAN RESOURCES
RESSOURCE HUMAINE
RECURSOS HUMANOS
UF HUMAN CAPITAL
RT 153

HUMAN RESOURCES DEVELOPMENT
DEVELOPPEMENT DES
  RESSOURCES HUMAINES
DESARROLLO DE RECURSOS
  HUMANOS
BT DEVELOPMENT
RT 151

HUMAN RIGHTS
DROITS DE L'HOMME
DERECHOS HUMANOS
UF CIVIL LIBERTIES
    INDIVIDUAL RIGHTS
NT FREEDOM OF SPEECH
RT 100
    CIVIL RIGHTS

HUMANISM
HUMANISME
HUMANISMO
RT 600

HUMANITIES
HUMANITES
HUMANIDADES
UF LIBERAL ARTS
RT 600

HUNGARY
HONGRIE
HUNGRIA
BT   EASTERN EUROPE

HUNGER
FAIM
HAMBRE
RT   503

HYDRAULICS
HYDRAULIQUE
HIDRAULICA
RT   647

HYGIENE
HYGIENE
HIGIENE
RT   502
     HEALTH

HYPOTHESIS TESTING
USE **STATISTICAL ANALYSIS**

IAMCR
AIERI
AIERI
SN   International Association for Mass Communication Research

IAU
AIU
AIU
SN   International Association of Universities

IBE
BIE
OIE
SN   International Bureau of Education

IBRD
BIRD
BIRF
SN   International Bank for Reconstruction and Development

ICE
CIE
CIE
SN   International Conference on Education

ICELAND
ISLANDE
ISLANDIA
BT   ATLANTIC OCEAN TERRITORIES
     SCANDINAVIA
     WESTERN EUROPE

ICET
CIPE
CIPE
SN   International Council on Education for Teaching

ICSSD
CIDSS
CIDCS
SN   International Committee for Social Science Information and Documentation

ICSUAB
ICSUAB
ICSUAB
SN   International Council of Scientific Unions Abstracting Board

ICVA
ICVA
CIAV
SN   International Council of Voluntary Agencies

IDA
IDA
AIF
SN   International Development Association

IDB
BID
BID
SN   Inter-American Development Bank

IDENTIFICATION
DEPISTAGE
IDENTIFICACION DE CASOS
RT 372

IDENTIFICATION (PSYCHOLOGICAL)
IDENTIFICATION (PSYCHOLOGIQUE)
IDENTIFICACION (PSICOLOGICA)
SN Process or state of imitating or merging emotionally with someone or something
BT PSYCHOLOGICAL PATTERNS
RT 555

IFFTU
SPIE
SPIE
SN International Federation of Free Teachers' Unions

IFLA
FIAB
FIAB
SN International Federation of Library Associations

IIALM
IIMAA
IIMAA
SN International Institute for Adult Literacy Methods

IIEP
IIPE
IIPE
SN International Institute for Educational Planning

ILCE
ILCE
ILCE
SN Latin American Institute for Educational Communication

ILLITERACY
ANALPHABETISME
ANALFABETISMO
SN Relates to the problem. Provision for resolving it should be handled by the "literacy" descriptors
RT 180

ILLITERATE ADULTS
ADULTE ANALPHABETE
ADULTO ANALFABETO
BT ADULTS
RT 402

ILLUSTRATIONS
ILLUSTRATION
ILUSTRACION
RT 733

ILO
OIT
OIT
SN International Labour Organization. Use to mean either the International Labour Organization or the International Labour Office

IMAGINATION
IMAGINATION
IMAGINACION
RT 522

IMMATURITY
IMMATURITE
INMADUREZ
RT 531

IMMIGRANTS
IMMIGRANT
INMIGRANTE
RT 470

IMMIGRATION
IMMIGRATION
INMIGRACION
RT 124

IMMUNIZATION PROGRAMMES
PROGRAMME DE VACCINATION
PROGRAMA DE VACUNACION
BT HEALTH PROGRAMMES
RT 161

INCENTIVE SYSTEMS
SYSTEME D'ENCOURAGEMENT
INCENTIVOS
RT 233

INCOME
REVENU
INGRESO
NT SALARIES
RT 153

INDEPENDENT READING
LECTURE PERSONNELLE
LECTURA PERSONAL
RT 661

INDEPENDENT SCHOOLS
USE **PRIVATE SCHOOLS**

INDEPENDENT STUDY
ETUDES LIBRES
ESTUDIOS LIBRES
SN Study carried on with a minimum or a complete absence of external guidance
RT 335

INDEXES (LOCATERS)
INDEX
INDICES
RT 721

INDEXING
INDEXAGE
INDIZADO
RT 202

INDIA
INDE
INDIA
BT SOUTH ASIA

INDIAN OCEAN TERRITORIES
TERRITOIRES DE L'OCEAN INDIEN
TERRITORIOS DEL OCEANO INDICO
May 1984
BT POLYNESIA
NT CHRISTMAS ISLAND
    COMOROS
    MADAGASCAR
    MAURITIUS
    REUNION ISLAND
    SEYCHELLES
RT EAST AFRICA
    SOUTHERN AFRICA

INDIVIDUAL CHARACTERISTICS
CARACTERISTIQUE INDIVIDUELLE
CARACTERISTICA INDIVIDUAL
NT CURIOSITY
    INDIVIDUAL DIFFERENCES
    PHYSICAL CHARACTERISTICS
RT 561

INDIVIDUAL COUNSELLING
CONSULTATION INDIVIDUELLE
ASESORAMIENTO INDIVIDUAL
BT COUNSELLING
RT 371

INDIVIDUAL DEVELOPMENT
DEVELOPPEMENT INDIVIDUEL
DESARROLLO INDIVIDUAL
UF PERSONAL DEVELOPMENT
RT 530

INDIVIDUAL DIFFERENCES
DIFFERENCE INDIVIDUELLE
DIFERENCIAS INDIVIDUALES
BT INDIVIDUAL CHARACTERISTICS
NT AGE DIFFERENCES
    SEX DIFFERENCES
RT 530

INDIVIDUAL LEARNING AREAS
AIRE DE TRAVAIL INDIVIDUEL
CAMPO DE ESTUDIO INDIVIDUAL
RT 711

INDIVIDUAL NEEDS
BESOIN INDIVIDUEL
NECESIDADES INDIVIDUALES
NT CHILDHOOD NEEDS
RT 536

INDIVIDUAL PSYCHOLOGY
PSYCHOLOGIE GENERALE
PSICOLOGIA GENERAL
BT PSYCHOLOGY
RT 642

INDIVIDUAL RIGHTS
USE HUMAN RIGHTS

INDIVIDUAL STUDY
ETUDES INDIVIDUELLES
ESTUDIOS INDIVIDUALES
RT 335

INDIVIDUALIZED CURRICULUM
PROGRAMMES INDIVIDUALISES
PROGRAMA INDIVIDUALIZADO
RT 332

INDIVIDUALIZED INSTRUCTION
ENSEIGNEMENT INDIVIDUALISE
ENSEÑANZA INDIVIDUALIZADA
BT INSTRUCTION
RT 352

INDO EUROPEAN LANGUAGES
LANGUES INDO-EUROPEENNES
LENGUAS INDOEUROPEAS
RT 625

INDONESIA
INDONESIE
INDONESIA
UF BORNEO
    CELEBES
    JAVA
    SUMATRA
BT SOUTH EAST ASIA

INDUCTION TRAINING
STAGE D'INITIATION
FORMACION PREVIA AL TRABAJO
SN Short training given by the employer to newly employed workers
BT TRAINING
RT 351

INDUCTIVE METHODS
METHODE INDUCTIVE
METODO INDUCTIVO
BT TEACHING METHODS
RT 355

INDUSTRIAL ARTS
ARTS INDUSTRIELS
ARTES INDUSTRIALES
RT 647

INDUSTRIAL EDUCATION
ENSEIGNEMENT INDUSTRIEL
ENSEÑANZA INDUSTRIAL
SN All types of education related to industry including industrial arts and education for occupations in industry at all levels
BT VOCATIONAL EDUCATION
RT 672

INDUSTRIAL OCCUPATIONS
METIER INDUSTRIEL
OCUPACION INDUSTRIAL
BT OCCUPATIONS
RT 155

INDUSTRIAL PERSONNEL
PERSONNEL DE L'INDUSTRIE
PERSONAL DE LA INDUSTRIA
RT 441

INDUSTRIAL TECHNOLOGY
TECHNOLOGIE INDUSTRIELLE
TECNOLOGIA INDUSTRIAL
BT TECHNOLOGY
RT 645

INDUSTRIALIZATION
INDUSTRIALISATION
INDUSTRIALIZACION
RT 150

INDUSTRIALIZED BUILDINGS
BATIMENT PREFABRIQUE
CONSTRUCCION PREFABRICADA
RT 253

INDUSTRY
INDUSTRIE
INDUSTRIA
NT CONSTRUCTION INDUSTRY
    FURNITURE INDUSTRY
    PUBLISHING INDUSTRY
    SMALL SCALE INDUSTRY
RT 150

INFANCY
PREMIER AGE
NIÑEZ
RT 500

INFANT BEHAVIOUR
COMPORTEMENT DU PREMIER AGE
CONDUCTA INFANTIL
BT BEHAVIOUR
RT 560

INFANT EDUCATION
USE **EARLY CHILDHOOD EDUCATION**

INFANTS
ENFANT DU PREMIER AGE
PARVULO
SN To age of approximately two years
RT 400

INFORMAL EDUCATION
EDUCATION DIFFUSE
EDUCACION INFORMAL
SN The process of learning which goes on continuously and incidentally for each individual, outside the organized situation of formal or non–formal education
RT 184

INFORMATION CENTRES
CENTRE D'INFORMATION
CENTRO DE INFORMACION
UF CLEARINGHOUSES
RT 310

INFORMATION DISSEMINATION
DIFFUSION DE L'INFORMATION
DIFUSION DE LA INFORMACION
BT INFORMATION UTILIZATION
RT 204

INFORMATION EXCHANGE
ECHANGE D'INFORMATION
INTERCAMBIO DE INFORMACION
RT 204

INFORMATION GATHERING
COLLECTE DE L'INFORMATION
ACOPIO DE INFORMACION
RT 204

INFORMATION NETWORKS
RESEAU D'INFORMATION
RED DE INFORMACION
RT 202

INFORMATION PROCESSING
TRAITEMENT DE L'INFORMATION
PROCESAMIENTO DE LA INFORMACION
SN Preparation, storage and retrieval
NT DATA PROCESSING
    INFORMATION UTILIZATION
RT 202

INFORMATION SCIENCE
SCIENCES DE L'INFORMATION
CIENCIAS DE LA INFORMACION
RT 630

INFORMATION SEEKING
RECHERCHE D'INFORMATION
BUSQUEDA DE INFORMACION
UF INQUIRY TRAINING
BT LEARNING PROCESSES
RT 541

INFORMATION SERVICES
SERVICES D'INFORMATION
SERVICIOS DE INFORMACION
BT   SERVICES
RT   107

INFORMATION SPECIALISTS
SPECIALISTE DE L'INFORMATION
ESPECIALISTA DE LA
   INFORMACION
RT   462

INFORMATION SYSTEMS
SYSTEME D'INFORMATION
SISTEMA DE INFORMACION
NT   FEEDBACK
RT   201

INFORMATION THEORY
THEORIE DE L'INFORMATION
TEORIA DE LA INFORMACION
                              May 1984
SN   Mathematical theory concerned
     with the rate and accuracy of
     information transmission within a
     system as affected by the number
     and width of channels, distorsion,
     noise, etc.
RT   204

INFORMATION UTILIZATION
UTILISATION DE L'INFORMATION
UTILIZACION DE LA
   INFORMACION
BT   INFORMATION PROCESSING
NT   INFORMATION
     DISSEMINATION
RT   204

INITIAL EMPLOYMENT
PREMIER EMPLOI
PRIMER EMPLEO
RT   154

INITIAL TEACHING ALPHABET
ALPHABET D'INITIATION
ENSEÑANZA INICIAL DEL
   ALFABETO
RT   661

INSERVICE EDUCATION

INNOVATION
INNOVATION
INNOVACION
SN   Applies to policies and
     management aspects
NT   EDUCATIONAL INNOVATIONS
RT   200

INPLANT PROGRAMMES
PROGRAMME DE FORMATION
   SUR LE TAS
PROGRAMA DE FORMACION EN
   EL TRABAJO
SN   Educational or training
     programmes carried on within
     commercial or industrial
     establishments
RT   673

INQUIRY TRAINING
USE **INFORMATION SEEKING**

INSECURITY
INSECURITE
INSEGURIDAD
BT   PSYCHOLOGICAL PATTERNS
RT   540

INSERVICE COURSES
COURS DE PERFECTIONNEMENT
CURSO DE PERFECCIONAMIENTO
BT   COURSES
NT   INSTITUTE TYPE COURSES
     REFRESHER TRAINING
RT   334

INSERVICE EDUCATION
FORMATION EN COURS D'EMPLOI
FORMACION EN EJERCICIO
SN   Courses or programmes providing
     sustained further study enabling
     professional persons to improve
     their qualifications
NT   INSERVICE TEACHER
     EDUCATION
RT   321

INSERVICE TEACHER EDUCATION

INSERVICE TEACHER EDUCATION
FORMATION DES MAITRES EN EXERCICE
FORMACION DE DOCENTES EN EJERCICIO
SN Designed to enable teachers to be retrained, or to obtain a higher level certificate, or even be initially trained when already in the field
BT INSERVICE EDUCATION
    TEACHER EDUCATION
RT 690

INSPECTION
USE **SUPERVISION**

INSPECTORS
INSPECTEUR
INSPECTOR
SN Officials with administrative and pedagogical responsibilities in respect of group of educational institutions
BT EDUCATIONAL PERSONNEL
NT PRIMARY SCHOOL INSPECTORS
    SECONDARY SCHOOL INSPECTORS
RT 420

INSTITUTE TYPE COURSES
STAGE DE PERFECTIONNEMENT
CURSILLO DE ESPECIALIZACION
SN Designed to provide advanced study in a subject field and lasting only a few days
BT INSERVICE COURSES
RT 334

INSTITUTIONAL FRAMEWORK
CADRE INSTITUTIONNEL
MARCO DE REFERENCIA INSTITUCIONAL
RT 260

INSTITUTIONAL SELF MANAGEMENT
AUTOGESTION
GESTION INSTITUCIONAL AUTONOMA
UF SELF GOVERNMENT
SN Arrangements giving educational establishment at any level a degree of autonomy in administrative and programme matters
RT 261

INSTITUTIONS
INSTITUTION
INSTITUCION
RT 125

INSTRUCTION
INSTRUCTION
INSTRUCCION
NT CONVENTIONAL INSTRUCTION
    GROUP INSTRUCTION
    INDIVIDUALIZED INSTRUCTION
    MASS EDUCATION
RT 352
    TEACHING

INSTRUCTIONAL FILMS
FILM DIDACTIQUE
PELICULA DIDACTICA
BT FILMS
RT 730

INSTRUCTIONAL IMPROVEMENT
PROGRES PEDAGOGIQUE
MEJORA PEDAGOGICA
RT 352

INSTRUCTIONAL INNOVATION
INNOVATION PEDAGOGIQUE
INNOVACION PEDAGOGICA
RT 352

INSTRUCTIONAL MATERIALS
MATERIEL DIDACTIQUE
MATERIAL DIDACTICO
UF   TEACHING MATERIALS
SN   All print and non-print materials used for teaching purposes
NT   MATERIALS SELECTION
     PROGRAMMED MATERIALS
     READING MATERIALS
RT   725
     AUDIOVISUAL AIDS

INSTRUCTIONAL MATERIALS CENTRES
USE **MEDIA RESOURCES CENTRES**

INSTRUCTIONAL PROGRAMME DIVISIONS
USE **GRADES (PROGRAMME DIVISIONS)**

INSTRUCTIONAL PROGRAMMES
PROGRAMME D'ENSEIGNEMENT
PROGRAMA DE ENSEÑANZA
SN   Outline of procedures, courses and subjects to be provided by an educational institution over a given period of time
NT   ACCELERATED PROGRAMMES
     ENRICHMENT PROGRAMMES
     SPECIAL PROGRAMMES
RT   320
     CURRICULUM

INSTRUCTIONAL PROGRAMMING
PROGRAMMATION PEDAGOGIQUE
PROGRAMACION PEDAGOGICA
RT   361

INSTRUCTIONAL TELEVISION
ENSEIGNEMENT TELEVISUEL
ENSEÑANZA POR TELEVISION
BT   EDUCATIONAL TELEVISION
NT   CLOSED CIRCUIT TELEVISION
RT   360

INSTRUCTIONAL TRIPS
EXCURSION PEDAGOGIQUE
EXCURSION DE ESTUDIOS
SN   As part of planned curriculum
RT   381

INSURANCE PROGRAMMES
PROGRAMME D'ASSURANCES
PROGRAMA DE SEGUROS
SN   Device for the reduction of economic risk
RT   241

INTEGRATED ACTIVITIES
ACTIVITE INTEGREE
ACTIVIDAD INTEGRADA
SN   Systematic organization of units into a meaningful pattern
BT   ACTIVITIES
RT   357

INTEGRATED CURRICULUM
PROGRAMMES INTEGRES
CURRICULO INTEGRADO
SN   Systematic organization of curriculum content and parts into a meaningful pattern
RT   332

INTEGRATED RURAL DEVELOPMENT
DEVELOPPEMENT RURAL INTEGRE
DESARROLLO RURAL INTEGRADO
BT   RURAL DEVELOPMENT
RT   151

INTELLECTUAL DEVELOPMENT
DEVELOPPEMENT INTELLECTUEL
DESARROLLO INTELECTUAL
BT   MENTAL DEVELOPMENT
RT   530

INTELLECTUALIZATION
USE **ABSTRACT REASONING**

INTELLIGENCE

INTELLIGENCE
INTELLIGENCE
INTELIGENCIA
UF   MENTAL ABILITY
BT   ABILITY
NT   COMPREHENSION
RT   520

INTELLIGENCE FACTORS
FACTEUR INTELLECTUEL
FACTOR INTELECTUAL
RT   285

INTELLIGENCE QUOTIENT
QUOTIENT INTELLECTUEL
CUOCIENTE INTELECTUAL
RT   520

INTELLIGENCE TESTS
TEST D'INTELLIGENCE
PRUEBA DE INTELIGENCIA
BT   PSYCHOLOGICAL TESTS
RT   394

INTENSIVE LANGUAGE COURSES
COURS INTENSIF DE LANGUE
CURSO INTENSIVO DE IDIOMA
RT   663

INTERACTION
INTERACTION
INTERACCION
SN   Of systems or factors, not people
RT   285
        RELATIONSHIP

INTERACTION PROCESS
PROCESSUS D'INTERACTION
   SOCIALE
PROCESO DE INTERACCION
SN   Restrict to people
BT   RELATIONSHIP
RT   352

INTERCULTURAL PROGRAMMES
PROGRAMME INTERCULTUREL
PROGRAMA INTERCULTURAL
RT   680

INTERDISCIPLINARITY
INTERDISCIPLINARITE
INTERDISCIPLINARIEDAD

May 1984

RT   331

INTERDISCIPLINARY APPROACH
APPROCHE INTERDISCIPLINAIRE
ENFOQUE INTERDISCIPLINARIO
RT   331

INTEREST
INTERET (REVENU)
INTERESES
SN   The price paid for the use of
       money over time
RT   241

INTEREST TESTS
TEST D'INTERET
PRUEBA DE INTERES
BT   EDUCATIONAL TESTS
RT   393

INTERESTS
INTERET
INTERES
NT   VOCATIONAL INTERESTS
RT   541

INTERGROUP RELATIONS
RELATIONS INTERGROUPES
RELACION ENTRE GRUPOS
BT   SOCIAL RELATIONS
RT   122

INTERINSTITUTIONAL
   COOPERATION
COOPERATION
   INTERINSTITUTIONNELLE
COOPERACION
   INTERINSTITUCIONAL
RT   262

INTERMEDIATE ADMINISTRATIVE
   UNITS
UNITE ADMINISTRATIVE
   INTERMEDIAIRE
UNIDAD ADMINISTRATIVA
   INTERMEDIA

SN Administering to districts rather than to individual institutions
RT 261

INTERMEDIATE EDUCATION
USE **LOWER SECONDARY EDUCATION**

INTERMEDIATE GRADES
CLASSE INTERMEDIAIRE
GRADO INTERMEDIO
BT GRADES (PROGRAMME DIVISIONS)
RT 342
    LOWER SECONDARY SCHOOLS

INTERMEDIATE TECHNOLOGIES
TECHNOLOGIE INTERMEDIAIRE
TECNOLOGIA INTERMEDIA
RT 360

INTERNAL ASSESSMENT
EVALUATION INTERNE
EVALUACION INTERNA
SN Evaluation of student performed within the institution
RT 391

INTERNATIONAL AGENCIES
ORGANISME INTERNATIONAL
ORGANISMO INTERNACIONAL
BT AGENCIES
RT 103

INTERNATIONAL CONVENTIONS
CONVENTION INTERNATIONALE
CONVENIO INTERNACIONAL
RT 170

INTERNATIONAL COOPERATION
COOPERATION INTERNATIONALE
COOPERACION INTERNACIONAL
RT 105

INTERNATIONAL EDUCATION
EDUCATION INTERNATIONALE
EDUCACION INTERNACIONAL
SN Study of the educational, social, political and economic forces in international relations
RT 640

INTERNATIONAL EDUCATION CONSULTANTS
CONSULTANT INTERNATIONAL EN EDUCATION
CONSULTOR INTERNACIONAL EN EDUCACION
BT CONSULTANTS
RT 430

INTERNATIONAL EXPERTS
EXPERT INTERNATIONAL
EXPERTO INTERNACIONAL
UF EXPERTS
BT EDUCATIONAL MISSIONS
   SPECIALISTS
RT 430

INTERNATIONAL ORGANIZATIONS
ORGANISATION INTERNATIONALE
ORGANIZACION INTERNACIONAL
SN Non-governmental bodies
BT ORGANIZATIONS
RT 110

INTERNATIONAL PROBLEMS
USE **WORLD PROBLEMS**

INTERNATIONAL PROGRAMMES
PROGRAMME INTERNATIONAL
PROGRAMA INTERNACIONAL
BT PROGRAMMES
RT 109

INTERNATIONAL RECOMMENDATIONS
RECOMMANDATION INTERNATIONALE
RECOMENDACION INTERNACIONAL
SN Adopted by international organizations
RT 170

INTERNATIONAL RELATIONS
RELATIONS INTERNATIONALES
RELACIONES INTERNACIONALES
SN As field of study, forming part of social sciences
RT 640

INTERNATIONAL SCHOOLS
ECOLE INTERNATIONALE
ESCUELA INTERNACIONAL
RT 302

INTERNATIONAL SURVEYS
ENQUETE INTERNATIONALE
ENCUESTA INTERNACIONAL
BT SURVEYS
RT 203

INTERNATIONAL UNDERSTANDING
COMPREHENSION INTERNATIONALE
COMPRENSION INTERNACIONAL
RT 101

INTERNSHIP PROGRAMMES
PROGRAMME DE STAGE
PROGRAMA DE CURSILLO
RT 222

INTERPERSONAL PROBLEMS
PROBLEME INTERPERSONNEL
PROBLEMA INTERPERSONAL
RT 554

INTERPERSONAL RELATIONSHIP
RELATIONS INTERPERSONNELLES
RELACIONES INTERPERSONALES
BT RELATIONSHIP
NT FAMILY RELATIONSHIP
    PEER RELATIONSHIP
    STUDENT TEACHER RELATIONSHIP
RT 553

INTERPRETERS
INTERPRETE
INTERPRETE
RT 462

INTERVENTION
INTERVENTION
INTERVENCION
SN Action performed to direct or influence behaviour
RT 355

INTERVIEWS
ENTRETIEN
ENTREVISTA
RT 221
        FIELD STUDIES

INTONATION
INTONATION
ENTONACION
RT 622

INVESTMENT
INVESTISSEMENT
INVERSION
RT 152

IPPF
IPPF
FIPP
SN International Planned Parenthood Federation

IRAN
May 1984
USE **IRAN (REPUBLIC ISLAMIC)**

IRAN (ISLAMIC REPUBLIC)
IRAN (REPUBLIQUE ISLAMIQUE)
IRAN (REPUBLICA ISLAMICA)
UF PERSIA
    IRAN
BT MIDDLE EAST

IRAQ
IRAK
IRAQ
BT ARAB COUNTRIES
    MIDDLE EAST

IRELAND
IRLANDE
IRLANDA
UF EIRE
      IRISH REPUBLIC
BT WESTERN EUROPE

IRISH REPUBLIC
May 1984
USE **IRELAND**

ISLAMIC EDUCATION
EDUCATION ISLAMIQUE
EDUCACION ISLAMICA
May 1984
RT 188

ISO
ISO
OIN
SN International Organization for Standardization

ISRAEL
ISRAEL
ISRAEL
BT MEDITERRANEAN
      COUNTRIES
      MIDDLE EAST

ITALY
ITALIE
ITALIA
BT MEDITERRANEAN
      COUNTRIES
      WESTERN EUROPE
RT HOLY SEE
      SAN MARINO

ITINERANT TEACHERS
MAITRE ITINERANT
MAESTRO ITINERANTE
RT 424

ITU
UIT
UIT
SN International Telecommunication Union

IVORY COAST
COTE D'IVOIRE
COSTA DE MARFIL
BT WEST AFRICA
RT FRENCH SPEAKING AFRICA

JAMAICA
JAMAIQUE
JAMAICA
BT CARIBBEAN

JAPAN
JAPON
JAPON
BT FAR EAST
NT RYUKU ISLANDS

JAVA
May 1984
USE **INDONESIA**

JEWS
JUIF
JUDIO
RT 475

JOB ANALYSIS
PROFIL D'EMPLOI
DESCRIPCION DEL EMPLEO
RT 221

JOB APPLICANTS
CANDIDAT A UN EMPLOI
CANDIDATO A UN EMPLEO
RT 451

JOB APPLICATION
DEMANDE D'EMPLOI
SOLICITUD DE EMPLEO
RT 221

JOB SATISFACTION
SATISFACTION PROFESSIONNELLE
SATISFACCION EN EL TRABAJO
RT 563

JOB TENURE

JOB TENURE
SECURITE D'EMPLOI
TITULARIDAD EN EL EMPLEO
RT 153

JOB TRAINING
USE **VOCATIONAL TRAINING**

JOHNSTON ISLAND
ILE JOHNSTON
ISLA JOHNSTON
May 1984
BT POLYNESIA

JORDAN
JORDANIE
JORDANIA
BT ARAB COUNTRIES
    MIDDLE EAST

JOURNALISM
JOURNALISME
PERIODISMO
RT 650
    PRESS

JUNIOR COLLEGES
COLLEGE POSTSECONDAIRE
INSTITUTO POSTSECUNDARIO
UF COMMUNITY COLLEGES
BT COLLEGES
RT 307

KAZAKH SSR
RSS DU KAZAKHSTAN
RSS DE KAZAKISTAN
May 1984
BT USSR

KENYA
KENYA
KENYA
BT EAST AFRICA
RT ENGLISH SPEAKING AFRICA

KERMADEC ISLANDS
ILES DE KERMADEC
ISLAS DE KERMADEC
May 1984
BT NEW ZEALAND

KHMER REPUBLIC
May 1984
USE **DEMOCRATIC KAMPUCHEA**

KINDERGARTEN
JARDIN D'ENFANTS
JARDIN INFANTIL
SN Applied to the grade, not the institution, for which use "nursery schools"
BT GRADES (PROGRAMME DIVISIONS)
RT 342

KINDERGARTEN CHILDREN
ELEVE DE JARDIN D'ENFANTS
ALUMNO DE JARDIN INFANTIL
BT PREPRIMARY CHILDREN
RT 411

KIRIBATI
KIRIBATI
KIRIBATI
May 1984
UF ELLICE ISLANDS
    PHOENIX ISLANDS
    GILBERT AND ELLICE
    ISLANDS
BT MICRONESIA

KNOWLEDGE LEVEL
NIVEAU DE CONNAISSANCE
NIVEL DE CONOCIMIENTO
SN Extent of knowledge gained
RT 535

KOREA DPR
COREE (REPUBLIQUE POPULAIRE DEMOCRATIQUE)
COREA (REPUBLICA POPULAR DEMOCRATICA)
UF NORTH KOREA
BT FAR EAST

KOREA R
COREE (REPUBLIQUE)
COREA (REPUBLICA)
UF SOUTH KOREA
BT FAR EAST

LABOUR RELATIONS

KUWAIT
KOWEIT
KUWAIT
BT   ARAB COUNTRIES
      GULF STATES

LABORATORIES
LABORATOIRE
LABORATORIO
RT   711

LABORATORY EQUIPMENT
EQUIPEMENT DE LABORATOIRE
EQUIPO DE LABORATORIO
BT   EQUIPMENT
RT   740

LABORATORY EXPERIMENTS
EXPERIENCES DE LABORATOIRE
EXPERIMENTO DE LABORATORIO
BT   EXPERIMENTS
RT   671

LABORATORY PROCEDURES
PROCEDE DE LABORATOIRE
METODO DE LABORATORIO
SN   Teaching procedures used in the laboratory phase of instruction
RT   671

LABORATORY SCHOOLS
ECOLE D'APPLICATION
ESCUELA DE APLICACION
UF   PRACTICE SCHOOLS
SN   School of primary and secondary grades attached to a university for purposes of research and teacher training
RT   305

LABORATORY TECHNIQUES
TECHNIQUE DE LABORATOIRE
TECNICA DE LABORATORIO
RT   671

LABORATORY TRAINING
FORMATION HUMAINE
FORMACION EN RELACIONES HUMANAS
SN   Method of training designed to facilitate self–insight, process awareness, interpersonal competence and dynamics of change
RT   352

LABOUR
TRAVAIL
TRABAJO
RT   153

LABOUR DEMANDS
REVENDICATION DES TRAVAILLEURS
REIVINDICACION DE LOS TRABAJADORES
RT   153

LABOUR FORCE
FORCE OUVRIERE
FUERZA DE TRABAJO
RT   153

LABOUR FORCE NONPARTICIPANTS
CHOMEUR VOLONTAIRE
FUERZA DE TRABAJO INACTIVA
RT   450

LABOUR LAWS
LEGISLATION DU TRAVAIL
LEGISLACION DEL TRABAJO
BT   LAWS
RT   170

LABOUR MARKET
MARCHE DU TRAVAIL
MERCADO DE TRABAJO
RT   154

LABOUR ORGANIZATIONS
USE **TRADE UNIONS**

LABOUR RELATIONS
RELATIONS INDUSTRIELLES
RELACIONES LABORALES
UF   EMPLOYER EMPLOYEE RELATIONSHIP
SN   Covers broad relations between: employers and employees;

management and organized labour; labour, management and the government. Excludes specific relationship between an employer and an individual employee (personnel management)
BT   SOCIAL RELATIONS
RT   153

LAND REFORM
USE **AGRARIAN REFORM**

LANGUAGE
LANGAGE
LENGUAJE
SN   Restrict to abstract sense of oral communication; for specific senses use "languages" or "national language"
NT   LANGUAGE USAGE
RT   131
    LANGUAGES

LANGUAGE ABILITY
APTITUDE LINGUISTIQUE
APTITUD LINGUISTICA
BT   ABILITY
RT   520

LANGUAGE ARTS
DISCIPLINE LINGUISTIQUE
DISCIPLINA LINGUISTICA
NT   LISTENING
    READING
    SPEAKING
    TRANSLATION
    WRITING
RT   620

LANGUAGE DEVELOPMENT
DEVELOPPEMENT DU LANGAGE
DESARROLLO DEL LENGUAJE
BT   MENTAL DEVELOPMENT
RT   530

LANGUAGE ENRICHMENT
ENRICHISSEMENT DU LANGAGE
ENRIQUECIMIENTO DEL LENGUAJE
RT   662

LANGUAGE HANDICAPS
HANDICAP LINGUISTIQUE
DEFICIENCIA LINGUISTICA
BT   HANDICAPS
NT   DYSLEXIA
RT   571

LANGUAGE INSTRUCTION
ENSEIGNEMENT DES LANGUES
ENSEÑANZA DE IDIOMAS
NT   MODERN LANGUAGE
       INSTRUCTION
    MOTHER TONGUE
       INSTRUCTION
    SECOND LANGUAGE
       INSTRUCTION
RT   662

LANGUAGE LABORATORIES
LABORATOIRE DE LANGUES
LABORATORIO DE IDIOMAS
RT   731

LANGUAGE PATTERNS
MODELE LINGUISTIQUE
MODELO LINGUISTICO
RT   621

LANGUAGE POLICY
POLITIQUE LINGUISTIQUE
POLITICA LINGUISTICA
SN   Covers development of a national language policy as well as planning and implementation phases
BT   SOCIAL POLICIES
RT   131

LANGUAGE PROFICIENCY
MAITRISE DE LA LANGUE
DOMINIO DEL IDIOMA
RT   535

LANGUAGE PROGRAMMES
PROGRAMME D'ENSEIGNEMENT DES LANGUES
PROGRAMA DE ENSEÑANZA DE IDIOMA
RT   662

LANGUAGE RESEARCH
RECHERCHE LINGUISTIQUE
INVESTIGACION LINGUISTICA
RT 280

LANGUAGE ROLE
ROLE DU LANGAGE
PAPEL DEL LENGUAJE
RT 285

LANGUAGE SKILLS
COMPETENCE LINGUISTIQUE
HABILIDAD LINGUISTICA
BT SKILLS
RT 533

LANGUAGE TEACHERS
PROFESSEUR DE LANGUE
PROFESOR DE IDIOMA
RT 425

LANGUAGE TESTS
TEST DE LANGAGE
PRUEBA DE LENGUAJE
BT EDUCATIONAL TESTS
RT 393

LANGUAGE TYPOLOGY
TYPOLOGIE DU LANGAGE
TIPOLOGIA DEL LENGUAJE
RT 621

LANGUAGE USAGE
USAGE LINGUISTIQUE
USO LINGUISTICO
BT LANGUAGE
RT 131

LANGUAGES
LANGUES
LENGUAS
NT CLASSICAL LANGUAGES
   MODERN LANGUAGES
   NATIONAL LANGUAGE
RT 625
   131
   LANGUAGE

LAO PDR
REPUBLIQUE DEMOCRATIQUE
   POPULAIRE LAO
REPUBLICA DEMOCRATICA
   POPULAR LAO

LAPLAND
LAPONIE
LAPONIA
                              May 1984
BT SCANDINAVIA

LARGE GROUP INSTRUCTION
ENSEIGNEMENT A DE LARGES
   GROUPES
ENSEÑANZA A GRANDES GRUPOS
BT GROUP INSTRUCTION
RT 352

LARGE TYPE MATERIALS
IMPRIME A GROS CARACTERES
IMPRESOS EN GRANDES
   CARACTERES
RT 734

LATERAL DOMINANCE
DOMINANCE LATERALE
ZURDERA
UF LEFT HANDEDNESS
RT 503

LATIN AMERICA
AMERIQUE LATINE
AMERICA LATINA
BT AMERICA
NT BERMUDA
   CARIBBEAN
   CENTRAL AMERICA
   MEXICO
   SOUTH AMERICA

LATVIAN SSR
RSS DE LATVIE
RSS DE LATVIA
                              May 1984
BT USSR

LAW ENFORCEMENT

LAW ENFORCEMENT
APPLICATION DE LA LOI
APLICACION DE LA LEY
RT 170

LAWS
LOI
LEY
NT CENTRAL GOVERNMENT
      LAWS
    EDUCATIONAL LEGISLATION
    LABOUR LAWS
    PROVINCIAL LAWS
    PUBLIC HEALTH LAWS
    RECREATION LEGISLATION
RT 170

LAWYERS
JURISTE
JURISTA
RT 460

LEADERSHIP
LEADERSHIP
LIDERAZGO
BT BEHAVIOUR
RT 554

LEADERSHIP TRAINING
FORMATION DES CHEFS DE
  GROUPE
FORMACION DE LIDERES
RT 681

LEAGUE OF ARAB STATES
LIGUE DES ETATS ARABES
LIGA DE LOS ESTADOS ARABES

LEARNING
APPRENTISSAGE
APRENDIZAJE
NT ACTIVITY LEARNING
    ADULT LEARNING
    ASSOCIATIVE LEARNING
    DISCOVERY LEARNING
    MULTISENSORY LEARNING
    PRESCHOOL LEARNING
    ROTE LEARNING
    SEQUENTIAL LEARNING
    SYMBOLIC LEARNING
    VERBAL LEARNING
    VISUAL LEARNING
RT 512

LEARNING ACTIVITIES
ACTIVITE D'APPRENTISSAGE
ACTIVIDAD DE APRENDIZAJE
RT 537

LEARNING CENTRES
USE **STUDY CENTRES**

LEARNING DIFFICULTIES
TROUBLE D'APPRENTISSAGE
DIFICULTADES EN EL
  APRENDIZAJE
RT 513

LEARNING DISABILITIES
DIFFICULTE DE L'APPRENTISSAGE
INCAPACIDAD PARA EL
  APRENDIZAJE
SN Distinguished by sharp imbalance
    within the student's cognitive
    development and by marked
    underachievement
RT 513

LEARNING NEEDS
CONNAISSANCES NECESSAIRES
NECESIDADES DE
  CONOCIMIENTOS
SN Knowledge, skills, attitudes
    required for adequate individual
    and social development
RT 536
    CURRICULUM DEVELOPMENT

LEARNING PROCESSES
PROCESSUS D'APPRENTISSAGE
PROCESO DE APRENDIZAJE
NT CONCEPT FORMATION
    FEEDBACK
    INFORMATION SEEKING
    RETENTION
RT 513

LESSER ANTILLES

LEARNING READINESS
APTITUDE A L'APPRENTISSAGE
MADUREZ PARA EL APRENDIZAJE
BT READINESS
RT 531

LEARNING SPECIALISTS
CENSEUR DES ETUDES
ENCARGADO DE CURSO
SN Person who assumes leadership of an instruction unit and is responsible for the learning efficiency of the students
BT SPECIALISTS
RT 430

LEARNING THEORIES
THEORIE DE L'APPRENTISSAGE
TEORIA DEL APRENDIZAJE
BT THEORIES
RT 513

LEAVE OF ABSENCE
CONGE
LICENCIA
UF SABBATICAL LEAVE
RT 222

LEBANON
LIBAN
LIBANO
BT ARAB COUNTRIES
    MEDITERRANEAN
      COUNTRIES
    MIDDLE EAST

LECTURE HALLS
SALLE DE CONFERENCE
SALA DE CONFERENCIA
RT 711

LECTURERS
MAITRE DE CONFERENCES
CONFERENCIANTE
BT COLLEGE TEACHERS
RT 422

LECTURES
COURS MAGISTRAL
CLASE MAGISTRAL
RT 355

LEEWARD ISLANDS
                                May 1984
USE **CARIBBEAN**

LEFT HANDEDNESS
USE **LATERAL DOMINANCE**

LEGAL AID
ASSISTANCE JUDICIAIRE
ASISTENCIA JUDICIAL
RT 170

LEGAL EDUCATION
ENSEIGNEMENT DU DROIT
ENSEÑANZA DEL DERECHO
RT 681

LEGAL RESPONSIBILITY
RESPONSABILITE LEGALE
RESPONSABILIDAD LEGAL
BT RESPONSIBILITY
RT 170

LEGISLATORS
LEGISLATEUR
LEGISLADOR
RT 460

LEISURE
LOISIR
TIEMPO LIBRE
RT 126

LESOTHO
LESOTHO
LESOTHO
BT SOUTHERN AFRICA
RT ENGLISH SPEAKING AFRICA

LESSER ANTILLES
                                May 1984
USE **CARIBBEAN**

LESSON OBSERVATION CRITERIA
CRITERE D'OBSERVATION D'UNE LECON
CRITERIOS DE OBSERVACION DE LA CLASE
RT 691

LESSON PLANS
PLAN DE LECON
PLAN DE CLASE
RT 356

LETTERS (CORRESPONDENCE)
MISSIVE
CARTA (CORRESPONDENCIA)
RT 721

LEVELS OF EDUCATION
NIVEAU D'ENSEIGNEMENT
NIVEL DE EDUCACION
SN Broad steps of formal educational progression from very elementary to more complicated learning experience. Used as a classification in educational organization and statistics
RT 185

LEXICOLOGY
LEXICOLOGIE
LEXICOLOGIA
RT 650

LIBERAL ARTS
USE **HUMANITIES**

LIBERIA
LIBERIA
LIBERIA
BT WEST AFRICA
RT ENGLISH SPEAKING AFRICA

LIBRARIANS
BIBLIOTHECAIRE
BIBLIOTECARIO
NT SCHOOL LIBRARIANS
RT 462

LIBRARIES
BIBLIOTHEQUE
BIBLIOTECA
NT COLLEGE LIBRARIES
   NATIONAL LIBRARIES
   PUBLIC LIBRARIES
   SCHOOL LIBRARIES
RT 310

LIBRARY COLLECTIONS
FONDS DE BIBLIOTHEQUE
FONDO BIBLIOGRAFICO
RT 722

LIBRARY EQUIPMENT
EQUIPEMENT DE BIBLIOTHEQUE
EQUIPO DE BIBLIOTECA
BT EQUIPMENT
RT 740

LIBRARY EXTENSION
RAYONNEMENT DES BIBLIOTHEQUES
EXTENSION CULTURAL DE LAS BIBLIOTECAS
SN Educational activities of public libraries
BT EXTENSION EDUCATION
RT 382

LIBRARY SCIENCE
BIBLIOTHECONOMIE
BIBLIOTECOLOGIA
RT 650

LIBRARY SCIENCE TRAINING
FORMATION DES BIBLIOTHECAIRES
FORMACION DE BIBLIOTECARIOS
SN Education or training of professional and non professional library personnel
RT 681

LIBRARY SERVICES
SERVICE DE BIBLIOTHEQUE
SERVICIO DE BIBLIOTECA
RT 270

LITERACY CENTRES

LIBYAN ARAB JAMAHIRIYA
JAMAHIRIYA ARABE LIBYENNE
JAMAHIRIYA ARABE LIBIA
                          May 1984
BT ARAB COUNTRIES
     MEDITERRANEAN
       COUNTRIES
     NORTH AFRICA

LIECHTENSTEIN
LIECHTENSTEIN
LIECHTENSTEIN
BT WESTERN EUROPE

LIFELONG EDUCATION
EDUCATION PERMANENTE
EDUCACION PERMANENTE
UF CONTINUING EDUCATION
     CONTINUOUS LEARNING
     PERMANENT EDUCATION
RT 180

LIGHTING
ECLAIRAGE
ILUMINACION
RT 252

LINE ISLANDS
ISLES DE LA LIGNE
ISLAS DE LA LINEA
                          May 1984
UF CHRISTMAS ISLAND (LINE
     ISLANDS)
BT POLYNESIA

LINEAR PROGRAMMES
PROGRAMME LINEAIRE
PROGRAMA LINEAL
RT 361

LINGUISTIC THEORY
THEORIE LINGUISTIQUE
TEORIA LINGUISTICA
RT 621

LINGUISTICS
LINGUISTIQUE
LINGUISTICA
NT CONTRASTIVE LINGUISTICS
     DESCRIPTIVE LINGUISTICS

RT 621

LIPREADING
LECTURE LABIALE
LECTURA LABIAL
RT 374

LISTENING
AUDITION
ESCUCHA
BT LANGUAGE ARTS
RT 620

LISTENING GROUPS
GROUPE D'AUDITEURS
GRUPO DE OYENTES
BT AUDIENCES
RT 343

LISTENING HABITS
MODE D'ECOUTE
MANERA DE ESCUCHAR
RT 542

LITERACY
ALPHABETISATION
ALFABETIZACION
NT FUNCTIONAL LITERACY
RT 180

LITERACY ACHIEVEMENT
PERFORMANCE DE
    L'ALPHABETISE
RENDIMIENTO DEL
    ALFABETIZADO
BT STUDENT ACHIEVEMENT
RT 535

LITERACY CAMPAIGNS
CAMPAGNE D'ALPHABETISATION
CAMPAÑA DE ALFABETIZACION
BT EDUCATIONAL PROGRAMMES
RT 271
     LITERACY PROGRAMMES

LITERACY CENTRES
CENTRE D'ALPHABETISATION
CENTRO DE ALFABETIZACION
RT 311

LITERACY CLASSES
CLASSE D'ALPHABETISATION
CLASE DE ALFABETIZACION
BT CLASSES
RT 343

LITERACY METHODS
METHODE D'ALPHABETISATION
METODO DE ALFABETIZACION
RT 661

LITERACY ORGANIZATIONS
ORGANISATION D'ALPHABETISATION
ORGANIZACION DE ALFABETIZACION
BT ORGANIZATIONS
RT 110

LITERACY PRIMERS
SYLLABAIRE
CARTILLA
May 1984
RT 725

LITERACY PROGRAMMES
PROGRAMME D'ALPHABETISATION
PROGRAMA DE ALFABETIZACION
SN Teaching of reading, writing and social skills to prepare persons to function at the fifth grade level
RT 321
    LITERACY CAMPAIGNS

LITERACY RETENTION
RETENTION D'ALPHABETISATION
RETENCION DE ALFABETIZACION
SN Skills retained after a literacy course
BT RETENTION
RT 535

LITERACY STATISTICS
STATISTIQUES DE L'ALPHABETISATION
ESTADISTICAS DE ALFABETIZACION
RT 284

LITERACY TEACHERS
May 1984
USE **LITERACY WORKERS**

LITERACY TESTS
TEST D'ALPHABETISATION
PRUEBA DE ALFABETIZACION
RT 393

LITERACY WORKERS
PERSONNEL DE L'ALPHABETISATION
ALFABETIZADOR
May 1984
UF LITERACY TEACHERS
RT 424

LITERARY ANALYSIS
ANALYSE LITTERAIRE
ANALISIS LITERARIO
RT 615

LITERARY CRITICISM
CRITIQUE LITTERAIRE
CRITICA LITERARIA
RT 615

LITERARY GENRES
GENRE LITTERAIRE
GENERO LITERARIO
SN Divisions of literature into categories or classes which group works by form or type, such as biographies, drama, essays, fiction or poetry, rather than by movements such as naturalism, realism, romanticism or by subject matter as in legends, myths, etc.
RT 616

LITERARY HISTORY
HISTOIRE LITTERAIRE
HISTORIA LITERARIA
SN Study of literature in historical context, term may also be linked with time identifiers
RT 615

LITERARY INFLUENCES
INFLUENCE LITTERAIRE
INFLUENCIA LITERARIA
RT 615

LITERATURE
LITTERATURE
LITERATURA
SN Used by itself or linked to term for specific languages or identifier for time or geographical location
RT 615

LITERATURE APPRECIATION
INITIATION LITTERAIRE
APRECIACION LITERARIA
RT 684

LITERATURE REVIEW
APERCU DE LA LITTERATURE
RESEÑA LITERARIA
RT 880

LITHUANIAN SSR
RSS DE LITHUANIE
RSS DE LITUANIA
May 1984
BT USSR

LIVESTOCK
BETAIL
GANADERIA
RT 750

LIVING STANDARDS
NIVEAU DE VIE
NIVEL DE VIDA
RT 150

LOCAL EDUCATION AUTHORITIES
AUTORITES SCOLAIRES LOCALES
AUTORIDADES ESCOLARES LOCALES
RT 263

LOCAL GOVERNMENT
GOUVERNEMENT LOCAL
GOBIERNO LOCAL
BT GOVERNMENT
RT 104

LOCAL MATERIALS
MATERIAUX LOCAUX
MATERIALES LOCALES
RT 253

LOGIC
LOGIQUE
LOGICA
RT 600

LOGICAL THINKING
PENSEE LOGIQUE
PENSAMIENTO LOGICO
BT THOUGHT PROCESSES
RT 521

LONGITUDINAL STUDIES
ETUDE LONGITUDINALE
ESTUDIO LONGITUDINAL
RT 282

LORD HOWE ISLAND
ILE LORD HOWE
ISLA DE LORD HOWE
May 1984
BT AUSTRALIA

LOW ABILITY STUDENTS
May 1984
USE **SLOW LEARNERS**

LOW ACHIEVERS
ELEVE MEDIOCRE
ALUMNO MEDIOCRE
UF UNDERACHIEVERS
RT 415

LOW INCOME GROUPS
GROUPE ECONOMIQUEMENT FAIBLE
GRUPO DE INGRESOS BAJOS
BT GROUPS
RT 443

LOWER SECONDARY EDUCATION
ENSEIGNEMENT SECONDAIRE (1ER CYCLE)
ENSEÑANZA SECUNDARIA (1ER CICLO)
UF INTERMEDIATE EDUCATION

LOWER SECONDARY SCHOOLS

BT SECONDARY EDUCATION
RT 185

LOWER SECONDARY SCHOOLS
ECOLE SECONDAIRE (1ER CYCLE)
ESCUELA SECUNDARIA (1ER CICLO)
BT SECONDARY SCHOOLS
RT 301
    INTERMEDIATE GRADES

LUXEMBOURG
LUXEMBOURG
LUXEMBURGO
BT WESTERN EUROPE

MACAO
MACAO
MACAO
BT FAR EAST

MACHINE TOOLS
MACHINE–OUTIL
MAQUINA HERRAMIENTA
RT 742

MADAGASCAR
MADAGASCAR
MADAGASCAR
BT EAST AFRICA
    INDIAN OCEAN TERRITORIES
    SOUTHERN AFRICA
RT FRENCH SPEAKING AFRICA

MADEIRA
MADERE
MADEIRA
BT ATLANTIC OCEAN TERRITORIES
    WESTERN EUROPE
RT NORTH AFRICA
    WEST AFRICA

MAINTENANCE
MAINTENANCE
MANTENIMIENTO
SN Preservation or continuance of a condition
NT SCHOOL MAINTENANCE
RT 251

MALADJUSTMENT
INADAPTATION
INADAPTACION
RT 551

MALAWI
MALAWI
MALAWI
UF NYASALAND
BT EAST AFRICA
    SOUTHERN AFRICA
RT ENGLISH SPEAKING AFRICA

MALAYA
MALAYA
MALAYA

May 1984

BT MALAYSIA

MALAYO POLYNESIAN LANGUAGES
LANGUES MALEO–POLYNESIENNES
LENGUAS MALAYOPOLINESICAS
RT 625

MALAYSIA
MALAISIE
MALASIA
BT SOUTH EAST ASIA
NT BRUNEI
    MALAYA
    SABAH
    SARAWAK
    SINGAPORE

MALDIVES
MALDIVES
MALDIVAS
BT SOUTH ASIA

MALE
SEXE MASCULIN
SEXO MASCULINO
RT 501

MALI
MALI
MALI
BT WEST AFRICA
RT FRENCH SPEAKING AFRICA

MALTA
MALTE
MALTA
BT MEDITERRANEAN
     COUNTRIES
   WESTERN EUROPE

MANAGEMENT
GESTION
GESTION
NT BUDGETING
   PERSONNEL MANAGEMENT
RT 201

MANAGEMENT EDUCATION
FORMATION DES GESTIONNAIRES
FORMACION DE
  ADMINISTRADORES
SN Educational programmes to increase managerial and supervisory skills of managers and management trainees
RT 672

MANAGEMENT SYSTEMS
SYSTEME DE GESTION
SISTEMA DE GESTION
RT 201

MANAGERS
GESTIONNAIRE
EMPRESARIO
RT 450

MANIHIKI ISLANDS
ILES MANAHIKI
ISLAS MANIHIKI
BT POLYNESIA

May 1984

MANIPULATIVE MATERIALS
MATERIEL DE MANIPULATION
MATERIAL MANIPULABLE
RT 725

MANPOWER DEVELOPMENT
DEVELOPPEMENT DE LA MAIN-D'OEUVRE
DESARROLLO DE LA MANO DE OBRA
BT DEVELOPMENT
RT 151

MANPOWER NEEDS
BESOIN EN MAIN-D'OEUVRE
NECESIDAD DE MANO DE OBRA
BT NEEDS
RT 154

MANPOWER PLANNING
PLANIFICATION DE LA MAIN-D'OEUVRE
PLANIFICACION DE RECURSOS HUMANOS
RT 154

MANPOWER POLICY
POLITIQUE DE LA MAIN-D'OEUVRE
POLITICA DE RECURSOS HUMANOS
RT 154

MANUAL
MANUEL
MANUAL
SN Concise reference book giving instructions on how to perform certain tasks
RT 880

MANUAL COMMUNICATION
COMMUNICATION GESTUELLE
COMUNICACION MANUAL
RT 374

MARIANA ISLANDS

MARIANA ISLANDS
ILES MARIANNES
ISLAS MARIANAS
May 1984
BT   MICRONESIA
NT   GUAM

MARITAL STATUS
ETAT CIVIL
ESTADO CIVIL
RT   126

MARKING
NOTATION
PUNTAJE
RT   391

MARQUESA ISLANDS
May 1984
USE **FRENCH POLYNESIA**

MARRIED STUDENTS
ETUDIANT MARIE
ESTUDIANTE CASADO
RT   413

MARRIED WOMEN RETURNERS
FEMME MARIEE REPRENANT UN EMPLOI
MUJER CASADA REINCORPORADA
RT   451

MARSHALL ISLANDS
ILES MARSHALL
ISLAS MARSHALL
May 1984
BT   MICRONESIA

MARTINIQUE
MARTINIQUE
MARTINICA
BT   CARIBBEAN

MASS EDUCATION
EDUCATION DE MASSE
ENSEÑANZA MASIVA
May 1984
BT   INSTRUCTION
RT   352

MASS MEDIA
MOYEN D'INFORMATION DE MASSE
MEDIOS DE COMUNICACION MASIVA
NT   FILMS
     PRESS
     RADIO
     TELEVISION
RT   145

MASTER TEACHERS
MAITRE D'APPLICATION
PROFESOR GUIA
SN   Regular teachers whose skill and experience qualify them to assist in preparation of student teachers
RT   426

MASTER THESES
MEMOIRE DE MAITRISE
TESIS DE MAESTRIA
RT   721

MASTERS DEGREES
DIPLOME UNIVERSITAIRE (2E CYCLE)
GRADO DE MAESTRIA
BT   DEGREES (TITLES)
RT   390

MATERIALS EVALUATION
EVALUATION DU MATERIEL DIDACTIQUE
EVALUACION DE MATERIALES DIDACTICOS
BT   EVALUATION
RT   213

MATERIALS PREPARATION
PREPARATION DU MATERIEL DIDACTIQUE
PREPARACION DE MATERIAL DIDACTICO
RT   213

MATERIALS SELECTION
SELECTION DU MATERIEL
  DIDACTIQUE
SELECCION DE MATERIAL
  DIDACTICO
BT INSTRUCTIONAL MATERIALS
RT 265

MATHEMATICAL CONCEPTS
CONCEPT MATHEMATIQUE
CONCEPTO MATEMATICO
NT ALGEBRAIC CONCEPTS
    GEOMETRIC CONCEPTS
    NUMBER CONCEPTS
RT 631

MATHEMATICS
MATHEMATIQUES
MATEMATICAS
NT APPLIED MATHEMATICS
    ARITHMETIC
    MODERN MATHEMATICS
    ALGEBRA
    GEOMETRY
RT 631

MATHEMATICS INSTRUCTION
ENSEIGNEMENT DES
  MATHEMATIQUES
ENSEÑANZA DE LAS
  MATEMATICAS
RT 670

MATHEMATICS TEACHERS
PROFESSEUR DE
  MATHEMATIQUES
PROFESOR DE MATEMATICAS
RT 425

MATURATION
MATURATION
MADURACION
RT 531

MAURITANIA
MAURITANIE
MAURITANIA
BT WEST AFRICA
RT FRENCH SPEAKING AFRICA

MAURITIUS
MAURICE
MAURICIO
BT INDIAN OCEAN TERRITORIES
RT ENGLISH SPEAKING AFRICA

MEASUREMENT
DOCIMOLOGIE
MEDICION
RT 391

MEASUREMENT AIMS
OBJECTIF DOCIMOLOGIQUE
OBJETIVO DE LA MEDICION
RT 391

MEASUREMENT INSTRUMENTS
INSTRUMENT DE MESURE
INSTRUMENTO DE MEDICION
RT 742

MEASUREMENT TECHNIQUES
TECHNIQUE DOCIMOLOGIQUE
TECNICA DE EVALUACION
RT 391

MECHANICAL EQUIPMENT
EQUIPEMENT MECANIQUE
EQUIPO MECANICO
SN Machinery or tools which
    automatically perform operations
    in controlling or producing a
    physical change in environment or
    in accomplishment of a given task
BT EQUIPMENT
RT 742

MECHANICAL SKILLS
HABILETE MECANIQUE
DESTREZA MECANICA
BT SKILLS
RT 533

MECHANICS (PROCESS)
MECANIQUE GENERALE
MECANICA GENERAL
RT 647

MEDIA RESEARCH
RECHERCHE SUR LES MEDIA
INVESTIGACION SOBRE MEDIOS
   DE COMUNICACION
RT 280

MEDIA RESOURCES CENTRES
CENTRE MULTIMEDIA
CENTRO DE MEDIOS DE
   COMUNICACION
UF INSTRUCTIONAL MATERIALS
      CENTRES
      MULTIMEDIA CENTRES
RT 312

MEDIA SPECIALISTS
SPECIALISTE DES MEDIA
ESPECIALISTA EN MEDIOS DE
   COMUNICACION
BT SPECIALISTS
RT 430

MEDIA TECHNOLOGY
TECHNOLOGIE DES MEDIA
TECNOLOGIA DE LOS MEDIOS DE
   COMUNICACION
RT 140

MEDIATION THEORY
THEORIE DE LA MEDIATION
TEORIA DE LA MEDIACION
SN Accounting for association of
     stimulus and response in terms of
     internal or mediating processes
BT THEORIES
RT 511

MEDICAL CONSULTANTS
CONSULTANT MEDICAL
CONSULTOR MEDICO
BT CONSULTANTS
RT 433

MEDICAL EDUCATION
FORMATION MEDICALE
FORMACION MEDICA
RT 681

MEDICAL EVALUATION
BILAN DE SANTE
EVALUACION DE LA SALUD
RT 391

MEDICAL SERVICES
SERVICE MEDICAL
SERVICIO MEDICO
BT HEALTH SERVICES
RT 160

MEDICAL SUPPLIES
FOURNITURE MEDICALE
SUMINISTROS MEDICOS
BT SUPPLIES
RT 751

MEDICAL TREATMENT
TRAITEMENT MEDICAL
TRATAMIENTO MEDICO
RT 373

MEDICINE
MEDECINE
MEDICINA
RT 651

MEDITERRANEAN AREAS
                              May 1984
USE **MEDITERRANEAN COUNTRIES**

MEDITERRANEAN COUNTRIES
PAYS MEDITERRANEENS
PAISES MEDITERRANEOS
UF MEDITERRANEAN AREAS
NT ALGERIA
    CYPRUS
    EGYPT
    FRANCE
    GREECE
    ISRAEL
    ITALY
    LEBANON
    LIBYAN ARAB JAMAHIRIYA
    MALTA
    MONACO
    MOROCCO
    SPAIN
    SYRIAN AR
    TUNISIA

METEOROLOGY

    TURKEY
RT ARAB COUNTRIES
    EUROPE
    MIDDLE EAST
    NORTH AFRICA

MEETINGS
REUNION
REUNION
RT 204

MELANESIA
MELANESIE
MELANESIA
BT OCEANIA
NT BANKS ISLANDS
    FIJI ISLANDS
    NEW CALEDONIA
    VANUATU
    SANTA CRUZ ISLANDS
    SOLOMON ISLANDS

MEMORIZING
MEMORISATION
MEMORIZACION
BT COGNITIVE PROCESSES
RT 521

MEN
HOMME
HOMBRE
BT ADULTS
RT 443

MENTAL ABILITY
USE **INTELLIGENCE**

MENTAL DEVELOPMENT
DEVELOPPEMENT MENTAL
DESARROLLO MENTAL
NT COGNITIVE DEVELOPMENT
    INTELLECTUAL
      DEVELOPMENT
    LANGUAGE DEVELOPMENT
RT 530

May 1984

MENTAL HANDICAPS
HANDICAP MENTAL
DEFICIENCIA MENTAL
BT HANDICAPS
RT 571

MENTAL HEALTH
SANTE MENTALE
SALUD MENTAL
BT HEALTH
RT 502

MENTAL HEALTH PROGRAMMES
PROGRAMME DE SANTE
   MENTALE
PROGRAMA DE SALUD MENTAL
RT 320

MENTAL ILLNESS
MALADIE MENTALE
ENFERMEDAD MENTAL
RT 570

MENTAL RETARDATION
ARRIERATION MENTALE
RETARDO MENTAL
RT 570

MENTAL TESTS
TEST MENTAL
PRUEBA MENTAL
BT PSYCHOLOGICAL TESTS
RT 394

MENTALLY RETARDED
USE **RETARDED CHILDREN**

METALWORKING
TRAVAIL DU METAL
TRABAJOS EN METAL
RT 647

METEOROLOGY
METEOROLOGIE
METEOROLOGIA
RT 633

METHODOLOGICAL PROBLEMS

METHODOLOGICAL PROBLEMS
PROBLEME METHODOLOGIQUE
PROBLEMA METODOLOGICO
SN   Relating to teaching methods
RT   281

METHODS COURSES
COURS DE METHODOLOGIE
CURSO DE METODOLOGIA
RT   691

METHODS TEACHERS
PROFESSEUR DE METHODOLOGIE
PROFESOR DE METODOLOGIA
RT   426

METRIC SYSTEM
SYSTEME METRIQUE
SISTEMA METRICO
RT   631

MEXICO
MEXIQUE
MEXICO
BT   LATIN AMERICA
RT   CENTRAL AMERICA

MICROFORM READERS
LECTEUR DE MICROFORMES
LECTOR DE MICROFORMATOS
RT   731

MICROFORMS
MICROFORMES
MICROFORMATOS
SN   Photographically reduced documents
RT   721

MICRONESIA
MICRONESIE
MICRONESIA

May 1984

BT   OCEANIA
NT   CANTON AND ENDERBY ISLANDS
     CAROLINE ISLANDS
     KIRIBATI
     MARIANA ISLANDS
     MARSHALL ISLANDS
     NAURU ISLAND

MICROTEACHING
MICRO–ENSEIGNEMENT
MICROENSEÑANZA
SN   An experimental teacher training method using small groups of students
RT   691

MIDDLE AGES
MOYEN AGE
MEDIOEVO

May 1984

MIDDLE CLASS
CLASSE MOYENNE
CLASE MEDIA
BT   SOCIAL CLASS
RT   121

MIDDLE CLASS PARENTS
PARENTS DE CONDITION MOYENNE
PADRES DE CLASE MEDIA
BT   PARENTS
RT   401

MIDDLE EAST
MOYEN–ORIENT
ORIENTE MEDIO
UF   CENTRAL AND WESTERN ASIA
     NEAR EAST
BT   ASIA
NT   AFGHANISTAN
     CYPRUS
     GULF STATES
     IRAN (ISLAMIC REPUBLIC)
     IRAQ
     ISRAEL
     JORDAN
     LEBANON
     OMAN
     SAUDI ARABIA
     SYRIAN AR
     TURKEY
     DEMOCRATIC YEMEN
     YEMEN
RT   ARAB COUNTRIES

MEDITERRANEAN
COUNTRIES

MIDDLE SCHOOLS
ETABLISSEMENT
D'ENSEIGNEMENT MOYEN
ESTABLECIMIENTO DE
ENSEÑANZA MEDIA
RT 301

MIDWAY ISLANDS
ILES MIDWAY
ISLAS MIDWAY
May 1984
BT POLYNESIA

MIGRANT EDUCATION
EDUCATION DES MIGRANTS
EDUCACION DEL MIGRANTE
RT 186

MIGRANT PROBLEMS
PROBLEME DE MIGRATION
PROBLEMAS DEL INMIGRANTE
RT 124

MIGRANT WORKERS
USE **FOREIGN WORKERS**

MIGRANTS
MIGRANT
MIGRANTE
RT 470

MIGRATION
MIGRATION
MIGRACION
SN Temporary movement within country or between countries
RT 124

MILITARY PERSONNEL
PERSONNEL MILITAIRE
PERSONAL MILITAR
SN Covers armed forces as well as ex–soldiers or veterans
RT 441

MILITARY SCIENCE
SCIENCE MILITAIRE
CIENCIA MILITAR
RT 630

MINICOURSES
May 1984
USE **SHORT COURSES**

MINIMAL BRAIN INJURY
LESION CEREBRALE MINEURE
LESION CEREBRAL MENOR
RT 570

MINISTRIES OF EDUCATION
USE **CENTRAL EDUCATIONAL AGENCIES**

MINISTRY OF EDUCATION
MINISTERE DE L'EDUCATION
MINISTERIO DE EDUCACION
SN Link to country location

MINISTRY OF EDUCATION REPORT
RAPPORT MINISTERE DE L'EDUCATION
INFORME DEL MINISTERIO DE EDUCACION
RT 880

MINORITY GROUP CHILDREN
ENFANT DE GROUPE MINORITAIRE
NIÑO DE GRUPO MINORITARIO
BT CHILDREN
RT 402

MINORITY GROUP TEACHERS
MAITRE DE GROUPE MINORITAIRE
MAESTRO DE GRUPO MINORITARIO
RT 424

MINORITY GROUPS
GROUPE MINORITAIRE
GRUPO MINORITARIO
BT GROUPS
RT 443

MINORITY ROLE
ROLE DES MINORITES
PAPEL DE LAS MINORIAS
RT 123

MIQUELON ISLAND
May 1984
USE **SAINT PIERRE AND MIQUELON ISLANDS**

MOBILE EDUCATIONAL SERVICES
SERVICES EDUCATIFS ITINERANTS
SERVICIO EDUCACIONAL ITINERANTE
RT 270

MOBILE SCHOOLS
ECOLE ITINERANTE
ESCUELA ITINERANTE
RT 303 RELOCATABLE FACILITIES

MOBILITY
MOBILITE
MOVILIDAD
NT FAMILY MOBILITY
    OCCUPATIONAL MOBILITY
    SOCIAL MOBILITY
    STUDENT MOBILITY
    TEACHER MOBILITY
RT 124

MOBILITY AIDS
AIDE A LA MOBILITE
AYUDAS PARA LA MOVILIDAD
RT 734

MODELS
MODELE REDUIT
MODELO
SN Representation of an object, principle or idea
RT 733

MODERN HISTORY
HISTOIRE MODERNE
HISTORIA MODERNA
BT HISTORY
RT 641

MODERN LANGUAGE INSTRUCTION
ENSEIGNEMENT D'UNE LANGUE VIVANTE
ENSEÑANZA DE UNA LENGUA MODERNA
BT LANGUAGE INSTRUCTION
RT 662

MODERN LANGUAGE PRIMARY PROGRAMMES
PROGRAMME PRIMAIRE DE LANGUE VIVANTE
PROGRAMA DE LENGUA MODERNA (PRIMARIA)
RT 662

MODERN LANGUAGES
LANGUES MODERNES
LENGUAS MODERNAS
BT LANGUAGES
RT 627

MODERN MATHEMATICS
MATHEMATIQUES MODERNES
MATEMATICAS MODERNAS
BT MATHEMATICS
RT 631

MODERN TIMES
TEMPS MODERNES
TIEMPOS MODERNOS
May 1984

MODULAR APPROACH
METHODE MODULAIRE
ENFOQUE MODULAR
SN Organization of instructional materials and procedures in self-contained units designed for management by the learner
NT MODULAR TRAINING
RT 331

MODULAR TRAINING
FORMATION PAR MODULES
FORMACION POR MODULOS
BT MODULAR APPROACH
    TRAINING
RT 351

MOLDAVIAN SSR
RSS DE MOLDAVIE
RSS DE MOLDAVIA
BT USSR

MONACO
MONACO
MONACO
BT MEDITERRANEAN
     COUNTRIES
    WESTERN EUROPE

MONGOLIA
MONGOLIE
MONGOLIA
BT FAR EAST

MONGOLISM
USE **DOWNS SYNDROME**

MONTSERRAT
MONTSERRAT
MONSERRAT
BT CARIBBEAN

MORAL EDUCATION
EDUCATION MORALE
EDUCACION MORAL
RT 682

MORAL ISSUES
PROBLEME MORAL
CUESTIONES MORALES
RT 100
    MORAL VALUES

MORAL VALUES
VALEUR MORALE
VALOR MORAL
BT VALUES
RT 555
    MORAL ISSUES

MOROCCO
MAROC
MARRUECOS
BT ARAB COUNTRIES
    MEDITERRANEAN
     COUNTRIES

May 1984

NORTH AFRICA

MORPHEMES
MORPHEME
MORFEMA
RT 622

MORPHOLOGY (LANGUAGES)
MORPHOLOGIE (LANGUE)
MORFOLOGIA (LENGUA)
RT 622

MOSLEMS
MUSULMAN
MUSULMAN
RT 475

MOTHER TONGUE
LANGUE MATERNELLE
LENGUA MATERNA
RT 131

MOTHER TONGUE INSTRUCTION
ENSEIGNEMENT DE LA LANGUE
    MATERNELLE
ENSEÑANZA DE LA LENGUA
    MATERNA
BT LANGUAGE INSTRUCTION
RT 662

MOTHERS
MERE
MADRE
BT PARENTS
RT 401

MOTIVATION
MOTIVATION
MOTIVACION
NT STUDENT MOTIVATION
    TEACHER MOTIVATION
RT 541

MOTOR DEVELOPMENT
DEVELOPPEMENT MOTEUR
DESARROLLO MOTOR
BT PHYSICAL DEVELOPMENT
RT 530

MOTOR REACTIONS

MOTOR REACTIONS
REACTION MOTRICE
REACCION MOTORA
BT   PHYSICAL ACTIVITIES
RT   511

MOTOR VEHICLES
VEHICULE A MOTEUR
VEHICULO A MOTOR
RT   743

MOZAMBIQUE
MOZAMBIQUE
MOZAMBIQUE
BT   EAST AFRICA
     SOUTHERN AFRICA

MULTILATERAL AID
AIDE MULTILATERALE
AYUDA MULTILATERAL
SN   Support channelled through
     international agencies
RT   106

MULTIMEDIA CENTRES
USE **MEDIA RESOURCES CENTRES**

MULTIMEDIA INSTRUCTION
ENSEIGNEMENT PAR
  MULTIMEDIA
ENSEÑANZA POR MEDIOS
  MULTIPLES
NT   SOUND SLIDE
       PRESENTATIONS
RT   360

MULTIPLE CHOICE TESTS
EPREUVE A CHOIX MULTIPLE
PRUEBA DE ELECCION MULTIPLE
RT   392

MULTIPLE CLASS TEACHING
ENSEIGNEMENT EN CLASSE
  UNIQUE
ENSEÑANZA EN CLASE UNICA
RT   340

MULTIPLE HANDICAPS
HANDICAPS ASSOCIES
DEFICIENCIAS MULTIPLES
BT   HANDICAPS
RT   571

MULTISENSORY LEARNING
APPRENTISSAGE MULTISENSORIEL
APRENDIZAJE MULTISENSORIAL
BT   LEARNING
RT   512

MUNICIPALITIES
MUNICIPALITE
MUNICIPIO
UF   CITIES
       TOWNS
RT   102
       CITY GOVERNMENT
       URBAN AREAS

MUSEUMS
MUSEE
MUSEO
RT   310

MUSIC
MUSIQUE
MUSICA
RT   610

MUSIC APPRECIATION
INITIATION MUSICALE
APRECIACION MUSICAL
RT   684

MUSIC EDUCATION
EDUCATION MUSICALE
EDUCACION MUSICAL
RT   684

MUSIC TEACHERS
PROFESSEUR DE MUSIQUE
PROFESOR DE MUSICA
RT   425

NATIONAL NORMS

MUSICAL INSTRUMENTS
INSTRUMENT DE MUSIQUE
INSTRUMENTO MUSICAL
RT 741

MUSICIANS
MUSICIEN
MUSICO
RT 461

MYTHOLOGY
MYTHOLOGIE
MITOLOGIA
RT 616

NAMIBIA
NAMIBIE
NAMIBIA
UF SOUTH WEST AFRICA
BT SOUTHERN AFRICA
RT ENGLISH SPEAKING AFRICA

NATION BUILDING
USE **NATIONAL INTEGRATION**

NATIONAL CADRES
CADRES NATIONAUX
FUNCIONARIOS NACIONALES
RT 441

NATIONAL COMMISSION FOR UNESCO
COMMISSION NATIONALE POUR L'UNESCO
COMISION NACIONAL DE COOPERACION CON LA UNESCO
SN Link to country location

NATIONAL DEMOGRAPHY
DEMOGRAPHIE NATIONALE
DEMOGRAFIA NACIONAL
RT 124

NATIONAL EDUCATIONAL SYSTEM
USE **EDUCATIONAL ORGANIZATION**

NATIONAL HISTORY
HISTOIRE NATIONALE
HISTORIA NACIONAL
SN Linked to geographical identifier
BT HISTORY
RT 641

NATIONAL INTEGRATION
INTEGRATION NATIONALE
INTEGRACION NACIONAL
UF NATION BUILDING
RT 101
   SOCIAL INTEGRATION

NATIONAL INTERAGENCY COORDINATION
COORDINATION NATIONALE INTERORGANISMES
COORDINACION NACIONAL DE ORGANISMOS
RT 105

NATIONAL LANGUAGE
LANGUE NATIONALE
LENGUA NACIONAL
SN Used by itself or linked to identifier for geographical location
BT LANGUAGES
RT 626

NATIONAL LIBRARIES
BIBLIOTHEQUE NATIONALE
BIBLIOTECA NACIONAL
BT LIBRARIES
RT 310

NATIONAL LITERATURE
LITTERATURE NATIONALE
LITERATURA NACIONAL
SN Used by itself or linked to identifier for geographical location
RT 615

NATIONAL NORMS
NORME NATIONALE
NORMA NACIONAL
RT 284

NATIONAL ORGANIZATIONS
ORGANISATION NATIONALE
ORGANIZACION NACIONAL
BT ORGANIZATIONS
NT PARENT ASSOCIATIONS
   PARENT TEACHER
      ASSOCIATIONS
   PROFESSIONAL
      ASSOCIATIONS
   RELIGIOUS ORGANIZATIONS
   STUDENT ORGANIZATIONS
   TEACHER ASSOCIATIONS
   TRADE UNIONS
   YOUTH ORGANIZATIONS
RT 110

NATIONAL PLANNING
PLANIFICATION NATIONALE
PLANIFICACION NACIONAL
BT PLANNING
NT NATIONAL REGIONAL
   PLANNING
RT 108

NATIONAL PROGRAMMES
PROGRAMME NATIONAL
PROGRAMA NACIONAL
BT PROGRAMMES
NT GOVERNMENT PROGRAMMES
   NATIONAL REGIONAL
      PROGRAMMES
RT 109

NATIONAL REGIONAL COOPERATION
COOPERATION NATIONALE
   INTERREGIONALE
COOPERACION NACIONAL
   INTERREGIONAL
SN Between geographical parts of
   single country
RT 105

NATIONAL REGIONAL DISPARITIES
DISPARITE NATIONALE
   INTERREGIONALE
DESIGUALDAD NACIONAL ENTRE
   REGIONES
RT 151

NATIONAL REGIONAL PLANNING
PLANIFICATION NATIONALE
   INTRAREGIONALE
PLANIFICACION NACIONAL
   REGIONAL
BT NATIONAL PLANNING
RT 108

NATIONAL REGIONAL PROGRAMMES
PROGRAMME NATIONAL
   INTRAREGIONAL
PROGRAMA NACIONAL
   INTERREGIONAL
SN At level of part of national
   territory
BT NATIONAL PROGRAMMES
RT 109

NATIONAL SERVICE
SERVICE NATIONAL
SERVICIO NACIONAL
RT 125

NATIONAL SURVEYS
ENQUETE NATIONALE
ENCUESTA NACIONAL
BT SURVEYS
NT PROVINCIAL SURVEYS
   SCHOOL SURVEYS
RT 203

NATIONALISM
NATIONALISME
NACIONALISMO
RT 101

NATURAL DISASTER
CATASTROPHE NATURELLE
CATASTROFE NATURAL
RT 250

NATURAL RESOURCES
RESSOURCE NATURELLE
RECURSOS NATURALES
BT RESOURCES
RT 700

NEW LITERATES

NAURU ISLAND
ILE NAURU
ISLA NAURU
UF PLEASANT ISLAND
BT MICRONESIA

NEAR EAST
May 1984
USE **MIDDLE EAST**

NEED GRATIFICATION
SATISFACTION DES BESOINS
SATISFACCION DE NECESIDADES
SN Satisfaction of basic needs
RT 536

NEEDS
BESOIN
NECESIDADES
SN Particular points or respects in which some necessity or want is present or felt
NT EDUCATIONAL NEEDS
    FINANCIAL NEEDS
    HEALTH NEEDS
    MANPOWER NEEDS
RT 100

NEEDS ASSESSMENT
ESTIMATION DES BESOINS
IDENTIFICACION DE NECESIDADES
May 1984
SN In relation to development programmes
RT 151

NEPAL
NEPAL
NEPAL
BT HIMALAYAN STATES

NERVOUS SYSTEM
SYSTEME NERVEUX
SISTEMA NERVIOSO
RT 502

NETHERLANDS
PAYS–BAS
PAISES BAJOS
UF HOLLAND
BT WESTERN EUROPE

NETHERLANDS ANTILLES
ANTILLES NEERLANDAISES
ANTILLAS HOLANDESAS
BT CARIBBEAN

NETWORK ANALYSIS
ANALYSE DE RESEAU
ANALISIS DE CIRCUITO
UF CRITICAL PATH METHOD
RT 201

NETWORKS
RESEAU
RED
RT 760

NEUROLOGICAL HANDICAPS
HANDICAP NEUROLOGIQUE
DAÑO NEUROLOGICO
SN Covers cerebral palsy and epilepsy
BT HANDICAPS
RT 571

NEUROTICS
NEVROSE
NEUROTICO
BT HANDICAPPED
RT 403

NEW CALEDONIA
NOUVELLE CALEDONIE
NUEVA CALEDONIA
UF NOUMEA
BT MELANESIA

NEW HEBRIDES
May 1984
USE **VANUATU**

NEW LITERATES
NEO–ALPHABETE
NEOALFABETIZADO
RT 412

NEW ZEALAND
NOUVELLE ZELANDE
NUEVA ZELANDIA
BT   AUSTRALASIA
NT   KERMADEC ISLANDS

NEWSPAPERS
JOURNAL
DIARIO
BT   PRESS
RT   720

NGO
ONG
ONG
SN   International Non Governmental Organization

NICARAGUA
NICARAGUA
NICARAGUA
BT   CENTRAL AMERICA

NIGER
NIGER
NIGER
BT   WEST AFRICA
RT   FRENCH SPEAKING AFRICA

NIGERIA
NIGERIA
NIGERIA
BT   WEST AFRICA
RT   ENGLISH SPEAKING AFRICA

NINETEENTH CENTURY
DIX–NEUVIEME SIECLE
SIGLO DIECINUEVE

NIUE ISLAND
ILE NIUE
ISLA NIUE
BT   POLYNESIA

NOMADISM
NOMADISME
NOMADISMO
RT   124

NOMADS
NOMADE
NOMADA
RT   470

NONCREDIT COURSES
COURS SANS UNITES CAPITALISABLES
CURSO SIN UNIDADES DE VALOR
BT   COURSES
RT   333

NONDISCRIMINATORY EDUCATION
USE **EQUAL EDUCATION**

NONFORMAL EDUCATION
EDUCATION NON FORMELLE
EDUCACION NO FORMAL
SN   Activities or programmes organized outside the framework of the established school system but directed to definite educational objectives
RT   184

NONGRADED CLASSES
CLASSE A NIVEAUX
CURSO DE ESCUELA SIN GRADOS
BT   CLASSES
RT   340

NONGRADED CURRICULUM
PROGRAMMES A PROGRESSION CONTINUE
CICLO ESCOLAR SIN GRADOS
RT   332
      CONTINUOUS PROGRESS PLAN

NONGRADED SCHOOLS
ECOLE A NIVEAUX
ESCUELA SIN GRADOS
RT   303

NONGRADED SYSTEM
SYSTEME A PROGRESSION CONTINUE
SISTEMA SIN GRADOS
RT   340

May 1984

**NONINSTRUCTIONAL
 RESPONSIBILITY**
RESPONSABILITE EXTRASCOLAIRE
RESPONSABILIDAD
 EXTRAESCOLAR
SN Teachers' duties in respect to out-of-school activities
BT RESPONSIBILITY
RT 231

NONPROFESSIONAL PERSONNEL
PERSONNEL NON
 PROFESSIONNEL
PERSONAL NO PROFESIONAL
RT 441

NORFOLK ISLAND
ILE NORFOLK
ISLA NORFOLK
                                           May 1984
BT AUSTRALIA

NORTH AFRICA
AFRIQUE DU NORD
AFRICA DEL NORTE
BT AFRICA
NT ALGERIA
    EGYPT
    LIBYAN ARAB JAMAHIRIYA
    MOROCCO
    TUNISIA
RT CANARY ISLANDS
    MADEIRA
    MEDITERRANEAN
     COUNTRIES

NORTH AMERICA
AMERIQUE DU NORD
AMERICA DEL NORTE
BT AMERICA
NT CANADA
    SAINT PIERRE AND
     MIQUELON ISLANDS
    USA
    GREENLAND

NORTH BORNEO
                                           May 1984
USE **SABAH**

NORTH KOREA
USE **KOREA DPR**

NORTH POLE
POLE NORD
POLO NORTE
                                           May 1984
BT POLAR REGIONS
RT ARCTIC REGIONS
    SOUTH POLE

NORTHERN HEMISPHERE
HEMISPHERE NORD
HEMISFERIO NORTE
                                           May 1984
RT SOUTHERN HEMISPHERE

NORWAY
NORVEGE
NORUEGA
BT SCANDINAVIA
    WESTERN EUROPE

NOUMEA
                                           May 1984
USE **NEW CALEDONIA**

NOVELS
ROMAN
NOVELA
RT 616

NUCLEAR PHYSICS
PHYSIQUE NUCLEAIRE
FISICA NUCLEAR
BT PHYSICS
RT 633

NUCLEAR PLANNING
PLANIFICATION NUCLEAIRE
PLANIFICACION NUCLEAR
SN Definition of a network of facilities and educational services for a locality
RT 250
    SCHOOL MAPPING

NUMBER CONCEPTS
CONCEPT DE NOMBRE
CONCEPTO DE NUMERO
BT MATHEMATICAL CONCEPTS
RT 631

NUMBERS
NOMBRE
NUMERO
RT 631

NUMERUS CLAUSUS
NUMERUS CLAUSUS
MATRICULA LIMITADA
SN Fixing by policy decision the number of entrants to be accepted for branches of higher education
BT QUOTA SYSTEM
RT 266

NURSERY SCHOOLS
ECOLE MATERNELLE
ESCUELA DE PARVULOS
BT PRESCHOOL CENTRES
RT 301

NURSES
INFIRMIERE
ENFERMERA
NT SCHOOL NURSES
RT 433

NUTRITION
NUTRITION
NUTRICION
RT 160

NYASALAND

May 1984

USE **MALAWI**

OAS
OEA
OEA
SN Organization of American States

OAU
OUA
OUA
SN Organization of African Unity

OBJECTIVE TESTS
TEST OBJECTIF
PRUEBA OBJETIVA
RT 392

OBSERVATION
OBSERVATION
OBSERVACION
RT 671

OBSERVATIONAL STUDIES
ETUDE FONDEE SUR L'OBSERVATION
ESTUDIO BASADO EN LA OBSERVACION
RT 282

OCAM
OCAM
OCAM
SN Common Afro Malagasy Organization

OCAS
OCAS
ODECA
SN Organization of Central American States

OCCUPATIONAL ADVANCEMENT
AVANCEMENT PROFESSIONNEL
ASCENSO EN EL EMPLEO
UF PROMOTION (OCCUPATIONAL)
NT TEACHER PROMOTION
RT 154

OCCUPATIONAL CHANGE
MODIFICATION DE L'EMPLOI
CAMBIO EN EL EMPLEO
SN Covers evolving nature of jobs
RT 155

OFFICIAL LANGUAGES

OCCUPATIONAL CLUSTERS
GROUPE DE METIERS
GRUPO DE OCUPACIONES
SN   Groups of related occupations
RT   155

OCCUPATIONAL GUIDANCE
USE **VOCATIONAL GUIDANCE**

OCCUPATIONAL INFORMATION
INFORMATION PROFESSIONNELLE
INFORMACION OCUPACIONAL
BT   CAREER COUNSELLING
RT   371

OCCUPATIONAL MOBILITY
MOBILITE PROFESSIONNELLE
MOVILIDAD OCUPACIONAL
SN   Covers change of job by the individual without referring to nature of the job
BT   MOBILITY
RT   563

OCCUPATIONAL SURVEYS
ENQUETE SUR L'EMPLOI
ENCUESTA OCUPACIONAL
BT   SURVEYS
RT   282

OCCUPATIONAL THERAPISTS
ERGOTHERAPEUTE
ERGOTERAPEUTA
BT   THERAPISTS
RT   432

OCCUPATIONS
METIER
OCUPACION
SN   Any distinct type of manual or non–manual work which can provide a means of livelihood. Occupational titles are given in the terminology used in the International Standard Classification of Occupations
NT   AGRICULTURAL OCCUPATIONS
     CLERICAL OCCUPATIONS
     INDUSTRIAL OCCUPATIONS
     PROFESSIONS
     SEMISKILLED OCCUPATIONS
     SERVICE OCCUPATIONS
     SKILLED OCCUPATIONS
     UNSKILLED OCCUPATIONS
RT   155

OCEANIA
OCEANIE
OCEANIA
UF   PACIFIC ISLANDS
     PACIFIC OCEAN TERRITORIES
NT   MELANESIA
     MICRONESIA
     POLYNESIA
     WAKE ISLANDS

OECD
OCDE
OCDE
SN   Organization for Economic Cooperation and Development

OEI
OEI
OEI
SN   Ibero–American Bureau of Education

OFF THE JOB TRAINING
FORMATION HORS DE L'EMPLOI
CAPACITACION FUERA DEL TRABAJO
SN   Conducted in company school or arranged with technical schools, colleges or professional agencies
BT   VOCATIONAL TRAINING
RT   351

OFFICE MACHINES
MACHINE DE BUREAU
MAQUINA DE OFICINA
RT   742

OFFICIAL LANGUAGES
LANGUE OFFICIELLE
LENGUA OFICIAL
RT   131

OFFICIAL REPORTS

OFFICIAL REPORTS
RAPPORT OFFICIEL
INFORME OFICIAL
RT 720

OKINAWA
USE **RYUKU ISLANDS**

May 1984

OMAN
OMAN
OMAN
BT   MIDDLE EAST

OMBUDSMEN
MEDIATEUR
MEDIADOR
RT 460

ON THE JOB TRAINING
FORMATION SUR LE TAS
FORMACION EN EL TRABAJO
BT   VOCATIONAL TRAINING
RT 351

ONE TEACHER SCHOOLS
ECOLE A MAITRE UNIQUE
ESCUELA DE MAESTRO UNICO
RT 303

OPEN COLLEGES
UNIVERSITE OUVERTE
UNIVERSIDAD ABIERTA
UF   OPEN UNIVERSITIES
       UNIVERSITIES WITHOUT
       WALLS
BT   COLLEGES
RT 307

OPEN LEARNING SYSTEMS
SYSTEME OUVERT
  D'ENSEIGNEMENT
SISTEMA DE ENSEÑANZA
  ABIERTO
SN   Systematic use of multimedia to
       reach unrestricted range of
       learners
RT 355

OPEN PLAN SCHOOLS
ECOLE SANS MURS
ESCUELA DE PLANTA ABIERTA
RT 340

OPEN UNIVERSITIES
USE **OPEN COLLEGES**

OPERATING EXPENSES
FRAIS D'EXPLOITATION
GASTOS DE EXPLOTACION
UF   RECURRENT COSTS
BT   EXPENDITURES
RT 241

OPERATIONS RESEARCH
RECHERCHE OPERATIONNELLE
INVESTIGACION OPERACIONAL
RT 282
       SYSTEMS ANALYSIS

OPINIONS
OPINION
OPINION
RT 552

OPPORTUNITIES
POSSIBILITE
OPORTUNIDAD
SN   Conditions favourable to an end
       or purpose
NT   EDUCATIONAL
         OPPORTUNITIES
       EMPLOYMENT
         OPPORTUNITIES
       EQUAL OPPORTUNITIES
         (JOBS)
       YOUTH OPPORTUNITIES
RT 100

OPPORTUNITY CLASSES
CLASSE DE RATTRAPAGE
CLASE DE RECUPERACION
SN   Designed to enable a group of
       students to reach normal grade
       performance and thus be
       integrated
BT   SPECIAL CLASSES
RT 343
       REMEDIAL INSTRUCTION

OPTICS
OPTIQUE
OPTICA
RT 633

OPTIONAL COURSES
COURS FACULTATIF
CURSO OPTATIVO
SN Any course which is not required by the curriculum being pursued
BT COURSES
RT 333

ORAL READING
LECTURE A HAUTE VOIX
LECTURA EN VOZ ALTA
BT READING
RT 620

OREALC
OREALC
OREALC
SN Regional Office of Education for Latin America and the Carribean (Santiago)

ORGANIGRAMS
USE **DIAGRAMS**

ORGANIZATIONS
ORGANISATION
ORGANIZACION
UF PRIVATE ORGANIZATIONS
   VOLUNTARY AGENCIES
SN Associations of people for pursuit of common interests, not officially established
NT COMMUNITY
     ORGANIZATIONS
   INTERNATIONAL
     ORGANIZATIONS
   LITERACY ORGANIZATIONS
   NATIONAL ORGANIZATIONS
RT 110

ORIENTATION COURSES
COURS D'ORIENTATION
CURSO DE ORIENTACION
BT COURSES
RT 333

ORIGINALITY
ORIGINALITE
ORIGINALIDAD
RT 522

ORTHOGRAPHIC SYMBOLS
SYMBOLE ORTHOGRAPHIQUE
SIMBOLO ORTOGRAFICO
RT 620

OUT OF SCHOOL ACTIVITIES
ACTIVITE EXTRASCOLAIRE
ACTIVIDAD EXTRAESCOLAR
BT ACTIVITIES
RT 357

OUT OF SCHOOL ACTIVITY CENTRES
CENTRE D'ACTIVITES
  EXTRASCOLAIRES
CENTRO DE ACTIVIDADES
  EXTRAESCOLARES
RT 311

OUT OF SCHOOL EDUCATION
EDUCATION EXTRASCOLAIRE
EDUCACION EXTRAESCOLAR
SN Covers institutions, programmes and activities for out-of-school youth and extra-curricular activities for those in school
RT 184

OUT OF SCHOOL YOUTH
JEUNESSE NON SCOLARISEE
JUVENTUD SIN ESCOLARIDAD
SN Children and young people not enrolled in school, including those who are no longer legally obliged to attend school
BT YOUTH
RT 412

OUTDOOR ACTIVITIES
ACTIVITE DE PLEIN AIR
ACTIVIDAD AL AIRE LIBRE
UF PLAYGROUND ACTIVITIES
BT RECREATIONAL ACTIVITIES
RT 357

OUTDOOR TEACHING AREAS
AIRE D'ENSEIGNEMENT EN
  PLEIN AIR
AREA DE ENSEÑANZA AL AIRE
  LIBRE
RT 711

OVERACHIEVERS
ELEVE BRILLANT
ALUMNO BRILLANTE
RT 415

OVERCROWDED CLASSES
CLASSE SURPEUPLEE
CLASE CON EXCESO DE
  ALUMNOS
RT 265

OVERHEAD PROJECTORS
RETROPROJECTEUR
RETROPROYECTOR
BT PROJECTION EQUIPMENT
RT 731

OVERTIME
HEURES SUPPLEMENTAIRES
HORAS EXTRAS
RT 222

PACIFIC ISLANDS
USE **OCEANIA**

PACIFIC OCEAN TERRITORIES
                              May 1984
USE **OCEANIA**

PAINTING
PEINTURE
PINTURA
RT 610

PAKISTAN
PAKISTAN
PAKISTAN
BT SOUTH ASIA

PANAMA
PANAMA
PANAMA
BT CENTRAL AMERICA

PANAMA CANAL ZONE
ZONE DU CANAL DE PANAMA
ZONA DEL CANAL DE PANAMA
BT CENTRAL AMERICA

PAPAL STATE
                              May 1984
USE **HOLY SEE**

PAPUA NEW GUINEA
PAPOUASIE-NOUVELLE-GUINEE
PAPUA NUEVA GUINEA
BT SOUTH EAST ASIA

PARAGUAY
PARAGUAY
PARAGUAY
BT SOUTH AMERICA

**PARAPROFESSIONAL SCHOOL
  PERSONNEL**
PERSONNEL PARAPEDAGOGIQUE
PERSONAL PARADOCENTE
SN Include non-teaching staff whose
    functions are professional
RT 423

PARENT ASSOCIATIONS
ASSOCIATION DE PARENTS
  D'ELEVES
ASOCIACION DE PADRES
BT NATIONAL ORGANIZATIONS
RT 110

PARENT CHILD RELATIONSHIP
RELATIONS PARENTS-ENFANTS
RELACION PADRES-HIJOS
BT FAMILY RELATIONSHIP
RT 553

**PARENT EDUCATION
  PROGRAMMES**
PROGRAMME D'EDUCATION DES
  PARENTS
PROGRAMA DE EDUCACION DE

LOS PADRES
RT 321

PARENT PARTICIPATION
PARTICIPATION DES PARENTS
PARTICIPACION DE LOS PADRES
BT PARTICIPATION
RT 380

PARENT RESPONSIBILITY
RESPONSABILITE DES PARENTS
RESPONSABILIDAD DE LOS PADRES
BT RESPONSIBILITY
RT 231

PARENT ROLE
ROLE DES PARENTS
PAPEL DE LOS PADRES
RT 553
  FAMILY INFLUENCE

PARENT STUDENT RELATIONSHIP
RELATIONS ELEVES–PARENTS
RELACION PADRES–ALUMNOS
BT FAMILY RELATIONSHIP
RT 380

PARENT TEACHER ASSOCIATIONS
ASSOCIATION PARENTS–MAITRES
ASOCIACION DE PADRES Y DOCENTES
BT NATIONAL ORGANIZATIONS
RT 110

PARENT TEACHER COOPERATION
COLLABORATION PARENTS–ENSEIGNANTS
COOPERACION PADRES–DOCENTES
RT 380

PARENTS
PARENTS
PADRES
NT FATHERS
   MIDDLE CLASS PARENTS
   MOTHERS
   WORKING CLASS PARENTS
   WORKING PARENTS

RT 401

PART TIME EDUCATION
EDUCATION A TEMPS PARTIEL
ENSEÑANZA DE MEDIA JORNADA
RT 184

PART TIME STUDENTS
ELEVE A TEMPS PARTIEL
ALUMNO DE MEDIA JORNADA
RT 410

PART TIME TEACHERS
MAITRE A TEMPS PARTIEL
DOCENTE DE TIEMPO PARCIAL
RT 424

PART TIME TRAINING
FORMATION A TEMPS PARTIEL
FORMACION A TIEMPO PARCIAL
BT VOCATIONAL TRAINING
RT 351

PARTIALLY SIGHTED
AMBLYOPE
AMBLIOPE
SN Children or adults
RT 403

PARTICIPANT INVOLVEMENT
ENGAGEMENT DU PARTICIPANT
COMPROMISO DEL PARTICIPANTE
SN Active participation of learner in design, execution and evaluation of educational activities
RT 554

PARTICIPANT SATISFACTION
SATISFACTION DU PARTICIPANT
SATISFACCION DEL PARTICIPANTE
SN The student's assessment of the degree to which a learning experience meets his needs
RT 554

PARTICIPATION

PARTICIPATION
PARTICIPATION
PARTICIPACION
NT CLASSROOM PARTICIPATION
    PARENT PARTICIPATION
    STUDENT PARTICIPATION
    TEACHER PARTICIPATION
    COMMUNITY PARTICIPATION
RT 554

PAST STUDENTS
ANCIEN ELEVE
EX ALUMNO
RT 410

PATIENTS (PERSONS)
MALADE
ENFERMO
RT 433

PATRIOTISM
PATRIOTISME
PATRIOTISMO
RT 101

PATTERN DRILLS (LANGUAGE)
EXERCICE STRUCTURAL
  (LANGAGE)
EJERCICIO ESTRUCTURAL
  (LENGUAJE)
RT 663

PATTERN RECOGNITION
RECONNAISSANCE DES FORMES
RECONOCIMIENTO DE FORMAS
BT RECOGNITION
RT 511

PAYROLL RECORDS
REGISTRE DE PAYE
REGISTRO DE SUELDOS
BT RECORDS (FORMS)
RT 723

PEACE EDUCATION
EDUCATION POUR LA PAIX
EDUCACION PARA LA PAZ
May 1984
RT 682

PEDAGOGY
PEDAGOGIE
PEDAGOGIA
RT 350

PEDIATRY
PEDIATRIE
PEDIATRIA
RT 651

PEER ACCEPTANCE
AGREMENT DES PAIRS
ACEPTACION DE CONDISCIPULOS
RT 554

PEER GROUPS
GROUPE DE PAIRS
GRUPO DE PARES
BT GROUPS
RT 443

PEER RELATIONSHIP
RELATIONS DES PAIRS
RELACION ENTRE PARES
BT INTERPERSONAL
    RELATIONSHIP
RT 554

PEER TEACHING
ENSEIGNEMENT MUTUEL
ENSEÑANZA MUTUA
BT TEACHING
RT 350

PEOPLES REPUBLIC OF CHINA
May 1984
USE **CHINA**

PERCEPTION
PERCEPTION
PERCEPCION
NT AUDITORY PERCEPTION
    VISUAL PERCEPTION
RT 510

PERCEPTUAL DISORDERS
TROUBLE DE LA PERCEPTION
ANOMALIAS DE LA PERCEPCION
SN Covers aural handicaps
BT HANDICAPS

RT 571

PERCEPTUAL MOTOR COORDINATION
COORDINATION IDEOMOTRICE
COORDINACION SENSOMOTRIZ
RT 510

PERFORMANCE
PERFORMANCE
RENDIMIENTO
RT 535

PERFORMANCE CRITERIA
CRITERE DE PERFORMANCE
CRITERIO DE RENDIMIENTO
SN Standards by which the efficacy of a system may be judged
RT 232

PERFORMANCE FACTORS
FACTEUR DE PERFORMANCE
FACTOR DE RENDIMIENTO
RT 535

PERFORMANCE SPECIFICATIONS
CARACTERISTIQUE DE PERFORMANCE
ESPECIFICACION DEL RENDIMIENTO
SN Statement of the operational characteristics of a system
BT SPECIFICATIONS
RT 232

PERFORMANCE TESTS
TEST DE PERFORMANCE
PRUEBA DE RENDIMIENTO
BT EDUCATIONAL TESTS
RT 393

PERIODICALS
PERIODIQUE
PERIODICO
BT SERIALS
RT 720

PERMANENT EDUCATION
USE **LIFELONG EDUCATION**

PERSIA   *May 1984*
USE **IRAN (ISLAMIC REPUBLIC)**

PERSISTENCE
PERSEVERANCE
PERSEVERANCIA
SN Used as antonym for dropping out, e.g. of school or employment
RT 535

PERSONAL DEVELOPMENT
USE **INDIVIDUAL DEVELOPMENT**

PERSONAL GROWTH
CROISSANCE PSYCHOLOGIQUE
MADUREZ PERSONAL
SN Development of psychological maturity
RT 531

PERSONALITY
PERSONNALITE
PERSONALIDAD
RT 555

PERSONALITY ASSESSMENT
EVALUATION DE LA PERSONNALITE
EVALUACION DE LA PERSONALIDAD
RT 221

PERSONALITY DEVELOPMENT
DEVELOPPEMENT DE LA PERSONNALITE
DESARROLLO DE LA PERSONALIDAD
RT 530

PERSONALITY PROBLEMS
PROBLEME DE PERSONNALITE
PROBLEMAS DE LA PERSONALIDAD
RT 572

PERSONALITY STUDIES

PERSONALITY STUDIES
ETUDE DE LA PERSONNALITE
ESTUDIO DE LA PERSONALIDAD
RT   282

PERSONALITY TESTS
TEST DE PERSONNALITE
PRUEBA DE PERSONALIDAD
BT   PSYCHOLOGICAL TESTS
RT   394

PERSONALITY THEORIES
THEORIE DE LA PERSONNALITE
TEORIA DE LA PERSONALIDAD
BT   THEORIES
RT   555

PERSONNEL DATA
RENSEIGNEMENT SUR LE
   PERSONNEL
DATOS SOBRE EL PERSONAL
RT   220

PERSONNEL EVALUATION
EVALUATION DU PERSONNEL
EVALUACION DEL PERSONAL
BT   EVALUATION
NT   TEACHER EVALUATION
RT   210

PERSONNEL MANAGEMENT
GESTION DU PERSONNEL
GESTION DEL PERSONAL
SN   Includes specific relationship
     between an employer or manager
     and an individual employee
BT   MANAGEMENT
RT   220

PERU
PEROU
PERU
BT   SOUTH AMERICA

PHILIPPINES
PHILIPPINES
FILIPINAS
BT   SOUTH EAST ASIA

PHILOSOPHY
PHILOSOPHIE
FILOSOFIA
RT   600

PHOENIX ISLANDS

USE **KIRIBATI**

PHONETICS
PHONETIQUE
FONETICA
RT   622

PHONICS
METHODE SYNTHETIQUE
METODO FONICO
RT   661

PHONOGRAPH RECORDS
DISQUE
DISCO
RT   730

PHONOLOGY
PHONOLOGIE
FONOLOGIA
RT   622

PHOTOGRAPHY
PHOTOGRAPHIE
FOTOGRAFIA
RT   647

PHYSICAL ACTIVITIES
ACTIVITE PHYSIQUE
ACTIVIDAD FISICA
NT   ATHLETIC ACTIVITIES
     EXERCISE (PHYSIOLOGY)
     MOTOR REACTIONS
RT   537

PHYSICAL CHARACTERISTICS
CARACTERISTIQUE PHYSIQUE
CARACTERISTICA FISICA
BT   INDIVIDUAL
        CHARACTERISTICS
RT   561

May 1984

PHYSICAL DEVELOPMENT
DEVELOPPEMENT PHYSIQUE
DESARROLLO FISICO
NT MOTOR DEVELOPMENT
RT 530

PHYSICAL EDUCATION
EDUCATION PHYSIQUE
EDUCACION FISICA
RT 683

PHYSICAL ENVIRONMENT
ENVIRONNEMENT PHYSIQUE
AMBIENTE FISICO
BT ENVIRONMENT
RT 550

PHYSICAL EXAMINATIONS
EXAMEN PHYSIQUE
EXAMEN FISICO
NT AUDIOVISUAL TESTS
RT 392

PHYSICAL HANDICAPS
HANDICAP PHYSIQUE
DEFICIENCIA FISICA
BT HANDICAPS
RT 571

PHYSICAL HEALTH
SANTE PHYSIQUE
SALUD FISICA
BT HEALTH
NT DENTAL HEALTH
RT 502

PHYSICAL PLANNING
URBANISME
PLANIFICACION FISICA
UF TOWN PLANNING
BT PLANNING
RT 108

PHYSICAL PLANS
PLAN D'AMENAGEMENT
PLAN FISICO
RT 250

PHYSICAL THERAPISTS
KINESITHERAPEUTE
KINESIOLOGO
BT THERAPISTS
RT 432

PHYSICALLY HANDICAPPED
HANDICAPE PHYSIQUE
DEFICIENTE FISICO
SN Children or adults
BT HANDICAPPED
RT 403

PHYSICIANS
MEDECIN
MEDICO
RT 433

PHYSICS
PHYSIQUE
FISICA
BT SCIENCES
NT NUCLEAR PHYSICS
RT 633

PHYSIOLOGY
PHYSIOLOGIE
FISIOLOGIA
BT BIOLOGY
RT 632

PILOT PROJECTS
PROJET PILOTE
PROYECTO PILOTO
SN Including experimental projects
BT PROJECTS
RT 272

PITCAIRN ISLANDS
ILES PITCAIRN
ISLAS PITCAIRN
May 1984
BT POLYNESIA

PLACEMENT
PLACEMENT
COLOCACION
SN In occupation
RT 154

PLANNING

PLANNING
PLANIFICATION
PLANIFICACION
NT COMMUNITY PLANNING
     EDUCATIONAL PLANNING
     NATIONAL PLANNING
     PHYSICAL PLANNING
     REGIONAL PLANNING
     SOCIAL PLANNING
RT 108
     POLICY MAKING

PLANNING BODIES
ORGANE DE PLANIFICATION
ORGANO DE PLANIFICACION
RT 261

PLAY
JEU
JUEGO
NT CHILDRENS GAMES
     EDUCATIONAL GAMES
RT 536

PLAY CENTRES
USE **PRESCHOOL CENTRES**

PLAYGROUND ACTIVITIES
USE **OUTDOOR ACTIVITIES**

PLEASANT ISLAND
May 1984
USE **NAURU ISLAND**

PLURICULTURALISM
PLURICULTURALISME
PLURICULTURALISMO
May 1984
RT 130

PLURILINGUALISM
PLURILINGUISME
PLURILINGUISMO
May 1984
RT 131

POETRY
POESIE
POESIA
RT 616

POLAND
POLOGNE
POLONIA
BT EASTERN EUROPE

POLAR REGIONS
REGIONS POLAIRES
REGIONES POLARES
May 1984
NT ANTARCTIC REGIONS
     ARCTIC REGIONS
     NORTH POLE
     SOUTH POLE

POLICE
POLICE
POLICIA
RT 460

POLICE SCHOOL RELATIONSHIP
RELATIONS ECOLE–POLICE
RELACION ESCUELA–POLICIA
RT 263

POLICIES
POLITIQUE
POLITICA
NT CULTURAL POLICIES
     ECONOMIC POLICIES
     EDUCATIONAL POLICIES
     SOCIAL POLICIES
RT 101
     POLICY MAKING

POLICY FORMATION
May 1984
USE **POLICY MAKING**

POLICY MAKING
ELABORATION DE POLITIQUES
ELABORACION DE POLITICAS
May 1984
UF POLICY FORMATION
SN Act of establishing principles to
     serve as guidelines for decision

making and action
RT 102
   PLANNING
   POLICIES

POLITICAL EDUCATION
EDUCATION POLITIQUE
FORMACION POLITICA
RT 680

POLITICAL FACTORS
FACTEUR POLITIQUE
FACTOR POLITICO
RT 285

POLITICAL ISSUES
PROBLEME POLITIQUE
PROBLEMA POLITICO
RT 100

POLITICAL SCIENCE
SCIENCES POLITIQUES
CIENCIAS POLITICAS
BT SOCIAL SCIENCES
RT 640

POLITICAL SOCIALIZATION
SOCIALISATION POLITIQUE
SOCIALIZACION POLITICA
BT SOCIALIZATION
RT 553

POLITICAL THEORIES
THEORIE POLITIQUE
TEORIAS POLITICAS
RT 101

POLYNESIA
POLYNESIE
POLINESIA

May 1984

BT OCEANIA
NT AMERICAN SAMOA
   COOK ISLANDS
   EASTER ISLAND
   FRENCH POLYNESIA
   HAWAII
   JOHNSTON ISLAND
   LINE ISLANDS
   MANIHIKI ISLANDS
   MIDWAY ISLANDS
   NIUE ISLAND
   PITCAIRN ISLANDS
   TOKELAU ISLANDS
   TONGA
   WALLIS AND FUTUNA
      ISLANDS
   SAMOA

POLYTECHNICAL EDUCATION
ENSEIGNEMENT POLYTECHNIQUE
ENSEÑANZA POLITECNICA
UF GENERAL TECHNICAL
      EDUCATION
SN Part of general education
   programme providing knowledge
   about main branches and scientific
   principles of production and
   equipping with basic practical
   skills necessary for participation in
   productive labour
RT 183

POPULATION DISTRIBUTION
REPARTITION DEMOGRAPHIQUE
DISTRIBUCION DE LA POBLACION
RT 124

POPULATION EDUCATION
EDUCATION EN MATIERE DE
   POPULATION
EDUCACION SOBRE POBLACION
UF FAMILY LIFE EDUCATION
RT 683

POPULATION PROBLEMS
PROBLEME DEMOGRAPHIQUE
PROBLEMAS DE POBLACION
RT 124

POPULATION TRENDS
TENDANCE DEMOGRAPHIQUE
TENDENCIA DEMOGRAFICA
RT 124

PORTUGAL
PORTUGAL
PORTUGAL
BT WESTERN EUROPE

PORTUGUESE TIMOR

PORTUGUESE TIMOR
TIMOR PORTUGAIS
TIMOR PORTUGUESA
May 1984
BT   SOUTH EAST ASIA

POST SECONDARY EDUCATION
USE **HIGHER EDUCATION**

POSTGRADUATE STUDENTS
ETUDIANT POSTUNIVERSITAIRE
ESTUDIANTE POSTUNIVERSITARIO
RT   413

POVERTY
PAUVRETE
POBREZA
RT   151

PRACTICE PERIODS
STAGE PRATIQUE
PERIODO DE PRACTICA
BT   WORK EXPERIENCE
      PROGRAMMES
NT   PRACTICE TEACHING
      SUPERVISED FARM PRACTICE
RT   673

PRACTICE SCHOOLS
USE **LABORATORY SCHOOLS**

PRACTICE TEACHING
LECON D'ESSAI
PRACTICA DOCENTE
UF   STUDENT TEACHING
BT   PRACTICE PERIODS
RT   690

PRACTICUMS
TRAVAUX PRATIQUES
TRABAJOS PRACTICOS
SN   Part of timetable where students
      do practical work in laboratory or
      workshop
RT   671

PREDICTION
PREDICTION
PRONOSTICO
RT   283

PREGNANCY
GROSSESSE
EMBARAZO
RT   502

PREMIUM PAY
PRIME
PRIMA
UF   SALARY DIFFERENTIALS
SN   Includes various forms of
      allowance in cash or kind
RT   242

PRENATAL INFLUENCES
INFLUENCE PRENATALE
INFLUENCIA PRENATAL
RT   550

PREPRIMARY CHILDREN
ELEVE DU PREPRIMAIRE
ALUMNO DE PREPRIMARIA
NT   KINDERGARTEN CHILDREN
RT   411

PREPRIMARY CURRICULUM
PROGRAMMES D'EDUCATION
    PRESCOLAIRE
CURRICULO DE EDUCACION
    PREESCOLAR
RT   330

PREPRIMARY EDUCATION
EDUCATION PREPRIMAIRE
EDUCACION PREESCOLAR
RT   185

PREPRIMARY PROGRAMMES
PROGRAMME PREPRIMAIRE
PROGRAMA PREESCOLAR
RT   320

PREPRIMARY TEACHERS
MAITRE DU PREPRIMAIRE
MAESTRO DE PREPRIMARIA
BT TEACHERS
RT 421

PRESCHOOL CENTRES
CENTRE PRESCOLAIRE
CENTRO PREESCOLAR
UF CRECHES
       PLAY CENTRES
NT NURSERY SCHOOLS
RT 311

PRESCHOOL LEARNING
APPRENTISSAGE PRESCOLAIRE
APRENDIZAJE PREESCOLAR
BT LEARNING
RT 514

PRESERVICE TEACHER EDUCATION
FORMATION PREALABLE DES ENSEIGNANTS
FORMACION INICIAL DE DOCENTES
BT TEACHER EDUCATION
RT 690

PRESIDENTS
RECTEUR
RECTOR
UF RECTORS
SN Heads of institutions of higher education
RT 422

PRESS
PRESSE
PRENSA
SN Covers all aspects of printed news media
BT MASS MEDIA
NT NEWSPAPERS
RT 145
      JOURNALISM

PRETECHNOLOGY PROGRAMMES
PROGRAMME D'INITIATION TECHNOLOGIQUE
PROGRAMA DE INICIACION TECNOLOGICA
SN Special curriculum to prepare individuals for technical training
RT 670

PREVOCATIONAL EDUCATION
ENSEIGNEMENT PREPROFESSIONNEL
ENSEÑANZA PREPROFESIONAL
RT 670

PRIESTS
PRETRE
SACERDOTE
SN Covers religious profession for all denominations and faiths
RT 462

PRIMARY EDUCATION
ENSEIGNEMENT PRIMAIRE
ENSEÑANZA PRIMARIA
UF ELEMENTARY EDUCATION
RT 185

PRIMARY GRADES
CLASSE DU PRIMAIRE
GRADOS DE PRIMARIA
BT GRADES (PROGRAMME DIVISIONS)
RT 342

PRIMARY SCHOOL CERTIFICATES
CERTIFICAT D'ETUDES PRIMAIRES
CERTIFICADO DE ESCUELA PRIMARIA
BT EDUCATIONAL CERTIFICATES
RT 390

PRIMARY SCHOOL COUNSELLORS
CONSEILLER SCOLAIRE (PRIMAIRE)
CONSEJERO ESCOLAR (PRIMARIA)
BT COUNSELLORS
RT 431

PRIMARY SCHOOL CURRICULUM

PRIMARY SCHOOL CURRICULUM
PROGRAMMES D'ETUDES
 PRIMAIRES
CURRICULO DE ESCUELA
 PRIMARIA
RT 330

PRIMARY SCHOOL INSPECTORS
INSPECTEUR DE
 L'ENSEIGNEMENT PRIMAIRE
INSPECTOR DE ESCUELAS
 PRIMARIAS
BT INSPECTORS
RT 420

PRIMARY SCHOOL MATHEMATICS
MATHEMATIQUES (NIVEAU
 PRIMAIRE)
MATEMATICA (NIVEL PRIMARIO)
RT 670

PRIMARY SCHOOL SCIENCE
SCIENCES (NIVEAU PRIMAIRE)
CIENCIAS (NIVEL PRIMARIO)
RT 670

PRIMARY SCHOOL STUDENTS
ELEVE DU PRIMAIRE
ALUMNO DE ESCUELA PRIMARIA
RT 411

PRIMARY SCHOOL TEACHERS
MAITRE DU PRIMAIRE
MAESTRO DE ESCUELA PRIMARIA
BT TEACHERS
RT 421

PRIMARY SCHOOLS
ECOLE PRIMAIRE
ESCUELA PRIMARIA
UF ELEMENTARY SCHOOLS
RT 301

PRINCIPALS
DIRECTEUR D'ETABLISSEMENT
DIRECTOR DE ESTABLECIMIENTO
UF SCHOOL HEADMASTERS
RT 423

PRINCIPE
May 1984
USE **SAO TOME AND PRINCIPE**

PRINCIPLES OF TEACHING
PRINCIPE PEDAGOGIQUE
PRINCIPIOS DE ENSEÑANZA
UF DIDACTICS
 EDUCATIONAL PRINCIPLES
RT 690

PRINTING
IMPRIMERIE
IMPRENTA
RT 647

PRIVATE COLLEGES
ETABLISSEMENT
 D'ENSEIGNEMENT SUPERIEUR
 PRIVE
UNIVERSIDAD PRIVADA
BT COLLEGES
RT 307

PRIVATE EDUCATION
ENSEIGNEMENT PRIVE
ENSEÑANZA PRIVADA
RT 187

PRIVATE FINANCIAL SUPPORT
AIDE FINANCIERE PRIVEE
AYUDA FINANCIERA PRIVADA
BT FINANCIAL SUPPORT
RT 240

PRIVATE ORGANIZATIONS
USE **ORGANIZATIONS**

PRIVATE SCHOOL TEACHERS
MAITRE DE L'ENSEIGNEMENT
 PRIVE
DOCENTE DE ESCUELA PRIVADA
RT 423

PRIVATE SCHOOLS
ECOLE PRIVEE
ESCUELA PRIVADA
UF CATHOLIC SCHOOLS
 DENOMINATIONAL
 SCHOOLS

INDEPENDENT SCHOOLS
NT   PROPRIETARY SCHOOLS
RT   302

PROBABILITY
PROBABILITE
PROBABILIDAD
RT   631

PROBATIONARY PERIOD
PERIODE PROBATOIRE
PERIODO DE PRUEBA
SN   Period in which a person must prove his ability to fulfil certain conditions as to achievement, behaviour or job assignment
RT   222

PROBLEM SOLVING
RESOLUTION DE PROBLEMES
RESOLUCION DE PROBLEMAS
BT   PRODUCTIVE THINKING
RT   522

PRODUCTIVE LIVING
VIE PRODUCTIVE
VIDA PRODUCTIVA
SN   A pattern of living, including work and leisure, which makes possible progress in human growth, capabilities and knowledge
RT   100

PRODUCTIVE THINKING
INTELLIGENCE PRATIQUE
INTELIGENCIA PRACTICA
BT   THOUGHT PROCESSES
NT   PROBLEM SOLVING
RT   521

PRODUCTIVITY
PRODUCTIVITE
PRODUCTIVIDAD
RT   150

PROFESSIONAL ASSOCIATIONS
ASSOCIATION PROFESSIONNELLE
ASOCIACION PROFESIONAL
BT   NATIONAL ORGANIZATIONS
RT   110

PROFESSIONAL EDUCATION
ENSEIGNEMENT SUPERIEUR PROFESSIONNEL
ENSEÑANZA PROFESIONAL SUPERIOR
SN   Covering all professions not specifically listed
RT   183

PROFESSIONAL PERSONNEL
PERSONNEL PROFESSIONNEL
PERSONAL PROFESIONAL
SN   To cover members of all professions not specifically listed
RT   441

PROFESSIONAL RECOGNITION
STATUT SOCIAL DE LA PROFESSION
RECONOCIMIENTO SOCIAL DE LA PROFESION
RT   121

PROFESSIONAL SERVICES
SERVICES PROFESSIONNELS
SERVICIOS PROFESIONALES
SN   Legal, management, testing and measurement services, etc., made available to educational institutions
NT   SOCIOPSYCHOLOGICAL SERVICES
RT   270

PROFESSIONS
PROFESSION
PROFESION
BT   OCCUPATIONS
RT   155

PROFESSORS
PROFESSEUR D'UNIVERSITE
PROFESOR UNIVERSITARIO
BT   COLLEGE TEACHERS
RT   422

PROGNOSTIC TESTS
TEST DE PRONOSTIC
PRUEBA DE PRONOSTICO
RT   392

PROGRAMME ADMINISTRATION

PROGRAMME ADMINISTRATION
ADMINISTRATION DU
  PROGRAMME
ADMINISTRACION DEL
  PROGRAMA
NT PROGRAMME COORDINATION
RT 262

PROGRAMME CONTENT
CONTENU DU PROGRAMME
CONTENIDO DEL PROGRAMA
SN Activities or subject matter of an
  instructional programme
RT 361

PROGRAMME COORDINATION
COORDINATION DES
  PROGRAMMES
COORDINACION DE LOS
  PROGRAMAS
BT COORDINATION
   PROGRAMME
     ADMINISTRATION
RT 205

PROGRAMME COSTS
COUT DU PROGRAMME
COSTO DEL PROGRAMA
BT COSTS
RT 243

PROGRAMME DESCRIPTIONS
DESCRIPTION DU PROGRAMME
DESCRIPCION DEL PROGRAMA
RT 203
   271
   PROGRAMME PLANNING

PROGRAMME DESIGN
CONCEPTION DE PROGRAMME
CONCEPCION DEL PROGRAMA
RT 205

PROGRAMME EVALUATION
EVALUATION DU PROGRAMME
EVALUACION DEL PROGRAMA
BT EVALUATION
NT FORMATIVE EVALUATION
   SUMMATIVE EVALUATION
RT 205

PROGRAMME LENGTH
DUREE DU PROGRAMME
EXTENSION DEL PROGRAMA
SN Length or duration of an
  instructional programme
RT 361

PROGRAMME PLANNING
PLANIFICATION DU PROGRAMME
PLANIFICACION DEL PROGRAMA
BT EDUCATIONAL PLANNING
RT 205
   PROGRAMME DESCRIPTIONS

PROGRAMMED INSTRUCTION
ENSEIGNEMENT PROGRAMME
ENSEÑANZA PROGRAMADA
RT 361

PROGRAMMED MATERIALS
MATERIEL D'ENSEIGNEMENT
  PROGRAMME
MATERIAL DE ENSEÑANZA
  PROGRAMADA
BT INSTRUCTIONAL MATERIALS
RT 725

PROGRAMMES
PROGRAMME
PROGRAMA
SN Plans of a series of intended
  activities, taken in the
  administrative sense
NT COMMUNITY PROGRAMMES
   EDUCATIONAL PROGRAMMES
   EMPLOYMENT PROGRAMMES
   FOUNDATION PROGRAMMES
   HEALTH PROGRAMMES
   INTERNATIONAL
     PROGRAMMES
   NATIONAL PROGRAMMES
   REGIONAL PROGRAMMES
RT 109

PROGRAMMING (FACILITIES)
PROGRAMMATION
  (INSTALLATIONS)
PROGRAMACION (EDIFICIOS Y
  EQUIPOS)
SN Preparation of description of

needs
RT 250

PROGRAMMING LANGUAGES
LANGAGE DE PROGRAMMATION
LENGUAJE DE PROGRAMACION
RT 621

PROJECT TRAINING METHODS
METHODE DE FORMATION
  INTEGREE
METODO DE FORMACION
  INTEGRADA
SN Programmes combining classroom instruction or vocational instruction with supervised and coordinated laboratory activities
RT 673

PROJECTION EQUIPMENT
EQUIPEMENT DE PROJECTION
EQUIPO DE PROYECCION
NT FILM PROJECTORS
    OVERHEAD PROJECTORS
RT 731

PROJECTIVE TESTS
TEST PROJECTIF
PRUEBA PROYECTIVA
BT PSYCHOLOGICAL TESTS
RT 394

PROJECTS
PROJET
PROYECTO
SN Component part of programme
NT DEMONSTRATION PROJECTS
    FAMILY PROJECTS
    PILOT PROJECTS
    RESEARCH PROJECTS
RT 272

PROMOTION (OCCUPATIONAL)
USE **OCCUPATIONAL ADVANCEMENT**

PROMOTION POLICIES
SYSTEME DE PROMOTION
SISTEMA DE PROMOCION
UF AUTOMATIC PROMOTION
SN Applied to students
RT 200
   FAILURE

PROMPTING
SOUFFLAGE
SOPLAR
RT 361

PRONUNCIATION
PRONONCIATION
PRONUNCIACION
RT 532

PROPERTY
USE **CAPITAL ASSETS**

PROPRIETARY SCHOOLS
ECOLE PRIVEE A CARACTERE
  LUCRATIF
ESCUELA PRIVADA PAGA
SN Private schools conducted for profit
BT PRIVATE SCHOOLS
RT 302

PROSE
PROSE
PROSA
RT 616

PROSTHESES
PROTHESE
PROTESIS
RT 734

PROTESTANTS
PROTESTANT
PROTESTANTE
RT 475

PROTOCOL MATERIALS
FILM DE SITUATIONS
  PEDAGOGIQUES
GRABACION AUDIOVISUAL DE
  SITUACIONES PEDAGOGICAS

141

PROVINCIAL AGENCIES

SN Audio and video recordings of behaviour which the preservice and inservice teacher education student can observe and analyse
RT 732

PROVINCIAL AGENCIES
ORGANISME PROVINCIAL
ORGANISMO PROVINCIAL
BT AGENCIES
RT 104

PROVINCIAL DEPARTMENTS OF EDUCATION
DIRECTION PROVINCIALE DE L'EDUCATION
DIRECCION PROVINCIAL DE EDUCACION
RT 261

PROVINCIAL GOVERNMENT
GOUVERNEMENT PROVINCIAL
GOBIERNO PROVINCIAL
SN Intermediate level of government for distinct part of national territory such as province or state
BT GOVERNMENT
RT 104
    PROVINCIAL LAWS
    PROVINCIAL POWERS

PROVINCIAL GOVERNMENT AID
AIDE DU GOUVERNEMENT PROVINCIAL
AYUDA DEL GOBIERNO PROVINCIAL
RT 106

PROVINCIAL LAWS
LEGISLATION PROVINCIALE
LEGISLACION PROVINCIAL
BT LAWS
RT 170
    PROVINCIAL GOVERNMENT

PROVINCIAL LOCAL RELATIONSHIP
RELATIONS PROVINCE-LOCALITES
RELACION PROVINCIA-LOCALIDADES
BT RELATIONSHIP
RT 262

PROVINCIAL POWERS
POUVOIR PROVINCIAL
PODER PROVINCIAL
RT 102
    PROVINCIAL GOVERNMENT

PROVINCIAL PROGRAMMES
PROGRAMME PROVINCIAL
PROGRAMA PROVINCIAL
RT 271

PROVINCIAL SURVEYS
ENQUETE PROVINCIALE
ENCUESTA PROVINCIAL
BT NATIONAL SURVEYS
RT 203

PSYCHIATRISTS
PSYCHIATRE
PSIQUIATRA
RT 462

PSYCHIATRY
PSYCHIATRIE
PSIQUIATRIA
RT 651

PSYCHOEDUCATIONAL CLINICS
CENTRE DE REEDUCATION
CENTRO DE REEDUCACION
SN Concerned primarily with behaviour problems of school children related to the school environment
RT 313

PSYCHOEDUCATIONAL PROCESSES
PROCESSUS PSYCHOPEDAGOGIQUE
PROCESO PSICOPEDAGOGICO
RT 350

PSYCHOLOGICAL CHARACTERISTICS
CARACTERISTIQUE PSYCHOLOGIQUE
CARACTERISTICA PSICOLOGICA

RT 561

PSYCHOLOGICAL EVALUATION
BILAN PSYCHOLOGIQUE
EVALUACION PSICOLOGICA
RT 391

PSYCHOLOGICAL NEEDS
BESOIN PSYCHOLOGIQUE
NECESIDADES PSICOLOGICAS
NT ACHIEVEMENT NEED
    AFFECTIVITY
    SECURITY
    STATUS NEED
RT 536

PSYCHOLOGICAL PATTERNS
MODELE PSYCHOLOGIQUE
MODELO PSICOLOGICO
NT ANXIETY
    FEAR
    IDENTIFICATION
      (PSYCHOLOGICAL)
    INSECURITY
    REJECTION
RT 551

PSYCHOLOGICAL STUDIES
ETUDE PSYCHOLOGIQUE
ESTUDIO PSICOLOGICO
RT 282

PSYCHOLOGICAL TESTING
ADMINISTRATION DE TESTS
    PSYCHOLOGIQUES
EXAMEN PSICOLOGICO
BT TESTING
RT 391

PSYCHOLOGICAL TESTS
TEST PSYCHOLOGIQUE
PRUEBA PSICOLOGICA
NT INTELLIGENCE TESTS
    MENTAL TESTS
    PERSONALITY TESTS
    PROJECTIVE TESTS
RT 392

PSYCHOLOGISTS
PSYCHOLOGUE
PSICOLOGO
NT SCHOOL PSYCHOLOGISTS
RT 462

PSYCHOLOGY
PSYCHOLOGIE
PSICOLOGIA
BT BEHAVIOURAL SCIENCES
NT CHILD PSYCHOLOGY
    DEVELOPMENTAL
      PSYCHOLOGY
    EDUCATIONAL PSYCHOLOGY
    EXPERIMENTAL
      PSYCHOLOGY
    INDIVIDUAL PSYCHOLOGY
    SOCIAL PSYCHOLOGY
RT 642

PSYCHOMETRICS
PSYCHOMETRIE
PSICOMETRIA
RT 391

PSYCHOMOTOR OBJECTIVES
OBJECTIF PSYCHOMOTEUR
OBJETIVO PSICOMOTOR
BT EDUCATIONAL OBJECTIVES
RT 300

PSYCHOMOTOR SKILLS
HABILETE PSYCHOMOTRICE
DESTREZA PSICOMOTORA
BT ABILITY
RT 533

PSYCHOPATHOLOGY
PSYCHOPATHOLOGIE
PSICOPATOLOGIA
RT 642

PSYCHOSOMATIC DISEASES
MALADIE PSYCHOSOMATIQUE
ENFERMEDAD PSICOSOMATICA
BT DISEASES
RT 570

PSYCHOTHERAPY
PSYCHOTHERAPIE
PSICOTERAPIA
BT THERAPY
RT 373

PSYCHOTICS
PSYCHOTIQUE
PSICOPATA
BT HANDICAPPED
RT 403

PUBLIC COLLEGES
ETABLISSEMENT
  D'ENSEIGNEMENT SUPERIEUR
  D'ETAT
UNIVERSIDAD ESTATAL
UF STATE UNIVERSITIES
BT COLLEGES
RT 307

PUBLIC EDUCATION
ENSEIGNEMENT PUBLIC
ENSEÑANZA PUBLICA
RT 187

PUBLIC HEALTH
SANTE PUBLIQUE
SALUD PUBLICA
BT HEALTH
RT 160

PUBLIC HEALTH LAWS
LEGISLATION SANITAIRE
LEGISLACION SANITARIA
BT LAWS
RT 170

PUBLIC LIBRARIES
BIBLIOTHEQUE PUBLIQUE
BIBLIOTECA PUBLICA
BT LIBRARIES
RT 310

PUBLIC RELATIONS
RELATIONS PUBLIQUES
RELACIONES PUBLICAS
RT 145

PUBLIC SCHOOL SYSTEMS
SYSTEME D'ECOLES PUBLIQUES
SISTEMA DE ESCUELAS PUBLICAS
BT SCHOOL SYSTEMS
RT 260

PUBLIC SCHOOL TEACHERS
MAITRE DE L'ENSEIGNEMENT
  PUBLIC
DOCENTE DE ESCUELA PUBLICA
RT 423

PUBLIC SCHOOLS
ECOLE PUBLIQUE
ESCUELA PUBLICA
UF STATE SCHOOLS
RT 302

PUBLIC SUPPORT
APPUI DE L'OPINION PUBLIQUE
APOYO DE LA OPINION PUBLICA
SN Includes public opinion
RT 100

PUBLICATION
PUBLICATION
PUBLICACION
RT 204

PUBLICATIONS
PUBLICATIONS
PUBLICACIONES
NT GOVERNMENT PUBLICATIONS
  SCHOOL PUBLICATIONS
RT 720

PUBLISHING INDUSTRY
EDITION
INDUSTRIA DEL LIBRO
BT INDUSTRY
RT 150

PUERTO RICO
PORTO RICO
PUERTO RICO
BT CARIBBEAN

PUNISHMENT
PUNITION
CASTIGO
RT 267

PUPILS
USE **STUDENTS**

PURCHASING
ACHAT
COMPRA
RT 241

QATAR
QATAR
QATAR
BT ARAB COUNTRIES
   GULF STATES

QUALIFICATIONS
QUALIFICATION
CALIFICACIONES
SN Required conditions, usually academic, for a post; the fulfilment of conditions
NT COUNSELLOR
     QUALIFICATIONS
   SUPERVISOR
     QUALIFICATIONS
   TEACHER QUALIFICATIONS
RT 221

QUANTITY SURVEYING
ARPENTAGE
AGRIMENSURA
RT 650

QUARTER SYSTEM
SYSTEME TRIMESTRIEL
SISTEMA TRIMESTRAL
BT SCHOOL CALENDARS
RT 344

QUESTIONING TECHNIQUES
TECHNIQUE D'INTERROGATION
TECNICA BASADA EN
   PREGUNTAS
BT TEACHING TECHNIQUES
RT 356

QUESTIONNAIRES
QUESTIONNAIRE
CUESTIONARIO
RT 203

QUOTA SYSTEM
SYSTEME DE QUOTA
SISTEMA DE CUOTA
SN Planned fixing of numbers for student intake as well as for placement of teachers
NT NUMERUS CLAUSUS
   TEACHER DISTRIBUTION
RT 205

RACE
RACE
RAZA
RT 123

RACE RELATIONS
RELATIONS INTERRACIALES
RELACIONES RACIALES
BT SOCIAL RELATIONS
RT 123

RACIAL DISCRIMINATION
DISCRIMINATION RACIALE
DISCRIMINACION RACIAL
RT 123

RACIAL INTEGRATION
INTEGRATION RACIALE
INTEGRACION RACIAL
RT 123

RACIAL SEGREGATION
SEGREGATION RACIALE
SEGREGACION RACIAL
RT 123

RACISM
RACISME
RACISMO
RT 101

RADIO

RADIO
RADIO
RADIO
BT MASS MEDIA
NT EDUCATIONAL RADIO
RT 145

RADIO TECHNOLOGY
RADIOTECHNIQUE
RADIOTECNIA
BT TECHNOLOGY
RT 645

RAPID READING
LECTURE RAPIDE
LECTURA RAPIDA
RT 660

RATING SCALES
BAREME DE CONVERSION
BAREMO DE CONVERSION
RT 392

REACTION TIME
TEMPS DE REACTION
TIEMPO DE REACCION
RT 511

READABILITY
LISIBILITE
LEGIBILIDAD
RT 660

READINESS
MATURITE
MADUREZ
SN Preparedness to respond or react
NT LEARNING READINESS
     READING READINESS
     SCHOOL READINESS
RT 531

READING
LECTURE
LECTURA
BT LANGUAGE ARTS
NT ORAL READING
RT 620

READING ABILITY
APTITUDE A LA LECTURE
APTITUD PARA LA LECTURA
BT ABILITY
RT 520

READING CONSULTANTS
CONSEILLER PEDAGOGIQUE EN
    LECTURE
CONSULTOR EN LECTURA
BT CONSULTANTS
RT 430

READING DEVELOPMENT
AMELIORATION EN LECTURE
MEJORAMIENTO EN LA LECTURA
UF READING IMPROVEMENT
RT 534

READING DIFFICULTY
DIFFICULTE EN LECTURE
DIFICULTAD EN LA LECTURA
RT 660

READING IMPROVEMENT
USE **READING DEVELOPMENT**

READING INSTRUCTION
ENSEIGNEMENT DE LA LECTURE
ENSEÑANZA DE LA LECTURA
RT 660

READING LEVEL
NIVEAU DE LECTURE
NIVEL DE LECTURA
RT 660

READING MATERIALS
MATERIEL DE LECTURE
MATERIAL DE LECTURA
BT INSTRUCTIONAL MATERIALS
NT SUPPLEMENTARY READING
     MATERIALS
RT 725

READING PROCESSES
PROCESSUS DE LECTURE
PROCESO DE LECTURA
NT FUNCTIONAL READING
RT 521

READING PROGRAMMES
PROGRAMME DE LECTURE
PROGRAMA DE LECTURA
NT ADULT READING
      PROGRAMMES
    REMEDIAL READING
      PROGRAMMES
RT 660

READING READINESS
MATURITE POUR LA LECTURE
MADUREZ PARA LA LECTURA
BT READINESS
RT 531

READING RESEARCH
RECHERCHE SUR LA LECTURE
INVESTIGACION SOBRE LA
  LECTURA
BT EDUCATIONAL RESEARCH
RT 280

READING TESTS
TEST DE LECTURE
PRUEBA DE LECTURA
BT EDUCATIONAL TESTS
RT 393

REAL ESTATE
USE CAPITAL ASSETS

REALISM
REALISME
REALISMO
SN Applied to literature
RT 615

RECALL (PSYCHOLOGICAL)
RAPPEL (MEMOIRE)
RECUERDO
RT 511

RECOGNITION
RECONNAISSANCE
  (PSYCHOLOGIE)
RECONOCIMIENTO (PSICOLOGIA)
NT PATTERN RECOGNITION
RT 511

RECORDKEEPING
CLASSEMENT (DOSSIERS)
REGISTRO (ACCION)
RT 202

RECORDS (FORMS)
REGISTRE
REGISTROS
NT ATTENDANCE RECORDS
    PAYROLL RECORDS
    STUDENT RECORDS
RT 723

RECREATION
RECREATION
RECREACION
RT 126

RECREATION LEGISLATION
LEGISLATION DES LOISIRS
LEGISLACION DE LA
  RECREACION
BT LAWS
RT 230

RECREATIONAL ACTIVITIES
ACTIVITE RECREATIVE
ACTIVIDAD RECREATIVA
BT ACTIVITIES
NT OUTDOOR ACTIVITIES
RT 357

RECREATIONAL FACILITIES
INSTALLATION RECREATIVE
INSTALACIONES DE RECREACION
BT EDUCATIONAL FACILITIES
RT 712

RECREATIONAL PROGRAMMES
PROGRAMME RECREATIF
PROGRAMA DE RECREACION
NT SCHOOL RECREATIONAL
    PROGRAMMES
RT 271

RECRUITMENT
RECRUTEMENT
RECLUTAMIENTO
SN Of educational personnel
RT 221

RECTORS
USE **PRESIDENTS**

RECURRENT COSTS
USE **OPERATING EXPENSES**

RECURRENT EDUCATION
FORMATION CONTINUE
EDUCACION RECURRENTE
SN   Periodic professional renewal, distinct from more general concept of lifelong education
RT   184

REDUNDANCY
REDONDANCE
EXCESO DE PERSONAL
RT   222

REFERENCE MATERIALS
OUVRAGE DE REFERENCE
DOCUMENTO DE REFERENCIA
SN   Covering dictionaries, encyclopaedias, thesauri, yearbooks
RT   720

REFERRAL
CONSULTATION
CONSULTA
SN   The process of referring to an appropriate agency or specialist
RT   372

REFRESHER TRAINING
MISE A JOUR DES CONNAISSANCES
ACTUALIZACION DE LOS CONOCIMIENTOS
BT   INSERVICE COURSES
RT   333

REFUGEES
REFUGIE
REFUGIADO
RT   470

REGIONAL AGENCIES
ORGANISME REGIONAL
ORGANISMO REGIONAL
SN   Intergovernmental bodies grouping a number of countries
BT   AGENCIES
RT   103

REGIONAL COOPERATION
COOPERATION REGIONALE
COOPERACION REGIONAL
SN   Extending over a group of countries
RT   105

REGIONAL PLANNING
PLANIFICATION REGIONALE
PLANIFICACION REGIONAL
SN   Involves group of countries
BT   PLANNING
RT   108

REGIONAL PROGRAMMES
PROGRAMME REGIONAL
PROGRAMA REGIONAL
BT   PROGRAMMES
RT   109

REGIONAL SURVEYS
ENQUETE REGIONALE
ENCUESTA REGIONAL
SN   Covering a group of countries
BT   SURVEYS
RT   203

REGULAR CLASS PLACEMENT
REINSERTION SCOLAIRE
REUBICACION EN CLASES REGULARES
SN   Placement of students identified as handicapped or gifted in regular classes
RT   341
         SPECIAL CLASSES
         SPECIAL SCHOOLS

REHABILITATION
READAPTATION
REHABILITACION
RT 373

REHABILITATION COUNSELLING
ORIENTATION POUR LA
   READAPTATION
ASESORAMIENTO PARA LA
   REHABILITACION
BT CAREER COUNSELLING
RT 370

REHABILITATION PROGRAMMES
PROGRAMME DE READAPTATION
PROGRAMA DE REHABILITACION
RT 271

REINFORCEMENT
RENFORCEMENT
REFUERZO
NT REWARDS
RT 511

REJECTION
REJET
RECHAZO
BT PSYCHOLOGICAL PATTERNS
RT 540

RELATIONSHIP
RELATIONS
RELACIONES
SN Restrict to people and institutions
NT CENTRAL PROVINCIAL
       RELATIONSHIP
    FAMILY RELATIONSHIP
    FAMILY SCHOOL
       RELATIONSHIP
    INTERACTION PROCESS
    INTERPERSONAL
       RELATIONSHIP
    PROVINCIAL LOCAL
       RELATIONSHIP
    SCHOOL INDUSTRY
       RELATIONSHIP
    STUDENT COLLEGE
       RELATIONSHIP
    STUDENT SCHOOL
       RELATIONSHIP

RELIGIOUS INSTITUTION ROLE

    TEACHER ADMINISTRATION
       RELATIONSHIP
RT 553
    INTERACTION

RELEASED TIME
TEMPS ACCORDE POUR L'ETUDE
LICENCIA DE ESTUDIOS
SN From work for study purposes
NT BLOCK RELEASE
    DAY RELEASE
RT 222

RELEVANCE (EDUCATION)
USE **EDUCATIONAL QUALITY**

RELIABILITY
FIABILITE
CONFIABILIDAD
SN Applied to measurement
    instruments
RT 283

RELIGION
RELIGION
RELIGION
RT 130

RELIGIOUS CULTURAL GROUPS
GROUPE D'OBEDIENCE
   RELIGIEUSE
GRUPO RELIGIOSO
BT GROUPS
RT 443

RELIGIOUS EDUCATION
EDUCATION RELIGIEUSE
EDUCACION RELIGIOSA
RT 682

RELIGIOUS FACTORS
FACTEUR RELIGIEUX
FACTOR RELIGIOSO
RT 285

RELIGIOUS INSTITUTION ROLE
ROLE DE L'INSTITUTION
   CONFESSIONNELLE
PAPEL DE LA INSTITUCION
   RELIGIOSA

RELIGIOUS INSTITUTIONS

RT 125

RELIGIOUS INSTITUTIONS
INSTITUTION CONFESSIONNELLE
INSTITUCION RELIGIOSA
UF CHURCHES
RT 125
    STATE CHURCH SEPARATION

RELIGIOUS ORGANIZATIONS
ORGANISATION RELIGIEUSE
ORGANIZACION RELIGIOSA
BT NATIONAL ORGANIZATIONS
RT 110

RELOCATABLE FACILITIES
INSTALLATION MOBILE
INSTALACIONES MOVILES
BT EDUCATIONAL FACILITIES
RT 710
    MOBILE SCHOOLS

REMEDIAL COURSES
COURS CORRECTIF
CURSO CORRECTIVO
BT COURSES
RT 333

REMEDIAL INSTRUCTION
ENSEIGNEMENT CORRECTIF
ENSEÑANZA CORRECTIVA
SN Special teaching for students with difficulties in particular curriculum areas
RT 352
    OPPORTUNITY CLASSES

REMEDIAL READING PROGRAMMES
PROGRAMME DE RATTRAPAGE EN LECTURE
PROGRAMA DE LECTURA CORRECTIVA
BT READING PROGRAMMES
RT 660

REMEDIAL TEACHERS
ORTHOPEDAGOGUE
ORTOPEDAGOGO
RT 426

REMUNERATION
USE **SALARIES**

RENAISSANCE
RENAISSANCE
RENACIMIENTO

REPETITION RATE
TAUX DE REDOUBLEMENT
TASA DE REPETICION
RT 206
    GRADE REPETITION

REPLICATION OF INNOVATIONS
TRANSFERT D'INNOVATIONS
TRANSFERENCIA DE INNOVACIONES
SN Deliberate attempt to adopt an innovatory practice from elsewhere in country or in another country
BT ADOPTION OF INNOVATIONS
RT 204

REPORT CARDS
CARNET SCOLAIRE
FICHA ESCOLAR
RT 723

REPORTING
ELABORATION DE RAPPORTS
ELABORACION DE INFORMES
RT 201

RESEARCH
RECHERCHE
INVESTIGACION
RT 140
    280

RESEARCH AND DEVELOPMENT
RECHERCHE ET DEVELOPPEMENT
INVESTIGACION Y DESARROLLO
May 1984
RT 282

RESEARCH REVIEWS

RESEARCH AND INSTRUCTION UNITS
UNITE D'ENSEIGNEMENT ET DE RECHERCHE
UNIDAD DE ENSEÑANZA E INVESTIGACION
SN An organization within a single school that is concerned with the improvement of teaching methods
RT 340

RESEARCH CENTRES
CENTRE DE RECHERCHE
CENTRO DE INVESTIGACION
May 1984
RT 312

RESEARCH COORDINATING UNITS
UNITE DE COORDINATION (RECHERCHE)
UNIDAD DE COORDINACION DE INVESTIGACIONES
RT 261

RESEARCH CRITERIA
CRITERE DE RECHERCHE
CRITERIO DE INVESTIGACION
BT CRITERIA
RT 283

RESEARCH DESIGN
PLAN DE RECHERCHE
PLAN DE INVESTIGACION
RT 283

RESEARCH DIRECTORS
DIRECTEUR DE RECHERCHE
DIRECTOR DE INVESTIGACION
RT 430

RESEARCH FINDINGS
RESULTAT DE RECHERCHE
RESULTADO DE LA INVESTIGACION
May 1984
RT 283

RESEARCH METHODOLOGY
METHODOLOGIE DE LA RECHERCHE
METODOLOGIA DE LA INVESTIGACION
RT 283

RESEARCH OPPORTUNITIES
POSSIBILITE DE RECHERCHE
OPORTUNIDADES DE INVESTIGACION
RT 223

RESEARCH POLICY
POLITIQUE DE RECHERCHE
POLITICA DE INVESTIGACION
May 1984
RT 140

RESEARCH PROBLEMS
PROBLEME DE RECHERCHE
PROBLEMA DE INVESTIGACION
RT 281

RESEARCH PROGRAMME
PROGRAMME DE RECHERCHE
PROGRAMA DE INVESTIGACION
May 1984
RT 140

RESEARCH PROJECTS
PROJET DE RECHERCHE
PROYECTO DE INVESTIGACION
BT PROJECTS
RT 272

RESEARCH REPORT
RAPPORT DE RECHERCHE
INFORME DE INVESTIGACION
May 1984
RT 880

RESEARCH REVIEWS
APERCU DE RECHERCHE
RESEÑA SOBRE INVESTIGACION
May 1984
RT 880

RESEARCH UTILIZATION

RESEARCH UTILIZATION
UTILISATION DE LA RECHERCHE
UTILIZACION DE LA
  INVESTIGACION
RT 204

RESEARCHERS
CHERCHEUR
INVESTIGADOR
NT EDUCATIONAL RESEARCHERS
RT 430

RESIDENT STUDENTS
RESIDENT UNIVERSITAIRE
ALUMNO RESIDENTE
RT 413

RESIDENTIAL CARE
SOINS HOSPITALIERS
ATENCION HOSPITALARIA
RT 374

RESIDENTIAL COLLEGES
INTERNAT UNIVERSITAIRE
INTERNADO UNIVERSITARIO
BT COLLEGES
RT 307

RESOURCE ALLOCATIONS
ALLOCATION DES RESSOURCES
DISTRIBUCION DE LOS RECURSOS
RT 243

RESOURCE MATERIALS
RESSOURCE DOCUMENTAIRE
MATERIALES DE CONSULTA
RT 700

RESOURCE TEACHERS
PROFESSEUR CONSULTANT
ASESOR PEDAGOGICO
SN Those with special competence who may be asked to assist other teachers
RT 426

RESOURCES
RESSOURCE
RECURSOS
NT COMMUNITY RESOURCES
    EDUCATIONAL RESOURCES
    NATURAL RESOURCES
RT 700

RESPONSE MODE
MODE DE REPONSE
MODO DE RESPUESTA
RT 511

RESPONSIBILITY
RESPONSABILITE
RESPONSABILIDAD
NT ADMINISTRATOR
      RESPONSIBILITY
    CHILD RESPONSIBILITY
    LEGAL RESPONSIBILITY
    NONINSTRUCTIONAL
      RESPONSIBILITY
    PARENT RESPONSIBILITY
    SCHOOL RESPONSIBILITY
    TEACHER RESPONSIBILITY
RT 231

RETARDATION
RETARD
RETRASO
RT 372

RETARDED CHILDREN
ENFANT RETARDE
NIÑO RETARDADO
UF MENTALLY RETARDED
BT HANDICAPPED
RT 403

RETENTION
RETENTION
RETENCION
BT LEARNING PROCESSES
NT LITERACY RETENTION
RT 535

RETIREMENT
RETRAITE
JUBILACION
RT 222

RETRAINING
RECYCLAGE
RECICLAJE
SN Training for a new occupation
BT TRAINING
RT 351

REUNION ISLAND
ILE DE LA REUNION
ISLA DE LA REUNION
May 1984
BT INDIAN OCEAN TERRITORIES

REVENUE
RESSOURCE FINANCIERE
RECURSOS FINANCIEROS
RT 240

REWARDS
GRATIFICATION
GRATIFICACION
BT REINFORCEMENT
RT 511

RHODESIA
May 1984
USE **ZIMBABWE**

RIGHT TO EDUCATION
DROIT A L'EDUCATION
DERECHO A LA EDUCACION
RT 180

ROEAO
ROEAO
ROEAO
SN Regional Office for Education in Asia and Oceania (Bangkok)

ROLE PERCEPTION
PERCEPTION DE ROLE
PERCEPCION DEL PAPEL
SN Awareness of behaviour patterns or functions expected of persons
RT 553

ROLE PLAYING
JEU DE ROLE
DESEMPEÑO DE UN PAPEL
RT 553

ROLE THEORY
THEORIE DES ROLES
TEORIA DE LAS FUNCIONES
    SOCIALES
RT 553

ROMANCE LANGUAGES
LANGUES ROMANES
LENGUAS ROMANCES
RT 625

ROMANIA
ROUMANIE
RUMANIA
UF RUMANIA
BT EASTERN EUROPE

ROMANTICISM
ROMANTISME
ROMANTICISMO
SN Applied to literature
RT 615

ROTE LEARNING
APPRENTISSAGE PAR COEUR
APRENDIZAJE DE MEMORIA
BT LEARNING
RT 512

RUANDA
May 1984
USE **RWANDA**

RUMANIA
May 1984
USE **ROMANIA**

RURAL AREAS
ZONE RURALE
ZONA RURAL
RT 122

RURAL DEVELOPMENT

RURAL DEVELOPMENT
DEVELOPPEMENT RURAL
DESARROLLO RURAL
BT DEVELOPMENT
NT INTEGRATED RURAL
      DEVELOPMENT
RT 151

RURAL EDUCATION
EDUCATION RURALE
EDUCACION RURAL
RT 186

RURAL EXTENSION
VULGARISATION EN MILIEU
  RURAL
EXTENSION EN MEDIO RURAL
UF AGRICULTURAL EXTENSION
SN Extension work in rural settings
BT EXTENSION EDUCATION
RT 382

RURAL FAMILY
FAMILLE RURALE
FAMILIA RURAL
BT FAMILY (SOCIOLOGICAL
      UNIT)
RT 126

RURAL POPULATION
POPULATION RURALE
POBLACION RURAL
RT 124

RURAL RESETTLEMENT
USE **AGRARIAN REFORM**

RURAL SCHOOL SYSTEMS
SYSTEME D'ECOLES RURALES
SISTEMA DE ESCUELAS RURALES
BT SCHOOL SYSTEMS
RT 260

RURAL SCHOOL TEACHERS
MAITRE D'ECOLE RURALE
MAESTRO DE ESCUELA RURAL
May 1984
BT TEACHERS
RT 421

RURAL SCHOOLS
ECOLE RURALE
ESCUELA RURAL
RT 303

RURAL URBAN DIFFERENCES
DIFFERENCE VILLE–CAMPAGNE
DIFERENCIA CIUDAD–CAMPO
RT 122

RURAL YOUTH
JEUNESSE RURALE
JUVENTUD RURAL
BT YOUTH
RT 400

RURAL–URBAN MIGRATION
USE **URBAN IMMIGRATION**

RUSSIA
May 1984
USE **USSR**

RUSSIAN
LANGUE RUSSE
LENGUA RUSA
RT 626

RUSSIAN SFSR
RSFS DE RUSSIE
RSFS DE RUSIA
May 1984
UF RUSSIAN SOVIET FEDERAL
      SOCIALIST REPUBLIC
BT USSR

RUSSIAN SOVIET FEDERAL
  SOCIALIST REPUBLIC
May 1984
USE **RUSSIAN SFSR**

RWANDA
RWANDA
RWANDA
UF RUANDA
BT CENTRAL AFRICA
      EAST AFRICA
RT FRENCH SPEAKING AFRICA

SALARY DIFFERENTIALS

RYUKU ISLANDS
ILES RYUKU
ISLAS RYUKU
May 1984
UF OKINAWA
BT JAPAN

SABAH
SABAH
SABAH
May 1984
UF NORTH BORNEO
BT MALAYSIA

SABBATICAL LEAVE
USE **LEAVE OF ABSENCE**

SAFETY
SECURITE
SEGURIDAD
SN Considered as a factor in administration of educational institutions
NT TRAFFIC SAFETY
RT 264

SAFETY EDUCATION
ENSEIGNEMENT DES MESURES DE SECURITE
ENSEÑANZA DE MEDIDAS DE SEGURIDAD
RT 683

SAINT BARTHELEMY
SAINT BARTHELEMY
SAN BARTOLOME
May 1984
BT CARIBBEAN

SAINT HELENA
SAINTE HELENE
SANTA ELENA
BT ATLANTIC OCEAN TERRITORIES
RT ENGLISH SPEAKING AFRICA

SAINT KITTS–NEVIS–ANGUILLA
SAINT CHRISTOPHE ET NIEVES ET ANGUILLA
SAN CRISTOBAL, NIEVES Y ANGUILA
May 1984
BT CARIBBEAN

SAINT LUCIA
SAINTE LUCIE
SANTA LUCIA
May 1984
BT CARIBBEAN

SAINT MARTIN
SAINT MARTIN
SAN MARTIN
May 1984
BT CARIBBEAN

SAINT PIERRE AND MIQUELON ISLANDS
ILES SAINT PIERRE ET MIQUELON
ISLAS SAN PEDRO Y MIQUELON
UF MIQUELON ISLAND
BT NORTH AMERICA

SAINT VINCENT
SAINT VINCENT
SAN VICENTE
May 1984
BT CARIBBEAN

SALARIES
SALAIRE
REMUNERACION
UF REMUNERATION
    SALARY SCALES
    WAGES
BT INCOME
NT TEACHER SALARIES
RT 242

SALARY DIFFERENTIALS
USE **PREMIUM PAY**

SALARY SCALES
USE **SALARIES**

SALVADOR
USE **EL SALVADOR**

SAMOA
SAMOA
SAMOA
May 1984
BT POLYNESIA

SAMPLING
ECHANTILLONNAGE
MUESTREO
RT 283

SAN MARINO
SAINT–MARIN
SAN MARINO
BT WESTERN EUROPE
RT ITALY

SANCTIONS
SANCTION
SANCION
RT 233

SANDWICH COURSES
COURS ALTERNES
CURSOS ALTERNADOS CON
   TRABAJO
SN Alternate periods of full–time
   work and full–time attendance at
   an educational institution
BT COURSES
RT 333

SANTA CRUZ ISLANDS
ILES SANTA CRUZ
ISLAS SANTA CRUZ
May 1984
BT MELANESIA

SAO TOME AND PRINCIPE
SAO TOME ET PRINCIPE
SANTO TOME Y PRINCIPE
UF PRINCIPE
BT CENTRAL AFRICA

SARAWAK
SARAWAK
SARAWAK
May 1984
BT MALAYSIA

SATIRE
SATIRE
SATIRA
RT 616

SAUDI ARABIA
ARABIE SAOUDITE
ARABIA SAUDITA
BT ARAB COUNTRIES
   MIDDLE EAST

SCANDINAVIA
SCANDINAVIE
ESCANDINAVIA
BT WESTERN EUROPE
NT DENMARK
   FAEROE ISLANDS
   FINLAND
   GREENLAND
   ICELAND
   LAPLAND
   NORWAY

SCHEDULING
ETABLISSEMENT DU CALENDRIER
ELABORACION DEL CALENDARIO
RT 201

SCHOLARSHIPS
BOURSE D'ETUDES
BECA DE ESTUDIOS
SN Reserve for school and
   undergraduate levels of education
BT GRANTS
RT 242

SCHOOL ACCOUNTING
COMPTABILITE SCOLAIRE
CONTABILIDAD ESCOLAR
BT ACCOUNTING
RT 243

SCHOOL ACTIVITIES
ACTIVITE SCOLAIRE
ACTIVIDAD ESCOLAR
BT   ACTIVITIES
NT   CLASS ACTIVITIES
RT   357

SCHOOL ADJUSTMENT
USE **STUDENT ADJUSTMENT**

SCHOOL ADMINISTRATION
ADMINISTRATION SCOLAIRE
ADMINISTRACION ESCOLAR
BT   EDUCATIONAL
       ADMINISTRATION
RT   265
       SCHOOL FUNDS

SCHOOL AGE POPULATION
POPULATION D'AGE SCOLAIRE
POBLACION EN EDAD ESCOLAR
RT   206

SCHOOL ATTENDANCE LAWS
LOI SUR LA FREQUENTATION
   SCOLAIRE
LEYES SOBRE ASISTENCIA
   ESCOLAR
BT   EDUCATIONAL LEGISLATION
RT   230

SCHOOL ATTITUDES
ATTITUDE DE L'ECOLE
ACTITUD DE LA ESCUELA
SN   Embodied in the school as
       institution
BT   ATTITUDES
RT   552

SCHOOL BUSES
CAR DE RAMASSAGE SCOLAIRE
OMNIBUS ESCOLAR
RT   743

SCHOOL CALENDARS
CALENDRIER SCOLAIRE
CALENDARIO ESCOLAR
NT   QUARTER SYSTEM
       SEMESTER DIVISIONS
RT   344

SCHOOL CLOSURE
FERMETURE D'ECOLE
CLAUSURA DE ESCUELA
SN   Temporarily or permanently for
       reasons of health, discipline,
       security or finance
RT   263

SCHOOL COMMUNITY
   COOPERATION
COOPERATION ECOLE–
   COLLECTIVITE
COOPERACION ESCUELA–
   COMUNIDAD
RT   263

SCHOOL COMMUNITY
   PROGRAMMES
PROGRAMME ECOLE–
   COLLECTIVITE
PROGRAMA ESCUELA–
   COMUNIDAD
RT   272

SCHOOL COMMUNITY
   RELATIONSHIP
RELATIONS ECOLE–COLLECTIVITE
RELACION ESCUELA–COMUNIDAD
RT   263

SCHOOL DISTRIBUTION
REPARTITION DES ECOLES
DISTRIBUCION DE ESCUELAS
SN   Actual location of schools, the
       planning process to be indexed
       under "school mapping"
RT   208

SCHOOL DISTRICT AUTONOMY
AUTONOMIE DES DISTRICTS
   SCOLAIRES
AUTONOMIA DE DISTRITOS
   ESCOLARES
SN   Area of control granted a school
       district or its officials through
       expressed or implied authority of
       central or provincial government
RT   263

SCHOOL DISTRICTS
DISTRICT SCOLAIRE
DISTRITO ESCOLAR
RT 264

SCHOOL FUNDS
FONDS SCOLAIRE
FONDOS ESCOLARES
RT 240
    SCHOOL ADMINISTRATION

SCHOOL GOVERNANCE
LEGISLATION SCOLAIRE
LEGISLACION ESCOLAR
SN Legal basis for control and management of categories of schools
NT SCHOOL REGULATIONS
RT 230

SCHOOL HEADMASTERS
USE **PRINCIPALS**

SCHOOL HEALTH SERVICES
SERVICE DE MEDECINE SCOLAIRE
SERVICIO ESCOLAR DE SALUD
BT HEALTH SERVICES
RT 270

SCHOOL HOLDING POWER
POUVOIR RETENTEUR DE L'ECOLE
PODER DE RETENCION DE LA ESCUELA
SN Measure of retention rate
RT 208

SCHOOL INDUSTRY RELATIONSHIP
RELATIONS ECOLE–INDUSTRIE
RELACION ESCUELA–INDUSTRIA
BT RELATIONSHIP
RT 263

SCHOOL INTEGRATION
INTEGRATION SCOLAIRE
INTEGRACION ESCOLAR
SN Referring to ethnic groups, covers also negative aspect of segregation

RT 230

SCHOOL LEAVERS
ELEVE SORTANT
EGRESADO ESCOLAR
RT 411

SCHOOL LEAVING
EXEAT SCOLAIRE
EGRESO DE LA ESCUELA
RT 266

SCHOOL LIBRARIANS
BIBLIOTHECAIRE SCOLAIRE
BIBLIOTECARIO ESCOLAR
BT LIBRARIANS
RT 462

SCHOOL LIBRARIES
BIBLIOTHEQUE SCOLAIRE
BIBLIOTECA ESCOLAR
BT LIBRARIES
RT 310

SCHOOL LOCATION
USE **SCHOOL MAPPING**

SCHOOL MAINTENANCE
ENTRETIEN DES ECOLES
MANTENIMIENTO DE ESCUELAS
BT MAINTENANCE
RT 265

SCHOOL MAPPING
CARTE SCOLAIRE
MAPA ESCOLAR
UF SCHOOL LOCATION
SN Planning further provisions of educational establishment in terms of demographic and geographical factors
RT 208
    NUCLEAR PLANNING

SCHOOL MEAL PROGRAMMES
PROGRAMME DE CANTINE SCOLAIRE
PROGRAMA DE COMEDORES ESCOLARES
RT 272

SCHOOL SERVICES

SCHOOL NURSES
INFIRMIERE SCOLAIRE
ENFERMERA ESCOLAR
BT NURSES
RT 433

SCHOOL ORGANIZATION
ORGANISATION SCOLAIRE
ORGANIZACION ESCOLAR
NT DEPARTMENTS (SCHOOL)
RT 340

SCHOOL PERSONNEL
PERSONNEL SCOLAIRE
PERSONAL ESCOLAR
RT 423

SCHOOL PLANNING
PLANIFICATION SCOLAIRE
PLANIFICACION ESCOLAR
SN In both programme and architectural senses
BT EDUCATIONAL PLANNING
RT 205

SCHOOL PSYCHOLOGISTS
PSYCHOLOGUE SCOLAIRE
PSICOLOGO ESCOLAR
BT PSYCHOLOGISTS
RT 430

SCHOOL PUBLICATIONS
PUBLICATION SCOLAIRE
PUBLICACION ESCOLAR
SN Publications for or by schools
BT PUBLICATIONS
RT 720

SCHOOL READINESS
APTITUDE A LA SCOLARITE
MADUREZ PARA LA ESCOLARIDAD
BT READINESS
RT 531

SCHOOL RECREATIONAL PROGRAMMES
PROGRAMME RECREATIF SCOLAIRE
PROGRAMA DE RECREACION ESCOLAR
BT RECREATIONAL PROGRAMMES
RT 272

SCHOOL REDISTRICTING
REDISTRIBUTION DES ECOLES
REDISTRIBUCION DE LAS ESCUELAS
RT 264

SCHOOL REGISTRATION
INSCRIPTION SCOLAIRE
INSCRIPCION ESCOLAR
RT 264

SCHOOL REGULATIONS
REGLEMENTATION SCOLAIRE
REGLAMENTACION ESCOLAR
BT SCHOOL GOVERNANCE
RT 230

SCHOOL RESPONSIBILITY
RESPONSABILITE DE L'ECOLE
RESPONSABILIDAD DE LA ESCUELA
BT RESPONSIBILITY
RT 231

SCHOOL ROLE
ROLE DE L'ECOLE
PAPEL DE LA ESCUELA
RT 187

SCHOOL SCHEDULES
USE **TIMETABLES**

SCHOOL SEGREGATION
SEGREGATION SCOLAIRE
SEGREGACION ESCOLAR
May 1984
SN At policy and practice level
RT 180

SCHOOL SERVICES
SERVICES SCOLAIRES
SERVICIOS ESCOLARES
BT SERVICES
NT ANCILLARY SERVICES
    STUDENT PERSONNEL

SCHOOL SHOPS

SERVICES
RT 270
COMMUNITY SERVICES
SOCIAL SERVICES

SCHOOL SHOPS
ATELIER SCOLAIRE
TALLER ESCOLAR
SN In sense of workshops
RT 742

SCHOOL SIZE
DIMENSION DE L'ECOLE
TAMAÑO DE LA ESCUELA
NT SMALL SCHOOLS
RT 208

SCHOOL STATISTICS
STATISTIQUES SCOLAIRES
ESTADISTICA ESCOLAR
SN At the level of the individual school
BT EDUCATIONAL STATISTICS
RT 208

SCHOOL SUPERVISION
INSPECTION DES ECOLES
INSPECCION DE ESCUELAS
BT SUPERVISION
RT 210

SCHOOL SURVEYS
ENQUETE SCOLAIRE
ENCUESTA ESCOLAR
BT NATIONAL SURVEYS
RT 203

SCHOOL SYSTEMS
SYSTEME SCOLAIRE
SISTEMA ESCOLAR
UF FORMAL EDUCATION
SN Relating particularly to structural aspects of institutions of formal education
BT EDUCATIONAL ORGANIZATION
NT PUBLIC SCHOOL SYSTEMS
RURAL SCHOOL SYSTEMS
RT 260

SCHOOL TAXES
TAXE SCOLAIRE
IMPUESTO ESCOLAR
BT TAXES
RT 240

SCHOOL ZONING
USE **CATCHMENT AREA**

SCHOOLS
ECOLE
ESCUELA
SN Educational institutions below higher level
RT 187

SCIENCE
SCIENCE
CIENCIA
SN Totality of systematic activity of the sciences as an institution involving processes, attitudes, ethics and interrelationships of science with other institutions
RT 140
SCIENCES

SCIENCE CONSULTANTS
CONSEILLER PEDAGOGIQUE EN SCIENCES
CONSULTOR EN CIENCIAS
BT CONSULTANTS
RT 430

SCIENCE EDUCATION
FORMATION SCIENTIFIQUE
FORMACION CIENTIFICA
RT 670

SCIENCE EQUIPMENT
EQUIPEMENT SCIENTIFIQUE
EQUIPO CIENTIFICO
BT EQUIPMENT
RT 740

SCIENCE EXPERIMENTS
EXPERIENCES SCIENTIFIQUES
EXPERIMENTO CIENTIFICO
BT EXPERIMENTS
RT 671

SCIENCE INSTRUCTION
ENSEIGNEMENT DES SCIENCES
ENSEÑANZA DE LA CIENCIA
RT 670

SCIENCE PROGRAMMES
PROGRAMME DE SCIENCES
PROGRAMA DE CIENCIAS
RT 670

SCIENCE TEACHERS
PROFESSEUR DE SCIENCES
PROFESOR DE CIENCIAS
RT 425

SCIENCE TEACHING CENTRES
CENTRE D'ENSEIGNEMENT DES
 SCIENCES
CENTRO DE ENSEÑANZA DE LAS
 CIENCIAS
RT 312

SCIENCE TESTS
TEST DE CONNAISSANCES
 SCIENTIFIQUES
PRUEBA DE CONOCIMIENTOS
 CIENTIFICOS
BT EDUCATIONAL TESTS
RT 393

SCIENCES
SCIENCES
CIENCIAS
NT ASTRONOMY
 BEHAVIOURAL SCIENCES
 BIOLOGY
 CHEMISTRY
 EARTH SCIENCES
 PHYSICS
 SOCIAL SCIENCES
RT 630
 SCIENCE

SCIENTIFIC CONCEPTS
CONCEPT SCIENTIFIQUE
CONCEPTO CIENTIFICO
RT 630

SCIENTIFIC MANPOWER
MAIN-D'OEUVRE SCIENTIFIQUE
PERSONAL CIENTIFICO
 DISPONIBLE
SN Resources in scientific personnel
RT 154

SCIENTIFIC PERSONNEL
PERSONNEL SCIENTIFIQUE
PERSONAL CIENTIFICO
RT 441

SCIENTIFIC PRINCIPLES
PRINCIPE SCIENTIFIQUE
PRINCIPIO CIENTIFICO
RT 140

SCIENTIFIC RESEARCH
RECHERCHE SCIENTIFIQUE
INVESTIGACION CIENTIFICA
SN Research conducted to advance
 knowledge in a scientific field
RT 140

SCIENTISTS
SCIENTIFIQUE
CIENTIFICO
RT 463

SCRIPTS
MANUSCRIT
MANUSCRITO
RT 721

SCULPTURE
SCULPTURE
ESCULTURA
RT 610

SEAMEO
SEAMEO
SEAMEO
SN Southeast Asian Ministers of
 Education Organization

SEASONAL EMPLOYMENT
TRAVAIL SAISONNIER
TRABAJO DE TEMPORADA
BT EMPLOYMENT
RT 154

SEASONAL WORKERS
TRAVAILLEUR SAISONNIER
TRABAJADOR DE TEMPORADA
BT WORKERS
RT 451

SECOND LANGUAGE INSTRUCTION
ENSEIGNEMENT D'UNE LANGUE
   SECONDE
ENSEÑANZA DE UNA SEGUNDA
   LENGUA
May 1984
BT LANGUAGE INSTRUCTION
RT 662

SECOND LANGUAGES
LANGUE SECONDE
SEGUNDA LENGUA
RT 131

SECONDARY EDUCATION
ENSEIGNEMENT SECONDAIRE
ENSEÑANZA SECUNDARIA
NT LOWER SECONDARY
       EDUCATION
    UPPER SECONDARY
       EDUCATION
RT 185

SECONDARY GRADES
CLASSE DU SECONDAIRE
GRADOS DE SECUNDARIA
BT GRADES (PROGRAMME
       DIVISIONS)
RT 342

**SECONDARY SCHOOL
    CERTIFICATES**
DIPLOME D'ETUDES
   SECONDAIRES
CERTIFICADO DE ESTUDIOS
   SECUNDARIOS
BT EDUCATIONAL CERTIFICATES
RT 390

**SECONDARY SCHOOL
    COUNSELLORS**
CONSEILLER SCOLAIRE
   (SECONDAIRE)
CONSEJERO ESCOLAR
   (SECUNDARIA)
BT COUNSELLORS
RT 431

**SECONDARY SCHOOL
    CURRICULUM**
PROGRAMMES D'ETUDES
   SECONDAIRES
CURRICULO DE ESCUELA
   SECUNDARIA
RT 330

SECONDARY SCHOOL GRADUATES
DIPLOME DE L'ENSEIGNEMENT
   SECONDAIRE
GRADUADO DE SECUNDARIA
BT GRADUATES
RT 411

SECONDARY SCHOOL INSPECTORS
INSPECTEUR DE
   L'ENSEIGNEMENT SECONDAIRE
INSPECTOR DE ENSEÑANZA
   SECUNDARIA
BT INSPECTORS
RT 420

**SECONDARY SCHOOL
    MATHEMATICS**
MATHEMATIQUES (NIVEAU
   SECONDAIRE)
MATEMATICA (NIVEL
   SECUNDARIO)
RT 670

SECONDARY SCHOOL SCIENCE
SCIENCES (NIVEAU SECONDAIRE)
CIENCIAS (NIVEL SECUNDARIO)
RT 670

SECONDARY SCHOOL STUDENTS
ELEVE DU SECONDAIRE
ALUMNO DE SECUNDARIA
RT 411

SECONDARY SCHOOL TEACHERS
MAITRE DU SECONDAIRE
PROFESOR DE SECUNDARIA
BT TEACHERS
RT 421

SELF INSTRUCTION

SECONDARY SCHOOLS
ECOLE SECONDAIRE
ESCUELA SECUNDARIA
UF   HIGH SCHOOLS
NT   COMPREHENSIVE
      SECONDARY SCHOOLS
     GENERAL SECONDARY
      SCHOOLS
     LOWER SECONDARY
      SCHOOLS
     TECHNICAL SECONDARY
      SCHOOLS
     UPPER SECONDARY SCHOOLS
     VOCATIONAL SECONDARY
      SCHOOLS
RT   301

SECULAR EDUCATION
ENSEIGNEMENT LAIC
EDUCACION LAICA
RT   180

SECURITY
SENTIMENT DE SECURITE
SENTIMIENTO DE SEGURIDAD
BT   PSYCHOLOGICAL NEEDS
RT   540

SECURITY COUNCIL
CONSEIL DE SECURITE
CONSEJO DE SEGURIDAD

SELECTION
SELECTION
SELECCION
SN   Applied to students
NT   COMPETITIVE SELECTION
     SELECTION PROCEDURES
RT   266

SELECTION PROCEDURES
PROCEDURE DE SELECTION
PROCEDIMIENTO DE SELECCION
BT   SELECTION
RT   266

SELF ACTUALIZATION
ACCOMPLISSEMENT DE SOI
REALIZACION DE SI MISMO
SN   The belief in or the process of
     developing the actuality of one's
     idealized image
BT   SELF CONCEPT
RT   555

SELF CONCEPT
IMAGE DE SOI
CONCEPTO DE SI MISMO
UF   SELF ESTEEM
NT   SELF ACTUALIZATION
RT   555

SELF CONTROL
CONTROLE DE SOI
AUTOCONTROL
RT   560

SELF DIRECTED GROUPS
GROUPE AUTO-GERE
GRUPO AUTODIRIGIDO
BT   GROUPS
RT   443

SELF ESTEEM
USE **SELF CONCEPT**

SELF EVALUATION
AUTO-EVALUATION
AUTOEVALUACION
RT   555

SELF EXPRESSION
EXPRESSION DE SOI
EXPRESION DE SI MISMO
RT   555

SELF GOVERNMENT
USE **INSTITUTIONAL SELF
     MANAGEMENT**

SELF INSTRUCTION
AUTODIDAXIE
AUTOAPRENDIZAJE

May 1984

RT   352
     SELF INSTRUCTIONAL

SELF INSTRUCTIONAL AIDS

    METHODS
    SELF INSTRUCTIONAL
      PROGRAMMES
    SELF INSTRUCTIONAL AIDS

SELF INSTRUCTIONAL AIDS
AUXILIAIRE AUTODIDACTIQUE
AUXILIAR AUTODIDACTICO
RT   730
    SELF INSTRUCTION

SELF INSTRUCTIONAL METHODS
METHODE AUTODIDACTIQUE
METODO AUTODIDACTICO
BT   EDUCATIONAL METHODS
RT   355
    SELF INSTRUCTION

**SELF INSTRUCTIONAL
   PROGRAMMES**
PROGRAMME D'AUTODIDAXIE
PROGRAMA DE
   AUTOAPRENDIZAJE
RT   320
    SELF INSTRUCTION

SEMANTICS
SEMANTIQUE
SEMANTICA
RT   622

SEMESTER DIVISIONS
DIVISION SEMESTRIELLE
DIVISION SEMESTRAL
BT   SCHOOL CALENDARS
RT   344

SEMINARS
SEMINAIRE
SEMINARIO
NT   EDUCATIONAL SEMINARS
     TEACHER SEMINARS
RT   355

SEMISKILLED OCCUPATIONS
METIER SPECIALISE
OCUPACION SEMICALIFICADA
BT   OCCUPATIONS
RT   155

SEMISKILLED WORKERS
OUVRIER SPECIALISE
TRABAJADOR SEMICALIFICADO
BT   WORKERS
RT   451

SENEGAL
SENEGAL
SENEGAL
BT   WEST AFRICA
RT   FRENCH SPEAKING AFRICA

SENIOR CIVIL SERVANTS
HAUT FONCTIONNAIRE
ALTO FUNCIONARIO
RT   460

SENSORY AIDS
AIDE SENSORIELLE
AYUDAS SENSORIALES
SN   All equipment and materials
     designed for the sensory capacities
     of the handicapped with a view to
     assisting their adaptation and
     education
RT   734

SENSORY DEPRIVATION
DEFICIT SENSORIEL
DEFICIENCIA SENSORIAL
RT   570

SENSORY EXPERIENCE
EXPERIENCE SENSORIELLE
EXPERIENCIA SENSORIAL
BT   EXPERIENCE
RT   562

SENSORY TRAINING
EDUCATION SENSORIELLE
EDUCACION SENSORIAL
RT   351

SENTENCE STRUCTURE
STRUCTURE DE LA PHRASE
ESTRUCTURA DE LA ORACION
SN   Covers punctuation
RT   622

SEQUENTIAL APPROACH
METHODE SEQUENTIELLE
METODO SECUENCIAL
RT 331

SEQUENTIAL LEARNING
APPRENTISSAGE SEQUENTIEL
APRENDIZAJE SECUENCIAL
BT LEARNING
RT 512

SERIALS
SERIE (PUBLICATIONS)
PUBLICACION SERIADA
NT PERIODICALS
RT 720

SERVICE OCCUPATIONS
METIER DU SECTEUR TERTIAIRE
OCUPACION EN EL SECTOR TERCIARIO
BT OCCUPATIONS
RT 155

SERVICE WORKERS
TRAVAILLEUR DU SECTEUR TERTIAIRE
EMPLEADO DEL SECTOR TERCIARIO
BT EMPLOYEES
RT 451

SERVICES
SERVICES
SERVICIOS
SN A series of activities undertaken in the public interest, by extension also the administrative structure responsible for them
NT COMMUNITY SERVICES
    EMPLOYMENT SERVICES
    FINANCIAL SERVICES
    FOOD SERVICES
    HEALTH SERVICES
    INFORMATION SERVICES
    SCHOOL SERVICES
    SOCIAL SERVICES
    WELFARE SERVICES
RT 107
    270

SEVENTEENTH CENTURY
DIX-SEPTIEME SIECLE
SIGLO DIECISIETE

May 1984

SEX (CHARACTERISTICS)
SEXE (CARACTERISTIQUES)
SEXO (CARACTERISTICAS)
RT 501

SEX DIFFERENCES
DIFFERENCE ENTRE SEXES
DIFERENCIA ENTRE SEXOS
BT INDIVIDUAL DIFFERENCES
RT 501

SEX EDUCATION
EDUCATION SEXUELLE
EDUCACION SEXUAL
RT 683

SEXUALITY
SEXUALITE
SEXUALIDAD
RT 502

SEYCHELLES
SEYCHELLES
SEYCHELLES
BT INDIAN OCEAN TERRITORIES

SHARED SERVICES
SERVICE COMMUN
SERVICIOS COMUNES
SN Between a number of educational institutions
RT 270

SHELTERED EMPLOYMENT
EMPLOI PROTEGE
EMPLEO VIGILADO
SN Special employment for handicapped people or those who are unable to take employment on the open market
BT EMPLOYMENT
RT 374

SHOP CURRICULUM
PROGRAMMES D'ATELIER
PROGRAMA DE TALLER
SN Relating to programmes in the workshop
RT 672

SHORT COURSES
COURS DE BREVE DUREE
CURSO DE CORTA DURACION
UF MINICOURSES
BT COURSES
NT VACATION COURSES
RT 334

SHORT STORIES
NOUVELLE
CUENTO
RT 616

SIAM
May 1984
USE **THAILAND**

SIBERIA
SIBERIE
SIBERIA
May 1984
BT USSR

SIBLINGS
ENFANTS DU MEME LIT
HERMANOS
RT 401

SIERRA LEONE
SIERRA LEONE
SIERRA LEONA
BT WEST AFRICA
RT ENGLISH SPEAKING AFRICA

SIGHT
VISION
VISION
May 1984
RT 503

SIGHT METHOD
METHODE DE VISUALISATION
METODO DE VISUALIZACION
RT 661

SIGHT VOCABULARY
VOCABULAIRE VISUEL
VOCABULARIO VISUAL
SN Words recognized immediately in reading without need for word and analysis procedures
RT 620

SIKKIM
SIKKIM
SIKKIM
May 1984
BT HIMALAYAN STATES

SILENT READING
LECTURE SILENCIEUSE
LECTURA SILENCIOSA
RT 661

SIMULATION
SIMULATION
SIMULACION
SN Duplication of the essential characteristics of a task or situation
RT 355

SINGAPORE
SINGAPOUR
SINGAPUR
BT MALAYSIA

SINGING
CHANT
CANTO
RT 610

SINGLE CONCEPT FILMS
FILM UNITHEMATIQUE
PELICULA DE TEMA UNICO
BT FILMS
RT 730

SINO TIBETAN LANGUAGES
LANGUES SINO–TIBETAINES
LENGUAS CHINOTIBETANAS
RT 625

SITE PLANNING
AMENAGEMENT DU TERRAIN
ACONDICIONAMIENTO DEL
   TERRENO
RT 250

SITES
TERRAIN
TERRENOS
RT 710

SKILL ANALYSIS
ANALYSE DES COMPETENCES
ANALISIS DE HABILIDADES
SN Breaking down manipulative skills
   into their components
RT 331

SKILL DEVELOPMENT
DEVELOPPEMENT DES
   COMPETENCES
DESARROLLO DE HABILIDADES
RT 534

SKILLED OCCUPATIONS
METIER QUALIFIE
OCUPACION CALIFICADA
BT OCCUPATIONS
RT 155

SKILLED WORKERS
OUVRIER QUALIFIE
TRABAJADOR CALIFICADO
BT WORKERS
RT 451

SKILLS
COMPETENCE
HABILIDAD
NT BASIC SKILLS
      COMMUNICATION SKILLS
      LANGUAGE SKILLS
      MECHANICAL SKILLS
      STUDY SKILLS
      TEACHING SKILLS

RT 533

SLAVIC LANGUAGES
LANGUES SLAVES
LENGUAS ESLAVAS
RT 625

SLEEP
SOMMEIL
SUEÑO
RT 503

SLIDES
DIAPOSITIVE
DIAPOSITIVA
RT 730

SLOW LEARNERS
ELEVE A APPRENTISSAGE LENT
ALUMNO DE APRENDIZAJE
   LENTO
UF EDUCATIONALLY RETARDED
      LOW ABILITY STUDENTS
RT 415

SLUMS
USE **DEPRESSED AREAS
   (ECONOMIC)**

SMALL SCALE INDUSTRY
PETITE INDUSTRIE
PEQUEÑA INDUSTRIA
BT INDUSTRY
RT 150

SMALL SCHOOLS
PETITE ECOLE
ESCUELA PEQUEÑA
BT SCHOOL SIZE
RT 208

SMOKING
USAGE DU TABAC
FUMAR
RT 542

SOCIAL ACTION

SOCIAL ACTION
ACTION SOCIALE
ACCION SOCIAL
RT 120

SOCIAL ADJUSTMENT
ADAPTATION SOCIALE
ADAPTACION SOCIAL
BT ADJUSTMENT
RT 551

SOCIAL ADVANCEMENT
PROMOTION SOCIALE
PROMOCION SOCIAL
RT 121

SOCIAL AGENCIES
ORGANISME SOCIAL
ORGANISMO SOCIAL
BT AGENCIES
RT 103

SOCIAL ATTITUDES
ATTITUDE SOCIALE
ACTITUD SOCIAL
BT ATTITUDES
RT 552

SOCIAL BACKGROUND
MILIEU SOCIAL
MEDIO SOCIAL
NT FAMILY BACKGROUND
RT 120

SOCIAL CHANGE
CHANGEMENT SOCIAL
CAMBIO SOCIAL
RT 120

SOCIAL CLASS
CLASSE SOCIALE
CLASE SOCIAL
NT MIDDLE CLASS
    UPPER CLASS
    WORKING CLASS
RT 121

SOCIAL DEVELOPMENT
DEVELOPPEMENT SOCIAL
DESARROLLO SOCIAL
May 1984
BT DEVELOPMENT
RT 151

SOCIAL DISADVANTAGEMENT
HANDICAP SOCIAL
MARGINACION SOCIAL
RT 121

SOCIAL DISCRIMINATION
DISCRIMINATION SOCIALE
DISCRIMINACION SOCIAL
RT 121

SOCIAL EDUCATION
USE **COMMUNITY EDUCATION**

SOCIAL ENVIRONMENT
ENVIRONNEMENT SOCIAL
AMBIENTE SOCIAL
BT CULTURAL ENVIRONMENT
RT 550

SOCIAL EXPERIENCE
EXPERIENCE SOCIALE
EXPERIENCIA SOCIAL
BT EXPERIENCE
RT 562

SOCIAL FACTORS
FACTEUR SOCIAL
FACTOR SOCIAL
RT 285

SOCIAL INTEGRATION
INTEGRATION SOCIALE
INTEGRACION SOCIAL
RT 121
    NATIONAL INTEGRATION

SOCIAL MATURITY
MATURITE SOCIALE
MADUREZ SOCIAL
RT 531

SOCIAL MOBILITY
MOBILITE SOCIALE
MOVILIDAD SOCIAL
BT MOBILITY
RT 121

SOCIAL PLANNING
PLANIFICATION SOCIALE
PLANIFICACION SOCIAL
BT PLANNING
NT FAMILY PLANNING
RT 120

SOCIAL POLICIES
POLITIQUE SOCIALE
POLITICA SOCIAL
BT POLICIES
NT LANGUAGE POLICY
RT 120
    EDUCATIONAL POLICIES

SOCIAL PROBLEMS
PROBLEME SOCIAL
PROBLEMA SOCIAL
RT 121

SOCIAL PSYCHOLOGY
PSYCHOLOGIE SOCIALE
PSICOLOGIA SOCIAL
BT PSYCHOLOGY
RT 642

SOCIAL RELATIONS
RELATIONS SOCIALES
RELACIONES SOCIALES
NT INTERGROUP RELATIONS
    LABOUR RELATIONS
    RACE RELATIONS
RT 553

SOCIAL SCIENCES
SCIENCES SOCIALES
CIENCIAS SOCIALES
BT SCIENCES
NT ANTHROPOLOGY
    DEMOGRAPHY
    ECONOMICS
    GEOGRAPHY
    HISTORY
    POLITICAL SCIENCE
    SOCIAL STUDIES
    SOCIOLOGY
RT 640

SOCIAL SCIENTISTS
SPECIALISTE DES SCIENCES
    SOCIALES
ESPECIALISTA EN CIENCIAS
    SOCIALES
RT 462

SOCIAL SERVICES
SERVICES SOCIAUX
SERVICIOS SOCIALES
BT SERVICES
RT 107
    SCHOOL SERVICES

SOCIAL STATUS
STATUT SOCIAL
POSICION SOCIAL
BT STATUS
RT 121

SOCIAL STUDIES
ETUDES SOCIALES
ESTUDIOS SOCIALES
SN Social studies consist of
    adaptations of knowledge from the
    social sciences for teaching
    purposes at the primary and
    secondary levels of education
BT SOCIAL SCIENCES
RT 640

SOCIAL SYSTEMS
SYSTEME SOCIAL
SISTEMA SOCIAL
RT 120

SOCIAL WELFARE
BIEN-ETRE SOCIAL
BIENESTAR SOCIAL
BT WELFARE
RT 100
    STUDENT WELFARE
    TEACHER WELFARE

SOCIAL WORK

SOCIAL WORK
TRAVAIL SOCIAL
TRABAJO SOCIAL
RT 120

SOCIAL WORKERS
TRAVAILLEUR SOCIAL
TRABAJADOR SOCIAL
RT 462

SOCIALIZATION
SOCIALISATION
SOCIALIZACION
NT POLITICAL SOCIALIZATION
RT 553

SOCIALLY DISADVANTAGED
DEFAVORISE SOCIAL
DESFAVORECIDO SOCIAL
RT 402

SOCIALLY MALADJUSTED
INADAPTE SOCIAL
INADAPTADO SOCIAL
SN Children or adults.
RT 403

SOCIETY ISLANDS
ILES DE LA SOCIETE
ISLAS DE LA SOCIEDAD
May 1984
UF TAHITI
BT FRENCH POLYNESIA

SOCIOCULTURAL PATTERNS
MODELE SOCIOCULTUREL
MODELO SOCIOCULTURAL
RT 120

SOCIOECONOMIC BACKGROUND
MILIEU SOCIO–ECONOMIQUE
MEDIO SOCIOECONOMICO
UF ECONOMIC BACKGROUND
RT 120

SOCIOECONOMIC STATUS
STATUT SOCIO–ECONOMIQUE
CONDICION SOCIOECONOMICA
BT STATUS
RT 121

SOCIOLOGY
SOCIOLOGIE
SOCIOLOGIA
BT BEHAVIOURAL SCIENCES
    SOCIAL SCIENCES
NT EDUCATIONAL SOCIOLOGY
RT 642

SOCIOMETRIC TECHNIQUES
TECHNIQUE SOCIOMETRIQUE
TECNICA SOCIOMETRICA
RT 283

SOCIOPSYCHOLOGICAL SERVICES
SERVICES PSYCHOSOCIAUX
SERVICIOS PSICOSOCIALES
BT PROFESSIONAL SERVICES
RT 270

SOIL CONSERVATION
CONSERVATION DU SOL
CONSERVACION DEL SUELO
RT 646

SOLOMON ISLANDS
ILES SALOMON
ISLAS SALOMON
May 1984
BT MELANESIA

SOMALIA
SOMALIE
SOMALIA
BT EAST AFRICA

SOUND FILMS
FILM SONORE
PELICULA SONORA
BT FILMS
RT 730

SOUND SLIDE PRESENTATIONS
DIAPORAMA
DIAPOSITIVAS CON SONIDO
BT MULTIMEDIA INSTRUCTION
RT 732

SOUTH AFRICA (REPUBLIC)
AFRIQUE DU SUD (REPUBLIQUE)
SUDAFRICA (REPUBLICA)
May 1984
BT SOUTHERN AFRICA
RT ENGLISH SPEAKING AFRICA

SOUTH AMERICA
AMERIQUE DU SUD
AMERICA DEL SUR
BT LATIN AMERICA
NT ARGENTINA
 BOLIVIA
 BRAZIL
 CHILE
 COLOMBIA
 ECUADOR
 FRENCH GUIANA
 GALAPAGOS ISLANDS
 GUYANA
 PARAGUAY
 PERU
 SURINAME
 URUGUAY
 VENEZUELA
RT FALKLAND ISLANDS

SOUTH ASIA
ASIE DU SUD
ASIA DEL SUR
May 1984
BT ASIA
NT BANGLADESH
 HIMALAYAN STATES
 INDIA
 MALDIVES
 PAKISTAN
 SRI LANKA
RT SOUTH EAST ASIA

SOUTH EAST ASIA
ASIE DU SUD-EST
ASIA SUDORIENTAL
BT ASIA
NT BURMA
 INDONESIA
 MALAYSIA
 PAPUA NEW GUINEA
 PHILIPPINES
 PORTUGUESE TIMOR

THAILAND
RT SOUTH ASIA

SOUTH KOREA
USE **KOREA R**

SOUTH POLE
POLE SUD
POLO SUR
May 1984
BT POLAR REGIONS
RT ANTARCTIC REGIONS
 NORTH POLE

SOUTH WEST AFRICA
USE **NAMIBIA**

SOUTHERN AFRICA
AFRIQUE MERIDIONALE
AFRICA MERIDIONAL
BT AFRICA SOUTH OF THE
 SAHARA
NT ANGOLA
 BOTSWANA
 LESOTHO
 MADAGASCAR
 MALAWI
 MOZAMBIQUE
 NAMIBIA
 ZIMBABWE
 SOUTH AFRICA (REPUBLIC)
 SWAZILAND
 ZAMBIA
 COMOROS
 MAURITIUS
 REUNION ISLAND
 SAINT HELENA
RT INDIAN OCEAN TERRITORIES

SOUTHERN HEMISPHERE
HEMISPHERE SUD
HEMISFERIO SUR
May 1984
RT NORTHERN HEMISPHERE

SOUTHERN YEMEN
USE **DEMOCRATIC YEMEN**

SPACE STANDARDS
NORME DE SURFACE
NORMAS REFERIDAS AL ESPACIO
RT   250

SPAIN
ESPAGNE
ESPAÑA
BT   MEDITERRANEAN
        COUNTRIES
      WESTERN EUROPE

SPANISH
LANGUE ESPAGNOLE
LENGUA ESPAÑOLA
RT   626

SPANISH GUINEA   May 1984
USE **EQUATORIAL GUINEA**

SPEAKING
EXPRESSION ORALE
EXPRESION ORAL
BT   LANGUAGE ARTS
RT   620

SPEAKING ACTIVITIES
ACTIVITE VERBALE
ACTIVIDAD DISCURSIVA
RT   537

SPECIAL CLASSES
CLASSE SPECIALE
CLASE ESPECIAL
BT   CLASSES
NT   OPPORTUNITY CLASSES
RT   343
        REGULAR CLASS PLACEMENT
        SPECIAL SCHOOLS

SPECIAL CLASSROOMS
SALLE SPECIALISEE
SALA DE CLASE ESPECIAL
BT   CLASSROOMS
RT   711

SPECIAL DEGREE PROGRAMMES
PROGRAMME UNIVERSITAIRE
   SPECIAL
PROGRAMA ESPECIAL
   UNIVERSITARIO
SN   Programmes geared to the needs
     of adult students admitted on the
     basis of previous experience or
     self–education rather than college
     credit
BT   COLLEGE PROGRAMMES
RT   320

SPECIAL EDUCATION
EDUCATION SPECIALE
EDUCACION ESPECIAL
NT   BLIND EDUCATION
     DEAF EDUCATION
RT   186

SPECIAL EDUCATION CENTRES
USE **SPECIAL SCHOOLS**

SPECIAL EDUCATION TEACHERS
EDUCATEUR SPECIALISE
MAESTRO DE EDUCACION
   ESPECIAL
BT   TEACHERS
RT   421

SPECIAL PROGRAMMES
PROGRAMME D'EDUCATION
   SPECIALE
PROGRAMA DE EDUCACION
   ESPECIAL
SN   Designed for handicapped students
BT   INSTRUCTIONAL
        PROGRAMMES
RT   320

SPECIAL SCHOOLS
ECOLE SPECIALE
ESCUELA ESPECIAL
UF   SPECIAL EDUCATION
        CENTRES
SN   For handicapped students
RT   304
        REGULAR CLASS PLACEMENT
        SPECIAL CLASSES

SPECIALIST IN EDUCATION DEGREES
LICENCE EN SCIENCES DE L'EDUCATION
LICENCIA EN CIENCIAS DE LA EDUCACION
SN Awarded for specialized study of two or more years in some field of education after first degree
BT DEGREES (TITLES)
RT 390

SPECIALISTS
SPECIALISTE
ESPECIALISTA
SN Professionals with a full-time specialized function in educational programmes
NT CHILD DEVELOPMENT SPECIALISTS
INTERNATIONAL EXPERTS
LEARNING SPECIALISTS
MEDIA SPECIALISTS
RT 430

SPECIFICATIONS
SPECIFICATION
ESPECIFICACION
NT EDUCATIONAL SPECIFICATIONS
PERFORMANCE SPECIFICATIONS
RT 232

SPEECH
PAROLE
HABLA
NT ARTICULATION (SPEECH)
CODED SPEECH
DICTION
RT 532

SPEECH HABITS
MODE D'EXPRESSION ORALE
MANERA DE HABLAR
RT 542

SPEECH HANDICAPS
TROUBLE DE LA PAROLE
TRASTORNOS DEL HABLA
BT HANDICAPS
RT 571

SPEECH INSTRUCTION
ENTRAINEMENT A L'EXPRESSION ORALE
EJERCITACION DE LA EXPRESION ORAL
RT 662

SPEECH PATHOLOGY
PATHOLOGIE DE LA PAROLE
PATOLOGIA DEL HABLA
RT 372

SPEECH THERAPISTS
ORTHOPHONISTE
ORTOFONOLOGO
BT THERAPISTS
RT 432

SPEECH THERAPY
ORTHOPHONIE
ORTOFONIA
BT THERAPY
RT 373

SPELLING
ORTHOGRAPHE
ORTOGRAFIA
RT 620

SPELLING INSTRUCTION
ENSEIGNEMENT DE L'ORTHOGRAPHE
ENSEÑANZA DE LA ORTOGRAFIA
RT 663

SPORTS
USE ATHLETIC ACTIVITIES

SPORTS FACILITIES
INSTALLATION SPORTIVE
INSTALACIONES DEPORTIVAS
BT EDUCATIONAL FACILITIES
RT 712

SRI LANKA
SRI LANKA
SRI LANKA
UF CEYLON
BT SOUTH ASIA

STAFF HOUSING
LOGEMENT DE FONCTION
ALOJAMIENTO PARA EL
   PERSONAL
BT HOUSING
RT 712

STANDARDIZED TESTS
TEST STANDARDISE
PRUEBA ESTANDARIZADA
RT 392

STANDARDS
NORMES
NORMAS
NT EQUIPMENT STANDARDS
RT 232

STATE AID
USE **CENTRAL GOVERNMENT AID**

STATE AID TO PROVINCES
AIDE DE L'ETAT AUX PROVINCES
AYUDA DEL ESTADO A LAS
   PROVINCIAS
BT CENTRAL GOVERNMENT AID
NT EQUALIZATION AID
RT 106

STATE CHURCH SEPARATION
SEPARATION EGLISE-ETAT
SEPARACION IGLESIA-ESTADO
RT 101
      RELIGIOUS INSTITUTIONS

STATE SCHOOLS
USE **PUBLIC SCHOOLS**

STATE UNIVERSITIES
USE **PUBLIC COLLEGES**

STATISTICAL ANALYSIS
ANALYSE STATISTIQUE
ANALISIS ESTADISTICO
UF ANALYSIS OF VARIANCE
      FACTOR ANALYSIS
      HYPOTHESIS TESTING
RT 284

STATISTICAL DATA
DONNEE STATISTIQUE
DATOS ESTADISTICOS
NT EDUCATIONAL STATISTICS
RT 284

STATISTICAL STUDIES
ETUDE STATISTIQUE
ESTUDIO ESTADISTICO
RT 282

STATISTICAL TABLES
TABLEAU STATISTIQUE
CUADRO ESTADISTICO
RT 880

STATUS
STATUT
STATUS
SN Individual's position in social
      system in respect of rights, duties
      and prestige
NT ECONOMIC STATUS
      SOCIAL STATUS
      SOCIOECONOMIC STATUS
      TEACHER STATUS
RT 121

STATUS NEED
BESOIN D'AFFIRMATION
NECESIDAD DE AFIRMACION
   PERSONAL
BT PSYCHOLOGICAL NEEDS
RT 536

STEREOTYPES
STEREOTYPE
ESTEREOTIPO
RT 552

STIMULANTS
STIMULANT
ESTIMULANTE
RT 751

STIMULI
STIMULUS
ESTIMULO
NT AURAL STIMULI
　　VISUAL STIMULI
RT 361

STIMULUS DEVICES
DISPOSITIF DE STIMULATION
DISPOSITIVO PARA ESTIMULAR
RT 734

STORY TELLING
NARRATION D'HISTOIRES
NARRACION DE CUENTOS
RT 663

STREAMING
USE **ABILITY GROUPING**

STRUCTURAL ANALYSIS
ANALYSE STRUCTURALE
ANALISIS ESTRUCTURAL
RT 331

STRUCTURAL GRAMMAR
GRAMMAIRE STRUCTURALE
GRAMATICA ESTRUCTURAL
BT GRAMMAR
RT 622

STUDENT ACHIEVEMENT
RENDEMENT DE L'ELEVE
RENDIMIENTO DEL ALUMNO
　　　　　　　　　　May 1984
NT LITERACY ACHIEVEMENT
RT 535

STUDENT ADJUSTMENT
ADAPTATION DE L'ELEVE
ADAPTACION DEL ALUMNO
UF SCHOOL ADJUSTMENT
BT ADJUSTMENT
RT 551

STUDENT ATTITUDES
ATTITUDE DE L'ELEVE
ACTITUD DEL ALUMNO
BT ATTITUDES
RT 552

STUDENT BEHAVIOUR
COMPORTEMENT DE L'ELEVE
COMPORTAMIENTO DEL ALUMNO
BT BEHAVIOUR
RT 560

STUDENT CHARACTERISTICS
CARACTERISTIQUE DE L'ELEVE
CARACTERISTICAS DEL
　　ESTUDIANTE
RT 561

**STUDENT COLLEGE
　RELATIONSHIP**
RELATIONS UNIVERSITE-
　　ETUDIANTS
RELACION ESTUDIANTE-
　　UNIVERSIDAD
SN The relationship between a college
　　and its students
BT RELATIONSHIP
RT 380

STUDENT DEVELOPED MATERIALS
MATERIEL ELABORE PAR LES
　　ELEVES
MATERIAL ELABORADO POR EL
　　ALUMNO
SN Instructional materials prepared by
　　students
RT 725

STUDENT EMPLOYMENT
EMPLOI DES ETUDIANTS
EMPLEO DEL ESTUDIANTE
RT 266

STUDENT EVALUATION
EVALUATION DES ETUDIANTS
EVALUACION DEL ALUMNO
RT 391

STUDENT GROUPING
USE **GROUPING (INSTRUCTIONAL PURPOSES)**

STUDENT HOUSING
LOGEMENT DES ETUDIANTS
ALOJAMIENTO PARA ESTUDIANTES
BT   BOARDING FACILITIES
RT   712

STUDENT LOANS
PRET D'ETUDE
PRESTAMO PARA ESTUDIOS
RT   242

STUDENT MOBILITY
MOBILITE DES ETUDIANTS
MOVILIDAD DEL ALUMNO
BT   MOBILITY
RT   206

STUDENT MOTIVATION
MOTIVATION DE L'ELEVE
MOTIVACION DEL ALUMNO
BT   MOTIVATION
RT   541

STUDENT NEEDS
BESOINS DE L'ELEVE
NECESIDADES DEL ALUMNO
RT   350

STUDENT ORGANIZATIONS
ORGANISATION D'ETUDIANTS
ORGANIZACION DE ESTUDIANTES
BT   NATIONAL ORGANIZATIONS
RT   110

STUDENT PARTICIPATION
PARTICIPATION DE L'ELEVE
PARTICIPACION DEL ALUMNO
BT   PARTICIPATION
RT   380

STUDENT PERSONNEL SERVICES
SERVICES SOCIAUX AUX ETUDIANTS
SERVICIOS SOCIALES PARA ESTUDIANTES
SN   Supportive, non-instructional services to school or college students in an institutional setting
BT   SCHOOL SERVICES
RT   270

STUDENT PLACEMENT
USE **GRADING**

STUDENT PROGRESS
CURSUS SCOLAIRE
TRAYECTORIA DEL ESTUDIANTE
SN   Movement of individual or of group through successive levels and forms of education
RT   266

STUDENT PROJECTS
PROJET D'ELEVE
PROYECTO DEL ALUMNO
RT   357

STUDENT PROMOTION
PROMOTION DES ELEVES
PROMOCION DE LOS ESTUDIANTES
SN   Process by which a student is passed to the next higher instruction or grade level
RT   266

STUDENT RECORDS
DOSSIER SCOLAIRE
HISTORIA DEL ALUMNO
BT   RECORDS (FORMS)
RT   723

STUDENT RESEARCH
RECHERCHE FAITE PAR LES ELEVES
INVESTIGACION REALIZADA POR ALUMNOS
RT   357

STUDENT ROLE
ROLE DE L'ELEVE
PAPEL DEL ALUMNO
RT   187

STUDENT SCHOOL RELATIONSHIP
RELATIONS ECOLE–ELEVES
RELACION ALUMNO–ESCUELA
BT   RELATIONSHIP
RT   380

STUDENT TEACHER RATIO
RAPPORT MAITRE–ELEVES
PROPORCION DOCENTES–
   ALUMNOS
RT   207

**STUDENT TEACHER
   RELATIONSHIP**
RELATIONS MAITRE–ELEVE
RELACION ALUMNO–DOCENTE
UF   TEACHER STUDENT
        RELATIONSHIP
BT   INTERPERSONAL
        RELATIONSHIP
RT   380

STUDENT TEACHERS
ELEVE–MAITRE
ALUMNO–DOCENTE
RT   424

STUDENT TEACHING
USE **PRACTICE TEACHING**

STUDENT TRANSFER
TRANSFERT D'ELEVES
TRANSFERENCIA DE
   ESTUDIANTES
SN   Applied to students
BT   TRANSFER POLICY
RT   266

STUDENT UNREST
CONTESTATION ESTUDIANTINE
AGITACION ESTUDIANTIL
RT   380

STUDENT WELFARE
PROTECTION DES ETUDIANTS
BIENESTAR DEL ALUMNO
BT   WELFARE
RT   200
        SOCIAL WELFARE

STUDENTS
ELEVE
ALUMNO
UF   PUPILS
RT   410

STUDY
ETUDE
ESTUDIO
RT   512

STUDY ABROAD
ETUDES A L'ETRANGER
ESTUDIOS EN EL EXTRANJERO
UF   TRAINING ABROAD
RT   335

STUDY CENTRES
CENTRE D'ETUDES
CENTRO DE ESTUDIOS
UF   LEARNING CENTRES
SN   Institutions organized on non–
        formal lines to provide human
        and material resources for those
        wishing to pursue a particular
        aspect of their education
BT   ADULT EDUCATION CENTRES
RT   311

STUDY GUIDE
LIVRE DE L'ELEVE
GUIA DEL ESTUDIANTE
SN   A form of textbook specifically
        designed for the learner, often to
        be written in; used in nonformal
        as well as formal education,
        covers such literacy material as
        primers or cartillas
BT   GUIDES
RT   880

STUDY HABITS
MODE D'ETUDE
MANERA DE ESTUDIAR
RT   542

STUDY LEAVE

STUDY LEAVE
USE **EDUCATIONAL LEAVE**

STUDY SKILLS
APTITUDE AUX ETUDES
APTITUD PARA LOS ESTUDIOS
BT SKILLS
RT 533

STUDY TOURS
VOYAGE D'ETUDES
VIAJE DE ESTUDIOS
RT 335

SUBJECTS OF STUDY
SUJET D'ETUDES
MATERIAS DE ESTUDIO
RT 331

SUBSTITUTE TEACHERS
MAITRE SUPPLEANT
DOCENTE SUPLENTE
RT 424

SUBURBAN SCHOOLS
ECOLE SUBURBAINE
ESCUELA SUBURBANA
RT 303

SUBVENTIONS
SUBVENTION
SUBVENCION
SN Funds made available to agencies, organizations or institutions by a public source of financing
RT 241

SUCCESS
SUCCES
EXITO
RT 535

SUCCESS FACTORS
FACTEUR DE SUCCES
FACTOR DE EXITO
RT 285

SUDAN
SOUDAN
SUDAN
BT ARAB COUNTRIES
    EAST AFRICA
RT ENGLISH SPEAKING AFRICA

SUMATRA
USE **INDONESIA**

SUMMATIVE EVALUATION
EVALUATION SOMMATIVE
EVALUACION ACUMULATIVA
BT PROGRAMME EVALUATION
RT 205

SUMMER SCHOOLS
ECOLE D'ETE
ESCUELA DE VERANO
RT 303
    VACATION COURSES

SUPERINTENDENT ROLE
ROLE DU DIRECTEUR REGIONAL
PAPEL DEL JEFE REGIONAL
RT 262

SUPERINTENDENTS
DIRECTEUR REGIONAL DE L'ENSEIGNEMENT
SUPERINTENDENTE ESCOLAR
SN In charge of unit, usually province or district of school system
BT EDUCATIONAL ADMINISTRATORS
RT 420

SUPERVISED FARM PRACTICE
STAGE AGRICOLE CONTROLE
PRACTICA AGRICOLA SUPERVISADA
SN Experience under school direction related to classroom instruction
BT PRACTICE PERIODS
RT 673

May 1984

SUPERVISION
INSPECTION
INSPECCION
UF INSPECTION
NT SCHOOL SUPERVISION
     TEACHER SUPERVISION
RT 210

SUPERVISOR QUALIFICATIONS
QUALIFICATION DE
  L'INSPECTEUR
CALIFICACION DEL INSPECTOR
BT QUALIFICATIONS
RT 223

SUPERVISORS
CONSEILLER PEDAGOGIQUE
CONSEJERO PEDAGOGICO
SN Professional staff with educational functions but no necessarily administrative responsibilities in respect of group of educational institutions or particular curriculum area
BT EDUCATIONAL PERSONNEL
RT 420

SUPERVISORY METHODS
METHODE D'INSPECTION
METODO DE INSPECCION
RT 210

SUPPLEMENTARY READING MATERIALS
MATERIEL COMPLEMENTAIRE DE LECTURE
MATERIAL COMPLEMENTARIO DE LECTURA
BT READING MATERIALS
RT 725

SUPPLEMENTARY TEXTBOOK
MANUEL COMPLEMENTAIRE
LIBRO DE TEXTO AUXILIAR
BT TEXTBOOK
RT 880

SUPPLIES
FOURNITURE
SUMINISTROS
NT AGRICULTURAL SUPPLIES
     MEDICAL SUPPLIES
RT 740

SURINAME
SURINAME
SURINAME
                                    May 1984
BT SOUTH AMERICA

SURVEYS
ENQUETE
ENCUESTA
NT INTERNATIONAL SURVEYS
     NATIONAL SURVEYS
     OCCUPATIONAL SURVEYS
     REGIONAL SURVEYS
RT 203

SWAZILAND
SWAZILAND
SWAZILANDIA
BT SOUTHERN AFRICA
RT ENGLISH SPEAKING AFRICA

SWEDEN
SUEDE
SUECIA
BT WESTERN EUROPE

SWITZERLAND
SUISSE
SUIZA
BT WESTERN EUROPE

SYLLABUSES
PROGRAMME D'ETUDES
PROGRAMA DE ESTUDIOS
RT 331

SYMBOLIC LEARNING
APPRENTISSAGE PAR SYMBOLES
APRENDIZAJE MEDIANTE
  SIMBOLOS
BT LEARNING
RT 512

SYMBOLS (LITERARY)
SYMBOLE (LITTERATURE)
SIMBOLO (LITERARIO)
RT 615

SYMPOSIA
SYMPOSIUM
SIMPOSIO
RT 204

SYNTAX
SYNTAXE
SINTAXIS
RT 622

SYRIAN AR
REPUBLIQUE ARABE SYRIENNE
REPUBLICA ARABE SIRIA
BT ARAB COUNTRIES
    MEDITERRANEAN
      COUNTRIES
    MIDDLE EAST

SYSTEMS ANALYSIS
ANALYSE SYSTEMIQUE
ANALISIS DE SISTEMA
RT 201
    OPERATIONS RESEARCH

TACTILE ADAPTATION
ADAPTATION TACTILE
ADAPTACION TACTIL
SN The conversion of educational materials for use with the instruction of the blind
RT 374

TAHITI
May 1984
USE **SOCIETY ISLANDS**

TAIWAN
TAIWAN
TAIWAN
May 1984
UF FORMOSA
BT FAR EAST

TALENT
TALENT
TALENTO
RT 520

TALENT IDENTIFICATION
DETECTION DES TALENTS
DETECCION DE TALENTOS
RT 211

TANZANIA UR
TANZANIE (REPUBLIQUE UNIE)
TANZANIA (REPUBLICA UNIDA)
BT EAST AFRICA

TAPE RECORDERS
MAGNETOPHONE
MAGNETOFONO
BT AUDIOVISUAL EQUIPMENT
RT 731

TAPE RECORDINGS
ENREGISTREMENT MAGNETIQUE
GRABACION MAGNETOFONICA
RT 732

TASMANIA
TASMANIE
TASMANIA
May 1984
BT AUSTRALIA

TAX ALLOCATION
AFFECTATION DES IMPOTS
ASIGNACION DE IMPUESTOS
RT 152

TAX EFFORT
EFFORT FISCAL
ESFUERZO TRIBUTARIO
RT 152

TAXES
IMPOT
IMPUESTOS
NT SCHOOL TAXES
RT 152

TEACHER DISTRIBUTION

TAXONOMY
TAXONOMIE
TAXONOMIA
RT 283

TEACHER ADMINISTRATION RELATIONSHIP
RELATIONS MAITRE-
 ADMINISTRATION
RELACION DOCENTE-
 ADMINISTRACION
BT RELATIONSHIP
RT 262

TEACHER AIDES
MAITRE AUXILIAIRE
AUXILIAR DOCENTE
SN Qualified or unqualified persons assisting in the instructional process
RT 424

TEACHER ASSOCIATIONS
ASSOCIATION D'ENSEIGNANTS
ASOCIACION DE DOCENTES
BT NATIONAL ORGANIZATIONS
RT 110

TEACHER ATTITUDES
ATTITUDE DE L'ENSEIGNANT
ACTITUD DEL DOCENTE
BT ATTITUDES
RT 350

TEACHER BACKGROUND
ACQUIS DE L'ENSEIGNANT
EXPERIENCIA DEL DOCENTE
RT 223

TEACHER BEHAVIOUR
COMPORTEMENT DE
 L'ENSEIGNANT
COMPORTAMIENTO DEL
 DOCENTE
BT BEHAVIOUR
RT 560

TEACHER CENTRES
CERCLE PEDAGOGIQUE
CENTRO PEDAGOGICO
SN Organized centres for teachers to meet, discuss, find resources and develop materials
RT 312

TEACHER CERTIFICATION
CERTIFICAT D'APTITUDE
 PEDAGOGIQUE
CERTIFICACION PARA LA
 DOCENCIA
BT CERTIFICATION
RT 390

TEACHER CHARACTERISTICS
CARACTERISTIQUE DE
 L'ENSEIGNANT
CARACTERISTICAS DEL DOCENTE
RT 350
    TEACHER PROFILE

TEACHER COUNSELLING
CONSULTATION D'ENSEIGNANTS
ASESORAMIENTO DE DOCENTES
RT 371

TEACHER DEVELOPED MATERIALS
MATERIEL ELABORE PAR LE
 MAITRE
MATERIAL ELABORADO POR EL
 DOCENTE
SN Instructional materials prepared by teachers
RT 725

TEACHER DISTRIBUTION
REPARTITION DES ENSEIGNANTS
DISTRIBUCION DE LOS
 DOCENTES
SN Covers both distribution among educational institutions and staffing ratios
BT QUOTA SYSTEM
RT 207

TEACHER EDUCATION
FORMATION DES ENSEIGNANTS
FORMACION DE DOCENTES
NT INSERVICE TEACHER
     EDUCATION
     PRESERVICE TEACHER
     EDUCATION
RT 690

TEACHER EDUCATION CURRICULUM
PROGRAMMES DE FORMATION DES MAITRES
CURRICULO DE FORMACION DE DOCENTES
RT 330

TEACHER EDUCATOR EDUCATION
FORMATION DES FORMATEURS
FORMACION DE FORMADORES DE DOCENTES
RT 690

TEACHER EDUCATORS
FORMATEUR D'ENSEIGNANTS
FORMADOR DE DOCENTES
RT 422

TEACHER EMPLOYMENT
EMPLOI DES ENSEIGNANTS
EMPLEO DEL DOCENTE
BT EMPLOYMENT
RT 223

TEACHER EVALUATION
EVALUATION DES ENSEIGNANTS
EVALUACION DEL DOCENTE
SN Judging teacher performance as related to established criteria
BT PERSONNEL EVALUATION
RT 212

TEACHER IMPROVEMENT
PERFECTIONNEMENT DES ENSEIGNANTS
PERFECCIONAMIENTO DEL DOCENTE
SN Education or training in the form of refresher courses designed to sustain and improve the professional quality of teachers
NT EDUCATIONAL READINGS
RT 212

TEACHER INFLUENCE
INFLUENCE DE L'ENSEIGNANT
INFLUENCIA DEL DOCENTE
RT 350

TEACHER INTERNS
MAITRE STAGIAIRE
DOCENTE PRACTICANTE
SN A trainee teacher under joint supervision of his college or university and the school system which employs him
RT 424

TEACHER MOBILITY
MOBILITE DES ENSEIGNANTS
MOVILIDAD DE LOS DOCENTES
BT MOBILITY
RT 207

TEACHER MOTIVATION
MOTIVATION DE L'ENSEIGNANT
MOTIVACION DEL DOCENTE
BT MOTIVATION
RT 350

TEACHER ORIENTATION
ORIENTATION PEDAGOGIQUE DES MAITRES
ORIENTACION PEDAGOGICA DE DOCENTES
RT 690

TEACHER PARTICIPATION
PARTICIPATION DE L'ENSEIGNANT
PARTICIPACION DEL DOCENTE
BT PARTICIPATION
RT 380

TEACHER PLACEMENT
AFFECTATION DES ENSEIGNANTS
ASIGNACION DE CARGO DOCENTE
RT 223

TEACHER PROFILE
PROFIL PROFESSIONNEL DE
  L'ENSEIGNANT
PERFIL PROFESIONAL DEL
  DOCENTE
                    May 1984
RT 223
    TEACHER CHARACTERISTICS
    690

TEACHER PROMOTION
PROMOTION DES ENSEIGNANTS
PROMOCION DE LOS DOCENTES
BT OCCUPATIONAL
      ADVANCEMENT
RT 223

TEACHER QUALIFICATIONS
QUALIFICATIONS DE
  L'ENSEIGNANT
CALIFICACIONES DEL DOCENTE
BT QUALIFICATIONS
RT 223

TEACHER RESPONSIBILITY
RESPONSABILITE DE
  L'ENSEIGNANT
RESPONSABILIDAD DEL DOCENTE
BT RESPONSIBILITY
RT 231

TEACHER ROLE
ROLE DE L'ENSEIGNANT
PAPEL DEL DOCENTE
RT 187

TEACHER SALARIES
SALAIRE DE L'ENSEIGNANT
REMUNERACION DEL DOCENTE
BT SALARIES
RT 242

TEACHER SELECTION
SELECTION DES ENSEIGNANTS
SELECCION DE DOCENTES
RT 223

TEACHER SEMINARS
SEMINAIRE DE FORMATION DES
  MAITRES
SEMINARIO DE DOCENTES
BT SEMINARS
RT 691

TEACHER SHORTAGE
PENURIE D'ENSEIGNANTS
ESCASEZ DE DOCENTES
RT 207

TEACHER STATUS
STATUT DE L'ENSEIGNANT
CONDICION DEL DOCENTE
BT STATUS
RT 187

TEACHER STRIKES
GREVE D'ENSEIGNANTS
HUELGA DE DOCENTES
RT 233

**TEACHER STUDENT
  RELATIONSHIP**
USE **STUDENT TEACHER
  RELATIONSHIP**

TEACHER SUPERVISION
INSPECTION DES ENSEIGNANTS
SUPERVISION DE LOS DOCENTES
BT SUPERVISION
RT 210

TEACHER SUPPLY AND DEMAND
OFFRE ET DEMANDE
  D'ENSEIGNANTS
OFERTA Y DEMANDA DE
  DOCENTES
RT 207

TEACHER TRAINING SCHOOLS
ECOLE NORMALE
ESCUELA NORMAL
                    May 1984
SN Utilized for undergraduate teachers
    colleges
RT 690

TEACHER TRANSFER

TEACHER TRANSFER
TRANSFERT D'ENSEIGNANTS
TRANSFERENCIA DE DOCENTES
BT TRANSFER POLICY
RT 223

TEACHER WELFARE
BIEN-ETRE DES ENSEIGNANTS
BIENESTAR DEL DOCENTE
BT WELFARE
RT 200
    SOCIAL WELFARE

TEACHERS
ENSEIGNANT
DOCENTE
BT EDUCATIONAL PERSONNEL
NT ADULT EDUCATORS
    COLLEGE TEACHERS
    PREPRIMARY TEACHERS
    PRIMARY SCHOOL TEACHERS
    SECONDARY SCHOOL
      TEACHERS
    SPECIAL EDUCATION
      TEACHERS
    RURAL SCHOOL TEACHERS
RT 421

TEACHERS COLLEGES
ECOLE NORMALE SUPERIEURE
ESCUELA NORMAL SUPERIOR
BT COLLEGES
RT 307

TEACHING
ENSEIGNEMENT
ENSEÑANZA
NT CONCEPT TEACHING
    CREATIVE TEACHING
    CROSS AGE TEACHING
    DIAGNOSTIC TEACHING
    PEER TEACHING
    TEAM TEACHING
RT 350
    TRAINING
    INSTRUCTION

TEACHING ASSIGNMENTS
TACHE PEDAGOGIQUE
TAREA ESCOLAR
BT ASSIGNMENTS
RT 356

TEACHING ASSISTANTS
ASSISTANT D'ENSEIGNEMENT
ASISTENTE
SN Graduate students assisting as instructors
RT 424

TEACHING CONDITIONS
CONDITION DE TRAVAIL DES MAITRES
CONDICIONES DE TRABAJO DEL DOCENTE
NT TEACHING LOAD
RT 212

TEACHING EXPERIENCE
EXPERIENCE DE L'ENSEIGNEMENT
EXPERIENCIA PEDAGOGICA
SN Actual and simulated experiences of preservice and inservice teachers
RT 690

TEACHING GUIDE
LIVRE DU MAITRE
GUIA DEL DOCENTE
SN Manual for teachers often accompanying textbooks
BT GUIDES
RT 880

TEACHING LOAD
CHARGE DE L'ENSEIGNANT
CARGA DOCENTE
BT TEACHING CONDITIONS
RT 265

TEACHING MACHINES
MACHINE A ENSEIGNER
MAQUINA DE ENSEÑAR
RT 731

TEACHING MATERIALS
USE **INSTRUCTIONAL MATERIALS**

TEACHING METHODS
METHODE PEDAGOGIQUE
METODO DE ENSEÑANZA
- SN Patterns of teacher behaviour that are recurrent, applicable to various subject matters, characteristic of more than one teacher and relevant to learning
- BT EDUCATIONAL METHODS
- NT ACTIVITY METHODS
  DEDUCTIVE METHODS
  INDUCTIVE METHODS
- RT 355

TEACHING PERSONNEL
CORPS ENSEIGNANT
PERSONAL DOCENTE
- UF FACULTY
- NT DIFFERENTIATED STAFFS
- RT 424

TEACHING PROCEDURES
PROCEDE PEDAGOGIQUE
PROCEDIMIENTO PEDAGOGICO
RT 356

TEACHING QUALITY
QUALITE DE L'ENSEIGNEMENT
CALIDAD DE LA ENSEÑANZA
RT 212

TEACHING SKILLS
COMPETENCE PEDAGOGIQUE
HABILIDAD PEDAGOGICA
- BT SKILLS
- RT 533

TEACHING STYLES
STYLE PEDAGOGIQUE
ESTILO PEDAGOGICO
RT 356

TEACHING TECHNIQUES
TECHNIQUE PEDAGOGIQUE
TECNICA DE ENSEÑANZA
- NT CLASSROOM TECHNIQUES
  QUESTIONING TECHNIQUES
- RT 356

TEACHING UNITS
UNITE D'ENSEIGNEMENT
UNIDAD DE ENSEÑANZA
- UF UNIT PLAN
- RT 356

TEAM LEADER (TEACHING)
ANIMATEUR D'EQUIPE PEDAGOGIQUE
ANIMADOR DE EQUIPO PEDAGOGICO
RT 426

TEAM TEACHING
ENSEIGNEMENT EN EQUIPE
ENSEÑANZA EN EQUIPO
- BT TEACHING
- RT 350

TEAM TRAINING
FORMATION EN EQUIPE
FORMACION EN EQUIPO
- BT TRAINING
- RT 351

TEAMWORK
TRAVAIL D'EQUIPE
TRABAJO EN EQUIPO
RT 554

TECHNICAL ASSISTANCE
ASSISTANCE TECHNIQUE
ASISTENCIA TECNICA
- SN Aid in form of personnel and training, not financial
- NT EDUCATIONAL MISSIONS
- RT 106

TECHNICAL COLLEGES
INSTITUT DE TECHNOLOGIE
ESCUELA TECNICA SUPERIOR
- SN Post secondary schools, at times with secondary courses, offering training for occupations at a level between the skilled trades and the professions
- BT COLLEGES
- RT 307

TECHNICAL DRAWING
DESSIN TECHNIQUE
DIBUJO TECNICO
RT 647

TECHNICAL EDUCATION
ENSEIGNEMENT TECHNIQUE
ENSEÑANZA TECNICA
SN Formal education designed to provide knowledge and skills underlying production processes with a wider connotation than vocational education at secondary or higher level
RT 183

TECHNICAL SECONDARY SCHOOLS
ECOLE SECONDAIRE TECHNIQUE
ESCUELA SECUNDARIA TECNICA
BT SECONDARY SCHOOLS
RT 306

TECHNICIANS
TECHNICIEN
TECNICO
SN Below level of professional but above clerical or labour levels
NT AGRICULTURAL TECHNICIANS
DRAFTSMEN
ELECTRONIC TECHNICIANS
ENGINEERING TECHNICIANS
RT 452

TECHNOLOGICAL ADVANCEMENT
PROGRES TECHNOLOGIQUE
PROGRESO TECNOLOGICO
RT 140

TECHNOLOGY
TECHNOLOGIE
TECNOLOGIA
NT AVIATION TECHNOLOGY
ELECTROMECHANICAL TECHNOLOGY
ENGINEERING TECHNOLOGY
INDUSTRIAL TECHNOLOGY
RADIO TECHNOLOGY
RT 140

TELECOMMUNICATION
TELECOMMUNICATIONS
TELECOMUNICACION
RT 145

TELEGRAPHIC MATERIALS
AIDE-MEMOIRE
AYUDA-MEMORIA
SN Highly abbreviated and condensed textual materials retaining all essential information
RT 725

TELEPHONE INSTRUCTION
ENSEIGNEMENT PAR TELEPHONE
ENSEÑANZA POR TELEFONO
SN Special education by use of the telephone
RT 360

TELEVISION
TELEVISION
TELEVISION
BT MASS MEDIA
NT EDUCATIONAL TELEVISION
TELEVISION VIEWING
RT 145

TELEVISION TEACHERS
MAITRE D'ENSEIGNEMENT TELEVISUEL
DOCENTE DE ENSEÑANZA POR TELEVISION
RT 426

TELEVISION VIEWING
SEANCE DE TELEVISION
SESION DE TELEVISION
BT TELEVISION
RT 360

TENURE
TITULARISATION
TITULARIDAD
SN Status granted to a person in a position, usually after serving a probationary period
RT 222

TERMINAL EDUCATION
ENSEIGNEMENT TERMINAL
ENSEÑANZA TERMINAL
RT   184

TERMINOLOGY
USE **GLOSSARY**

TERTIARY EDUCATION
USE **HIGHER EDUCATION**

TEST CONSTRUCTION
ELABORATION DE TESTS
ELABORACION DE PRUEBAS
RT   392

TEST RESULTS
RESULTAT DE TEST
RESULTADO DE PRUEBAS
RT   392

TESTING
ADMINISTRATION DE TESTS
PRUEBAS
NT   EDUCATIONAL TESTING
     PSYCHOLOGICAL TESTING
RT   391

TESTS
USE **EXAMINATIONS**

TESTS OF SIGNIFICANCE
EPREUVE DE VALIDATION
PRUEBA DE VERIFICACION
SN   Determination of the probability of rejecting a hypothesis when it is actually true
RT   284

TEXTBOOK
MANUEL SCOLAIRE
LIBRO DE TEXTO
SN   Designed for class use, usually in a particular subject
BT   BOOKS
NT   SUPPLEMENTARY TEXTBOOK
RT   880

TEXTBOOK AUTHORIZATION
VISA DES MANUELS SCOLAIRES
AUTORIZACION DE TEXTOS DE ESTUDIO
RT   213

TEXTBOOK CONTENT
CONTENU DES MANUELS SCOLAIRES
CONTENIDO DE LOS LIBROS DE TEXTO
RT   331

TEXTBOOK SHORTAGE
PENURIE DE MANUELS SCOLAIRES
CARENCIA DE LIBROS DE TEXTO
RT   205

THAILAND
THAILANDE
TAILANDIA
UF   SIAM
BT   SOUTH EAST ASIA

THEATRE ARTS
ART THEATRAL
ARTE TEATRAL
RT   610

THEATRES
THEATRE
TEATRO
RT   310

THEMATIC APPROACH
APPROCHE THEMATIQUE
ENFOQUE TEMATICO
SN   Teaching approach which organizes subject matter around broad themes
RT   331

THEOLOGICAL EDUCATION
FORMATION THEOLOGIQUE
FORMACION TEOLOGICA
RT   681

THEORIES
THEORIE
TEORIA
NT BEHAVIOUR THEORIES
    GUIDANCE THEORIES
    EDUCATIONAL THEORIES
    LEARNING THEORIES
    MEDIATION THEORY
    PERSONALITY THEORIES
RT 522

THERAPISTS
THERAPEUTE
TERAPEUTA
NT HEARING THERAPISTS
    OCCUPATIONAL THERAPISTS
    PHYSICAL THERAPISTS
    SPEECH THERAPISTS
RT 432

THERAPY
THERAPIE
TERAPIA
NT HEARING THERAPY
    PSYCHOTHERAPY
    SPEECH THERAPY
RT 373

THERMAL COMFORT
CONFORT THERMIQUE
CONFORT TERMICO
RT 252

THESAURUS
USE **GLOSSARY**

THOUGHT PROCESSES
PROCESSUS DE LA PENSEE
PROCESO DEL PENSAMIENTO
NT ABSTRACT REASONING
    CREATIVE THINKING
    CRITICAL THINKING
    LOGICAL THINKING
    PRODUCTIVE THINKING
RT 521

TIME FACTORS (LEARNING)
FACTEUR TEMPS
  (APPRENTISSAGE)
FACTOR TIEMPO (APRENDIZAJE)
RT 511

TIME SHARING
EMPLOI PARTAGE (ORDINATEUR)
TIEMPO COMPARTIDO
  (COMPUTADORA)
SN Use of a device for two or more
   purposes during same time interval
   with interspersing component
   actions in time
BT DATA PROCESSING
RT 284

TIMETABLES
EMPLOI DU TEMPS
HORARIO
UF SCHOOL SCHEDULES
NT FLEXIBLE TIMETABLING
RT 340

TOBAGO
May 1984
USE **TRINIDAD AND TOBAGO**

TOGO
TOGO
TOGO
BT WEST AFRICA
RT FRENCH SPEAKING AFRICA

TOKELAU ISLANDS
ILES TOKELAU
ISLAS TOKELAU
May 1984
BT POLYNESIA

TONGA
TONGA
TONGA
UF FRIENDLY ISLANDS
BT POLYNESIA

TOURISM
TOURISME
TURISMO
RT   145

TOWN PLANNING
USE **PHYSICAL PLANNING**

TOWNS
USE **MUNICIPALITIES**

TOYS
JOUET
JUGUETE
RT   741

TRADE UNIONS
SYNDICAT
SINDICATOS
UF   LABOUR ORGANIZATIONS
BT   NATIONAL ORGANIZATIONS
RT   125

TRADITIONAL EDUCATION
EDUCATION TRADITIONNELLE
EDUCACION TRADICIONAL
SN   That provided by societies before or alongside the introduction of a formal educational system
RT   180

TRADITIONAL GRAMMAR
GRAMMAIRE TRADITIONNELLE
GRAMATICA TRADICIONAL
BT   GRAMMAR
RT   622

TRAFFIC SAFETY
SECURITE DE LA CIRCULATION
SEGURIDAD EN EL TRANSITO
BT   SAFETY
RT   264

TRAINEES
STAGIAIRE
PARTICIPANTE EN UN SEMINARIO–TALLER
SN   Participants in vocational, administrative or technical training programmes for purpose of developing job related skills
RT   410

TRAINERS
FORMATEUR
INSTRUCTOR
SN   Persons who direct the practice of skills toward immediate improvement in some art or task
BT   EDUCATIONAL PERSONNEL
RT   421

TRAINING
FORMATION
FORMACION
SN   Systematic educative process by which one learns new skills
NT   BASIC TRAINING
     FURTHER TRAINING
     INDUCTION TRAINING
     MODULAR TRAINING
     RETRAINING
     TEAM TRAINING
     VOCATIONAL TRAINING
     TRAINING PROGRAMMES
RT   351
     TEACHING

TRAINING ABROAD
USE **STUDY ABROAD**

TRAINING ALLOWANCES
INDEMNITE DE FORMATION
ASIGNACION PARA FORMACION
BT   GRANTS
RT   242

TRAINING BY STAGES
FORMATION PAR ETAPES
FORMACION POR ETAPAS
BT   VOCATIONAL TRAINING
RT   351

TRAINING OBJECTIVES
OBJECTIF DE LA FORMATION
OBJETIVO DE LA FORMACION
BT   EDUCATIONAL OBJECTIVES
RT   300

TRAINING PROGRAMMES
PROGRAMMES DE FORMATION
PROGRAMA DE FORMACION
                           May 1984
BT   TRAINING
RT   351

TRAINING TECHNIQUES
TECHNIQUE DE FORMATION
TECNICA DE CAPACITACION
SN   Specific teaching formats designed for learning new skills
RT   356

TRANSACTIONAL ANALYSIS
ANALYSE TRANSACTIONNELLE
ANALISIS TRANSACCIONAL
                           May 1984
RT   352

TRANSFER CLASSES
CLASSE PREPARATOIRE
CLASE ESPECIAL PARA PROMOCION
UF   BRIDGE CLASSES
SN   Special provision for progression from one stage to the next
BT   CLASSES
RT   343

TRANSFER OF TRAINING
TRANSFERT DE LA FORMATION
TRANSFERENCIA DE LA FORMACION
RT   511

TRANSFER POLICY
POLITIQUE DE TRANSFERT
POLITICA DE TRANSFERENCIA
SN   Policy governing the movement of teachers or students from one school or instructional programme to another
NT   ARTICULATION
       STUDENT TRANSFER
       TEACHER TRANSFER
RT   200

TRANSFER STUDENTS
ELEVE TRANSFERE
ALUMNO TRASLADADO
RT   411

TRANSFORMATION THEORY (LANGUAGE)
THEORIE DE LA TRANSFORMATION
TEORIA DE LA TRANSFORMACION (LENGUA)
RT   622

TRANSLATION
TRADUCTION
TRADUCCION
SN   One language to another
BT   LANGUAGE ARTS
RT   620

TRANSPARENCIES
DOCUMENT TRANSPARENT
TRANSPARENCIA
RT   730

TRANSPORTATION
TRANSPORT
TRANSPORTE
RT   264

TRAVEL
VOYAGE
VIAJE
RT   145

TRIBES
TRIBU
TRIBU
RT   122

TRINIDAD AND TOBAGO
TRINITE ET TOBAGO
TRINIDAD Y TABAGO
UF   TOBAGO
BT   CARIBBEAN

TRUANCY
ECOLE BUISSONNIERE
INASISTENCIA INJUSTIFICADA
RT 267

TRUCIAL STATES
USE **UNITED ARAB EMIRATES**

TRUSTEESHIP COUNCIL
CONSEIL DE TUTELLE
CONSEJO DE ADMINISTRACION
   FIDUCIARIA

TUAMOTU ISLANDS
ILES TOUAMOTOU
ISLAS TUAMOTU
May 1984
BT   FRENCH POLYNESIA

TUBUAI ISLANDS
ILES TUBUAI
ISLAS TUBUAI
May 1984
BT   FRENCH POLYNESIA

TUNISIA
TUNISIE
TUNEZ
BT   ARAB COUNTRIES
      MEDITERRANEAN
        COUNTRIES
      NORTH AFRICA

TURKEY
TURQUIE
TURQUIA
BT   MEDITERRANEAN
      COUNTRIES
      MIDDLE EAST
      WESTERN EUROPE

TURKS AND CAICOS ISLANDS
ILES TURKS ET CAICOS
ISLAS TURCAS Y CAICOS
BT   CARIBBEAN

TUTORING
DIRECTION D'ETUDES
TUTORIA
RT 355

TWENTIETH CENTURY
VINGTIEME SIECLE
SIGLO VEINTE

TWENTY FIRST CENTURY
VINGT ET UNIEME SIECLE
SIGLO VEINTIUNO
May 1984

TWINS
JUMEAU
GEMELOS
RT 401

UGANDA
OUGANDA
UGANDA
BT   EAST AFRICA

UIEH
IUEH
IUEH
SN   Unesco Institute for Education,
      Hamburg

UK
ROYAUME-UNI
REINO UNIDO
UF   UNITED KINGDOM
      ENGLAND
BT   WESTERN EUROPE

UKRAINIAN SSR
RSS D'UKRAINE
RSS DE UCRANIA
BT   USSR

UN
ONU
ONU
SN   United Nations

UNDERACHIEVERS
UF LOW ACHIEVERS

UNDEREMPLOYED
SOUS-EMPLOYE
SUBEMPLEADO
RT 450

UNDEREMPLOYMENT
SOUS-EMPLOI
SUBEMPLEO
RT 154

UNDERGRADUATE STUDY
ETUDES UNIVERSITAIRES (1ER CYCLE)
ESTUDIOS UNIVERSITARIOS DE PRIMER CICLO
BT COLLEGE CURRICULUM
RT 330

UNDERGRADUATES
USE **COLLEGE STUDENTS**

UNDP
PNUD
PNUD
SN United Nations Development Programme

UNEDBAS
UNEDBAS
UNEDBAS
SN Unesco Regional Office for Education in Arab States (Beirut)

UNEMPLOYMENT
CHOMAGE
DESEMPLEO
NT EDUCATED UNEMPLOYMENT
    YOUTH UNEMPLOYMENT
RT 154

UNEP
PNUE
PNUMA
SN United Nations Environment Programme

UNESCO
UNESCO
UNESCO
SN United Nations Educational, Scientific and Cultural Organization

UNESCO EDUCATION SECTOR
SECTEUR DE L'EDUCATION DE L'UNESCO
SECTOR DE EDUCACION DE LA UNESCO

UNESCO EXECUTIVE BOARD
CONSEIL EXECUTIF DE L'UNESCO
CONSEJO EJECUTIVO DE LA UNESCO

UNESCO GENERAL CONFERENCE
CONFERENCE GENERALE DE L'UNESCO
CONFERENCIA GENERAL DE LA UNESCO

UNESCO SECRETARIAT
SECRETARIAT DE L'UNESCO
SECRETARIA DE LA UNESCO

UNFPA
FNUAP
FNUAP
SN United Nations Fund for Population Activities

UNHCR
UNHCR
ACNUR
SN United Nations Office of the High Commissioner for Refugees

UNICEF
UNICEF
UNICEF
SN United Nations Children's Fund

UNIDO
ONUDI
ONUDI
SN United Nations Industrial Development Organization

UNILINGUAL STUDENTS
ELEVE UNILINGUE
ALUMNO UNILINGUE
RT 414

UNION MEMBERS
SYNDIQUE
SINDICADO
RT 450

UNION OF SOVIET SOCIALIST
 REPUBLICS
USE **USSR**

UNISIST
UNISIST
UNISIST
SN World Science and Technical Information System

UNIT COSTS
COUT UNITAIRE
COSTO UNITARIO
BT COSTS
RT 243

UNIT PLAN
USE **TEACHING UNITS**

UNITAR
UNITAR
UNITAR
SN United Nations Institute for Training and Research

UNITED ARAB EMIRATES
EMIRATS ARABES UNIS
EMIRATOS ARABES UNIDOS
UF TRUCIAL STATES
BT ARAB COUNTRIES
 GULF STATES

UNITED KINGDOM
USE **UK**

UNITED STATES OF AMERICA
USE **USA**

UNITS OF STUDY (SUBJECT FIELDS)
UNITE D'ETUDES (DISCIPLINES)
UNIDADES DE ESTUDIO (DISCIPLINAS)
RT 331

UNIVERSAL EDUCATION
EDUCATION UNIVERSELLE
EDUCACION UNIVERSAL
SN System of education extending opportunities to all
RT 180

UNIVERSITIES
UNIVERSITE
UNIVERSIDAD
SN Institutions of higher education with legal right to confer degrees; preferred generic term is "colleges", hence use only when text refers to questions specific to universities
BT COLLEGES
RT 187

UNIVERSITIES WITHOUT WALLS
USE **OPEN COLLEGES**

UNIVERSITY EXTENSION
EDUCATION PERI–UNIVERSITAIRE
EXTENSION UNIVERSITARIA
UF EXTRA MURAL EDUCATION
SN Extension activity of universities and colleges including agricultural and cooperative extension
BT EXTENSION EDUCATION
RT 382

UNRISD
IRNU
UNRISD
SN United Nations Research Institute for Social Development

UNRWA
UNRWA
UNRWA
SN United Nations Relief and Works Agency for Palestine Refugees in

UNSKILLED OCCUPATIONS

the Near East

UNSKILLED OCCUPATIONS
METIER NON QUALIFIE
OCUPACION NO CALIFICADA
BT   OCCUPATIONS
RT   155

UNSKILLED WORKERS
OUVRIER NON QUALIFIE
TRABAJADOR NO CALIFICADO
BT   WORKERS
RT   451

UNU
UNU
UNU
SN   United Nations University

UNWRITTEN LANGUAGES
LANGUE NON ECRITE
LENGUA NO ESCRITA
RT   621

UPBRINGING
EDUCATION DE L'ENFANT
EDUCACION DEL NIÑO
UF   CHILD REARING
RT   180

UPPER CLASS
CLASSE SUPERIEURE
CLASE ALTA
BT   SOCIAL CLASS
RT   121

UPPER SECONDARY EDUCATION
ENSEIGNEMENT SECONDAIRE (2E CYCLE)
ENSEÑANZA SECUNDARIA (2DO CICLO)
BT   SECONDARY EDUCATION
RT   185

UPPER SECONDARY SCHOOLS
ECOLE SECONDAIRE (2E CYCLE)
ESCUELA SECUNDARIA (2DO CICLO)
BT   SECONDARY SCHOOLS
RT   301

UPPER VOLTA
HAUTE VOLTA
ALTO VOLTA
BT   WEST AFRICA
RT   FRENCH SPEAKING AFRICA

URALIC ALTAIC LANGUAGES
LANGUES OURALO–ALTAIQUES
LENGUAS URALALTAICAS
RT   625

URBAN AREAS
ZONE URBAINE
ZONA URBANA
RT   122
       MUNICIPALITIES

URBAN CULTURE
CIVILISATION URBAINE
CULTURA URBANA
BT   CULTURE
RT   130

URBAN EDUCATION
EDUCATION URBAINE
EDUCACION URBANA
RT   186

URBAN EXTENSION
VULGARISATION EN MILIEU URBAIN
EXTENSION CULTURAL URBANA
SN   Extension work in urban settings
BT   EXTENSION EDUCATION
RT   382

URBAN IMMIGRATION
EXODE RURAL
EXODO RURAL
UF   RURAL–URBAN MIGRATION
RT   124

URBAN POPULATION
POPULATION URBAINE
POBLACION URBANA
RT   124

URBAN SCHOOLS
ECOLE URBAINE
ESCUELA URBANA
RT 303

URBAN YOUTH
JEUNESSE URBAINE
JUVENTUD URBANA
BT YOUTH
RT 400

URBANIZATION
URBANISATION
URBANIZACION
RT 122

URUGUAY
URUGUAY
URUGUAY
BT SOUTH AMERICA

USA
ETATS–UNIS D'AMERIQUE
ESTADOS UNIDOS DE AMERICA
UF UNITED STATES OF AMERICA
BT NORTH AMERICA
NT HAWAII

USER GROUPS
GROUPE D'UTILISATEURS
GRUPO DE USUARIOS
RT 443

USSR
URSS
URSS
UF UNION OF SOVIET SOCIALIST
　　REPUBLICS
　　RUSSIA
BT EASTERN EUROPE
NT ARMENIAN SSR
　　BYELORUSSIAN SSR
　　ESTONIAN SSR
　　GEORGIAN SSR
　　KAZAKH SSR
　　LATVIAN SSR
　　LITHUANIAN SSR
　　MOLDAVIAN SSR
　　RUSSIAN SFSR
　　SIBERIA

　　UKRAINIAN SSR

VACATION COURSES
COURS DE VACANCES
CURSO DE VACACIONES
BT SHORT COURSES
RT 334
　　SUMMER SCHOOLS

VACATIONS
VACANCES
VACACIONES
RT 344

VALIDITY
VALIDITE
VALIDEZ
SN Applied to measurement
　　instruments
RT 283

VALUES
VALEUR
VALOR
NT MORAL VALUES
RT 555

VANUATU
VANUATU
VANUATU
UF NEW HEBRIDES
BT MELANESIA

VATICAN CITY
USE **HOLY SEE**

VENEZUELA
VENEZUELA
VENEZUELA
BT SOUTH AMERICA

VERBAL COMMUNICATION
COMMUNICATION VERBALE
COMUNICACION VERBAL
BT COMMUNICATION
RT 662

May 1984

VERBAL LEARNING
APPRENTISSAGE VERBAL
APRENDIZAJE VERBAL
BT LEARNING
RT 512

VERBAL TESTS
TEST VERBAL
PRUEBA VERBAL
BT EDUCATIONAL TESTS
RT 393

VETERINARIANS
VETERINAIRE
VETERINARIO
RT 433

VIDEO TAPE RECORDINGS
ENREGISTREMENT VIDEO
GRABACION VIDEO
RT 732

VIET NAM SR
VIETNAM (REPUBLIQUE
  SOCIALISTE)
VIETNAM (REPUBLICA
  SOCIALISTA)

VIRGIN ISLANDS (UK)
ILES VIERGES (RU)
ISLAS VIRGENES (RU)
BT CARIBBEAN

VIRGIN ISLANDS (USA)
ILES VIERGES (EUA)
ISLAS VIRGENES (EE.UU)
BT CARIBBEAN

VISUAL HANDICAPS
DEFICIENCE VISUELLE
DEFICIENCIA VISUAL
BT HANDICAPS
RT 571

VISUAL LEARNING
APPRENTISSAGE VISUEL
APRENDIZAJE VISUAL
BT LEARNING
RT 512

VISUAL PERCEPTION
PERCEPTION VISUELLE
PERCEPCION VISUAL
BT PERCEPTION
RT 510

VISUAL STIMULI
STIMULUS VISUEL
ESTIMULO VISUAL
BT STIMULI
RT 510

VISUALIZATION
VISUALISATION
VISUALIZACION
SN Act or power of forming mentally
    visual images of objects not
    present to the eye
RT 521

VOCABULARY
VOCABULAIRE
VOCABULARIO
RT 620

VOCABULARY DEVELOPMENT
DEVELOPPEMENT DU
  VOCABULAIRE
DESARROLLO DEL VOCABULARIO
RT 534

VOCATIONAL ADJUSTMENT
ADAPTATION PROFESSIONNELLE
ADAPTACION PROFESIONAL
BT ADJUSTMENT
RT 551

**VOCATIONAL AGRICULTURE
  TEACHERS**
PROFESSEUR D'ENSEIGNEMENT
  AGRICOLE
PROFESOR DE ENSEÑANZA
  AGRICOLA
BT VOCATIONAL EDUCATION
    TEACHERS
RT 425

VOCATIONAL APTITUDES
APTITUDE PROFESSIONNELLE
APTITUD PROFESIONAL
BT   APTITUDE
RT   520

VOCATIONAL DEVELOPMENT
DEVELOPPEMENT
   PROFESSIONNEL
DESARROLLO PROFESIONAL
NT   CAREER CHOICE
RT   534

VOCATIONAL EDUCATION
ENSEIGNEMENT PROFESSIONNEL
ENSEÑANZA PROFESIONAL
SN   Formal education designed to prepare for skilled occupations in industry, agriculture and commerce, generally at secondary level
NT   AGRICULTURAL EDUCATION
       COMMERCIAL EDUCATION
       DISTRIBUTIVE EDUCATION
       INDUSTRIAL EDUCATION
       VOCATIONAL TRAINING
RT   183

VOCATIONAL EDUCATION TEACHERS
MAITRE D'ENSEIGNEMENT
   PROFESSIONNEL
PROFESOR DE ENSEÑANZA
   PROFESIONAL
NT   VOCATIONAL AGRICULTURE
       TEACHERS
RT   425

VOCATIONAL GUIDANCE
ORIENTATION PROFESSIONNELLE
ORIENTACION PROFESIONAL
UF   OCCUPATIONAL GUIDANCE
       VOCATIONAL ORIENTATION
SN   Help given to the individual inside or outside the school system in choosing a career or occupation
RT   211
       CAREERS

VOCATIONAL INTERESTS
INTERET PROFESSIONNEL
INTERES PROFESIONAL
BT   INTERESTS
RT   541

VOCATIONAL MATURITY
MATURITE PROFESSIONNELLE
MADUREZ PROFESIONAL
RT   531

VOCATIONAL ORIENTATION
USE **VOCATIONAL GUIDANCE**

VOCATIONAL SCHOOL CERTIFICATES
CERTIFICAT D'APTITUDE
   PROFESSIONNEL
CERTIFICADO DE ESCUELA
   PROFESIONAL
BT   EDUCATIONAL CERTIFICATES
RT   390

VOCATIONAL SCHOOL CURRICULUM
PROGRAMMES D'ENSEIGNEMENT
   PROFESSIONNEL
CURRICULO DE ESCUELA
   PROFESIONAL
RT   330

VOCATIONAL SCHOOLS
ECOLE PROFESSIONNELLE
ESCUELA PROFESIONAL
RT   306

VOCATIONAL SECONDARY SCHOOLS
ECOLE SECONDAIRE
   PROFESSIONNELLE
ESCUELA SECUNDARIA
   PROFESIONAL
BT   SECONDARY SCHOOLS
RT   306

VOCATIONAL TRAINING
FORMATION PROFESSIONNELLE
FORMACION PROFESIONAL
UF   JOB TRAINING
BT   TRAINING

VOCATIONAL TRAINING CENTRES

      VOCATIONAL EDUCATION
NT FULL TIME TRAINING
      OFF THE JOB TRAINING
      ON THE JOB TRAINING
      PART TIME TRAINING
      TRAINING BY STAGES
RT 351

VOCATIONAL TRAINING CENTRES
CENTRE DE FORMATION
  PROFESSIONNELLE
CENTRO DE FORMACION
  PROFESIONAL
RT 306

VOLUNTARY AGENCIES
USE **ORGANIZATIONS**

VOLUNTEERS
VOLONTAIRE
VOLUNTARIO
RT 440

VOTING
VOTE
VOTO
UF ELECTIONS
RT 102

WAGES
USE **SALARIES**

WAKE ISLANDS
ILES WAKE
ISLAS WAKE
                    May 1984
BT OCEANIA

WALLIS AND FUTUNA ISLANDS
ILES WALLIS ET FUTUNA
ISLAS WALLIS Y FUTUNA
                    May 1984
UF FUTUNA ISLANDS
BT POLYNESIA

WCC
COE
CMI
SN World Council of Churches

WCOTP
CMOPE
CMOPE
SN World Confederation of
      Organizations of the Teaching
      Profession

WEIGHT
USE **BODY WEIGHT**

WELFARE
BIEN-ETRE
BIENESTAR
SN Well-being of a community or
      person
NT CHILD WELFARE
      SOCIAL WELFARE
      STUDENT WELFARE
      TEACHER WELFARE
      YOUTH WELFARE
RT 100

WELFARE AGENCIES
ORGANISME DE BIEN-ETRE
  SOCIAL
ORGANISMO DE BIENESTAR
  SOCIAL
BT AGENCIES
RT 103

WELFARE PROBLEMS
PROBLEME DE BIEN-ETRE
PROBLEMA DE BIENESTAR
RT 281

WELFARE SERVICES
SERVICES DE BIEN-ETRE SOCIAL
SERVICIOS DE BIENESTAR SOCIAL
BT SERVICES
RT 107

WEST AFRICA
AFRIQUE OCCIDENTALE
AFRICA OCCIDENTAL
BT AFRICA SOUTH OF THE
      SAHARA
NT BENIN
      CAMEROON UR
      GAMBIA
      GHANA

GUINEA
GUINEA-BISSAU
IVORY COAST
LIBERIA
MALI
MAURITANIA
NIGER
NIGERIA
SENEGAL
SIERRA LEONE
WESTERN SAHARA
TOGO
UPPER VOLTA
CAPE VERDE
RT CANARY ISLANDS
   MADEIRA

WEST GERMANY
May 1984
USE **GERMANY FR**

WEST INDIES
USE **CARIBBEAN**

WESTERN EUROPE
EUROPE OCCIDENTALE
EUROPA OCCIDENTAL
BT EUROPE
NT ANDORRA
   AUSTRIA
   BELGIUM
   CHANNEL ISLANDS
   CYPRUS
   DENMARK
   FAEROE ISLANDS
   FINLAND
   FRANCE
   GERMANY FR
   GIBRALTAR
   GREECE
   HOLY SEE
   IRELAND
   ITALY
   LIECHTENSTEIN
   LUXEMBOURG
   MALTA
   MONACO
   NETHERLANDS
   NORWAY
   PORTUGAL

SAN MARINO
SCANDINAVIA
SPAIN
SWEDEN
SWITZERLAND
TURKEY
UK
ICELAND

WESTERN HEMISPHERE
HEMISPHERE OCCIDENTAL
HEMISFERIO OCCIDENTAL
May 1984
RT EASTERN HEMISPHERE

WESTERN SAHARA
SAHARA OCCIDENTAL
SAHARA ESPANOL
May 1984
BT WEST AFRICA

WFP
PAM
PMA
SN World Food Programme

WHO
OMS
OMS
SN World Health Organization

WINDWARD ISLANDS
May 1984
USE **CARIBBEAN**

WOMEN
FEMME
MUJER
BT ADULTS
RT 443

WOMEN PROFESSORS
PROFESSEUR D'UNIVERSITE
  (FEMME)
PROFESORA UNIVERSITARIA
RT 422

WOMEN TEACHERS
ENSEIGNANTE
DOCENTE (MUJER)
RT 421

WOMEN WORKERS
TRAVAILLEUSE
TRABAJADORA
BT WORKERS
RT 451

WOMENS EDUCATION
EDUCATION DES FEMMES
EDUCACION DE LA MUJER
RT 180

WOODWORKING
TRAVAIL DU BOIS
TRABAJOS EN MADERA
RT 647

WORD FREQUENCY
FREQUENCE DE MOTS
FRECUENCIA DE PALABRAS
RT 620

WORD LISTS
LISTE DE MOTS
LISTA DE PALABRAS
RT 721

WORK ATTITUDES
ATTITUDE FACE AU TRAVAIL
ACTITUD ANTE EL TRABAJO
BT ATTITUDES
RT 552

WORK EDUCATION
EDUCATION POUR LE TRAVAIL
EDUCACION PARA EL TRABAJO
SN Cultivation of positive attitudes towards work
RT 682

WORK ENVIRONMENT
ENVIRONNEMENT PROFESSIONNEL
AMBIENTE LABORAL
BT ENVIRONMENT
RT 550

WORK EXPERIENCE
EXPERIENCE DU TRAVAIL
EXPERIENCIA LABORAL
BT EXPERIENCE
RT 562

WORK EXPERIENCE PROGRAMMES
PROGRAMME INTEGRE ETUDE-TRAVAIL
PROGRAMA INTEGRADO ESTUDIO-TRABAJO
UF COOPERATIVE EDUCATION
SN Instructional programmes providing for some part of the students' time to be spent in one of the sectors of production
NT PRACTICE PERIODS
RT 673

WORKER TRAITS
CARACTERISTIQUE DE L'OUVRIER
CARACTERISTICAS DEL TRABAJADOR
RT 561

WORKERS
TRAVAILLEUR
TRABAJADOR
NT AGRICULTURAL WORKERS
    FOREIGN WORKERS
    SEASONAL WORKERS
    SEMISKILLED WORKERS
    SKILLED WORKERS
    UNSKILLED WORKERS
    WOMEN WORKERS
RT 451

WORKERS EDUCATION
EDUCATION OUVRIERE
EDUCACION OBRERA
SN Includes education and training of trade union members sponsored by unions sometimes in cooperation with educational institutions
RT 186

WORKING CLASS
CLASSE OUVRIERE
CLASE TRABAJADORA
BT SOCIAL CLASS
RT 121

WORKING CLASS PARENTS
PARENTS DE CONDITION
   OUVRIERE
PADRES OBREROS
BT PARENTS
RT 401

WORKING CONDITIONS
CONDITION DE TRAVAIL
CONDICIONES DE TRABAJO
RT 153

WORKING HOURS
HEURE DE TRAVAIL
HORA DE TRABAJO
RT 153

WORKING PARENTS
PARENTS TRAVAILLANT AU
   DEHORS
PADRES QUE TRABAJAN
BT PARENTS
RT 401

WORKSHOPS
ATELIER
TALLER
RT 742

WORLD HISTORY
HISTOIRE MONDIALE
HISTORIA UNIVERSAL
BT HISTORY
RT 641

WORLD LITERATURE
LITTERATURE MONDIALE
LITERATURA UNIVERSAL
RT 615

WORLD PROBLEMS
PROBLEME MONDIAL
PROBLEMAS MUNDIALES
UF INTERNATIONAL PROBLEMS
RT 101

WRITING
ECRITURE
ESCRITURA
BT LANGUAGE ARTS
RT 620

YEAR ROUND SCHOOLS
ECOLE FONCTIONNANT TOUTE
   L'ANNEE
ESCUELA QUE FUNCIONA TODO
   EL AÑO
RT 303

YEARBOOK
ANNUAIRE
ANUARIO
RT 880

YEMEN
YEMEN
YEMEN
BT ARAB COUNTRIES
     MIDDLE EAST

YOUTH
JEUNESSE
JUVENTUD
NT OUT OF SCHOOL YOUTH
    RURAL YOUTH
    URBAN YOUTH
RT 400

YOUTH AGENCIES
ORGANISME DE JEUNESSE
ORGANISMO DE LA JUVENTUD
BT AGENCIES
RT 103

YOUTH CLUBS
CLUB DE JEUNES
CLUB JUVENIL
BT CLUBS
RT 381

May 1984

YOUTH LEADERS

YOUTH LEADERS
ANIMATEUR DE GROUPE DE
  JEUNES
ANIMADOR DE GRUPO DE
  JOVENES
RT 440

YOUTH OPPORTUNITIES
POSSIBILITE OFFERTE AUX
  JEUNES
OPORTUNIDAD PARA LA
  JUVENTUD
BT OPPORTUNITIES
RT 100
     EDUCATIONAL
       OPPORTUNITIES
     EQUAL OPPORTUNITIES
       (JOBS)

YOUTH ORGANIZATIONS
ORGANISATION DE JEUNESSE
ORGANIZACION DE LA
  JUVENTUD
BT NATIONAL ORGANIZATIONS
RT 110

YOUTH PROBLEMS
PROBLEME DES JEUNES
PROBLEMAS DE LA JUVENTUD
RT 572

YOUTH PROGRAMMES
PROGRAMME POUR LA JEUNESSE
PROGRAMA PARA LA JUVENTUD
RT 381

YOUTH SERVICES
SERVICES DE JEUNESSE
SERVICIOS PARA LA JUVENTUD
RT 107

YOUTH UNEMPLOYMENT
CHOMAGE DES JEUNES
DESOCUPACION DE LOS JOVENES
BT UNEMPLOYMENT
RT 154

YOUTH WELFARE
BIEN-ETRE DE LA JEUNESSE
BIENESTAR DE LA JUVENTUD
BT WELFARE
RT 100

YUGOSLAVIA
YOUGOSLAVIE
YUGOSLAVIA
BT EASTERN EUROPE

ZAIRE
ZAIRE
ZAIRE
UF CONGO (KINSHASA)
     CONGO DR
BT CENTRAL AFRICA
RT FRENCH SPEAKING AFRICA

ZAMBIA
ZAMBIE
ZAMBIA
BT EAST AFRICA
     SOUTHERN AFRICA

ZIMBABWE
ZIMBABWE
ZIMBABWE

May 1984

UF RHODESIA
BT EAST AFRICA
     SOUTHERN AFRICA
RT ENGLISH SPEAKING AFRICA

ZOOLOGY
ZOOLOGIE
ZOOLOGIA
BT BIOLOGY
RT 632

III. Alphabetical array of adult education descriptors

ACCELERATED VOCATIONAL TRAINING
FORMATION PROFESSIONNELLE ACCELEREE
FORMACION PROFESIONAL ACELERADA
RT 351

ADMINISTRATOR EDUCATION
FORMATION DES ADMINISTRATEURS
FORMACION DE ADMINISTRADORES
RT 672

ADULT COLLEGES
INSTITUTION D'ENSEIGNEMENT SUPERIEUR (ADULTES)
INSTITUTO DE ENSEÑANZA SUPERIOR PARA ADULTOS
RT 187

ADULT COUNSELLORS
CONSEILLER D'ORIENTATION (ADULTES)
CONSEJO DE ADULTOS
RT 431

ADULT DEVELOPMENT
DEVELOPPEMENT DES ADULTES
DESARROLLO DEL ADULTO
RT 530

ADULT EDUCATION ACCOMMODATION
INSTALLATION D'ENSEIGNEMENT (ADULTES)
DISPONIBILIDADES PARA LA EDUCACION DE ADULTOS
RT 711

ADULT EDUCATION AGENCIES
ORGANISME DE L'EDUCATION DES ADULTES
ORGANISMO DE EDUCACION DE ADULTOS
RT 103

ADULT EDUCATION ASSOCIATIONS
ASSOCIATION D'EDUCATION DES ADULTES
ASOCIACION DE EDUCACION DE ADULTOS
RT 110

ADULT EDUCATION REGULATIONS
REGLEMENTATION (EDUCATION DES ADULTES)
REGLAMENTO SOBRE EDUCACION DE ADULTOS
RT 230

ADULT EDUCATION SCHOOL COOPERATION
COOPERATION ECOLE-EDUCATION DES ADULTES
COOPERACION ESCUELA-EDUCACION DE ADULTOS
RT 263

ADULT EDUCATION TAXES
TAXE D'EDUCATION DES ADULTES
CONTRIBUCION PARA LA EDUCACION DE ADULTOS
RT 240

ADULT EDUCATION–COMMUNITY RELATIONS
RELATION EDUCATION DES ADULTES–COLLECTIVITE
RELACION EDUCACION ADULTOS–COMUNIDAD
RT 263

ADULT EDUCATION–INDUSTRY COOPERATION
COOPERATION EDUCATION DES ADULTES–INDUSTRIE
COOPERACION INDUSTRIA–EDUCACION DE ADULTOS
RT 263

ADULT POPULATION
POPULATION ADULTE
POBLACION ADULTA
RT 124

ADULT PROGRAMME COMMITTEES
COMITE DE PROGRAMMATION (ADULTES)
COMISION DE PROGRAMACION (EDUCACION DE ADULTOS)
RT 442

ADULT SCHOOLS
ECOLE D'ADULTES
ESCUELA PARA ADULTOS
RT 187

ADULT SERVICES
SERVICES POUR ADULTES
SERVICIOS PARA ADULTOS
RT 107

ADULT STUDENT–INSTITUTION RELATIONSHIP
RELATION ELEVES ADULTES–INSTITUTION
RELACION ALUMNOS ADULTOS–INSTITUCION
RT 380

ADULT TEACHING
ENSEIGNEMENT DES ADULTES
ENSEÑANZA DE ADULTOS
RT 352

ADULTHOOD
AGE ADULTE
EDAD ADULTA
RT 500

AEROSPACE INDUSTRY
INDUSTRIE AEROSPATIALE
INDUSTRIA AEROESPACIAL
RT 150

AGE SEGREGATION
SEGREGATION EN FONCTION DE L'AGE
SEGREGACION POR EDAD
RT 341

AGEING
PROCESSUS DE MATURATION
ENVEJECIMIENTO
RT 531

ALIENATION
ALIENATION
ALIENACION
RT 554

ANIMATEUR SELECTION
SELECTION DES ANIMATEURS
SELECCION DE ANIMADORES
RT 223

ANIMATION
ANIMATION
ANIMACION
RT 181

ANIMATION METHODS
METHODE D'ANIMATION
METODO DE ANIMACION
RT 355

CASE STUDY METHODS
METHODE D'ETUDE DE CAS
METODO DE ESTUDIOS DE CASOS
RT 355

CHEMICAL ENGINEERS
INGENIEUR CHIMISTE
INGENIERO QUIMICO
RT 463

CHEMICAL INDUSTRY
INDUSTRIE CHIMIQUE
INDUSTRIA QUIMICA
RT 150

CHEMICAL WORKERS
OUVRIER CHIMISTE
TRABAJADOR QUIMICO
RT 451

CHEMISTS
CHIMISTE
QUIMICO
RT 463

CLOTHING INDUSTRY
INDUSTRIE DU VETEMENT
INDUSTRIA DEL VESTIDO
RT 150

CLOTHING WORKERS
OUVRIER DU VETEMENT
TRABAJADOR DE LA INDUSTRIA
  DEL VESTIDO
RT 451

COLLECTIVE ADVANCEMENT
PROMOTION COLLECTIVE
PROMOCION COLECTIVA
RT 121

COMMUNITY ACTION
ACTION COMMUNAUTAIRE
ACCION COMUNITARIA
RT 102

COMMUNITY CENTRES
CENTRE COMMUNAUTAIRE
CENTRO COMUNITARIO
RT 311

COMPULSORY COURSES
COURS OBLIGATOIRE
CURSO OBLIGATORIO
RT 331

CONDITIONS OF GRANT
CONDITIONS POUR BOURSE
CONDICIONES DE LA BECA
RT 232

CONDITIONS OF SUBSIDY
CONDITIONS POUR SUBVENTION
CONDICIONES DEL SUBSIDIO
RT 241

CONSTRUCTION WORKERS
OUVRIER DU BATIMENT
TRABAJADOR DE LA
  CONSTRUCCION
RT 451

COORDINATING AGENCIES
ORGANISME OFFICIEL DE
  COORDINATION
ORGANISMO COORDINADOR
RT 103

COORDINATING ORGANIZATIONS
ORGANISME DE COORDINATION
ORGANIZACION DE
  COORDINACION
RT 110

COURSE COMPLETION
ACHEVEMENT DU COURS
TERMINO DEL CURSO
RT 266

CULTURAL DEVELOPMENT
DEVELOPPEMENT CULTUREL
DESARROLLO CULTURAL
RT 151

DAY TIME PROGRAMMES
PROGRAMME DE JOUR
PROGRAMA DIURNO
RT 321

DEFICIT FINANCING
FINANCEMENT DEFICITAIRE
FINANCIAMIENTO DEFICITARIO
RT 243

DENTISTS
DENTISTE
DENTISTA
RT 433

DIRECT TEACHING
ENSEIGNEMENT DIRECT
ENSEÑANZA DIRECTA
RT 352

DIRECTED STUDY
ETUDE DIRIGEE
ESTUDIO DIRIGIDO
RT 335

DISTANCE STUDY
ETUDE A DISTANCE
ESTUDIO A DISTANCIA
RT 335

DISTANCE TEACHING
ENSEIGNEMENT A DISTANCE
ENSEÑANZA A DISTANCIA
RT 352

DISTANCE TEACHING INSTITUTIONS
INSTITUTION DE TELE-ENSEIGNEMENT
INSTITUCION DE ENSEÑANZA A DISTANCIA
RT 311

DISTRIBUTIVE WORKERS
EMPLOYE D'UNE ENTREPRISE DE VENTE
TRABAJADOR DE LA DISTRIBUCION
RT 451

EARLY ADULTHOOD
PREMIER AGE ADULTE
JUVENTUD
RT 500

ECONOMICALLY DISADVANTAGED
ECONOMIQUEMENT FAIBLE
DESFAVORECIDO ECONOMICAMENTE
RT 402

EDUCATIONAL ALLOWANCES
BOURSE DE FORMATION
SUBSIDIO PARA FORMACION
RT 242

EDUCATIONAL ATTITUDES
ATTITUDE EDUCATIVE
ACTITUD EDUCATIVA
RT 181

EDUCATIONAL CHOICE
CHOIX DE FORMATION
OPCION EDUCACIONAL
RT 181

EDUCATIONAL LEISURE
LOISIR EDUCATIF
TIEMPO LIBRE EDUCATIVO
RT 357

EDUCATIONAL PUBLICITY
PUBLICITE EDUCATIVE
PUBLICIDAD EDUCATIVA
RT 182

EDUCATIONAL RECREATION
RECREATION EDUCATIVE
RECREACION EDUCATIVA
RT 357

EDUCATIONAL VOUCHERS
CREDIT EDUCATION
ALOCACIONES EDUCACIONALES
RT 242

ELECTRICAL ENGINEERS
INGENIEUR ELECTRICIEN
INGENIERO ELECTRICISTA
RT 463

ELECTRICAL INDUSTRY
INDUSTRIE ELECTRIQUE
INDUSTRIA DE LA ELECTRICIDAD
RT 150

ELECTRONICS INDUSTRY
INDUSTRIE ELECTRONIQUE
INDUSTRIA ELECTRONICA
RT 150

ENTERPRISES
ENTREPRISE
EMPRESA
RT 110

EXTENSION PROGRAMMES
PROGRAMME PERISCOLAIRE
PROGRAMA DE EXTENSION
RT 321

EXTENSION TEACHERS
ENSEIGNANT PERISCOLAIRE
DOCENTE DE EXTENSION
   EDUCACIONAL
RT 422

FAILURE RATE
TAUX D'ECHEC
TASA DE FRACASOS
RT 266

FEMINISM
FEMINISME
FEMINISMO
RT 101

FINANCIAL RESOURCES
RESSOURCES FINANCIERES
RECURSOS FINANCIEROS
RT 240

FIREFIGHTERS
POMPIER
BOMBERO
RT 460

FOOD INDUSTRY
INDUSTRIE ALIMENTAIRE
INDUSTRIA ALIMENTICIA
RT 150

FOOD INDUSTRY WORKERS
OUVRIER DE L'INDUSTRIE
   ALIMENTAIRE
TRABAJADOR DE LA
   ALIMENTACION
RT 451

FOREIGN WORKER EDUCATION
EDUCATION DES TRAVAILLEURS
   ETRANGERS
EDUCACION PARA
   TRABAJADORES EXTRANJEROS
RT 186

FOREMEN
CONTREMAITRE
CAPATAZ
RT 451

FORESTRY WORKERS
TRAVAILLEUR FORESTIER
TRABAJADOR FORESTAL
RT 451

FREEDOM OF ASSOCIATION
LIBERTE D'ASSOCIATION
LIBERTAD DE ASOCIACION
RT 100

FULL TIME EDUCATION
EDUCATION A PLEIN TEMPS
EDUCACION DE TIEMPO
   COMPLETO
RT 184

FULL TIME EDUCATORS
EDUCATEUR PERMANENT
EDUCADORES DE TIEMPO
   COMPLETO
RT 424

FULL TIME EMPLOYMENT
EMPLOI A PLEIN TEMPS
EMPLEO DE TIEMPO COMPLETO
RT 222

FULL TIME STUDENTS
ETUDIANT A PLEIN TEMPS
ESTUDIANTE DE TIEMPO
   COMPLETO
RT 410

GERIATRICS
GERIATRIE
GERIATRIA
RT 651

GOVERNMENT SUPERVISION
INSPECTION GOUVERNEMENTALE
SUPERVISION GUBERNAMENTAL
RT 105

GROUP LEADERSHIP
DIRECTION DE GROUPE
LIDERAZGO DE GRUPOS
RT 554

HANDICAPPED EDUCATION
EDUCATION DES HANDICAPES
EDUCACION PARA DEFICIENTES
RT 322

HORIZONTAL INTEGRATION (LEARNING)
INTEGRATION HORIZONTALE (APPRENTISSAGE)
INTEGRACION HORIZONTAL (APRENDIZAJE)
RT 514

HOTEL WORKERS
EMPLOYE DE L'HOTELLERIE
TRABAJADOR DE HOTEL
RT 451

INDEPENDANT LEARNERS
AUTODIDACTE
AUTODIDACTA
RT 412

INDIVIDUAL DEVELOPMENT EDUCATION
FORMATION AU DEVELOPPEMENT INDIVIDUEL
EDUCACION PARA EL DESARROLLO INDIVIDUAL
RT 183

INDIVIDUAL DEVELOPMENT PROGRAMMES
PROGRAMME DE DEVELOPPEMENT INDIVIDUEL
PROGRAMA DE DESARROLLO INDIVIDUAL
RT 321

INSTRUCTIONAL LEVEL
NIVEAU D'INSTRUCTION
NIVEL DE INSTRUCCION
RT 352

INTELLECTUAL DETERIORATION
DETERIORATION INTELLECTUELLE
DETERIORO INTELECTUAL
RT 520

INTERGENERATIONAL EQUALITY
EGALITE ENTRE GENERATIONS
IGUALDAD ENTRE GENERACIONES
RT 181

INTERORGANIZATIONAL COOPERATION
COOPERATION INTERORGANISATIONS
COOPERACION INTERINSTITUCIONAL
RT 262

KNOWLEDGE OBSOLESCENCE
OBSOLESCENCE DES CONNAISSANCES
OBSOLENCIA DEL CONOCIMIENTO
RT 181

KNOWLEDGE TRANSMISSION
TRANSMISSION DES CONNAISSANCES
TRANSMISION DE CONOCIMIENTOS
RT 512

LAITY
LAICITE
LAICIDAD
RT 475

LEARNING INTEGRATION
INTEGRATION DE L'APPRENTISSAGE
INTEGRACION DEL APRENDIZAJE
RT 514

LEARNING SPEED
RAPIDITE D'APPRENTISSAGE
RAPIDEZ DE APRENDIZAJE
RT 513

LEATHERWORKERS
OUVRIER DU CUIR
TRABAJADOR DEL CUERO
RT 451

LOCAL AUTONOMY
AUTONOMIE LOCALE
AUTONOMIA LOCAL
RT 263

LOCAL GOVERNMENT AID
AIDE DES AUTORITES LOCALES
AYUDA DEL GOBIERNO LOCAL
RT 106

LOCAL PROGRAMMING
PROGRAMMATION LOCALE
PROGRAMACION LOCAL
RT 271

LONG COURSES
COURS DE LONGUE DUREE
CURSO LARGO
RT 333

LOSS OF EARNINGS PAYMENTS
COMPENSATION DE PERTE DE SALAIRE
COMPENSACION POR PERDIDA DE SALARIO
RT 242

MANAGEMENT GAMES
JEU DE GESTION
JUEGOS DE GESTION
RT 355

MANUAL WORKERS
TRAVAILLEUR MANUEL
TRABAJADOR MANUAL
RT 451

MANUFACTURED INDUSTRY
INDUSTRIE MANUFACTURIERE
INDUSTRIA MANUFACTURERA
RT 150

MARKETING
VENTE
COMERCIALIZACION
RT 150

MARRIAGE COUNSELLING
CONSULTATION CONJUGALE
CONSEJO MATRIMONIAL
RT 371

MECHANICAL ENGINEERING
CONSTRUCTION MECANIQUE
INGENIERIA MECANICA
RT 647

MECHANICAL ENGINEERS
INGENIEUR MECANICIEN
INGENIERO MECANICO
RT 463

MENTAL SET
REGIDITE MENTALE
RIGIDEZ MENTAL
RT 513

MENTALLY HANDICAPPED
DEFICIENT MENTAL
DEFICIENTE MENTAL
RT 403

METAL INDUSTRY
INDUSTRIE METALLURGIQUE
INDUSTRIA METALURGICA
RT 150

METALLURGISTS
METALLURGISTE
INGENIERO METALURGICO
RT 463

METALWORKERS
OUVRIER METALLURGIQUE
TRABAJADOR METALURGICO
RT 451

MIDDLE AGE
AGE MUR
EDAD MADURA
RT 500

MIDDLE AGE PEOPLE
PERSONNE D'AGE MUR
PERSONA DE EDAD MADURA
RT 400

MILITARY TRAINING
FORMATION MILITAIRE
ENTRENAMIENTO MILITAR
RT 351

MINERS
MINEUR
TRABAJADOR MINERO
RT 451

MINIMUM AGE
AGE MINIMUM
EDAD MINIMA
RT 500

MINING ENGINEERS
INGENIEUR DES MINES
INGENIERO DE MINAS
RT 463

MINING INDUSTRY
INDUSTRIE MINIERE
INDUSTRIA MINERA
RT 150

MIXED SYSTEMS
SYSTEME MIXTE
SISTEMA MIXTO
RT 260

MOTOR VEHICLE INDUSTRY
INDUSTRIE DE L'AUTOMOBILE
INDUSTRIA DE VEHICULOS A
  MOTOR
RT 150

MULTI PURPOSE CENTRES
CENTRE POLYVALENT
CENTRO POLIVALENTE
RT 311

MULTIMEDIA ORGANIZATIONS
ORGANISME D'ENSEIGNEMENT
  PAR MULTIMEDIA
ORGANIZACION DE ENSEÑANZA
  POR MEDIOS MULTIPLES
RT 187

NON PARTICIPATION
NON-PARTICIPATION
NO PARTICIPACION
RT 554

**NON SUBSIDIZED
  ORGANIZATIONS**
ORGANISATION NON
  SUBVENTIONNEE
ORGANIZACION NO
  SUBVENCIONADA
RT 110

NON VOCATIONAL COURSES
COURS NON PROFESSIONNEL
CURSO NO PROFESIONAL
RT 333

NONMANUAL WORKERS
TRAVAILLEUR NON MANUEL
TRABAJADOR NO MANUAL
RT 451

NON-PARTICIPANTS
NON PARTICIPANT
NO PARTICIPANTES
RT 410

NURSING
PROFESSION D'INFIRMIERE
ENFERMERIA
RT 155

OLD AGE
VIEILLESSE
VEJEZ
RT 500

OPEN ENROLMENT
RECRUTEMENT OUVERT
MATRICULA LIBRE
RT 266

OPTICIANS
OPTICIEN
OPTICO
RT 433

PAID EDUCATIONAL LEAVE
CONGE PAYE DE FORMATION
LICENCIA DE ESTUDIOS CON
 SUELDO
RT 222

PARENT EDUCATION
EDUCATION DES PARENTS
EDUCACION PARA PADRES
RT 186

PART TIME EDUCATORS
EDUCATEUR A TEMPS PARTIEL
EDUCADORES DE TIEMPO
 PARCIAL
RT 424

PART TIME EMPLOYMENT
EMPLOI A TEMPS PARTIEL
EMPLEO DE TIEMPO PARCIAL
RT 222

PARTICIPATION DETERRENTS
OBSTACLE A LA PARTICIPATION
OBSTACULO A LA PARTICIPACION
RT 285

PARTICIPATION INCENTIVES
STIMULANT A LA PARTICIPATION
INCENTIVOS PARA LA
 PARTICIPACION
RT 285

PARTICIPATION PROBLEMS
PROBLEME DE PARTICIPATION
PROBLEMAS DE PARTICIPACION
RT 281

PARTICIPATION RATE
TAUX DE PARTICIPATION
TASA DE PARTICIPACION
RT 206

PERFORMANCE INCENTIVES
STIMULANT A BON RENDEMENT
INCENTIVOS DE RENDIMIENTO
RT 266

PERSONNEL
PERSONNEL
PERSONAL
RT 441

PETROLEUM INDUSTRY
INDUSTRIE PETROLIERE
INDUSTRIA PETROLIFERA
RT 150

PETROLEUM WORKERS
OUVRIER DU PETROLE
TRABAJADOR DEL PETROLEO
RT 451

PHARMACISTS
PHARMACIEN
FARMACEUTICO
RT 433

PHYSICISTS
PHYSICIEN
FISICO
RT 463

PLANTATION WORKERS
TRAVAILLEUR DES PLANTATIONS
TRABAJADOR DE LAS
 PLANTACIONES
RT 451

POLITICAL ORGANIZATIONS
ORGANISATION POLITIQUE
ORGANIZACION POLITICA
RT 110

POST INDUSTRIAL SOCIETY
SOCIETE POSTINDUSTRIELLE
SOCIEDAD POSTINDUSTRIAL
RT 150

PRE INDUSTRIAL SOCIETY
SOCIETE PRE-INDUSTRIELLE
SOCIEDAD PREINDUSTRIAL
RT 150

PRE RETIREMENT EDUCATION
PREPARATION A LA RETRAITE
PREPARACION PARA LA JUBILACION
RT 183

PRE RETIREMENT PROGRAMMES
PROGRAMME DE PREPARATION A LA RETRAITE
PROGRAMA DE PREPARACION PARA LA JUBILACION
RT 321

PRINTING INDUSTRY
INDUSTRIE GRAPHIQUE
INDUSTRIA GRAFICA
RT 150

PRINTING WORKERS
OUVRIER DE L'INDUSTRIE GRAPHIQUE
TRABAJADOR GRAFICO
RT 451

PRIOR KNOWLEDGE LEVEL
NIVEAU DE CONNAISSANCE INITIALE
NIVEL DE CONOCIMIENTOS PREVIOS
RT 391

PRISONERS
DETENU
PRESO
RT 403

PRIVATE ADULT EDUCATION
ENSEIGNEMENT PRIVE DES ADULTES
ENSEÑANZA PRIVADA DE ADULTOS
RT 187

PRIVATE EDUCATION SYSTEMS
SYSTEME PRIVE DE FORMATION
SISTEMA DE ENSEÑANZA PRIVADA
RT 260

PRIVATE ENTERPRISES
ENTREPRISE PRIVEE
EMPRESA PRIVADA
RT 150

PRODUCTION WORKERS
OUVRIER D'INDUSTRIE MANUFACTURIERE
TRABAJADOR DE LA INDUSTRIA MANUFACTURERA
RT 451

PUBLIC EDUCATION SYSTEMS
SYSTEME PUBLIC D'EDUCATION
SISTEMA DE ENSEÑANZA PUBLICA
RT 260

PUBLIC ENTERPRISES
ENTREPRISE PUBLIQUE
EMPRESA PUBLICA
RT 150

PUBLIC FINANCE
FINANCES PUBLIQUES
FINANZA PUBLICA
RT 240

RAILWAY WORKERS
EMPLOYE DE CHEMIN DE FER
TRABAJADOR FERROVIARIO
RT 451

READING HABITS
HABITUDE DE LECTURE
HABITO DE LECTURA
RT 542

RESIDENCE CHARGES
PRIX D'INTERNAT
PRECIO DEL INTERNADO
RT 240

RESIDENTIAL ADULT CENTRES
CENTRE RESIDENTIEL POUR
  ADULTES
INTERNADO DE EDUCACION DE
  ADULTOS
RT 311

RESIDENTIAL ADULT EDUCATION
EDUCATION D'ADULTES EN
  RESIDENCE
EDUCACION DE ADULTOS EN
  INTERNADO
RT 184

RESIDENTIAL PROGRAMMES
PROGRAMME EN RESIDENCE
PROGRAMA EN INTERNADO
RT 321

RESOURCE PERSONS
ANIMATEURS
ANIMADOR
May 1984
RT 421

RETIRED PERSONS
PERSONNE A LA RETRAITE
PERSONA JUBILADA
RT 400

ROLE CONFLICT
CONFLIT DE ROLE
CONFLICTO DE FUNCIONES
RT 553

ROLE EDUCATION
FORMATION A UN ROLE
EDUCACION PARA UNA FUNCION
RT 183

RURAL EXTENSION PROGRAMMES
PROGRAMME VULGARISATION
  MILIEU RURAL
PROGRAMA DE EXTENSION
  RURAL
RT 321

SALESMEN
VENDEUR
VENDEDOR
RT 451

SEAFARER EDUCATION
EDUCATION DES MARINS
EDUCACION PARA MARINEROS
RT 186

SEAFARERS
MARIN
MARINERO
RT 451

SELF EMPLOYED
TRAVAILLEUR INDEPENDANT
TRABAJADOR POR CUENTA
  PROPIA
RT 450

SENESCENCE
SENESCENCE
SENECTUD
RT 531

SERVICE INDUSTRIES
INDUSTRIE DE SERVICE
INDUSTRIA DE SERVICIOS
RT 150

SHORT TERM MEMORY
MEMOIRE IMMEDIATE
MEMORIA IMMEDIATA
RT 521

SKILL OBSOLESCENCE
OBSOLESCENCE DES
  COMPETENCES
OBSOLECENCIA DE UNA
  DESTREZA
RT 181

SOCIAL DISENGAGEMENT
DESENGAGEMENT SOCIAL
DESINTERES POR ACTIVIDADES
   SOCIALES
RT 531

SOCIOCULTURAL FACILITIES
EQUIPEMENT SOCIOCULTUREL
FACILIDADES SOCIOCULTURALES
RT 710

STUDENT RECRUITMENT
RECRUTEMENT D'ETUDIANTS
MATRICULACION ESTUDIANTIL
RT 266

STUDENT TURNOVER
TAUX DE MOBILITE DES ELEVES
ROTACION DEL ALUMNO
RT 206

SUBSCRIPTIONS
COTISATIONS
CUOTA
SN Membership dues
RT 240

SURGEONS
CHIRURGIEN
CIRUJANO
RT 433

SURVEYORS
GEOMETRE
AGRIMENSOR
RT 452

TARGET GROUPS
GROUPE CIBLE
GRUPO DESTINATARIO
RT 443

TEACHABLE MOMENTS
MOMENT FAVORABLE A
   L'INSTRUCTION
MOMENTO APROPRIADO PARA LA
   ENSEÑANZA
RT 531

TEXTILE INDUSTRY
INDUSTRIE TEXTILE
INDUSTRIA TEXTIL
RT 150

TEXTILE WORKERS
OUVRIER DU TEXTILE
TRABAJADOR TEXTIL
RT 451

TRANSPORT WORKERS
EMPLOYE DES TRANSPORTS
TRABAJADOR DEL TRANSPORTE
RT 451

UNEMPLOYED
CHOMEUR
DESOCUPADO
RT 450

**UNEMPLOYED EDUCATION
   PROGRAMMES**
PROGRAMME D'EDUCATION
   POUR CHOMEURS
PROGRAMA DE EDUCACION
   PARA DESEMPLEADOS
RT 321

**UNIVERSITY EXTENSION
   DEPARTMENTS**
DEPARTEMENT D'EDUCATION
   PERI–UNIVERSITAIRE
DEPARTAMENTO DE EXTENSION
   UNIVERSITARIA
RT 307

**UNIVERSITY EXTENSION
   PROGRAMMES**
PROGRAMME D'EDUCATION
   PERI–UNIVERSITAIRE
PROGRAMA DE EXTENSION
   UNIVERSITARIA
RT 321

**UNIVERSITY EXTENSION
   TEACHERS**
ENSEIGNANT EDUCATION PERI–
   UNIVERSITAIRE
PROFESOR DE EXTENSION
   UNIVERSITARIA

RT 422

VERTICAL INTEGRATION (LEARNING)
INTEGRATION VERTICALE (APPRENTISSAGE)
INTEGRACION VERTICAL (APRENDIZAJE)
RT 514

VOCATIONAL REHABILITATION
READAPTATION PROFESSIONNELLE
READAPTACION PROFESIONAL
RT 373

VOCATIONAL TRAINING PROGRAMMES
PROGRAMME DE FORMATION PROFESSIONNELLE
PROGRAMA DE FORMACION PROFESIONAL
RT 321

VOCATIONAL TRAINING TAXES
TAXE DE FORMATION PROFESSIONNELLE
CONTRIBUCION PARA LA CAPACITACION PROFESIONAL
RT 240

VOLUNTARILY PROVIDED ADULT EDUCATION
EDUCATION BENEVOLE DES ADULTES
EDUCACION DE ADULTOS IMPARTIDA BENEVOLAMENTE
RT 187

VOLUNTARY EDUCATION
EDUCATION VOLONTAIRE
EDUCACION VOLUNTARIA
RT 180

VOLUNTARY ORGANIZATIONS
ORGANISATION BENEVOLE
ORGANIZACION BENEVOLA
RT 110A

VOLUNTARY SERVICES
SERVICE VOLONTAIRE
SERVICIO VOLONTARIO
RT 154

WEEKEND SCHOOLS
STAGE DE WEEKEND
ESCUELA DE FIN DE SEMANA
RT 303

WOODWORKERS
OUVRIER DU BOIS
TRABAJADOR DE LA MADERA
RT 451

WORKING LIFE
VIE ACTIVE
VIDA ACTIVA
RT 154

YOUNG ADULTS
JEUNE ADULTE
JOVENES
RT 400

IV. Facetted array of descriptors and identifiers

100 ABSTRACT IDEAS

CHILD WELFARE
EDUCATIONAL FUTUROLOGY
FREEDOM OF SPEECH
HUMAN DIGNITY
HUMAN RIGHTS
MORAL ISSUES
NEEDS
OPPORTUNITIES
POLITICAL ISSUES
PRODUCTIVE LIVING
PUBLIC SUPPORT
SOCIAL WELFARE
WELFARE
YOUTH OPPORTUNITIES
YOUTH WELFARE
  A FREEDOM OF ASSOCIATION

101 POLICIES

CITIZENSHIP
COLLECTIVISM
COLONIALISM
DEMOCRACY
DEVELOPED COUNTRIES
DEVELOPING COUNTRIES
INTERNATIONAL
    UNDERSTANDING
NATIONAL INTEGRATION
NATIONALISM
PATRIOTISM
POLICIES
POLITICAL THEORIES
RACISM
STATE CHURCH SEPARATION
WORLD PROBLEMS
  A FEMINISM

102 POLITICAL STRUCTURE

COMMUNITY
COMMUNITY CONTROL
COORDINATION
FEDERATIVE STRUCTURE
FOREIGN POLICY
GEOGRAPHIC REGIONS
GOVERNMENT
MUNICIPALITIES
POLICY MAKING
PROVINCIAL POWERS
VOTING
  A COMMUNITY ACTION

103 CENTRAL AGENCIES

AGENCIES
CENTRAL GOVERNMENT
GOVERNMENTAL STRUCTURE
INTERNATIONAL AGENCIES
REGIONAL AGENCIES
SOCIAL AGENCIES
WELFARE AGENCIES
YOUTH AGENCIES
  A ADULT EDUCATION
    AGENCIES
  A COORDINATING AGENCIES

104 INTERMEDIATE, LOCAL AGENCIES

CITY GOVERNMENT
COMMUNITY AGENCIES
  (PUBLIC)
LOCAL GOVERNMENT
PROVINCIAL AGENCIES
PROVINCIAL GOVERNMENT

105 AGENCY ROLE, RELATIONSHIP

AGENCY ROLE
CENTRAL PROVINCIAL
  RELATIONSHIP
CITIZEN PARTICIPATION

CITIZEN ROLE
COMMUNITY ROLE
GOVERNMENT ROLE
INTERNATIONAL COOPERATION
NATIONAL INTERAGENCY
   COORDINATION
NATIONAL REGIONAL
   COOPERATION
REGIONAL COOPERATION
   A GOVERNMENT
   SUPERVISION

106 AID

BILATERAL AID
CENTRAL GOVERNMENT AID
MULTILATERAL AID
PROVINCIAL GOVERNMENT
   AID
STATE AID TO PROVINCES
TECHNICAL ASSISTANCE
   A LOCAL GOVERNMENT AID

107 SERVICES

COMMUNITY SERVICES
HEALTH SERVICES
INFORMATION SERVICES
SERVICES
SOCIAL SERVICES
WELFARE SERVICES
YOUTH SERVICES
   A ADULT SERVICES

108 PLANNING

COMMUNITY PLANNING
NATIONAL PLANNING
NATIONAL REGIONAL
   PLANNING
PHYSICAL PLANNING
PLANNING
REGIONAL PLANNING

109 PROGRAMMES

COMMUNITY PROGRAMMES
FOUNDATION PROGRAMMES
GOVERNMENT PROGRAMMES
INTERNATIONAL PROGRAMMES
NATIONAL PROGRAMMES
NATIONAL REGIONAL
   PROGRAMMES
PROGRAMMES
REGIONAL PROGRAMMES

110 ORGANIZATIONS

COMMUNITY ORGANIZATIONS
INTERNATIONAL
   ORGANIZATIONS
LITERACY ORGANIZATIONS
NATIONAL ORGANIZATIONS
ORGANIZATIONS
PARENT ASSOCIATIONS
PARENT TEACHER
   ASSOCIATIONS
PROFESSIONAL ASSOCIATIONS
RELIGIOUS ORGANIZATIONS
STUDENT ORGANIZATIONS
TEACHER ASSOCIATIONS
YOUTH ORGANIZATIONS
   A ADULT EDUCATION
   ASSOCIATIONS
   A COORDINATING
   ORGANIZATIONS
   A ENTERPRISES
   A NON SUBSIDIZED
   ORGANIZATIONS
   A POLITICAL
   ORGANIZATIONS
   A VOLUNTARY
   ORGANIZATIONS

120 SOCIETY

SOCIAL ACTION
SOCIAL BACKGROUND
SOCIAL CHANGE
SOCIAL PLANNING
SOCIAL POLICIES
SOCIAL SYSTEMS
SOCIAL WORK
SOCIOCULTURAL PATTERNS
SOCIOECONOMIC
   BACKGROUND

121 DIVISIONS

ECONOMIC STATUS
MIDDLE CLASS
PROFESSIONAL RECOGNITION
SOCIAL ADVANCEMENT
SOCIAL CLASS
SOCIAL DISADVANTAGEMENT
SOCIAL DISCRIMINATION
SOCIAL INTEGRATION
SOCIAL MOBILITY
SOCIAL PROBLEMS
SOCIAL STATUS
SOCIOECONOMIC STATUS
STATUS
UPPER CLASS
WORKING CLASS
   A COLLECTIVE ADVANCEMENT

122 COMMUNITY

COLLECTIVE SETTLEMENTS
COMMUNITY INFLUENCE
COMMUNITY PARTICIPATION
COMMUNITY PROBLEMS
GROUP STRUCTURE
GROUP UNITY
HUMAN RELATIONS
INTERGROUP RELATIONS
RURAL AREAS
RURAL URBAN DIFFERENCES
TRIBES
URBAN AREAS
URBANIZATION

123 ETHNIC DISTRIBUTION

ETHNIC CONFLICT
ETHNIC DISTRIBUTION
MINORITY ROLE
RACE
RACE RELATIONS
RACIAL DISCRIMINATION
RACIAL INTEGRATION
RACIAL SEGREGATION

124 DEMOGRAPHY

BRAIN DRAIN
CENSUS DATA
EMIGRATION
FAMILY MOBILITY
GEOGRAPHIC DISTRIBUTION
IMMIGRATION
MIGRANT PROBLEMS
MIGRATION
MOBILITY
NATIONAL DEMOGRAPHY
NOMADISM
POPULATION DISTRIBUTION
POPULATION PROBLEMS
POPULATION TRENDS
RURAL POPULATION
URBAN IMMIGRATION
URBAN POPULATION
   A ADULT POPULATION

125 INSTITUTIONS

EDUCATIONAL INSTITUTIONS
INSTITUTIONS
NATIONAL SERVICE
RELIGIOUS INSTITUTION ROLE
RELIGIOUS INSTITUTIONS
TRADE UNIONS

126 FAMILY

CHILD CARE
FAMILY BACKGROUND
FAMILY PLANNING
FAMILY ROLE
FAMILY (SOCIOLOGICAL UNIT)
FAMILY STRUCTURE
FOSTER FAMILY
FOSTER HOMES
HOUSING
LEISURE
MARITAL STATUS
RECREATION
RURAL FAMILY

130 CULTURE

ACCULTURATION

BICULTURALISM
CULTURAL BACKGROUND
CULTURAL
    DISADVANTAGEMENT
CULTURAL EXCHANGE
CULTURAL
    INTERRELATIONSHIPS
CULTURAL ISOLATION
CULTURAL POLICIES
CULTURE
PLURICULTURALISM
RELIGION
URBAN CULTURE

131 LANGUAGE

BILINGUALISM
LANGUAGE
LANGUAGE POLICY
LANGUAGE USAGE
MOTHER TONGUE
OFFICIAL LANGUAGES
PLURILINGUALISM
SECOND LANGUAGES

140 RESEARCH AND TECHNOLOGY

AUTOMATION
ENVIRONMENT
HUMAN ENGINEERING
MEDIA TECHNOLOGY
RESEARCH
RESEARCH POLICY
RESEARCH PROGRAMME
SCIENCE
SCIENTIFIC PRINCIPLES
SCIENTIFIC RESEARCH
TECHNOLOGICAL
    ADVANCEMENT
TECHNOLOGY

145 COMMUNICATIONS

COMMUNICATIONS
MASS MEDIA
PRESS
PUBLIC RELATIONS
RADIO
TELECOMMUNICATION
TELEVISION
TOURISM
TRAVEL

150 ECONOMY

AGRICULTURAL PRODUCTION
CAPITAL
COMMERCE
CONSTRUCTION INDUSTRY
COOPERATIVES
ECONOMIC CLIMATE
ECONOMIC POLICIES
ECONOMIC PROGRESS
FINANCIAL SERVICES
FURNITURE INDUSTRY
INDUSTRIALIZATION
INDUSTRY
LIVING STANDARDS
PRODUCTIVITY
PUBLISHING INDUSTRY
SMALL SCALE INDUSTRY
    A AEROSPACE INDUSTRY
    A CHEMICAL INDUSTRY
    A CLOTHING INDUSTRY
    A ELECTRICAL INDUSTRY
    A ELECTRONICS INDUSTRY
    A FOOD INDUSTRY
    A MANUFACTURED
       INDUSTRY
    A MARKETING
    A METAL INDUSTRY
    A MINING INDUSTRY
    A MOTOR VEHICLE
       INDUSTRY
    A PETROLEUM INDUSTRY
    A POST INDUSTRIAL SOCIETY
    A PRE INDUSTRIAL SOCIETY
    A PRINTING INDUSTRY
    A PRIVATE ENTERPRISES
    A PUBLIC ENTERPRISES
    A SERVICE INDUSTRIES
    A TEXTILE INDUSTRY

151 DEVELOPMENT

AGRARIAN REFORM
AGRICULTURAL DEVELOPMENT
COMMUNITY DEVELOPMENT

DEPRESSED AREAS (ECONOMIC) DEVELOPMENT
ECONOMIC DEVELOPMENT
HUMAN RESOURCES DEVELOPMENT
INTEGRATED RURAL DEVELOPMENT
MANPOWER DEVELOPMENT
NATIONAL REGIONAL DISPARITIES
NEEDS ASSESSMENT
POVERTY
RURAL DEVELOPMENT
SOCIAL DEVELOPMENT
  A CULTURAL DEVELOPMENT

152 FINANCIAL

EQUALIZATION AID
FINANCIAL NEEDS
FINANCIAL POLICY
FISCAL MANAGEMENT
INVESTMENT
TAX ALLOCATION
TAX EFFORT
TAXES

153 LABOUR

CHILD LABOUR
COLLECTIVE AGREEMENTS
EQUAL OPPORTUNITIES (JOBS)
HUMAN RESOURCES
INCOME
JOB TENURE
LABOUR
LABOUR DEMANDS
LABOUR FORCE
LABOUR RELATIONS
WORKING CONDITIONS
WORKING HOURS

154 EMPLOYMENT

EDUCATED UNEMPLOYMENT
EMPLOYMENT
EMPLOYMENT OPPORTUNITIES
EMPLOYMENT PROGRAMMES
EMPLOYMENT SERVICES
EMPLOYMENT STATISTICS
EMPLOYMENT STRATEGIES
INITIAL EMPLOYMENT
LABOUR MARKET
MANPOWER NEEDS
MANPOWER PLANNING
MANPOWER POLICY
OCCUPATIONAL ADVANCEMENT
PLACEMENT
SCIENTIFIC MANPOWER
SEASONAL EMPLOYMENT
UNDEREMPLOYMENT
UNEMPLOYMENT
YOUTH UNEMPLOYMENT
  A VOLUNTARY SERVICES
  A WORKING LIFE

155 OCCUPATIONS

AGRICULTURAL OCCUPATIONS
BUILDING TRADES
CLERICAL OCCUPATIONS
INDUSTRIAL OCCUPATIONS
OCCUPATIONAL CHANGE
OCCUPATIONAL CLUSTERS
OCCUPATIONS
PROFESSIONS
SEMISKILLED OCCUPATIONS
SERVICE OCCUPATIONS
SKILLED OCCUPATIONS
UNSKILLED OCCUPATIONS
  A NURSING

160 HEALTH

FOOD
FOOD SERVICES
HEALTH
HEALTH NEEDS
HEALTH PROGRAMMES
MEDICAL SERVICES
NUTRITION
PUBLIC HEALTH

161 DISEASES

COMMUNICABLE DISEASES
DISEASE CONTROL

DISEASE RATE
DISEASES
IMMUNIZATION PROGRAMMES

170 LEGAL TERMS

AGREEMENTS
CENTRAL GOVERNMENT LAWS
CIVIL RIGHTS
COPYRIGHTS
CORRECTIONAL INSTITUTIONS
COURT LITIGATION
COURTS
INTERNATIONAL
    CONVENTIONS
INTERNATIONAL
    RECOMMENDATIONS
LABOUR LAWS
LAW ENFORCEMENT
LAWS
LEGAL AID
LEGAL RESPONSIBILITY
PROVINCIAL LAWS
PUBLIC HEALTH LAWS

180 BROAD EDUCATIONAL CONCEPTS

ACADEMIC FREEDOM
COMPULSORY EDUCATION
DEMOCRATIZATION OF
    EDUCATION
EDUCATION
EDUCATIONAL GOALS
EDUCATIONAL OPPORTUNITIES
EDUCATIONAL PHILOSOPHY
EDUCATIONAL THEORIES
ELITIST EDUCATION
EQUAL EDUCATION
FREE EDUCATION
FUNCTIONAL LITERACY
ILLITERACY
LIFELONG EDUCATION
LITERACY
RIGHT TO EDUCATION
SCHOOL SEGREGATION
SECULAR EDUCATION
TRADITIONAL EDUCATION
UNIVERSAL EDUCATION
UPBRINGING

WOMENS EDUCATION
A VOLUNTARY EDUCATION

181 NARROWER EDUCATIONAL CONCEPTS

ACCESS TO EDUCATION
EDUCATIONAL BENEFITS
EDUCATIONAL DEMAND
EDUCATIONAL
    DISADVANTAGEMENT
EDUCATIONAL
    DISCRIMINATION
EDUCATIONAL
    INFRASTRUCTURE
EDUCATIONAL NEEDS
EDUCATIONAL OUTPUT
EDUCATIONAL QUALITY
A ANIMATION
A EDUCATIONAL ATTITUDES
A EDUCATIONAL CHOICE
A INTERGENERATIONAL
    EQUALITY
A KNOWLEDGE
    OBSOLESCENCE
A SKILL OBSOLESCENCE

182 EDUCATIONAL POLICIES

EDUCATION WORK
    RELATIONSHIP
EDUCATIONAL DEVELOPMENT
EDUCATIONAL DEVELOPMENT
    TRENDS
EDUCATIONAL IMPROVEMENT
EDUCATIONAL POLICIES
EDUCATIONAL POLICY TRENDS
EDUCATIONAL PRACTICE
EDUCATIONAL PRIORITIES
EDUCATIONAL PROBLEMS
EDUCATIONAL STRATEGIES
A EDUCATIONAL PUBLICITY

183 EDUCATION BY TYPE

BASIC EDUCATION
BILINGUAL EDUCATION
CAREER EDUCATION
GENERAL EDUCATION

POLYTECHNICAL EDUCATION
PROFESSIONAL EDUCATION
TECHNICAL EDUCATION
VOCATIONAL EDUCATION
  A INDIVIDUAL
    DEVELOPMENT EDUCATION
  A PRE RETIREMENT
    EDUCATION
  A ROLE EDUCATION

184 EDUCATION BY FORM

ACTIVE SCHOOLS
ALTERNATIVE EDUCATION
COMPLEMENTARY EDUCATION
CONTINUATION EDUCATION
INFORMAL EDUCATION
NONFORMAL EDUCATION
OUT OF SCHOOL EDUCATION
PART TIME EDUCATION
RECURRENT EDUCATION
TERMINAL EDUCATION
  A FULL TIME EDUCATION
  A RESIDENTIAL ADULT
    EDUCATION

185 LEVELS OF EDUCATION

HIGHER EDUCATION
LEVELS OF EDUCATION
LOWER SECONDARY
  EDUCATION
PREPRIMARY EDUCATION
PRIMARY EDUCATION
SECONDARY EDUCATION
UPPER SECONDARY
  EDUCATION

186 EDUCATION BY GROUP, LOCALITY

ADULT EDUCATION
ARMED FORCES EDUCATION
COEDUCATION
COMMUNITY EDUCATION
COMPENSATORY EDUCATION
CONSUMER EDUCATION
CORRECTIONAL EDUCATION
EARLY CHILDHOOD
  EDUCATION
FAMILY EDUCATION
GIRLS ENROLMENT
MIGRANT EDUCATION
RURAL EDUCATION
SPECIAL EDUCATION
URBAN EDUCATION
WORKERS EDUCATION
  A FOREIGN WORKER
    EDUCATION
  A PARENT EDUCATION
  A SEAFARER EDUCATION

187 EDUCATION BY AGENTS

COLLEGE ROLE
COLLEGES
EDUCATIONAL COMPLEXES
PRIVATE EDUCATION
PUBLIC EDUCATION
SCHOOL ROLE
SCHOOLS
STUDENT ROLE
TEACHER ROLE
TEACHER STATUS
UNIVERSITIES
  A ADULT COLLEGES
  A ADULT SCHOOLS
  A MULTIMEDIA
    ORGANIZATIONS
  A PRIVATE ADULT
    EDUCATION
  A VOLUNTARILY PROVIDED
    ADULT EDUCATION

188 EDUCATION BY IDEOLOGY

ATHEISTIC EDUCATION
CHRISTIAN EDUCATION
COMMUNIST EDUCATION
ISLAMIC EDUCATION

200 ADMINISTRATIVE POLICIES

ADMINISTRATION
ADMINISTRATIVE POLICIES
ADMINISTRATIVE PRINCIPLES
ADOPTION OF INNOVATIONS
CENTRALIZATION

DECENTRALIZATION
EDUCATIONAL
   ADMINISTRATION
EDUCATIONAL AIMS
EDUCATIONAL COORDINATION
EDUCATIONAL INFORMATION
EDUCATIONAL INNOVATIONS
EDUCATIONAL REFORM
INNOVATION
PROMOTION POLICIES
STUDENT WELFARE
TEACHER WELFARE
TRANSFER POLICY

201 MANAGEMENT

DECISION MAKING
INFORMATION SYSTEMS
MANAGEMENT
MANAGEMENT SYSTEMS
NETWORK ANALYSIS
REPORTING
SCHEDULING
SYSTEMS ANALYSIS

202 RECORD KEEPING

ABSTRACTING
CATALOGUING
CLASSIFICATION
DOCUMENTATION
EDUCATIONAL
   DOCUMENTATION
FILING
INDEXING
INFORMATION NETWORKS
INFORMATION PROCESSING
RECORDKEEPING

203 SURVEYS

DATA COLLECTION
INTERNATIONAL SURVEYS
NATIONAL SURVEYS
PROGRAMME DESCRIPTIONS
PROVINCIAL SURVEYS
QUESTIONNAIRES
REGIONAL SURVEYS
SCHOOL SURVEYS

SURVEYS

204 INFORMATION DISSEMINATION

COMMUNICATION
COMMUNICATION PROBLEMS
CONFERENCES
DIFFUSION
EDUCATIONAL SEMINARS
FEEDBACK
INFORMATION DISSEMINATION
INFORMATION EXCHANGE
INFORMATION GATHERING
INFORMATION THEORY
INFORMATION UTILIZATION
MEETINGS
PUBLICATION
REPLICATION OF INNOVATIONS
RESEARCH UTILIZATION
SYMPOSIA

205 EDUCATIONAL PLANNING

ARTICULATION
COLLEGE PLANNING
EDUCATIONAL MISSIONS
EDUCATIONAL PLANNING
EDUCATIONAL WASTAGE
FORMATIVE EVALUATION
PROGRAMME COORDINATION
PROGRAMME DESIGN
PROGRAMME EVALUATION
PROGRAMME PLANNING
QUOTA SYSTEM
SCHOOL PLANNING
SUMMATIVE EVALUATION
TEXTBOOK SHORTAGE

206 STUDENT ACCOUNTING

ATTENDANCE RATE
DROPOUT RATE
DUAL ENROLMENT
ENROLMENT PROJECTIONS
ENROLMENT RATIO
ENROLMENT TRENDS
REPETITION RATE
SCHOOL AGE POPULATION

STUDENT MOBILITY
  A PARTICIPATION RATE
  A STUDENT TURNOVER

207 TEACHER ACCOUNTING

STUDENT TEACHER RATIO
TEACHER DISTRIBUTION
TEACHER MOBILITY
TEACHER SHORTAGE
TEACHER SUPPLY AND
   DEMAND

208 SCHOOL ACCOUNTING

COLLEGE LOCATION
SCHOOL DISTRIBUTION
SCHOOL HOLDING POWER
SCHOOL MAPPING
SCHOOL SIZE
SCHOOL STATISTICS
SMALL SCHOOLS

210 SUPERVISION

ACCREDITATION
   (INSTITUTIONS)
EVALUATION
EVALUATION CRITERIA
EVALUATION METHODS
PERSONNEL EVALUATION
SCHOOL SUPERVISION
SUPERVISION
SUPERVISORY METHODS
TEACHER SUPERVISION

211 GUIDANCE

EDUCATIONAL GUIDANCE
GUIDANCE
GUIDANCE AIMS
GUIDANCE FUNCTIONS
GUIDANCE THEORIES
TALENT IDENTIFICATION
VOCATIONAL GUIDANCE

212 TEACHER EVALUATION

TEACHER EVALUATION
TEACHER IMPROVEMENT
TEACHING CONDITIONS
TEACHING QUALITY

213 CURRICULUM EVALUATION

CURRICULUM EVALUATION
CURRICULUM PLANNING
MATERIALS EVALUATION
MATERIALS PREPARATION
TEXTBOOK AUTHORIZATION

220 PERSONNEL ADMINISTRATION

PERSONNEL DATA
PERSONNEL MANAGEMENT

221 RECRUITMENT

EDUCATIONAL BACKGROUND
EMPLOYMENT EXPERIENCE
INTERVIEWS
JOB ANALYSIS
JOB APPLICATION
PERSONALITY ASSESSMENT
QUALIFICATIONS
RECRUITMENT

222 TENURE

BLOCK RELEASE
DAY RELEASE
EDUCATIONAL LEAVE
INTERNSHIP PROGRAMMES
LEAVE OF ABSENCE
OVERTIME
PROBATIONARY PERIOD
REDUNDANCY
RELEASED TIME
RETIREMENT
TENURE
  A FULL TIME EMPLOYMENT
  A PAID EDUCATIONAL LEAVE
  A PART TIME EMPLOYMENT

223 TEACHER EMPLOYMENT

ADMINISTRATOR SELECTION
COUNSELLOR QUALIFICATIONS
RESEARCH OPPORTUNITIES
SUPERVISOR QUALIFICATIONS
TEACHER BACKGROUND
TEACHER EMPLOYMENT
TEACHER PLACEMENT
TEACHER PROFILE
TEACHER PROMOTION
TEACHER QUALIFICATIONS
TEACHER SELECTION
TEACHER TRANSFER
   A ANIMATEUR SELECTION

230 LEGISLATION

CODIFICATION
EDUCATIONAL LEGISLATION
RECREATION LEGISLATION
SCHOOL ATTENDANCE LAWS
SCHOOL GOVERNANCE
SCHOOL INTEGRATION
SCHOOL REGULATIONS
   A ADULT EDUCATION
      REGULATIONS

231 RESPONSIBILITY

ACCOUNTABILITY
ADMINISTRATOR
   RESPONSIBILITY
CHILD RESPONSIBILITY
DISCIPLINE POLICY
NONINSTRUCTIONAL
   RESPONSIBILITY
PARENT RESPONSIBILITY
RESPONSIBILITY
SCHOOL RESPONSIBILITY
TEACHER RESPONSIBILITY

232 STANDARDS

ADMISSION REQUIREMENTS
CREDENTIALS
EDUCATIONAL SPECIFICATIONS
EQUIPMENT STANDARDS
EQUIVALENCES
FACILITY GUIDELINES
PERFORMANCE CRITERIA
PERFORMANCE
   SPECIFICATIONS
SPECIFICATIONS
STANDARDS
   A CONDITIONS OF GRANT

233 SANCTIONS

DISPUTE SETTLEMENT
DISQUALIFICATION
FINES (PENALTIES)
INCENTIVE SYSTEMS
SANCTIONS
TEACHER STRIKES

240 REVENUE

BOND ISSUES
FEES
FINANCIAL SUPPORT
FUNDS IN TRUST
PRIVATE FINANCIAL SUPPORT
REVENUE
SCHOOL FUNDS
SCHOOL TAXES
   A ADULT EDUCATION TAXES
   A FINANCIAL RESOURCES
   A PUBLIC FINANCE
   A RESIDENCE CHARGES
   A SUBSCRIPTIONS
   A VOCATIONAL TRAINING
      TAXES

241 EXPENDITURE

CAPITAL OUTLAY (FOR FIXED
   ASSETS)
CONTRACTS
COSTS
EXPENDITURES
GRANTS
INSURANCE PROGRAMMES
INTEREST
OPERATING EXPENSES
PURCHASING
SUBVENTIONS
   A CONDITIONS OF SUBSIDY

242 SALARIES

FELLOWSHIPS
PREMIUM PAY
SALARIES
SCHOLARSHIPS
STUDENT LOANS
TEACHER SALARIES
TRAINING ALLOWANCES
  A EDUCATIONAL
    ALLOWANCES
  A EDUCATIONAL VOUCHERS
  A LOSS OF EARNINGS
    PAYMENTS

243 ACCOUNTING AND BUDGETING

ACCOUNTING
ALLOCATION PER STUDENT
BUDGETING
BUDGETS
COST EFFECTIVENESS
COST REDUCTION
EDUCATIONAL FINANCE
ESTIMATED COSTS
EXPENDITURE PER STUDENT
PROGRAMME COSTS
RESOURCE ALLOCATIONS
SCHOOL ACCOUNTING
UNIT COSTS
  A DEFICIT FINANCING

250 PHYSICAL FACILITIES PLANNING

DEFICIT (FACILITIES)
FACILITY REQUIREMENTS
NATURAL DISASTER
NUCLEAR PLANNING
PHYSICAL PLANS
PROGRAMMING (FACILITIES)
SITE PLANNING
SPACE STANDARDS

251 FACILITIES MANAGEMENT

BUILDING EVALUATION
BUILDING FINANCE
BUILDING USE
CIRCULATION
CONSTRUCTION COSTS
FACILITIES MANAGEMENT
MAINTENANCE

252 FACILITIES DESIGN

ACOUSTICS
ARCHITECTURAL CONCEPTS
ARCHITECTURAL DRAWINGS
AREA ANALYSIS
BUILDING DESIGN
BUILDING ENGINEERING
DESIGN PROCEDURE
ERGONOMICS
FACILITIES DESIGN
FURNITURE DESIGN
LIGHTING
THERMAL COMFORT

253 CONSTRUCTION PROGRAMMES

BUILDING ELEMENTS
BUILDING IMPROVEMENT
BUILDING MATERIALS
CONSTRUCTION EQUIPMENT
CONSTRUCTION PRACTICES
CONSTRUCTION PROCEDURES
CONSTRUCTION PROGRAMMES
FINISHES
INDUSTRIALIZED BUILDINGS
LOCAL MATERIALS

260 SCHOOL SYSTEMS

ADULT EDUCATION SYSTEMS
EDUCATIONAL ORGANIZATION
INSTITUTIONAL FRAMEWORK
PUBLIC SCHOOL SYSTEMS
RURAL SCHOOL SYSTEMS
SCHOOL SYSTEMS
  A MIXED SYSTEMS
  A PRIVATE EDUCATION
    SYSTEMS
  A PUBLIC EDUCATION
    SYSTEMS

261 ADMINISTRATIVE ORGANIZATION

ADMINISTRATIVE ORGANIZATION
CENTRAL EDUCATIONAL AGENCIES
CONSORTIA
GOVERNING BOARDS
INSTITUTIONAL SELF MANAGEMENT
INTERMEDIATE ADMINISTRATIVE UNITS
PLANNING BODIES
PROVINCIAL DEPARTMENTS OF EDUCATION
RESEARCH COORDINATING UNITS

262 ROLES AND RELATIONSHIPS

ADMINISTRATOR ROLE
INTERINSTITUTIONAL COOPERATION
PROGRAMME ADMINISTRATION
PROVINCIAL LOCAL RELATIONSHIP
SUPERINTENDENT ROLE
TEACHER ADMINISTRATION RELATIONSHIP
  A INTERORGANIZATIONAL COOPERATION

263 LOCAL RELATIONSHIPS

LOCAL EDUCATION AUTHORITIES
POLICE SCHOOL RELATIONSHIP
SCHOOL CLOSURE
SCHOOL COMMUNITY COOPERATION
SCHOOL COMMUNITY RELATIONSHIP
SCHOOL DISTRICT AUTONOMY
SCHOOL INDUSTRY RELATIONSHIP
  A ADULT EDUCATION SCHOOL COOPERATION
  A ADULT EDUCATION– COMMUNITY RELATIONS
  A ADULT EDUCATION– INDUSTRY COOPERATION
  A LOCAL AUTONOMY

264 SCHOOL DISTRICTS

CATCHMENT AREA
CONSOLIDATION OF SCHOOLS
DISTANCE
SAFETY
SCHOOL DISTRICTS
SCHOOL REDISTRICTING
SCHOOL REGISTRATION
TRAFFIC SAFETY
TRANSPORTATION

265 SCHOOL ADMINISTRATION

ACCIDENTS
COLLEGE ADMINISTRATION
COLLEGE SCHOOL COOPERATION
MATERIALS SELECTION
OVERCROWDED CLASSES
SCHOOL ADMINISTRATION
SCHOOL MAINTENANCE
TEACHING LOAD

266 STUDENT PROGRESS

ACCELERATION
ADMISSION
ATTENDANCE
COLLEGE PLACEMENT
COMPETITIVE SELECTION
DROPPING OUT
ENROLMENT
NUMERUS CLAUSUS
SCHOOL LEAVING
SELECTION
SELECTION PROCEDURES
STUDENT EMPLOYMENT
STUDENT PROGRESS
STUDENT PROMOTION
STUDENT TRANSFER
  A COURSE COMPLETION
  A FAILURE RATE
  A OPEN ENROLMENT
  A PERFORMANCE

INCENTIVES
A STUDENT RECRUITMENT

267 DISCIPLINE

DISCIPLINE
EXPULSION
FAILURE
GRADE REPETITION
PUNISHMENT
TRUANCY

270 SCHOOL SERVICES

ANCILLARY SERVICES
DAY CARE SERVICES
GUIDANCE SERVICES
LIBRARY SERVICES
MOBILE EDUCATIONAL
    SERVICES
PROFESSIONAL SERVICES
SCHOOL HEALTH SERVICES
SCHOOL SERVICES
SHARED SERVICES
SOCIOPSYCHOLOGICAL
    SERVICES
STUDENT PERSONNEL
    SERVICES

271 EDUCATIONAL PROGRAMMES

COMPENSATORY EDUCATION
    PROGRAMMES
EDUCATIONAL PROGRAMMES
EMERGENCY PROGRAMMES
EXCHANGE PROGRAMMES
GUIDANCE PROGRAMMES
LITERACY CAMPAIGNS
PROVINCIAL PROGRAMMES
RECREATIONAL PROGRAMMES
REHABILITATION
    PROGRAMMES
A LOCAL PROGRAMMING

272 SPECIFIC PROGRAMMES AND PROJECTS

DEMONSTRATION PROJECTS
FAMILY PROJECTS
PILOT PROJECTS
PROJECTS
RESEARCH PROJECTS
SCHOOL COMMUNITY
    PROGRAMMES
SCHOOL MEAL PROGRAMMES
SCHOOL RECREATIONAL
    PROGRAMMES

280 FIELD OF RESEARCH

BEHAVIOURAL SCIENCE
    RESEARCH
CLASSROOM RESEARCH
CURRICULUM RESEARCH
ECONOMIC RESEARCH
EDUCATIONAL RESEARCH
EXCEPTIONAL CHILD
    RESEARCH
EXPERIMENTAL EDUCATION
LANGUAGE RESEARCH
MEDIA RESEARCH
READING RESEARCH

281 PROBLEMS

ADMINISTRATIVE PROBLEMS
BEHAVIOUR PROBLEMS
CURRICULUM PROBLEMS
DELINQUENCY PREVENTION
DISCIPLINE PROBLEMS
FAMILY PROBLEMS
METHODOLOGICAL PROBLEMS
RESEARCH PROBLEMS
WELFARE PROBLEMS
A PARTICIPATION PROBLEMS

282 TYPE OF RESEARCH

ACTION PROGRAMMES
    (COMMUNITY)
ACTION RESEARCH
APPLIED RESEARCH
CASE STUDIES
COMPARATIVE ANALYSIS
CROSS CULTURAL STUDIES
EDUCATIONAL EXPERIMENTS

EMPIRICAL RESEARCH
EXPERIMENTAL RESEARCH
EXPERIMENTAL TEACHING
FEASIBILITY STUDIES
FIELD RESEARCH
FIELD STUDIES
FOLLOWUP STUDIES
FUNDAMENTAL RESEARCH
LONGITUDINAL STUDIES
OBSERVATIONAL STUDIES
OCCUPATIONAL SURVEYS
OPERATIONS RESEARCH
PERSONALITY STUDIES
PSYCHOLOGICAL STUDIES
RESEARCH AND DEVELOPMENT
STATISTICAL STUDIES

283 RESEARCH METHODOLOGY

CONTROL GROUPS
CORRELATION
CRITERIA
DATA BASE
EXPERIMENTAL GROUPS
PREDICTION
RELIABILITY
RESEARCH CRITERIA
RESEARCH DESIGN
RESEARCH FINDINGS
RESEARCH METHODOLOGY
SAMPLING
SOCIOMETRIC TECHNIQUES
TAXONOMY
VALIDITY

284 DATA

DATA ANALYSIS
DATA PROCESSING
EDUCATIONAL STATISTICS
GROUP NORMS
LITERACY STATISTICS
NATIONAL NORMS
STATISTICAL ANALYSIS
STATISTICAL DATA
TESTS OF SIGNIFICANCE
TIME SHARING

285 VARIABLES

CLIMATIC FACTORS
COMMUNITY
    CHARACTERISTICS
CULTURAL FACTORS
DELINQUENCY CAUSES
ECONOMIC FACTORS
ENROLMENT INFLUENCES
ETIOLOGY
FAILURE FACTORS
INTELLIGENCE FACTORS
INTERACTION
LANGUAGE ROLE
POLITICAL FACTORS
RELIGIOUS FACTORS
SOCIAL FACTORS
SUCCESS FACTORS
  A PARTICIPATION
    DETERRENTS
  A PARTICIPATION
    INCENTIVES

300 EDUCATIONAL OBJECTIVES

AFFECTIVE OBJECTIVES
BEHAVIOURAL OBJECTIVES
COGNITIVE OBJECTIVES
COURSE OBJECTIVES
EDUCATIONAL OBJECTIVES
PSYCHOMOTOR OBJECTIVES
TRAINING OBJECTIVES

301 SCHOOLS — BY LEVEL

BASIC SCHOOLS
LOWER SECONDARY SCHOOLS
MIDDLE SCHOOLS
NURSERY SCHOOLS
PRIMARY SCHOOLS
SECONDARY SCHOOLS
UPPER SECONDARY SCHOOLS

302 SCHOOLS — BY ADMINISTRATION

COMMUNITY SCHOOLS
INTERNATIONAL SCHOOLS
PRIVATE SCHOOLS

PROPRIETARY SCHOOLS
PUBLIC SCHOOLS

303 SCHOOLS — BY ORGANIZING PRINCIPLE

BOARDING SCHOOLS
COEDUCATIONAL SCHOOLS
CORRESPONDENCE SCHOOLS
DAY SCHOOLS
DOUBLE SHIFT SCHOOLS
EVENING SCHOOLS
EXTENDED DAY SCHOOLS
MOBILE SCHOOLS
NONGRADED SCHOOLS
ONE TEACHER SCHOOLS
RURAL SCHOOLS
SUBURBAN SCHOOLS
SUMMER SCHOOLS
URBAN SCHOOLS
YEAR ROUND SCHOOLS
   A WEEKEND SCHOOLS

304 SCHOOLS — SPECIAL

CORRECTIONAL SCHOOLS
DISADVANTAGED SCHOOLS
HOSPITAL SCHOOLS
SPECIAL SCHOOLS

305 SCHOOLS — EXPERIMENTAL

AFFILIATED SCHOOLS
ASSOCIATED SCHOOLS (UNESCO)
EXPERIMENTAL SCHOOLS
LABORATORY SCHOOLS

306 SCHOOLS — BY CURRICULUM

COMPREHENSIVE SCHOOLS
COMPREHENSIVE SECONDARY SCHOOLS
GENERAL SECONDARY SCHOOLS
TECHNICAL SECONDARY SCHOOLS
VOCATIONAL SCHOOLS
VOCATIONAL SECONDARY SCHOOLS
VOCATIONAL TRAINING CENTRES

307 COLLEGES

AGRICULTURAL COLLEGES
EVENING COURSES
JUNIOR COLLEGES
OPEN COLLEGES
PRIVATE COLLEGES
PUBLIC COLLEGES
RESIDENTIAL COLLEGES
TEACHERS COLLEGES
TECHNICAL COLLEGES
   A UNIVERSITY EXTENSION DEPARTMENTS

310 OTHER INSTITUTIONS

COLLEGE LIBRARIES
CULTURAL CENTRES
DOCUMENTATION CENTRES
INFORMATION CENTRES
LIBRARIES
MUSEUMS
NATIONAL LIBRARIES
PUBLIC LIBRARIES
SCHOOL LIBRARIES
THEATRES

311 CENTRES

ADULT EDUCATION CENTRES
CHILD CARE CENTRES
COUNSELLING CENTRES
GROUP TRAINING CENTRES
LITERACY CENTRES
OUT OF SCHOOL ACTIVITY CENTRES
PRESCHOOL CENTRES
STUDY CENTRES
   A COMMUNITY CENTRES
   A DISTANCE TEACHING INSTITUTIONS
   A MULTI PURPOSE CENTRES
   A RESIDENTIAL ADULT

CENTRES

312 RESEARCH CENTRES

CURRICULUM STUDY CENTRES
MEDIA RESOURCES CENTRES
RESEARCH CENTRES
SCIENCE TEACHING CENTRES
TEACHER CENTRES

313 CLINICS

CLINICS
HOSPITALS
PSYCHOEDUCATIONAL CLINICS

320 INSTRUCTIONAL PROGRAMMES

ACCELERATED PROGRAMMES
COLLEGE PROGRAMMES
DOCTORAL PROGRAMMES
DROPOUT PROGRAMMES
ENRICHMENT PROGRAMMES
INSTRUCTIONAL PROGRAMMES
MENTAL HEALTH
  PROGRAMMES
PREPRIMARY PROGRAMMES
SELF INSTRUCTIONAL
  PROGRAMMES
SPECIAL DEGREE
  PROGRAMMES
SPECIAL PROGRAMMES

321 ADULT PROGRAMMES

ADULT EDUCATION
  PROGRAMMES
FUNCTIONAL LITERACY
  PROGRAMMES
FUNCTIONAL LITERACY
  PROJECTS
INSERVICE EDUCATION
LITERACY PROGRAMMES
PARENT EDUCATION
  PROGRAMMES
  A DAY TIME PROGRAMMES
  A EXTENSION PROGRAMMES
  A INDIVIDUAL
    DEVELOPMENT
    PROGRAMMES
  A PRE RETIREMENT
    PROGRAMMES
  A RESIDENTIAL
    PROGRAMMES
  A RURAL EXTENSION
    PROGRAMMES
  A UNEMPLOYED EDUCATION
    PROGRAMMES
  A UNIVERSITY EXTENSION
    PROGRAMMES
  A VOCATIONAL TRAINING
    PROGRAMMES

322 SPECIAL PROGRAMMES

BLIND EDUCATION
DEAF EDUCATION
EXCEPTIONAL CHILD
  EDUCATION
A HANDICAPPED EDUCATION

330 CURRICULUM

COLLEGE CURRICULUM
COLLEGE PREPARATION
CORE CURRICULUM
CURRICULUM
GRADUATE STUDY
PREPRIMARY CURRICULUM
PRIMARY SCHOOL
  CURRICULUM
SECONDARY SCHOOL
  CURRICULUM
TEACHER EDUCATION
  CURRICULUM
UNDERGRADUATE STUDY
VOCATIONAL SCHOOL
  CURRICULUM

331 CURRICULUM DEVELOPMENT

CENTRES OF INTEREST
CONTENT ANALYSIS
CONTINUOUS PROGRESS PLAN
CURRICULUM DEVELOPMENT

INTERDISCIPLINARITY
INTERDISCIPLINARY
    APPROACH
MODULAR APPROACH
SEQUENTIAL APPROACH
SKILL ANALYSIS
STRUCTURAL ANALYSIS
SUBJECTS OF STUDY
SYLLABUSES
TEXTBOOK CONTENT
THEMATIC APPROACH
UNITS OF STUDY (SUBJECT
    FIELDS)
  A COMPULSORY COURSES

332 CURRICULUM TYPE

EXPERIMENTAL CURRICULUM
INDIVIDUALIZED CURRICULUM
INTEGRATED CURRICULUM
NONGRADED CURRICULUM

333 COURSES

ACCELERATED COURSES
COLLEGE MAJORS
COLLEGE MINORS
CORE COURSES
CORRESPONDENCE COURSES
COURSE DURATION
COURSE EVALUATION
COURSE ORGANIZATION
COURSES
CREDIT COURSES
ELECTIVE COURSES
NONCREDIT COURSES
OPTIONAL COURSES
ORIENTATION COURSES
REFRESHER TRAINING
REMEDIAL COURSES
SANDWICH COURSES
  A LONG COURSES
  A NON VOCATIONAL
    COURSES

334 SHORT COURSES

INSERVICE COURSES
INSTITUTE TYPE COURSES

SHORT COURSES
VACATION COURSES

335 INDIVIDUAL STUDY

CORRESPONDENCE TUITION
HOME STUDY
INDEPENDENT STUDY
INDIVIDUAL STUDY
STUDY ABROAD
STUDY TOURS
  A DIRECTED STUDY
  A DISTANCE STUDY

340 SCHOOL ORGANIZATION

DEPARTMENTAL TEACHING
    PLANS
DEPARTMENTS (SCHOOL)
FLEXIBLE TIMETABLING
MULTIPLE CLASS TEACHING
NONGRADED CLASSES
NONGRADED SYSTEM
OPEN PLAN SCHOOLS
RESEARCH AND INSTRUCTION
    UNITS
SCHOOL ORGANIZATION
TIMETABLES

341 GROUPING

ABILITY GROUPING
GROUPING (INSTRUCTIONAL
    PURPOSES)
GROUPING PROCEDURES
HETEROGENEOUS GROUPING
HOMOGENEOUS GROUPING
REGULAR CLASS PLACEMENT
  A AGE SEGREGATION

342 GRADE ORGANIZATION

COMMON CORE
GRADE ORGANIZATION
GRADES (PROGRAMME
    DIVISIONS)
INTERMEDIATE GRADES
KINDERGARTEN

PRIMARY GRADES
SECONDARY GRADES

343 CLASSES

CLASS SIZE
CLASSES
DISCUSSION GROUPS
LISTENING GROUPS
LITERACY CLASSES
OPPORTUNITY CLASSES
SPECIAL CLASSES
TRANSFER CLASSES

344 SCHOOL CALENDARS

EXTENDED SCHOOL YEAR
QUARTER SYSTEM
SCHOOL CALENDARS
SEMESTER DIVISIONS
VACATIONS

350 TEACHING

CONCEPT TEACHING
CREATIVE TEACHING
CROSS AGE TEACHING
DIAGNOSTIC TEACHING
PEDAGOGY
PEER TEACHING
PSYCHOEDUCATIONAL
    PROCESSES
STUDENT NEEDS
TEACHER ATTITUDES
TEACHER CHARACTERISTICS
TEACHER INFLUENCE
TEACHER MOTIVATION
TEACHING
TEAM TEACHING

351 TRAINING

APPRENTICESHIP
BASIC TRAINING
FULL TIME TRAINING
FURTHER TRAINING
INDUCTION TRAINING
MODULAR TRAINING
OFF THE JOB TRAINING
ON THE JOB TRAINING
PART TIME TRAINING
RETRAINING
SENSORY TRAINING
TEAM TRAINING
TRAINING
TRAINING BY STAGES
TRAINING PROGRAMMES
VOCATIONAL TRAINING
  A ACCELERATED
     VOCATIONAL TRAINING
  A MILITARY TRAINING

352 INSTRUCTION

COLLEGE INSTRUCTION
COMPETENCY-BASED
    EDUCATION
CONVENTIONAL INSTRUCTION
GROUP INSTRUCTION
HOME INSTRUCTION
INDIVIDUALIZED INSTRUCTION
INSTRUCTION
INSTRUCTIONAL
    IMPROVEMENT
INSTRUCTIONAL INNOVATION
INTERACTION PROCESS
LABORATORY TRAINING
LARGE GROUP INSTRUCTION
MASS EDUCATION
REMEDIAL INSTRUCTION
SELF INSTRUCTION
TRANSACTIONAL ANALYSIS
  A ADULT TEACHING
  A DIRECT TEACHING
  A DISTANCE TEACHING
  A INSTRUCTIONAL LEVEL

355 EDUCATIONAL METHODS

ACTIVITY METHODS
CLASSROOM COMMUNICATION
DEDUCTIVE METHODS
DISTANCE EDUCATION
EDUCATIONAL METHODS
GROUP DYNAMICS
INDUCTIVE METHODS
INTERVENTION
LECTURES

OPEN LEARNING SYSTEMS
SELF INSTRUCTIONAL
  METHODS
SEMINARS
SIMULATION
TEACHING METHODS
TUTORING
  A ANIMATION METHODS
  A CASE STUDY METHODS
  A MANAGEMENT GAMES

356 CLASSROOM TECHNIQUES

ASSIGNMENTS
CLASSROOM ARRANGEMENT
CLASSROOM PARTICIPATION
CLASSROOM TECHNIQUES
DISCUSSION (TEACHING
  TECHNIQUE)
EDUCATIONAL GAMES
GROUP DISCUSSION
HOMEWORK
LESSON PLANS
QUESTIONING TECHNIQUES
TEACHING ASSIGNMENTS
TEACHING PROCEDURES
TEACHING STYLES
TEACHING TECHNIQUES
TEACHING UNITS
TRAINING TECHNIQUES

357 ACTIVITIES

ACTIVITIES
ATHLETIC ACTIVITIES
CLASS ACTIVITIES
EXTRACURRICULAR ACTIVITIES
GROUP ACTIVITIES
HEALTH ACTIVITIES
INTEGRATED ACTIVITIES
OUT OF SCHOOL ACTIVITIES
OUTDOOR ACTIVITIES
RECREATIONAL ACTIVITIES
SCHOOL ACTIVITIES
STUDENT PROJECTS
STUDENT RESEARCH
  A EDUCATIONAL LEISURE
  A EDUCATIONAL
    RECREATION

360 EDUCATIONAL MEDIA

AUDIOVISUAL
  COMMUNICATION
AUDIOVISUAL INSTRUCTION
CLOSED CIRCUIT TELEVISION
EDUCATIONAL MEDIA
EDUCATIONAL RADIO
EDUCATIONAL TECHNOLOGY
EDUCATIONAL TELEVISION
INSTRUCTIONAL TELEVISION
INTERMEDIATE TECHNOLOGIES
MULTIMEDIA INSTRUCTION
TELEPHONE INSTRUCTION
TELEVISION VIEWING

361 PROGRAMMED INSTRUCTION

BRANCHING PROGRAMMES
COMPUTER ASSISTED
  INSTRUCTION
INSTRUCTIONAL
  PROGRAMMING
LINEAR PROGRAMMES
PROGRAMME CONTENT
PROGRAMME LENGTH
PROGRAMMED INSTRUCTION
PROMPTING
STIMULI

370 COUNSELLING

BEHAVIOURAL COUNSELLING
CAREER COUNSELLING
COUNSELLING
COUNSELLING OBJECTIVES
COUNSELLOR FUNCTIONS
EDUCATIONAL COUNSELLING
REHABILITATION
  COUNSELLING

371 COUNSELLING — SPECIFIC GROUPS

ADULT COUNSELLING
FAMILY COUNSELLING
GROUP COUNSELLING
INDIVIDUAL COUNSELLING

OCCUPATIONAL INFORMATION
TEACHER COUNSELLING
  A MARRIAGE COUNSELLING

372 IDENTIFICATION

CLINICAL DIAGNOSIS
HANDICAP DETECTION
IDENTIFICATION
REFERRAL
RETARDATION
SPEECH PATHOLOGY

373 THERAPY

HEARING THERAPY
MEDICAL TREATMENT
PSYCHOTHERAPY
REHABILITATION
SPEECH THERAPY
THERAPY
  A VOCATIONAL
    REHABILITATION

374 SPECIAL METHODS

BRAILLE
CODED SPEECH
LIPREADING
MANUAL COMMUNICATION
RESIDENTIAL CARE
SHELTERED EMPLOYMENT
TACTILE ADAPTATION

380 EDUCATIONAL ENVIRONMENT

CLASSROOM ENVIRONMENT
EDUCATIONAL ENVIRONMENT
FAMILY SCHOOL
  RELATIONSHIP
PARENT PARTICIPATION
PARENT STUDENT
  RELATIONSHIP
PARENT TEACHER
  COOPERATION
STUDENT COLLEGE
  RELATIONSHIP
STUDENT PARTICIPATION
STUDENT SCHOOL
  RELATIONSHIP
STUDENT TEACHER
  RELATIONSHIP
STUDENT UNREST
TEACHER PARTICIPATION
  A ADULT STUDENT-
    INSTITUTION
    RELATIONSHIP

381 EXTRACURRICULAR

CLUBS
DRAMA WORKSHOPS
INSTRUCTIONAL TRIPS
YOUTH CLUBS
YOUTH PROGRAMMES

382 EXTENSION EDUCATION

EXTENSION EDUCATION
LIBRARY EXTENSION
RURAL EXTENSION
UNIVERSITY EXTENSION
URBAN EXTENSION

390 CERTIFICATION

BACHELORS DEGREES
CERTIFICATION
CREDIT SYSTEM
DEGREE REQUIREMENTS
DEGREES (TITLES)
DIPLOMAS
DOCTORAL DEGREES
EDUCATIONAL CERTIFICATES
EMPLOYMENT QUALIFICATIONS
GRADUATION
MASTERS DEGREES
PRIMARY SCHOOL
  CERTIFICATES
SECONDARY SCHOOL
  CERTIFICATES
SPECIALIST IN EDUCATION
  DEGREES
TEACHER CERTIFICATION
VOCATIONAL SCHOOL
  CERTIFICATES

391 TESTING

ACADEMIC STANDARDS
ACHIEVEMENT RATING
CONTINUOUS ASSESSMENT
EDUCATIONAL DIAGNOSIS
EDUCATIONAL TESTING
GRADING
INTERNAL ASSESSMENT
MARKING
MEASUREMENT
MEASUREMENT AIMS
MEASUREMENT TECHNIQUES
MEDICAL EVALUATION
PSYCHOLOGICAL EVALUATION
PSYCHOLOGICAL TESTING
PSYCHOMETRICS
STUDENT EVALUATION
TESTING
   A PRIOR KNOWLEDGE LEVEL

392 TESTS — GENERAL

COLLEGE ENTRANCE
   EXAMINATIONS
CRITERION REFERENCED
   TESTS
DIAGNOSTIC TESTS
EDUCATIONAL TESTS
ENTRANCE EXAMINATIONS
ESSAY TESTS
EXAMINATIONS
MULTIPLE CHOICE TESTS
OBJECTIVE TESTS
PHYSICAL EXAMINATIONS
PROGNOSTIC TESTS
PSYCHOLOGICAL TESTS
RATING SCALES
STANDARDIZED TESTS
TEST CONSTRUCTION
TEST RESULTS

393 EDUCATIONAL TESTS

ACHIEVEMENT TESTS
APTITUDE TESTS
AUDIOVISUAL TESTS
INTEREST TESTS
LANGUAGE TESTS
LITERACY TESTS
PERFORMANCE TESTS
READING TESTS
SCIENCE TESTS
VERBAL TESTS

394 PSYCHOLOGICAL TESTS

INTELLIGENCE TESTS
MENTAL TESTS
PERSONALITY TESTS
PROJECTIVE TESTS

400 STAGES OF MAN

ADOLESCENTS
ADULTS
CHILDREN
ELDERLY PEOPLE
INFANTS
RURAL YOUTH
URBAN YOUTH
YOUTH
   A MIDDLE AGE PEOPLE
   A RETIRED PERSONS
   A YOUNG ADULTS

401 FAMILIES

ADOPTED CHILDREN
FATHERS
HEADS OF HOUSEHOLDS
MIDDLE CLASS PARENTS
MOTHERS
PARENTS
SIBLINGS
TWINS
WORKING CLASS PARENTS
WORKING PARENTS

402 DISADVANTAGED

CULTURALLY DISADVANTAGED
EDUCATIONALLY
   DISADVANTAGED
ILLITERATE ADULTS
MINORITY GROUP CHILDREN
SOCIALLY DISADVANTAGED
   A ECONOMICALLY

DISADVANTAGED

403 HANDICAPPED

BLIND
CRIPPLES
DEAF
DELINQUENTS
EMOTIONALLY DISTURBED
HANDICAPPED
HARD OF HEARING
HOMEBOUND PERSONS
HOSPITALIZED PERSONS
NEUROTICS
PARTIALLY SIGHTED
PHYSICALLY HANDICAPPED
PSYCHOTICS
RETARDED CHILDREN
SOCIALLY MALADJUSTED
   A MENTALLY HANDICAPPED
   A PRISONERS

410 STUDENTS

BOARDERS
DAY STUDENTS
EVENING STUDENTS
GRADUATES
PART TIME STUDENTS
PAST STUDENTS
STUDENTS
TRAINEES
   A FULL TIME STUDENTS
   A NON-PARTICIPANTS

411 SCHOOL STUDENTS

DROPOUTS
HANDICAPPED STUDENTS
KINDERGARTEN CHILDREN
PREPRIMARY CHILDREN
PRIMARY SCHOOL STUDENTS
SCHOOL LEAVERS
SECONDARY SCHOOL
   GRADUATES
SECONDARY SCHOOL
   STUDENTS
TRANSFER STUDENTS

412 NONFORMAL STUDENTS

ADULT STUDENTS
CONTINUATION STUDENTS
EXTERNAL CANDIDATES
NEW LITERATES
OUT OF SCHOOL YOUTH
   A INDEPENDANT LEARNERS

413 COLLEGE STUDENTS

COLLEGE GRADUATES
COLLEGE STUDENTS
FOREIGN STUDENTS
MARRIED STUDENTS
POSTGRADUATE STUDENTS
RESIDENT STUDENTS

414 LANGUAGE OF STUDENTS

BILINGUAL STUDENTS
UNILINGUAL STUDENTS

415 ACHIEVERS

HIGH ACHIEVERS
LOW ACHIEVERS
OVERACHIEVERS
SLOW LEARNERS

416 ABILITY OF STUDENTS

ABLE STUDENTS
ADVANCED STUDENTS
AVERAGE STUDENTS
EXCEPTIONAL STUDENTS
GIFTED STUDENTS

420 EDUCATIONAL PERSONNEL

ATTENDANCE OFFICERS
EDUCATIONAL
   ADMINISTRATORS
EDUCATIONAL PERSONNEL
EXAMINERS
INSPECTORS
PRIMARY SCHOOL INSPECTORS

SECONDARY SCHOOL
    INSPECTORS
SUPERINTENDENTS
SUPERVISORS

421 TEACHERS

ADULT EDUCATORS
PREPRIMARY TEACHERS
PRIMARY SCHOOL TEACHERS
RURAL SCHOOL TEACHERS
SECONDARY SCHOOL
    TEACHERS
SPECIAL EDUCATION
    TEACHERS
TEACHERS
TRAINERS
WOMEN TEACHERS
  A RESOURCE PERSONS

422 COLLEGE TEACHERS

COLLEGE DEANS
COLLEGE TEACHERS
LECTURERS
PRESIDENTS
PROFESSORS
TEACHER EDUCATORS
WOMEN PROFESSORS
  A EXTENSION TEACHERS
  A UNIVERSITY EXTENSION
    TEACHERS

423 SCHOOL PERSONNEL

HEADS OF DEPARTMENT
    (SCHOOL)
PARAPROFESSIONAL SCHOOL
    PERSONNEL
PRINCIPALS
PRIVATE SCHOOL TEACHERS
PUBLIC SCHOOL TEACHERS
SCHOOL PERSONNEL

424 INSTRUCTIONAL STAFF

BEGINNING TEACHERS
DIFFERENTIATED STAFFS

FORMER TEACHERS
GIFTED TEACHERS
ITINERANT TEACHERS
LITERACY WORKERS
MINORITY GROUP TEACHERS
PART TIME TEACHERS
STUDENT TEACHERS
SUBSTITUTE TEACHERS
TEACHER AIDES
TEACHER INTERNS
TEACHING ASSISTANTS
TEACHING PERSONNEL
  A FULL TIME EDUCATORS
  A PART TIME EDUCATORS

425 SUBJECT TEACHERS

ART TEACHERS
COACHING TEACHERS
GEOGRAPHY TEACHERS
HISTORY TEACHERS
HOME ECONOMICS TEACHERS
LANGUAGE TEACHERS
MATHEMATICS TEACHERS
MUSIC TEACHERS
SCIENCE TEACHERS
VOCATIONAL AGRICULTURE
    TEACHERS
VOCATIONAL EDUCATION
    TEACHERS

426 METHODS TEACHERS

BILINGUAL TEACHERS
COLLEGE SUPERVISORS
MASTER TEACHERS
METHODS TEACHERS
REMEDIAL TEACHERS
RESOURCE TEACHERS
TEAM LEADER (TEACHING)
TELEVISION TEACHERS

430 CONSULTANTS

CHILD CARE WORKERS
CHILD DEVELOPMENT
    SPECIALISTS
CONSULTANTS
EDUCATIONAL RESEARCHERS

INTERNATIONAL EDUCATION
    CONSULTANTS
INTERNATIONAL EXPERTS
LEARNING SPECIALISTS
MEDIA SPECIALISTS
READING CONSULTANTS
RESEARCH DIRECTORS
RESEARCHERS
SCHOOL PSYCHOLOGISTS
SCIENCE CONSULTANTS
SPECIALISTS

431 COUNSELLORS

COUNSELLORS
EMPLOYMENT COUNSELLORS
FOREIGN STUDENT ADVISERS
GUIDANCE PERSONNEL
PRIMARY SCHOOL
    COUNSELLORS
SECONDARY SCHOOL
    COUNSELLORS
  A ADULT COUNSELLORS

432 THERAPISTS

HEARING THERAPISTS
OCCUPATIONAL THERAPISTS
PHYSICAL THERAPISTS
SPEECH THERAPISTS
THERAPISTS

433 HEALTH PERSONNEL

HEALTH PERSONNEL
MEDICAL CONSULTANTS
NURSES
PATIENTS (PERSONS)
PHYSICIANS
SCHOOL NURSES
VETERINARIANS
  A DENTISTS
  A OPTICIANS
  A PHARMACISTS
  A SURGEONS

440 LEADERS

ADULT LEADERS
CHANGE AGENTS
COMMUNITY LEADERS
EXTENSION AGENTS
VOLUNTEERS
YOUTH LEADERS

441 PERSONNEL

INDUSTRIAL PERSONNEL
MILITARY PERSONNEL
NATIONAL CADRES
NONPROFESSIONAL
    PERSONNEL
PROFESSIONAL PERSONNEL
SCIENTIFIC PERSONNEL
  A PERSONNEL

442 COMMITTEES

ADVISORY COMMITTEES
AUDIENCES
COMMITTEES
  A ADULT PROGRAMME
    COMMITTEES

443 GROUPS

AGE GROUPS
DISADVANTAGED GROUPS
ETHNIC GROUPS
GROUPS
LOW INCOME GROUPS
MEN
MINORITY GROUPS
PEER GROUPS
RELIGIOUS CULTURAL GROUPS
SELF DIRECTED GROUPS
USER GROUPS
WOMEN
  A TARGET GROUPS

450 WORKERS COLLECTIVELY

EMPLOYEES
EMPLOYERS

LABOUR FORCE
  NONPARTICIPANTS
MANAGERS
UNDEREMPLOYED
UNION MEMBERS
  A SELF EMPLOYED
  A UNEMPLOYED

451 CLASSES OF WORKERS

ADMINISTRATIVE WORKERS
AGRICULTURAL WORKERS
CLERICAL WORKERS
COMMERCIAL WORKERS
FARMERS
HOUSEWIVES
JOB APPLICANTS
MARRIED WOMEN RETURNERS
SEASONAL WORKERS
SEMISKILLED WORKERS
SERVICE WORKERS
SKILLED WORKERS
UNSKILLED WORKERS
WOMEN WORKERS
WORKERS
  A CHEMICAL WORKERS
  A CLOTHING WORKERS
  A CONSTRUCTION WORKERS
  A DISTRIBUTIVE WORKERS
  A FOOD INDUSTRY WORKERS
  A FOREMEN
  A FORESTRY WORKERS
  A HOTEL WORKERS
  A LEATHERWORKERS
  A MANUAL WORKERS
  A METALWORKERS
  A MINERS
  A NONMANUAL WORKERS
  A PETROLEUM WORKERS
  A PLANTATION WORKERS
  A PRINTING WORKERS
  A PRODUCTION WORKERS
  A RAILWAY WORKERS
  A SALESMEN
  A SEAFARERS
  A TEXTILE WORKERS
  A TRANSPORT WORKERS
  A WOODWORKERS

452 TECHNICIANS

AGRICULTURAL TECHNICIANS
DRAFTSMEN
ELECTRICIANS
ELECTRONIC TECHNICIANS
ENGINEERING TECHNICIANS
TECHNICIANS
  A SURVEYORS

460 LAW AND ORDER PROFESSIONS

ACCOUNTANTS
CIVIL SERVANTS
LAWYERS
LEGISLATORS
OMBUDSMEN
POLICE
SENIOR CIVIL SERVANTS
  A FIREFIGHTERS

461 ARTS AND PHYSICAL PROFESSIONS

ARCHITECTS
ARTISTS
ATHLETES
AUTHORS
MUSICIANS

462 SOCIAL PROFESSIONS

DOCUMENTALISTS
INFORMATION SPECIALISTS
INTERPRETERS
LIBRARIANS
PRIESTS
PSYCHIATRISTS
PSYCHOLOGISTS
SCHOOL LIBRARIANS
SOCIAL SCIENTISTS
SOCIAL WORKERS

463 SCIENTIFIC PROFESSIONS

ENGINEERS
SCIENTISTS

A CHEMICAL ENGINEERS
A CHEMISTS
A ELECTRICAL ENGINEERS
A MECHANICAL ENGINEERS
A METALLURGISTS
A MINING ENGINEERS
A PHYSICISTS

470 MIGRANTS

FOREIGN WORKERS
IMMIGRANTS
MIGRANTS
NOMADS
REFUGEES

475 RELIGIOUS GROUPS

BUDDHISTS
CATHOLICS
JEWS
MOSLEMS
PROTESTANTS
  A LAITY

500 AGE

ADOLESCENCE
AGE
AGE DIFFERENCES
BIRTH ORDER
CHILDHOOD
DEATH
EARLY CHILDHOOD
INFANCY
  A ADULTHOOD
  A EARLY ADULTHOOD
  A MIDDLE AGE
  A MINIMUM AGE
  A OLD AGE

501 SEX

FEMALE
MALE
SEX (CHARACTERISTICS)
SEX DIFFERENCES

502 GROWTH PATTERNS

BODY HEIGHT
BODY WEIGHT
CARDIOVASCULAR SYSTEM
DENTAL HEALTH
GROWTH PATTERNS
HEREDITY
HUMAN BODY
HYGIENE
MENTAL HEALTH
NERVOUS SYSTEM
PHYSICAL HEALTH
PREGNANCY
SEXUALITY

503 PHYSIOLOGY

AUDITION (PHYSIOLOGY)
EXERCISE (PHYSIOLOGY)
EYE MOVEMENTS
FATIGUE
HUNGER
LATERAL DOMINANCE
SIGHT
SLEEP

510 PERCEPTION

AUDITORY PERCEPTION
AURAL STIMULI
PERCEPTION
PERCEPTUAL MOTOR
  COORDINATION
VISUAL PERCEPTION
VISUAL STIMULI

511 RESPONSE

CONDITIONED RESPONSE
EIDETIC IMAGES
EXTINCTION (PSYCHOLOGY)
MEDIATION THEORY
MOTOR REACTIONS
PATTERN RECOGNITION
REACTION TIME
RECALL (PSYCHOLOGICAL)
RECOGNITION
REINFORCEMENT

RESPONSE MODE
REWARDS
TIME FACTORS (LEARNING)
TRANSFER OF TRAINING

512 LEARNING

ACTIVITY LEARNING
ASSOCIATIVE LEARNING
DISCOVERY LEARNING
LEARNING
MULTISENSORY LEARNING
ROTE LEARNING
SEQUENTIAL LEARNING
STUDY
SYMBOLIC LEARNING
VERBAL LEARNING
VISUAL LEARNING
  A KNOWLEDGE
    TRANSMISSION

513 LEARNING PROCESSES

CONCEPT FORMATION
LEARNING DIFFICULTIES
LEARNING DISABILITIES
LEARNING PROCESSES
LEARNING THEORIES
  A LEARNING SPEED
  A MENTAL SET

514 STAGES OF LEARNING

ADULT LEARNING
PRESCHOOL LEARNING
  A HORIZONTAL
    INTEGRATION (LEARNING)
  A LEARNING INTEGRATION
  A VERTICAL INTEGRATION
    (LEARNING)

520 ABILITY

ABILITY
APTITUDE
COGNITIVE ABILITY
CREATIVE ABILITY
INTELLIGENCE
INTELLIGENCE QUOTIENT
LANGUAGE ABILITY
READING ABILITY
TALENT
VOCATIONAL APTITUDES
  A INTELLECTUAL
    DETERIORATION

521 THOUGHT PROCESSES

COGNITIVE PROCESSES
COMPREHENSION
CREATIVE THINKING
CRITICAL THINKING
FUNCTIONAL READING
LOGICAL THINKING
MEMORIZING
PRODUCTIVE THINKING
READING PROCESSES
THOUGHT PROCESSES
VISUALIZATION
  A SHORT TERM MEMORY

522 ABSTRACT REASONING

ABSTRACT REASONING
COMPLEXITY LEVEL
CONCEPTUAL SCHEMES
CREATIVITY
FUNDAMENTAL CONCEPTS
GENERALIZATION
IMAGINATION
ORIGINALITY
PROBLEM SOLVING
THEORIES

530 PERSONALITY DEVELOPMENT

BEHAVIOUR DEVELOPMENT
CHILD DEVELOPMENT
COGNITIVE DEVELOPMENT
CREATIVE DEVELOPMENT
EMOTIONAL DEVELOPMENT
INDIVIDUAL DEVELOPMENT
INDIVIDUAL DIFFERENCES
INTELLECTUAL DEVELOPMENT
LANGUAGE DEVELOPMENT
MENTAL DEVELOPMENT

MOTOR DEVELOPMENT
PERSONALITY DEVELOPMENT
PHYSICAL DEVELOPMENT
  A ADULT DEVELOPMENT

531 MATURATION

IMMATURITY
LEARNING READINESS
MATURATION
PERSONAL GROWTH
READINESS
READING READINESS
SCHOOL READINESS
SOCIAL MATURITY
VOCATIONAL MATURITY
  A AGEING
  A SENESCENCE
  A SOCIAL DISENGAGEMENT
  A TEACHABLE MOMENTS

532 SPEECH

ARTICULATION (SPEECH)
CHILD LANGUAGE
DICTION
PRONUNCIATION
SPEECH

533 BASIC SKILLS

BASIC SKILLS
COMMUNICATION SKILLS
LANGUAGE SKILLS
MECHANICAL SKILLS
PSYCHOMOTOR SKILLS
SKILLS
STUDY SKILLS
TEACHING SKILLS

534 SKILL DEVELOPMENT

HANDWRITING DEVELOPMENT
READING DEVELOPMENT
SKILL DEVELOPMENT
VOCABULARY DEVELOPMENT
VOCATIONAL DEVELOPMENT

535 ACHIEVEMENT

ATTENTION
ATTENTION SPAN
KNOWLEDGE LEVEL
LANGUAGE PROFICIENCY
LITERACY ACHIEVEMENT
LITERACY RETENTION
PERFORMANCE
PERFORMANCE FACTORS
PERSISTENCE
RETENTION
STUDENT ACHIEVEMENT
SUCCESS

536 INDIVIDUAL NEEDS

ACHIEVEMENT NEED
CHILDHOOD NEEDS
INDIVIDUAL NEEDS
LEARNING NEEDS
NEED GRATIFICATION
PLAY
PSYCHOLOGICAL NEEDS
STATUS NEED

537 LEARNING ACTIVITIES

CHILDRENS GAMES
CULTURAL ACTIVITIES
LEARNING ACTIVITIES
PHYSICAL ACTIVITIES
SPEAKING ACTIVITIES

540 AFFECTION

AFFECTIVE BEHAVIOUR
AFFECTIVITY
AGGRESSION
ANXIETY
EMOTIONAL PROBLEMS
FEAR
INSECURITY
REJECTION
SECURITY

541 INTERESTS

ASPIRATION
EDUCATIONAL EXPECTATIONS
EDUCATIONAL INTEREST
GOAL ORIENTATION
INFORMATION SEEKING
INTERESTS
MOTIVATION
STUDENT MOTIVATION
VOCATIONAL INTERESTS

542 HABITS

HABIT FORMATION
LISTENING HABITS
SMOKING
SPEECH HABITS
STUDY HABITS
  A READING HABITS

550 ENVIRONMENTAL INFLUENCES

CULTURAL ENVIRONMENT
ENVIRONMENTAL INFLUENCES
ETHNIC ORIGINS
FAMILY INFLUENCE
HOME ENVIRONMENT
PHYSICAL ENVIRONMENT
PRENATAL INFLUENCES
SOCIAL ENVIRONMENT
WORK ENVIRONMENT

551 ADJUSTMENT

ADJUSTMENT
ADJUSTMENT PROBLEMS
EMOTIONAL ADJUSTMENT
MALADJUSTMENT
PSYCHOLOGICAL PATTERNS
SOCIAL ADJUSTMENT
STUDENT ADJUSTMENT
VOCATIONAL ADJUSTMENT

552 ATTITUDES

ATTITUDES
BIAS
CHANGING ATTITUDES
CHILDHOOD ATTITUDES
CLASS ATTITUDES
FAMILY ATTITUDES
OPINIONS
SCHOOL ATTITUDES
SOCIAL ATTITUDES
STEREOTYPES
STUDENT ATTITUDES
WORK ATTITUDES

553 RELATIONSHIP

FAMILY RELATIONSHIP
INTERPERSONAL RELATIONSHIP
PARENT CHILD RELATIONSHIP
PARENT ROLE
POLITICAL SOCIALIZATION
RELATIONSHIP
ROLE PERCEPTION
ROLE PLAYING
ROLE THEORY
SOCIAL RELATIONS
SOCIALIZATION
  A ROLE CONFLICT

554 GROUP MEMBERSHIP

CONFORMITY
GROUP MEMBERSHIP
INTERPERSONAL PROBLEMS
LEADERSHIP
PARTICIPANT INVOLVEMENT
PARTICIPANT SATISFACTION
PARTICIPATION
PEER ACCEPTANCE
PEER RELATIONSHIP
TEAMWORK
  A ALIENATION
  A GROUP LEADERSHIP
  A NON PARTICIPATION

555 SELF CONCEPT

IDENTIFICATION
  (PSYCHOLOGICAL)
MORAL VALUES

PERSONALITY
PERSONALITY THEORIES
SELF ACTUALIZATION
SELF CONCEPT
SELF EVALUATION
SELF EXPRESSION
VALUES

560 BEHAVIOUR

BEHAVIOUR
BEHAVIOUR CHANGE
BEHAVIOUR THEORIES
GROUP BEHAVIOUR
INFANT BEHAVIOUR
SELF CONTROL
STUDENT BEHAVIOUR
TEACHER BEHAVIOUR

561 INDIVIDUAL CHARACTERISTICS

ADULT CHARACTERISTICS
CULTURAL TRAITS
CURIOSITY
INDIVIDUAL CHARACTERISTICS
PHYSICAL CHARACTERISTICS
PSYCHOLOGICAL
    CHARACTERISTICS
STUDENT CHARACTERISTICS
WORKER TRAITS

562 EXPERIENCE

EDUCATIONAL EXPERIENCE
EMOTIONAL EXPERIENCE
EXPERIENCE
SENSORY EXPERIENCE
SOCIAL EXPERIENCE
WORK EXPERIENCE

563 CAREERS

CAREER CHOICE
CAREER PLANNING
CAREERS
JOB SATISFACTION
OCCUPATIONAL MOBILITY

570 STATES OF HANDICAP

AMETROPIA
DOWNS SYNDROME
DYSLEXIA
MENTAL ILLNESS
MENTAL RETARDATION
MINIMAL BRAIN INJURY
PSYCHOSOMATIC DISEASES
SENSORY DEPRIVATION

571 HANDICAPS

HANDICAPS
LANGUAGE HANDICAPS
MENTAL HANDICAPS
MULTIPLE HANDICAPS
NEUROLOGICAL HANDICAPS
PERCEPTUAL DISORDERS
PHYSICAL HANDICAPS
SPEECH HANDICAPS
VISUAL HANDICAPS

572 EMOTIONAL DISTURBANCE

ANTI SOCIAL BEHAVIOUR
AUTISM
CONFLICT
CONFLICT RESOLUTION
DELINQUENCY
DRUG ABUSE
EMOTIONAL DISTURBANCE
PERSONALITY PROBLEMS
YOUTH PROBLEMS

600 LIBERAL ARTS

CULTURES
ETHICS
HUMANISM
HUMANITIES
LOGIC
PHILOSOPHY

610 FINE ARTS

ART
CINEMA

COMMERCIAL ART
DANCE
FINE ARTS
GRAPHIC ARTS
HANDICRAFTS
MUSIC
PAINTING
SCULPTURE
SINGING
THEATRE ARTS

615 LITERATURE

LITERARY ANALYSIS
LITERARY CRITICISM
LITERARY HISTORY
LITERARY INFLUENCES
LITERATURE
NATIONAL LITERATURE
REALISM
ROMANTICISM
SYMBOLS (LITERARY)
WORLD LITERATURE

616 LITERARY GENRES

BIOGRAPHIES
DRAMA
ESSAYS
FABLES
FICTION
LITERARY GENRES
MYTHOLOGY
NOVELS
POETRY
PROSE
SATIRE
SHORT STORIES

620 LANGUAGE ARTS

ALPHABETS
COMPOSITION (LITERARY)
CONNECTED DISCOURSE
FIGURATIVE LANGUAGE
HANDWRITING
LANGUAGE ARTS
LISTENING
ORAL READING
ORTHOGRAPHIC SYMBOLS
READING
SIGHT VOCABULARY
SPEAKING
SPELLING
TRANSLATION
VOCABULARY
WORD FREQUENCY
WRITING

621 LINGUISTICS

CONTRASTIVE LINGUISTICS
DESCRIPTIVE LINGUISTICS
LANGUAGE PATTERNS
LANGUAGE TYPOLOGY
LINGUISTIC THEORY
LINGUISTICS
PROGRAMMING LANGUAGES
UNWRITTEN LANGUAGES

622 GRAMMAR

ETYMOLOGY
FORM CLASSES (LANGUAGES)
GENERATIVE GRAMMAR
GRAMMAR
INTONATION
MORPHEMES
MORPHOLOGY (LANGUAGES)
PHONETICS
PHONOLOGY
SEMANTICS
SENTENCE STRUCTURE
STRUCTURAL GRAMMAR
SYNTAX
TRADITIONAL GRAMMAR
TRANSFORMATION THEORY
    (LANGUAGE)

625 LANGUAGE FAMILIES

AFRICAN LANGUAGES
AFRO ASIATIC LANGUAGES
AMERICAN INDIAN
    LANGUAGES
CAUCASIAN LANGUAGES
CREOLES
DIALECTS

DRAVIDIAN LANGUAGES
GERMANIC LANGUAGES
INDO EUROPEAN LANGUAGES
LANGUAGES
MALAYO POLYNESIAN
    LANGUAGES
ROMANCE LANGUAGES
SINO TIBETAN LANGUAGES
SLAVIC LANGUAGES
URALIC ALTAIC LANGUAGES

626 LANGUAGES

ARABIC
CHINESE
ENGLISH
FRENCH
GERMAN
NATIONAL LANGUAGE
RUSSIAN
SPANISH

627 LANGUAGES IN TIME

CLASSICAL LANGUAGES
MODERN LANGUAGES

630 SCIENCES

COMPUTER SCIENCES
INFORMATION SCIENCE
MILITARY SCIENCE
SCIENCES
SCIENTIFIC CONCEPTS

631 MATHEMATICS

ALGEBRA
ALGEBRAIC CONCEPTS
APPLIED MATHEMATICS
ARITHMETIC
ARITHMETICAL CONCEPTS
CALCULATION
GEOMETRIC CONCEPTS
GEOMETRY
MATHEMATICAL CONCEPTS
MATHEMATICS
METRIC SYSTEM

MODERN MATHEMATICS
NUMBER CONCEPTS
NUMBERS
PROBABILITY

632 BIOLOGICAL SCIENCES

ANATOMY
BIOLOGY
BOTANY
ECOLOGY
GENETICS
PHYSIOLOGY
ZOOLOGY

633 PHYSICAL SCIENCES

ASTRONOMY
CHEMISTRY
EARTH SCIENCES
ELECTRICITY
ELECTRONICS
GEOLOGY
METEOROLOGY
NUCLEAR PHYSICS
OPTICS
PHYSICS

640 SOCIAL SCIENCES

ANTHROPOLOGY
CIVICS
COMPARATIVE EDUCATION
DEMOGRAPHY
DEVELOPMENT STUDIES
ECONOMICS
EDUCATIONAL ECONOMICS
EDUCATIONAL SCIENCES
GEOGRAPHIC CONCEPTS
GEOGRAPHY
HOME ECONOMICS
INTERNATIONAL EDUCATION
INTERNATIONAL RELATIONS
POLITICAL SCIENCE
SOCIAL SCIENCES
SOCIAL STUDIES

641 HISTORY

EDUCATIONAL HISTORY
HISTORY
MODERN HISTORY
NATIONAL HISTORY
WORLD HISTORY

642 BEHAVIOURAL SCIENCES

BEHAVIOURAL SCIENCES
CHILD PSYCHOLOGY
DEVELOPMENTAL PSYCHOLOGY
EDUCATIONAL
   ANTHROPOLOGY
EDUCATIONAL PSYCHOLOGY
EDUCATIONAL SOCIOLOGY
EXPERIMENTAL PSYCHOLOGY
INDIVIDUAL PSYCHOLOGY
PSYCHOLOGY
PSYCHOPATHOLOGY
SOCIAL PSYCHOLOGY
SOCIOLOGY

645 TECHNOLOGY

AVIATION TECHNOLOGY
ELECTROMECHANICAL
   TECHNOLOGY
ENGINEERING TECHNOLOGY
INDUSTRIAL TECHNOLOGY
RADIO TECHNOLOGY

646 AGRONOMY

AGRICULTURAL ENGINEERING
AGRICULTURE
AGRONOMY
ANIMAL SCIENCE
FORESTRY
HORTICULTURE
SOIL CONSERVATION

647 ENGINEERING

CIVIL ENGINEERING
ENGINEERING
HYDRAULICS

INDUSTRIAL ARTS
MECHANICS (PROCESS)
METALWORKING
PHOTOGRAPHY
PRINTING
TECHNICAL DRAWING
WOODWORKING
  A MECHANICAL
    ENGINEERING

650 PROFESSIONAL

ARCHITECTURE
CYBERNETICS
FACILITIES PLANNING
JOURNALISM
LEXICOLOGY
LIBRARY SCIENCE
QUANTITY SURVEYING

651 HEALTH

ATHLETICS
CALISTHENICS
DENTISTRY
MEDICINE
PEDIATRY
PSYCHIATRY
  A GERIATRICS

660 READING INSTRUCTION

ADULT READING
   PROGRAMMES
BEGINNING READING
CORRECTIVE READING
RAPID READING
READABILITY
READING DIFFICULTY
READING INSTRUCTION
READING LEVEL
READING PROGRAMMES
REMEDIAL READING
   PROGRAMMES

661 READING METHODS

GLOBAL METHOD

INDEPENDENT READING
INITIAL TEACHING ALPHABET
LITERACY METHODS
PHONICS
SIGHT METHOD
SILENT READING

662 LANGUAGE INSTRUCTION

LANGUAGE ENRICHMENT
LANGUAGE INSTRUCTION
LANGUAGE PROGRAMMES
MODERN LANGUAGE
    INSTRUCTION
MODERN LANGUAGE PRIMARY
    PROGRAMMES
MOTHER TONGUE
    INSTRUCTION
SECOND LANGUAGE
    INSTRUCTION
SPEECH INSTRUCTION
VERBAL COMMUNICATION

663 LANGUAGE METHODS

CONVERSATIONAL LANGUAGE
    COURSES
HANDWRITING INSTRUCTION
INTENSIVE LANGUAGE
    COURSES
PATTERN DRILLS (LANGUAGE)
SPELLING INSTRUCTION
STORY TELLING

670 SCIENCE INSTRUCTION

ELEMENTARY SCIENCE
GENERAL SCIENCE
MATHEMATICS INSTRUCTION
PRETECHNOLOGY
    PROGRAMMES
PREVOCATIONAL EDUCATION
PRIMARY SCHOOL
    MATHEMATICS
PRIMARY SCHOOL SCIENCE
SCIENCE EDUCATION
SCIENCE INSTRUCTION
SCIENCE PROGRAMMES
SECONDARY SCHOOL
    MATHEMATICS
SECONDARY SCHOOL SCIENCE

671 SCIENCE METHODS

DEMONSTRATIONS
    (EDUCATIONAL)
EXPERIMENTS
FIELD EXPERIENCE
    PROGRAMMES
LABORATORY EXPERIMENTS
LABORATORY PROCEDURES
LABORATORY TECHNIQUES
OBSERVATION
PRACTICUMS
SCIENCE EXPERIMENTS

672 VOCATIONAL INSTRUCTION

AGRICULTURAL EDUCATION
COMMERCIAL EDUCATION
DISTRIBUTIVE EDUCATION
INDUSTRIAL EDUCATION
MANAGEMENT EDUCATION
SHOP CURRICULUM
A ADMINISTRATOR
    EDUCATION

673 VOCATIONAL METHODS

ACCIDENT PREVENTION
AGRICULTURAL TRAINING
BUSINESS SUBJECTS
INPLANT PROGRAMMES
PRACTICE PERIODS
PROJECT TRAINING METHODS
SUPERVISED FARM PRACTICE
WORK EXPERIENCE
    PROGRAMMES

680 SOCIAL STUDIES

AREA STUDIES
COMMUNITY STUDY
GEOGRAPHY INSTRUCTION
HISTORY INSTRUCTION
INTERCULTURAL PROGRAMMES
POLITICAL EDUCATION

681 PROFESSIONAL EDUCATION

COUNSELLOR TRAINING
ENGINEERING EDUCATION
LEADERSHIP TRAINING
LEGAL EDUCATION
LIBRARY SCIENCE TRAINING
MEDICAL EDUCATION
THEOLOGICAL EDUCATION

682 MORAL EDUCATION

DEVELOPMENT EDUCATION
DISARMAMENT EDUCATION
ETHICAL INSTRUCTION
MORAL EDUCATION
PEACE EDUCATION
RELIGIOUS EDUCATION
WORK EDUCATION

683 HEALTH EDUCATION

ALCOHOL EDUCATION
DRUG EDUCATION
ENVIRONMENTAL EDUCATION
FIRST AID
HEALTH EDUCATION
HOME ECONOMICS EDUCATION
PHYSICAL EDUCATION
POPULATION EDUCATION
SAFETY EDUCATION
SEX EDUCATION

684 AESTHETIC EDUCATION

AESTHETIC EDUCATION
ART APPRECIATION
ART EDUCATION
LITERATURE APPRECIATION
MUSIC APPRECIATION
MUSIC EDUCATION

690 TEACHER EDUCATION

EDUCATIONAL READINGS
INSERVICE TEACHER
    EDUCATION
PRACTICE TEACHING

PRESERVICE TEACHER
    EDUCATION
PRINCIPLES OF TEACHING
TEACHER EDUCATION
TEACHER EDUCATOR
    EDUCATION
TEACHER ORIENTATION
TEACHER TRAINING SCHOOLS
TEACHING EXPERIENCE

691 EDUCATION COURSES

CLASS MANAGEMENT
EDUCATION COURSES
LESSON OBSERVATION
    CRITERIA
METHODS COURSES
MICROTEACHING
TEACHER SEMINARS

700 RESOURCES

COMMUNITY RESOURCES
EDUCATIONAL RESOURCES
NATURAL RESOURCES
RESOURCE MATERIALS
RESOURCES

710 CAPITAL ASSETS

BUILDINGS
CAPITAL ASSETS
EDUCATIONAL FACILITIES
RELOCATABLE FACILITIES
SITES
    A SOCIOCULTURAL
    FACILITIES

711 EDUCATIONAL SPACES

CLASSROOMS
EDUCATIONAL SPACES
EXHIBITION AREAS
INDIVIDUAL LEARNING AREAS
LABORATORIES
LECTURE HALLS
OUTDOOR TEACHING AREAS
SPECIAL CLASSROOMS

A ADULT EDUCATION
ACCOMMODATION

712 ANCILLARY SPACES

ANCILLARY SPACES
BOARDING FACILITIES
RECREATIONAL FACILITIES
SPORTS FACILITIES
STAFF HOUSING
STUDENT HOUSING

720 PUBLICATIONS

GOVERNMENT PUBLICATIONS
NEWSPAPERS
OFFICIAL REPORTS
PERIODICALS
PUBLICATIONS
REFERENCE MATERIALS
SCHOOL PUBLICATIONS
SERIALS

721 DOCUMENTS

DOCTORAL THESES
DOCUMENTS
INDEXES (LOCATERS)
LETTERS (CORRESPONDENCE)
MASTER THESES
MICROFORMS
SCRIPTS
WORD LISTS

722 BOOKS

ANTHOLOGIES
ATLASES
BOOKS
CHILDRENS BOOKS
LIBRARY COLLECTIONS

723 RECORDS

ATTENDANCE RECORDS
PAYROLL RECORDS
RECORDS (FORMS)

REPORT CARDS
STUDENT RECORDS

724 GUIDES

CURRICULUM GUIDES
GUIDES

725 INSTRUCTIONAL MATERIALS

INSTRUCTIONAL MATERIALS
LITERACY PRIMERS
MANIPULATIVE MATERIALS
PROGRAMMED MATERIALS
READING MATERIALS
STUDENT DEVELOPED
    MATERIALS
SUPPLEMENTARY READING
    MATERIALS
TEACHER DEVELOPED
    MATERIALS
TELEGRAPHIC MATERIALS

730 AUDIOVISUAL AIDS

AUDIOVISUAL AIDS
FILMS
FILMSTRIPS
INSTRUCTIONAL FILMS
PHONOGRAPH RECORDS
SELF INSTRUCTIONAL AIDS
SINGLE CONCEPT FILMS
SLIDES
SOUND FILMS
TRANSPARENCIES

731 AUDIOVISUAL EQUIPMENT

AUDIOVISUAL EQUIPMENT
COMMUNICATIONS SATELLITES
FILM PROJECTORS
LANGUAGE LABORATORIES
MICROFORM READERS
OVERHEAD PROJECTORS
PROJECTION EQUIPMENT
TAPE RECORDERS
TEACHING MACHINES

732 AUDIOVISUAL PROGRAMMES

AUDIOVISUAL PROGRAMMES
PROTOCOL MATERIALS
SOUND SLIDE PRESENTATIONS
TAPE RECORDINGS
VIDEO TAPE RECORDINGS

733 EXHIBITS

CHARTS
DIAGRAMS
EXHIBITS
ILLUSTRATIONS
MODELS

734 SPECIAL AIDS

HEARING AIDS
LARGE TYPE MATERIALS
MOBILITY AIDS
PROSTHESES
SENSORY AIDS
STIMULUS DEVICES

740 SUPPLIES

ATHLETIC EQUIPMENT
CLOTHING
EDUCATIONAL EQUIPMENT
EQUIPMENT
LABORATORY EQUIPMENT
LIBRARY EQUIPMENT
SCIENCE EQUIPMENT
SUPPLIES

741 CLASSROOM MATERIALS

CHALKBOARDS
CLASSROOM MATERIALS
DISPLAY BOARDS
FURNITURE
MUSICAL INSTRUMENTS
TOYS

742 SCHOOL SHOPS

ENGINES
HAND TOOLS
MACHINE TOOLS
MEASUREMENT INSTRUMENTS
MECHANICAL EQUIPMENT
OFFICE MACHINES
SCHOOL SHOPS
WORKSHOPS

743 MOTOR VEHICLES

BOOKMOBILES
MOTOR VEHICLES
SCHOOL BUSES

750 AGRICULTURAL SUPPLIES

AGRICULTURAL SUPPLIES
FISHERIES
LIVESTOCK

751 MEDICAL SUPPLIES

MEDICAL SUPPLIES
STIMULANTS

760 COMPUTERS

COMPUTER LANGUAGES
COMPUTER PROGRAMMES
COMPUTERS
NETWORKS

800 CONTINENTS

AFRICA
AMERICA
ASIA
EUROPE
OCEANIA

801 REGIONS AND SUBREGIONS

AFRICA SOUTH OF THE

SAHARA
ANTARCTIC REGIONS
ARAB COUNTRIES
ARCTIC REGIONS
ATLANTIC OCEAN TERRITORIES
AUSTRALASIA
CARIBBEAN
CENTRAL AFRICA
CENTRAL AMERICA
COMMONWEALTH
EAST AFRICA
EASTERN EUROPE
EASTERN HEMISPHERE
ENGLISH SPEAKING AFRICA
FAR EAST
FRENCH SPEAKING AFRICA
INDIAN OCEAN TERRITORIES
LATIN AMERICA
MEDITERRANEAN COUNTRIES
MELANESIA
MICRONESIA
MIDDLE EAST
NORTH AFRICA
NORTH AMERICA
NORTH POLE
NORTHERN HEMISPHERE
POLAR REGIONS
POLYNESIA
SCANDINAVIA
SOUTH AMERICA
SOUTH EAST ASIA
SOUTH POLE
SOUTHERN AFRICA
SOUTHERN HEMISPHERE
WEST AFRICA
WESTERN EUROPE
WESTERN HEMISPHERE
WESTERN SAHARA

802 AFRICA — COUNTRIES AND TERRITORIES

ANGOLA
BENIN
BOTSWANA
BURUNDI
CAMEROON UR
CENTRAL AFRICAN REPUBLIC
CHAD
CONGO
DJIBOUTI
EQUATORIAL GUINEA
ETHIOPIA
GABON
GAMBIA
GHANA
GUINEA
GUINEA–BISSAU
IVORY COAST
KENYA
LESOTHO
LIBERIA
MADAGASCAR
MALAWI
MALI
MAURITANIA
MOZAMBIQUE
NAMIBIA
NIGER
NIGERIA
RWANDA
SAO TOME AND PRINCIPE
SENEGAL
SIERRA LEONE
SOMALIA
SOUTH AFRICA (REPUBLIC)
SWAZILAND
TANZANIA UR
TOGO
UGANDA
UPPER VOLTA
ZAIRE
ZAMBIA
ZIMBABWE

803 AMERICA — COUNTRIES AND TERRITORIES

ANTIGUA AND BARBUDA
ARGENTINA
BAHAMAS
BARBADOS
BELIZE
BERMUDA
BOLIVIA
BRAZIL
CANADA
CAYMAN ISLANDS
CHILE
COLOMBIA
COSTA RICA
CUBA

DOMINICA
DOMINICAN REPUBLIC
ECUADOR
EL SALVADOR
FRENCH GUIANA
GALAPAGOS ISLANDS
GRENADA
GUADELOUPE
GUATEMALA
GUYANA
HAITI
HONDURAS
JAMAICA
MARTINIQUE
MEXICO
MONTSERRAT
NETHERLANDS ANTILLES
NICARAGUA
PANAMA
PANAMA CANAL ZONE
PARAGUAY
PERU
PUERTO RICO
SAINT BARTHELEMY
SAINT KITTS–NEVIS–ANGUILLA
SAINT LUCIA
SAINT MARTIN
SAINT PIERRE AND MIQUELON ISLANDS
SAINT VINCENT
SURINAME
TRINIDAD AND TOBAGO
TURKS AND CAICOS ISLANDS
URUGUAY
USA
VENEZUELA
VIRGIN ISLANDS (UK)
VIRGIN ISLANDS (USA)

804 ASIA — COUNTRIES AND TERRITORIES

AFGHANISTAN
BANGLADESH
BHUTAN
BRUNEI
BURMA
CHINA
DEMOCRATIC KAMPUCHEA
HIMALAYAN STATES
HONG KONG
INDIA
INDONESIA
IRAN (ISLAMIC REPUBLIC)
ISRAEL
JAPAN
KOREA DPR
KOREA R
LAO PDR
MACAO
MALAYA
MALAYSIA
MALDIVES
MONGOLIA
NEPAL
OMAN
PAKISTAN
PAPUA NEW GUINEA
PHILIPPINES
PORTUGUESE TIMOR
RYUKU ISLANDS
SABAH
SARAWAK
SIKKIM
SINGAPORE
SOUTH ASIA
SRI LANKA
TAIWAN
THAILAND
VIET NAM SR

805 EUROPE — COUNTRIES AND TERRITORIES

ALBANIA
ANDORRA
ARMENIAN SSR
AUSTRIA
BELGIUM
BULGARIA
BYELORUSSIAN SSR
CHANNEL ISLANDS
CYPRUS
CZECHOSLOVAKIA
DENMARK
ESTONIAN SSR
FAEROE ISLANDS
FINLAND
FRANCE
GEORGIAN SSR
GERMAN DR
GERMANY FR

GIBRALTAR
GREECE
GREENLAND
HOLY SEE
HUNGARY
ICELAND
IRELAND
ITALY
KAZAKH SSR
LAPLAND
LATVIAN SSR
LIECHTENSTEIN
LITHUANIAN SSR
LUXEMBOURG
MALTA
MOLDAVIAN SSR
MONACO
NETHERLANDS
NORWAY
POLAND
PORTUGAL
ROMANIA
RUSSIAN SFSR
SAN MARINO
SIBERIA
SPAIN
SWEDEN
SWITZERLAND
TURKEY
UK
UKRAINIAN SSR
USSR
YUGOSLAVIA

806 OCEANIA — COUNTRIES AND TERRITORIES

AMERICAN SAMOA
AUSTRALIA
BANKS ISLANDS
CANTON AND ENDERBY ISLANDS
CAROLINE ISLANDS
COOK ISLANDS
EASTER ISLAND
FIJI ISLANDS
FRENCH POLYNESIA
GUAM
HAWAII
JOHNSTON ISLAND
KERMADEC ISLANDS
KIRIBATI
LINE ISLANDS
LORD HOWE ISLAND
MANIHIKI ISLANDS
MARIANA ISLANDS
MARSHALL ISLANDS
MIDWAY ISLANDS
NAURU ISLAND
NEW CALEDONIA
NEW ZEALAND
NIUE ISLAND
NORFOLK ISLAND
PITCAIRN ISLANDS
SAMOA
SANTA CRUZ ISLANDS
SOCIETY ISLANDS
SOLOMON ISLANDS
TASMANIA
TOKELAU ISLANDS
TONGA
TUAMOTU ISLANDS
TUBUAI ISLANDS
VANUATU
WAKE ISLANDS
WALLIS AND FUTUNA ISLANDS

807 ARAB COUNTRIES

ALGERIA
BAHRAIN
DEMOCRATIC YEMEN
EGYPT
GULF STATES
IRAQ
JORDAN
KUWAIT
LEBANON
LIBYAN ARAB JAMAHIRIYA
MOROCCO
QATAR
SAUDI ARABIA
SUDAN
SYRIAN AR
TUNISIA
UNITED ARAB EMIRATES
YEMEN

808 ATLANTIC OCEAN TERRITORIES

ASCENSION ISLAND
AZORES
BOUVET ISLAND
CANARY ISLANDS
CAPE VERDE
FALKLAND ISLANDS
MADEIRA
SAINT HELENA

809 INDIAN OCEAN TERRITORIES

CHRISTMAS ISLAND
COMOROS
MAURITIUS
REUNION ISLAND
SEYCHELLES

840 TIME LOCATION

ANCIENT TIME
EIGHTEENTH CENTURY
FUTURE
MIDDLE AGES
MODERN TIMES
NINETEENTH CENTURY
RENAISSANCE
SEVENTEENTH CENTURY
TWENTIETH CENTURY
TWENTY FIRST CENTURY

850 UN INTERNATIONAL AGENCIES

CLADES
ECA
ECE
ECLA
ECOSOC
ESCAP
FAO
GENERAL ASSEMBLY
IBRD
IDA
ILO
ITU
SECURITY COUNCIL
TRUSTEESHIP COUNCIL
UN

UNDP
UNEP
UNESCO
UNFPA
UNHCR
UNICEF
UNIDO
UNITAR
UNRISD
UNRWA
UNU
WHO

851 UNESCO ASSOCIATED UNITS

ASFEC
BREDA
IBE
ICE
IIALM
IIEP
OREALC
ROEAO
UIEH
UNEDBAS
UNESCO EDUCATION SECTOR
UNESCO EXECUTIVE BOARD
UNESCO GENERAL CONFERENCE
UNESCO SECRETARIAT
UNISIST

852 OTHER INTERGOVERNMENTAL AGENCIES

ALECSO
CELC
CIECC
COLOMBO PLAN
COMECON
COMMONWEALTH SECRETARIAT
CONESCAL
COUNCIL OF EUROPE
CREFAL
ECWA
EEC
EUROPEAN COMMUNITIES
FED

IDB
ILCE
LEAGUE OF ARAB STATES
OAS
OAU
OCAM
OCAS
OECD
OEI
SEAMEO

GLOSSARY
LITERATURE REVIEW
MANUAL
MINISTRY OF EDUCATION
    REPORT
RESEARCH REPORT
RESEARCH REVIEWS
STATISTICAL TABLES
STUDY GUIDE
SUPPLEMENTARY TEXTBOOK
TEACHING GUIDE
TEXTBOOK
YEARBOOK

853 NON GOVERNMENTAL ORGANIZATIONS

CSME
FID
FISE
IAMCR
IAU
ICET
ICSSD
ICSUAB
ICVA
IFFTU
IFLA
IPPF
ISO
NGO
WCC
WCOTP

860 NATIONAL AGENCIES

MINISTRY OF EDUCATION
NATIONAL COMMISSION FOR
    UNESCO

880 FORM TERMS FOR DOCUMENTS

ABSTRACTS
ANNOTATED BIBLIOGRAPHY
BIBLIOGRAPHY
CATALOGUE
COMMISSION REPORT
CONFERENCE REPORT
DICTIONARY
DIRECTORY
ENCYCLOPAEDIA

V. Rotated list of descriptors

ABILITY
    ABILITY 520
    ABILITY GROUPING 341
    COGNITIVE ABILITY 520
    CREATIVE ABILITY 520
    LANGUAGE ABILITY 520
    READING ABILITY 520
ABLE
    ABLE STUDENTS 416
ABROAD
    STUDY ABROAD 335
ABSENCE
    LEAVE OF ABSENCE 222
ABSTRACT
    ABSTRACT REASONING 522
ABSTRACTING
    ABSTRACTING 202
ABSTRACTS
    ABSTRACTS 880
ABUSE
    DRUG ABUSE 572
ACADEMIC
    ACADEMIC FREEDOM 180
    ACADEMIC STANDARDS 391
ACCELERATED
    ACCELERATED COURSES 333
    ACCELERATED PROGRAMMES 320
    ACCELERATED VOCATIONAL TRAINING 351
ACCELERATION
    ACCELERATION 266
ACCEPTANCE
    PEER ACCEPTANCE 554
ACCESS
    ACCESS TO EDUCATION 181
ACCIDENT
    ACCIDENT PREVENTION 673
ACCIDENTS
    ACCIDENTS 265
ACCOMMODATION
    ADULT EDUCATION ACCOMMODATION 711
ACCOUNTABILITY
    ACCOUNTABILITY 231

ACCOUNTANTS
    ACCOUNTANTS 460
ACCOUNTING
    ACCOUNTING 243
    SCHOOL ACCOUNTING 243
ACCREDITATION
    ACCREDITATION (INSTITUTIONS) 210
ACCULTURATION
    ACCULTURATION 130
ACHIEVEMENT
    ACHIEVEMENT NEED 536
    ACHIEVEMENT RATING 391
    ACHIEVEMENT TESTS 393
    LITERACY ACHIEVEMENT 535
    STUDENT ACHIEVEMENT 535
ACHIEVERS
    HIGH ACHIEVERS 415
    LOW ACHIEVERS 415
ACOUSTICS
    ACOUSTICS 252
ACTION
    ACTION PROGRAMMES (COMMUNITY) 282
    ACTION RESEARCH 282
    COMMUNITY ACTION 102
    SOCIAL ACTION 120
ACTIVE
    ACTIVE SCHOOLS 184
ACTIVITIES
    ACTIVITIES 357
    ATHLETIC ACTIVITIES 357
    CLASS ACTIVITIES 357
    CULTURAL ACTIVITIES 537
    EXTRACURRICULAR ACTIVITIES 357
    GROUP ACTIVITIES 357
    HEALTH ACTIVITIES 357
    INTEGRATED ACTIVITIES 357
    LEARNING ACTIVITIES 537
    OUT OF SCHOOL ACTIVITIES 357
    OUTDOOR ACTIVITIES 357
    PHYSICAL ACTIVITIES 537

ACTIVITIES
    RECREATIONAL ACTIVITIES 357
    SCHOOL ACTIVITIES 357
    SPEAKING ACTIVITIES 537
ACTIVITY
    ACTIVITY LEARNING 512
    ACTIVITY METHODS 355
    OUT OF SCHOOL ACTIVITY CENTRES 311
ACTUALIZATION
    SELF ACTUALIZATION 555
ADAPTATION
    TACTILE ADAPTATION 374
ADJUSTMENT
    ADJUSTMENT 551
    ADJUSTMENT PROBLEMS 551
    EMOTIONAL ADJUSTMENT 551
    SOCIAL ADJUSTMENT 551
    STUDENT ADJUSTMENT 551
    VOCATIONAL ADJUSTMENT 551
ADMINISTRATION
    ADMINISTRATION 200
    COLLEGE ADMINISTRATION 265
    EDUCATIONAL ADMINISTRATION 200
    PROGRAMME ADMINISTRATION 262
    SCHOOL ADMINISTRATION 265
    TEACHER ADMINISTRATION RELATIONSHIP 262
ADMINISTRATIVE
    ADMINISTRATIVE ORGANIZATION 261
    ADMINISTRATIVE POLICIES 200
    ADMINISTRATIVE PRINCIPLES 200
    ADMINISTRATIVE PROBLEMS 281
    ADMINISTRATIVE WORKERS 451
    INTERMEDIATE ADMINISTRATIVE UNITS 261
ADMINISTRATOR
    ADMINISTRATOR EDUCATION 672
    ADMINISTRATOR RESPONSIBILITY 231
    ADMINISTRATOR ROLE 262
    ADMINISTRATOR SELECTION 223
ADMINISTRATORS
    EDUCATIONAL ADMINISTRATORS 420
ADMISSION
    ADMISSION 266
    ADMISSION REQUIREMENTS 232
ADOLESCENCE
    ADOLESCENCE 500
ADOLESCENTS
    ADOLESCENTS 400
ADOPTED
    ADOPTED CHILDREN 401
ADOPTION
    ADOPTION OF INNOVATIONS 200
ADULT
    ADULT CHARACTERISTICS 561
    ADULT COLLEGES 187
    ADULT COUNSELLING 371
    ADULT COUNSELLORS 431
    ADULT DEVELOPMENT 530
    ADULT EDUCATION 186
    ADULT EDUCATION ACCOMMODATION 711
    ADULT EDUCATION AGENCIES 103
    ADULT EDUCATION ASSOCIATIONS 110
    ADULT EDUCATION CENTRES 311
    ADULT EDUCATION PROGRAMMES 321
    ADULT EDUCATION REGULATIONS 230
    ADULT EDUCATION SCHOOL COOPERATION 263
    ADULT EDUCATION SYSTEMS 260
    ADULT EDUCATION TAXES 240
    ADULT EDUCATION– COMMUNITY RELATIONS 263
    ADULT EDUCATION–

ADULT
- INDUSTRY COOPERATION 263
- ADULT EDUCATORS 421
- ADULT LEADERS 440
- ADULT LEARNING 514
- ADULT POPULATION 124
- ADULT PROGRAMME COMMITTEES 442
- ADULT READING PROGRAMMES 660
- ADULT SCHOOLS 187
- ADULT SERVICES 107
- ADULT STUDENT–INSTITUTION RELATIONSHIP 380
- ADULT STUDENTS 412
- ADULT TEACHING 352
- PRIVATE ADULT EDUCATION 187
- RESIDENTIAL ADULT CENTRES 311
- RESIDENTIAL ADULT EDUCATION 184
- VOLUNTARILY PROVIDED ADULT EDUCATION 187

ADULTHOOD
- ADULTHOOD 500
- EARLY ADULTHOOD 500

ADULTS
- ADULTS 400
- ILLITERATE ADULTS 402
- YOUNG ADULTS 400

ADVANCED
- ADVANCED STUDENTS 416

ADVANCEMENT
- COLLECTIVE ADVANCEMENT 121
- OCCUPATIONAL ADVANCEMENT 154
- SOCIAL ADVANCEMENT 121
- TECHNOLOGICAL ADVANCEMENT 140

ADVISERS
- FOREIGN STUDENT ADVISERS 431

ADVISORY
- ADVISORY COMMITTEES 442

AEROSPACE
- AEROSPACE INDUSTRY 150

AESTHETIC
- AESTHETIC EDUCATION 684

AFFECTIVE
- AFFECTIVE BEHAVIOUR 540
- AFFECTIVE OBJECTIVES 300

AFFECTIVITY
- AFFECTIVITY 540

AFFILIATED
- AFFILIATED SCHOOLS 305

AFGHANISTAN
- AFGHANISTAN 804

AFRICA
- AFRICA 800
- AFRICA SOUTH OF THE SAHARA 801
- CENTRAL AFRICA 801
- EAST AFRICA 801
- ENGLISH SPEAKING AFRICA 801
- FRENCH SPEAKING AFRICA 801
- NORTH AFRICA 801
- SOUTH AFRICA (REPUBLIC) 802
- SOUTHERN AFRICA 801
- WEST AFRICA 801

AFRICAN
- AFRICAN LANGUAGES 625
- CENTRAL AFRICAN REPUBLIC 802

AFRO
- AFRO ASIATIC LANGUAGES 625

AGE
- AGE 500
- AGE DIFFERENCES 500
- AGE GROUPS 443
- AGE SEGREGATION 341
- CROSS AGE TEACHING 350
- MIDDLE AGE 500
- MIDDLE AGE PEOPLE 400
- MINIMUM AGE 500
- OLD AGE 500
- SCHOOL AGE POPULATION 206

AGEING
- AGEING 531

AGENCIES
- ADULT EDUCATION AGENCIES 103
- AGENCIES 103
- CENTRAL EDUCATIONAL AGENCIES 261

AGENCIES
   COMMUNITY AGENCIES (PUBLIC) 104
   COORDINATING AGENCIES 103
   INTERNATIONAL AGENCIES 103
   PROVINCIAL AGENCIES 104
   REGIONAL AGENCIES 103
   SOCIAL AGENCIES 103
   WELFARE AGENCIES 103
   YOUTH AGENCIES 103
AGENCY
   AGENCY ROLE 105
AGENTS
   CHANGE AGENTS 440
   EXTENSION AGENTS 440
AGES
   MIDDLE AGES 840
AGGRESSION
   AGGRESSION 540
AGRARIAN
   AGRARIAN REFORM 151
AGREEMENTS
   AGREEMENTS 170
   COLLECTIVE AGREEMENTS 153
AGRICULTURAL
   AGRICULTURAL COLLEGES 307
   AGRICULTURAL DEVELOPMENT 151
   AGRICULTURAL EDUCATION 672
   AGRICULTURAL ENGINEERING 646
   AGRICULTURAL OCCUPATIONS 155
   AGRICULTURAL PRODUCTION 150
   AGRICULTURAL SUPPLIES 750
   AGRICULTURAL TECHNICIANS 452
   AGRICULTURAL TRAINING 673
   AGRICULTURAL WORKERS 451
AGRICULTURE
   AGRICULTURE 646
   VOCATIONAL AGRICULTURE TEACHERS 425

AGRONOMY
   AGRONOMY 646
AID
   BILATERAL AID 106
   CENTRAL GOVERNMENT AID 106
   EQUALIZATION AID 152
   FIRST AID 683
   LEGAL AID 170
   LOCAL GOVERNMENT AID 106
   MULTILATERAL AID 106
   PROVINCIAL GOVERNMENT AID 106
   STATE AID TO PROVINCES 106
AIDES
   TEACHER AIDES 424
AIDS
   AUDIOVISUAL AIDS 730
   HEARING AIDS 734
   MOBILITY AIDS 734
   SELF INSTRUCTIONAL AIDS 730
   SENSORY AIDS 734
AIMS
   EDUCATIONAL AIMS 200
   GUIDANCE AIMS 211
   MEASUREMENT AIMS 391
ALBANIA
   ALBANIA 805
ALCOHOL
   ALCOHOL EDUCATION 683
ALECSO
   ALECSO 852
ALGEBRA
   ALGEBRA 631
ALGEBRAIC
   ALGEBRAIC CONCEPTS 631
ALGERIA
   ALGERIA 807
ALIENATION
   ALIENATION 554
ALLOCATION
   ALLOCATION PER STUDENT 243
   TAX ALLOCATION 152
ALLOCATIONS
   RESOURCE ALLOCATIONS 243
ALLOWANCES
   EDUCATIONAL ALLOWANCES 242

ALLOWANCES
    TRAINING ALLOWANCES 242
ALPHABET
    INITIAL TEACHING ALPHABET 661
ALPHABETS
    ALPHABETS 620
ALTAIC
    URALIC ALTAIC LANGUAGES 625
ALTERNATIVE
    ALTERNATIVE EDUCATION 184
AMERICA
    AMERICA 800
    CENTRAL AMERICA 801
    LATIN AMERICA 801
    NORTH AMERICA 801
    SOUTH AMERICA 801
AMERICAN
    AMERICAN INDIAN LANGUAGES 625
    AMERICAN SAMOA 806
AMETROPIA
    AMETROPIA 570
ANALYSIS
    AREA ANALYSIS 252
    COMPARATIVE ANALYSIS 282
    CONTENT ANALYSIS 331
    DATA ANALYSIS 284
    JOB ANALYSIS 221
    LITERARY ANALYSIS 615
    NETWORK ANALYSIS 201
    SKILL ANALYSIS 331
    STATISTICAL ANALYSIS 284
    STRUCTURAL ANALYSIS 331
    SYSTEMS ANALYSIS 201
    TRANSACTIONAL ANALYSIS 352
ANATOMY
    ANATOMY 632
ANCIENT
    ANCIENT TIME 840
ANCILLARY
    ANCILLARY SERVICES 270
    ANCILLARY SPACES 712
ANDORRA
    ANDORRA 805
ANGOLA
    ANGOLA 802
ANGUILLA

ANGUILLA
    SAINT KITTS–NEVIS–ANGUILLA 803
ANIMAL
    ANIMAL SCIENCE 646
ANIMATEUR
    ANIMATEUR SELECTION 223
ANIMATION
    ANIMATION 181
    ANIMATION METHODS 355
ANNOTATED
    ANNOTATED BIBLIOGRAPHY 880
ANTARCTIC
    ANTARCTIC REGIONS 801
ANTHOLOGIES
    ANTHOLOGIES 722
ANTHROPOLOGY
    ANTHROPOLOGY 640
    EDUCATIONAL ANTHROPOLOGY 642
ANTI
    ANTI SOCIAL BEHAVIOUR 572
ANTIGUA
    ANTIGUA AND BARBUDA 803
ANTILLES
    NETHERLANDS ANTILLES 803
ANXIETY
    ANXIETY 540
APPLICANTS
    JOB APPLICANTS 451
APPLICATION
    JOB APPLICATION 221
APPLIED
    APPLIED MATHEMATICS 631
    APPLIED RESEARCH 282
APPRECIATION
    ART APPRECIATION 684
    LITERATURE APPRECIATION 684
    MUSIC APPRECIATION 684
APPRENTICESHIP
    APPRENTICESHIP 351
APPROACH
    INTERDISCIPLINARY APPROACH 331
    MODULAR APPROACH 331
    SEQUENTIAL APPROACH 331
    THEMATIC APPROACH 331
APTITUDE
    APTITUDE 520
    APTITUDE TESTS 393

APTITUDES
    VOCATIONAL APTITUDES 520
ARAB
    ARAB COUNTRIES 801
    LEAGUE OF ARAB STATES 852
    LIBYAN ARAB JAMAHIRIYA 807
    UNITED ARAB EMIRATES 807
ARABIA
    SAUDI ARABIA 807
ARABIC
    ARABIC 626
ARCHITECTS
    ARCHITECTS 461
ARCHITECTURAL
    ARCHITECTURAL CONCEPTS 252
    ARCHITECTURAL DRAWINGS 252
ARCHITECTURE
    ARCHITECTURE 650
ARCTIC
    ARCTIC REGIONS 801
AREA
    AREA ANALYSIS 252
    AREA STUDIES 680
    CATCHMENT AREA 264
AREAS
    DEPRESSED AREAS (ECONOMIC) 151
    EXHIBITION AREAS 711
    INDIVIDUAL LEARNING AREAS 711
    OUTDOOR TEACHING AREAS 711
    RURAL AREAS 122
    URBAN AREAS 122
ARGENTINA
    ARGENTINA 803
ARITHMETIC
    ARITHMETIC 631
ARITHMETICAL
    ARITHMETICAL CONCEPTS 631
ARMED
    ARMED FORCES EDUCATION 186
ARMENIAN
    ARMENIAN SSR 805
ARRANGEMENT
    CLASSROOM ARRANGEMENT 356

ART
    ART 610
    ART APPRECIATION 684
    ART EDUCATION 684
    ART TEACHERS 425
    COMMERCIAL ART 610
ARTICULATION
    ARTICULATION 205
    ARTICULATION (SPEECH) 532
ARTISTS
    ARTISTS 461
ARTS
    FINE ARTS 610
    GRAPHIC ARTS 610
    INDUSTRIAL ARTS 647
    LANGUAGE ARTS 620
    THEATRE ARTS 610
ASCENSION
    ASCENSION ISLAND 808
ASFEC
    ASFEC 851
ASIA
    ASIA 800
    SOUTH ASIA 804
    SOUTH EAST ASIA 801
ASIATIC
    AFRO ASIATIC LANGUAGES 625
ASPIRATION
    ASPIRATION 541
ASSEMBLY
    GENERAL ASSEMBLY 850
ASSESSMENT
    CONTINUOUS ASSESSMENT 391
    INTERNAL ASSESSMENT 391
    NEEDS ASSESSMENT 151
    PERSONALITY ASSESSMENT 221
ASSETS
    CAPITAL ASSETS 710
    CAPITAL OUTLAY (FOR FIXED ASSETS) 241
ASSIGNMENTS
    ASSIGNMENTS 356
    TEACHING ASSIGNMENTS 356
ASSISTANCE
    TECHNICAL ASSISTANCE 106
ASSISTANTS
    TEACHING ASSISTANTS 424
ASSISTED

ASSISTED
    COMPUTER ASSISTED INSTRUCTION 361
ASSOCIATED
    ASSOCIATED SCHOOLS (UNESCO) 305
ASSOCIATION
    FREEDOM OF ASSOCIATION 100
ASSOCIATIONS
    ADULT EDUCATION ASSOCIATIONS 110
    PARENT ASSOCIATIONS 110
    PARENT TEACHER ASSOCIATIONS 110
    PROFESSIONAL ASSOCIATIONS 110
    TEACHER ASSOCIATIONS 110
ASSOCIATIVE
    ASSOCIATIVE LEARNING 512
ASTRONOMY
    ASTRONOMY 633
ATHEISTIC
    ATHEISTIC EDUCATION 188
ATHLETES
    ATHLETES 461
ATHLETIC
    ATHLETIC ACTIVITIES 357
    ATHLETIC EQUIPMENT 740
ATHLETICS
    ATHLETICS 651
ATLANTIC
    ATLANTIC OCEAN TERRITORIES 801
ATLASES
    ATLASES 722
ATTENDANCE
    ATTENDANCE 266
    ATTENDANCE OFFICERS 420
    ATTENDANCE RATE 206
    ATTENDANCE RECORDS 723
    SCHOOL ATTENDANCE LAWS 230
ATTENTION
    ATTENTION 535
    ATTENTION SPAN 535
ATTITUDES
    ATTITUDES 552
    CHANGING ATTITUDES 552
    CHILDHOOD ATTITUDES 552
    CLASS ATTITUDES 552

ATTITUDES
    EDUCATIONAL ATTITUDES 181
    FAMILY ATTITUDES 552
    SCHOOL ATTITUDES 552
    SOCIAL ATTITUDES 552
    STUDENT ATTITUDES 552
    TEACHER ATTITUDES 350
    WORK ATTITUDES 552
AUDIENCES
    AUDIENCES 442
AUDIOVISUAL
    AUDIOVISUAL AIDS 730
    AUDIOVISUAL COMMUNICATION 360
    AUDIOVISUAL EQUIPMENT 731
    AUDIOVISUAL INSTRUCTION 360
    AUDIOVISUAL PROGRAMMES 732
    AUDIOVISUAL TESTS 393
AUDITION
    AUDITION (PHYSIOLOGY) 503
AUDITORY
    AUDITORY PERCEPTION 510
AURAL
    AURAL STIMULI 510
AUSTRALASIA
    AUSTRALASIA 801
AUSTRALIA
    AUSTRALIA 806
AUSTRIA
    AUSTRIA 805
AUTHORITIES
    LOCAL EDUCATION AUTHORITIES 263
AUTHORIZATION
    TEXTBOOK AUTHORIZATION 213
AUTHORS
    AUTHORS 461
AUTISM
    AUTISM 572
AUTOMATION
    AUTOMATION 140
AUTONOMY
    LOCAL AUTONOMY 263
    SCHOOL DISTRICT AUTONOMY 263
AVERAGE
    AVERAGE STUDENTS 416

AVIATION
    AVIATION TECHNOLOGY 645
AZORES
    AZORES 808
BACHELORS
    BACHELORS DEGREES 390
BACKGROUND
    CULTURAL BACKGROUND 130
    EDUCATIONAL BACKGROUND 221
    FAMILY BACKGROUND 126
    SOCIAL BACKGROUND 120
    SOCIOECONOMIC BACKGROUND 120
    TEACHER BACKGROUND 223
BAHAMAS
    BAHAMAS 803
BAHRAIN
    BAHRAIN 807
BANGLADESH
    BANGLADESH 804
BANKS
    BANKS ISLANDS 806
BARBADOS
    BARBADOS 803
BARBUDA
    ANTIGUA AND BARBUDA 803
BARTHELEMY
    SAINT BARTHELEMY 803
BASE
    DATA BASE 283
BASED
    COMPETENCY-BASED EDUCATION 352
BASIC
    BASIC EDUCATION 183
    BASIC SCHOOLS 301
    BASIC SKILLS 533
    BASIC TRAINING 351
BEGINNING
    BEGINNING READING 660
    BEGINNING TEACHERS 424
BEHAVIOUR
    AFFECTIVE BEHAVIOUR 540
    ANTI SOCIAL BEHAVIOUR 572
    BEHAVIOUR 560
    BEHAVIOUR CHANGE 560
    BEHAVIOUR DEVELOPMENT 530
    BEHAVIOUR PROBLEMS 281
    BEHAVIOUR THEORIES 560
    GROUP BEHAVIOUR 560

BEHAVIOUR
    INFANT BEHAVIOUR 560
    STUDENT BEHAVIOUR 560
    TEACHER BEHAVIOUR 560
BEHAVIOURAL
    BEHAVIOURAL COUNSELLING 370
    BEHAVIOURAL OBJECTIVES 300
    BEHAVIOURAL SCIENCE RESEARCH 280
    BEHAVIOURAL SCIENCES 642
BELGIUM
    BELGIUM 805
BELIZE
    BELIZE 803
BENEFITS
    EDUCATIONAL BENEFITS 181
BENIN
    BENIN 802
BERMUDA
    BERMUDA 803
BHUTAN
    BHUTAN 804
BIAS
    BIAS 552
BIBLIOGRAPHY
    ANNOTATED BIBLIOGRAPHY 880
    BIBLIOGRAPHY 880
BICULTURALISM
    BICULTURALISM 130
BILATERAL
    BILATERAL AID 106
BILINGUAL
    BILINGUAL EDUCATION 183
    BILINGUAL STUDENTS 414
    BILINGUAL TEACHERS 426
BILINGUALISM
    BILINGUALISM 131
BIOGRAPHIES
    BIOGRAPHIES 616
BIOLOGY
    BIOLOGY 632
BIRTH
    BIRTH ORDER 500
BISSAU
    GUINEA-BISSAU 802
BLIND
    BLIND 403
    BLIND EDUCATION 322

BLOCK
   BLOCK RELEASE 222
BOARD
   UNESCO EXECUTIVE BOARD 851
BOARDERS
   BOARDERS 410
BOARDING
   BOARDING FACILITIES 712
   BOARDING SCHOOLS 303
BOARDS
   DISPLAY BOARDS 741
   GOVERNING BOARDS 261
BODIES
   PLANNING BODIES 261
BODY
   BODY HEIGHT 502
   BODY WEIGHT 502
   HUMAN BODY 502
BOLIVIA
   BOLIVIA 803
BOND
   BOND ISSUES 240
BOOKMOBILES
   BOOKMOBILES 743
BOOKS
   BOOKS 722
   CHILDRENS BOOKS 722
BOTANY
   BOTANY 632
BOTSWANA
   BOTSWANA 802
BOUVET
   BOUVET ISLAND 808
BRAILLE
   BRAILLE 374
BRAIN
   BRAIN DRAIN 124
   MINIMAL BRAIN INJURY 570
BRANCHING
   BRANCHING PROGRAMMES 361
BRAZIL
   BRAZIL 803
BREDA
   BREDA 851
BRUNEI
   BRUNEI 804
BUDDHISTS
   BUDDHISTS 475
BUDGETING
   BUDGETING 243

BUDGETS
   BUDGETS 243
BUILDING
   BUILDING DESIGN 252
   BUILDING ELEMENTS 253
   BUILDING ENGINEERING 252
   BUILDING EVALUATION 251
   BUILDING FINANCE 251
   BUILDING IMPROVEMENT 253
   BUILDING MATERIALS 253
   BUILDING TRADES 155
   BUILDING USE 251
BUILDINGS
   BUILDINGS 710
   INDUSTRIALIZED BUILDINGS 253
BULGARIA
   BULGARIA 805
BURMA
   BURMA 804
BURUNDI
   BURUNDI 802
BUSES
   SCHOOL BUSES 743
BUSINESS
   BUSINESS SUBJECTS 673
BYELORUSSIAN
   BYELORUSSIAN SSR 805
CADRES
   NATIONAL CADRES 441
CAICOS
   TURKS AND CAICOS ISLANDS 803
CALCULATION
   CALCULATION 631
CALEDONIA
   NEW CALEDONIA 806
CALENDARS
   SCHOOL CALENDARS 344
CALISTHENICS
   CALISTHENICS 651
CAMEROON
   CAMEROON UR 802
CAMPAIGNS
   LITERACY CAMPAIGNS 271
CANADA
   CANADA 803
CANAL
   PANAMA CANAL ZONE 803
CANARY
   CANARY ISLANDS 808

CANDIDATES
    EXTERNAL CANDIDATES 412
CANTON
    CANTON AND ENDERBY ISLANDS 806
CAPE
    CAPE VERDE 808
CAPITAL
    CAPITAL 150
    CAPITAL ASSETS 710
    CAPITAL OUTLAY (FOR FIXED ASSETS) 241
CARDIOVASCULAR
    CARDIOVASCULAR SYSTEM 502
CARDS
    REPORT CARDS 723
CARE
    CHILD CARE 126
    CHILD CARE CENTRES 311
    CHILD CARE WORKERS 430
    DAY CARE SERVICES 270
    RESIDENTIAL CARE 374
CAREER
    CAREER CHOICE 563
    CAREER COUNSELLING 370
    CAREER EDUCATION 183
    CAREER PLANNING 563
CAREERS
    CAREERS 563
CARIBBEAN
    CARIBBEAN 801
    CARIBBEAN
CAROLINE
    CAROLINE ISLANDS 806
CASE
    CASE STUDIES 282
    CASE STUDY METHODS 355
CATALOGUE
    CATALOGUE 880
CATALOGUING
    CATALOGUING 202
CATCHMENT
    CATCHMENT AREA 264
CATHOLICS
    CATHOLICS 475
CAUCASIAN
    CAUCASIAN LANGUAGES 625
CAUSES
    DELINQUENCY CAUSES 285
CAYMAN
    CAYMAN ISLANDS 803

CELC
    CELC 852
CENSUS
    CENSUS DATA 124
CENTRAL
    CENTRAL AFRICA 801
    CENTRAL AFRICAN REPUBLIC 802
    CENTRAL AMERICA 801
    CENTRAL EDUCATIONAL AGENCIES 261
    CENTRAL GOVERNMENT 103
    CENTRAL GOVERNMENT AID 106
    CENTRAL GOVERNMENT LAWS 170
    CENTRAL PROVINCIAL RELATIONSHIP 105
CENTRALIZATION
    CENTRALIZATION 200
CENTRES
    ADULT EDUCATION CENTRES 311
    CENTRES OF INTEREST 331
    CHILD CARE CENTRES 311
    COMMUNITY CENTRES 311
    COUNSELLING CENTRES 311
    CULTURAL CENTRES 310
    CURRICULUM STUDY CENTRES 312
    DOCUMENTATION CENTRES 310
    GROUP TRAINING CENTRES 311
    INFORMATION CENTRES 310
    LITERACY CENTRES 311
    MEDIA RESOURCES CENTRES 312
    MULTI PURPOSE CENTRES 311
    OUT OF SCHOOL ACTIVITY CENTRES 311
    PRESCHOOL CENTRES 311
    RESEARCH CENTRES 312
    RESIDENTIAL ADULT CENTRES 311
    SCIENCE TEACHING CENTRES 312
    STUDY CENTRES 311
    TEACHER CENTRES 312
    VOCATIONAL TRAINING CENTRES 306

CENTURY
 EIGHTEENTH CENTURY 840
 NINETEENTH CENTURY 840
 SEVENTEENTH CENTURY 840
 TWENTIETH CENTURY 840
 TWENTY FIRST CENTURY 840
CERTIFICATES
 EDUCATIONAL CERTIFICATES 390
 PRIMARY SCHOOL CERTIFICATES 390
 SECONDARY SCHOOL CERTIFICATES 390
 VOCATIONAL SCHOOL CERTIFICATES 390
CERTIFICATION
 CERTIFICATION 390
 TEACHER CERTIFICATION 390
CHAD
 CHAD 802
CHALKBOARDS
 CHALKBOARDS 741
CHANGE
 BEHAVIOUR CHANGE 560
 CHANGE AGENTS 440
 OCCUPATIONAL CHANGE 155
 SOCIAL CHANGE 120
CHANGING
 CHANGING ATTITUDES 552
CHANNEL
 CHANNEL ISLANDS 805
CHARACTERISTICS
 ADULT CHARACTERISTICS 561
 COMMUNITY CHARACTERISTICS 285
 INDIVIDUAL CHARACTERISTICS 561
 PHYSICAL CHARACTERISTICS 561
 PSYCHOLOGICAL CHARACTERISTICS 561
 SEX (CHARACTERISTICS) 501
 STUDENT CHARACTERISTICS 561
 TEACHER CHARACTERISTICS 350
CHARGES
 RESIDENCE CHARGES 240
CHARTS
 CHARTS 733
CHEMICAL
 CHEMICAL ENGINEERS 463

CHEMICAL
 CHEMICAL INDUSTRY 150
 CHEMICAL WORKERS 451
CHEMISTRY
 CHEMISTRY 633
CHEMISTS
 CHEMISTS 463
CHILD
 CHILD CARE 126
 CHILD CARE CENTRES 311
 CHILD CARE WORKERS 430
 CHILD DEVELOPMENT 530
 CHILD DEVELOPMENT SPECIALISTS 430
 CHILD LABOUR 153
 CHILD LANGUAGE 532
 CHILD PSYCHOLOGY 642
 CHILD RESPONSIBILITY 231
 CHILD WELFARE 100
 EXCEPTIONAL CHILD EDUCATION 322
 EXCEPTIONAL CHILD RESEARCH 280
 PARENT CHILD RELATIONSHIP 553
CHILDHOOD
 CHILDHOOD 500
 CHILDHOOD ATTITUDES 552
 CHILDHOOD NEEDS 536
 EARLY CHILDHOOD 500
 EARLY CHILDHOOD EDUCATION 186
CHILDREN
 ADOPTED CHILDREN 401
 CHILDREN 400
 KINDERGARTEN CHILDREN 411
 MINORITY GROUP CHILDREN 402
 PREPRIMARY CHILDREN 411
 RETARDED CHILDREN 403
CHILDRENS
 CHILDRENS BOOKS 722
 CHILDRENS GAMES 537
CHILE
 CHILE 803
CHINA
 CHINA 804
CHINESE
 CHINESE 626
CHOICE
 CAREER CHOICE 563

CHOICE
    EDUCATIONAL CHOICE 181
    MULTIPLE CHOICE TESTS 392
CHRISTIAN
    CHRISTIAN EDUCATION 188
CHRISTMAS
    CHRISTMAS ISLAND 809
CHURCH
    STATE CHURCH SEPARATION 101
CIECC
    CIECC 852
CINEMA
    CINEMA 610
CIRCUIT
    CLOSED CIRCUIT TELEVISION 360
CIRCULATION
    CIRCULATION 251
CITIZEN
    CITIZEN PARTICIPATION 105
    CITIZEN ROLE 105
CITIZENSHIP
    CITIZENSHIP 101
CITY
    CITY GOVERNMENT 104
CIVICS
    CIVICS 640
CIVIL
    CIVIL ENGINEERING 647
    CIVIL RIGHTS 170
    CIVIL SERVANTS 460
    SENIOR CIVIL SERVANTS 460
CLADES
    CLADES 850
CLASS
    CLASS ACTIVITIES 357
    CLASS ATTITUDES 552
    CLASS MANAGEMENT 691
    CLASS SIZE 343
    MIDDLE CLASS 121
    MIDDLE CLASS PARENTS 401
    MULTIPLE CLASS TEACHING 340
    REGULAR CLASS PLACEMENT 341
    SOCIAL CLASS 121
    UPPER CLASS 121
    WORKING CLASS 121
    WORKING CLASS PARENTS 401

CLASSES
    CLASSES 343
    FORM CLASSES (LANGUAGES) 622
    LITERACY CLASSES 343
    NONGRADED CLASSES 340
    OPPORTUNITY CLASSES 343
    OVERCROWDED CLASSES 265
    SPECIAL CLASSES 343
    TRANSFER CLASSES 343
CLASSICAL
    CLASSICAL LANGUAGES 627
CLASSIFICATION
    CLASSIFICATION 202
CLASSROOM
    CLASSROOM ARRANGEMENT 356
    CLASSROOM COMMUNICATION 355
    CLASSROOM ENVIRONMENT 380
    CLASSROOM MATERIALS 741
    CLASSROOM PARTICIPATION 356
    CLASSROOM RESEARCH 280
    CLASSROOM TECHNIQUES 356
CLASSROOMS
    CLASSROOMS 711
    SPECIAL CLASSROOMS 711
CLAUSUS
    NUMERUS CLAUSUS 266
CLERICAL
    CLERICAL OCCUPATIONS 155
    CLERICAL WORKERS 451
CLIMATE
    ECONOMIC CLIMATE 150
CLIMATIC
    CLIMATIC FACTORS 285
CLINICAL
    CLINICAL DIAGNOSIS 372
CLINICS
    CLINICS 313
    PSYCHOEDUCATIONAL CLINICS 313
CLOSED
    CLOSED CIRCUIT TELEVISION 360
CLOSURE
    SCHOOL CLOSURE 263
CLOTHING
    CLOTHING 740
    CLOTHING INDUSTRY 150

CLOTHING
   CLOTHING WORKERS 451
CLUBS
   CLUBS 381
   YOUTH CLUBS 381
CLUSTERS
   OCCUPATIONAL CLUSTERS 155
COACHING
   COACHING TEACHERS 425
COAST
   IVORY COAST 802
CODED
   CODED SPEECH 374
CODIFICATION
   CODIFICATION 230
COEDUCATION
   COEDUCATION 186
COEDUCATIONAL
   COEDUCATIONAL SCHOOLS 303
COGNITIVE
   COGNITIVE ABILITY 520
   COGNITIVE DEVELOPMENT 530
   COGNITIVE OBJECTIVES 300
   COGNITIVE PROCESSES 521
COLLECTION
   DATA COLLECTION 203
COLLECTIONS
   LIBRARY COLLECTIONS 722
COLLECTIVE
   COLLECTIVE ADVANCEMENT 121
   COLLECTIVE AGREEMENTS 153
   COLLECTIVE SETTLEMENTS 122
COLLECTIVISM
   COLLECTIVISM 101
COLLEGE
   COLLEGE ADMINISTRATION 265
   COLLEGE CURRICULUM 330
   COLLEGE DEANS 422
   COLLEGE ENTRANCE EXAMINATIONS 392
   COLLEGE GRADUATES 413
   COLLEGE INSTRUCTION 352
   COLLEGE LIBRARIES 310
   COLLEGE LOCATION 208
   COLLEGE MAJORS 333

COLLEGE
   COLLEGE MINORS 333
   COLLEGE PLACEMENT 266
   COLLEGE PLANNING 205
   COLLEGE PREPARATION 330
   COLLEGE PROGRAMMES 320
   COLLEGE ROLE 187
   COLLEGE SCHOOL COOPERATION 265
   COLLEGE STUDENTS 413
   COLLEGE SUPERVISORS 426
   COLLEGE TEACHERS 422
   STUDENT COLLEGE RELATIONSHIP 380
COLLEGES
   ADULT COLLEGES 187
   AGRICULTURAL COLLEGES 307
   COLLEGES 187
   JUNIOR COLLEGES 307
   OPEN COLLEGES 307
   PRIVATE COLLEGES 307
   PUBLIC COLLEGES 307
   RESIDENTIAL COLLEGES 307
   TEACHERS COLLEGES 307
   TECHNICAL COLLEGES 307
COLOMBIA
   COLOMBIA 803
COLOMBO
   COLOMBO PLAN 852
COLONIALISM
   COLONIALISM 101
COMECON
   COMECON 852
COMFORT
   THERMAL COMFORT 252
COMMERCE
   COMMERCE 150
COMMERCIAL
   COMMERCIAL ART 610
   COMMERCIAL EDUCATION 672
   COMMERCIAL WORKERS 451
COMMISSION
   COMMISSION REPORT 880
   NATIONAL COMMISSION FOR UNESCO 860
COMMITTEES
   ADULT PROGRAMME COMMITTEES 442
   ADVISORY COMMITTEES 442
   COMMITTEES 442

COMMON
    COMMON CORE 342
COMMONWEALTH
    COMMONWEALTH 801
    COMMONWEALTH
      SECRETARIAT 852
COMMUNICABLE
    COMMUNICABLE DISEASES
      161
COMMUNICATION
    AUDIOVISUAL
      COMMUNICATION 360
    CLASSROOM
      COMMUNICATION 355
    COMMUNICATION 204
    COMMUNICATION PROBLEMS
      204
    COMMUNICATION SKILLS 533
    MANUAL COMMUNICATION
      374
    VERBAL COMMUNICATION
      662
COMMUNICATIONS
    COMMUNICATIONS 145
    COMMUNICATIONS
      SATELLITES 731
COMMUNIST
    COMMUNIST EDUCATION 188
COMMUNITIES
    EUROPEAN COMMUNITIES
      852
COMMUNITY
    ACTION PROGRAMMES
      (COMMUNITY) 282
    ADULT EDUCATION–
      COMMUNITY RELATIONS
      263
    COMMUNITY 102
    COMMUNITY ACTION 102
    COMMUNITY AGENCIES
      (PUBLIC) 104
    COMMUNITY CENTRES 311
    COMMUNITY
      CHARACTERISTICS 285
    COMMUNITY CONTROL 102
    COMMUNITY DEVELOPMENT
      151
    COMMUNITY EDUCATION 186
    COMMUNITY INFLUENCE 122
    COMMUNITY LEADERS 440
    COMMUNITY
      ORGANIZATIONS 110

COMMUNITY
    COMMUNITY PARTICIPATION
      122
    COMMUNITY PLANNING 108
    COMMUNITY PROBLEMS 122
    COMMUNITY PROGRAMMES
      109
    COMMUNITY RESOURCES 700
    COMMUNITY ROLE 105
    COMMUNITY SCHOOLS 302
    COMMUNITY SERVICES 107
    COMMUNITY STUDY 680
    SCHOOL COMMUNITY
      COOPERATION 263
    SCHOOL COMMUNITY
      PROGRAMMES 272
    SCHOOL COMMUNITY
      RELATIONSHIP 263
COMOROS
    COMOROS 809
COMPARATIVE
    COMPARATIVE ANALYSIS 282
    COMPARATIVE EDUCATION
      640
COMPENSATORY
    COMPENSATORY EDUCATION
      186
    COMPENSATORY EDUCATION
      PROGRAMMES 271
COMPETENCY
    COMPETENCY-BASED
      EDUCATION 352
COMPETITIVE
    COMPETITIVE SELECTION 266
COMPLEMENTARY
    COMPLEMENTARY
      EDUCATION 184
COMPLETION
    COURSE COMPLETION 266
COMPLEXES
    EDUCATIONAL COMPLEXES
      187
COMPLEXITY
    COMPLEXITY LEVEL 522
COMPOSITION
    COMPOSITION (LITERARY) 620
COMPREHENSION
    COMPREHENSION 521
COMPREHENSIVE
    COMPREHENSIVE SCHOOLS
      306

COMPREHENSIVE
    COMPREHENSIVE
       SECONDARY SCHOOLS 306
COMPULSORY
    COMPULSORY COURSES 331
    COMPULSORY EDUCATION
       180
COMPUTER
    COMPUTER ASSISTED
       INSTRUCTION 361
    COMPUTER LANGUAGES 760
    COMPUTER PROGRAMMES 760
    COMPUTER SCIENCES 630
COMPUTERS
    COMPUTERS 760
CONCEPT
    CONCEPT FORMATION 513
    CONCEPT TEACHING 350
    SELF CONCEPT 555
    SINGLE CONCEPT FILMS 730
CONCEPTS
    ALGEBRAIC CONCEPTS 631
    ARCHITECTURAL CONCEPTS
       252
    ARITHMETICAL CONCEPTS
       631
    FUNDAMENTAL CONCEPTS
       522
    GEOGRAPHIC CONCEPTS 640
    GEOMETRIC CONCEPTS 631
    MATHEMATICAL CONCEPTS
       631
    NUMBER CONCEPTS 631
    SCIENTIFIC CONCEPTS 630
CONCEPTUAL
    CONCEPTUAL SCHEMES 522
CONDITIONED
    CONDITIONED RESPONSE 511
CONDITIONS
    CONDITIONS OF GRANT 232
    CONDITIONS OF SUBSIDY 241
    TEACHING CONDITIONS 212
    WORKING CONDITIONS 153
CONESCAL
    CONESCAL 852
CONFERENCE
    CONFERENCE REPORT 880
    UNESCO GENERAL
       CONFERENCE 851
CONFERENCES
    CONFERENCES 204

CONFLICT
    CONFLICT 572
    CONFLICT RESOLUTION 572
    ETHNIC CONFLICT 123
    ROLE CONFLICT 553
CONFORMITY
    CONFORMITY 554
CONGO
    CONGO 802
CONNECTED
    CONNECTED DISCOURSE 620
CONSERVATION
    SOIL CONSERVATION 646
CONSOLIDATION
    CONSOLIDATION OF
       SCHOOLS 264
CONSORTIA
    CONSORTIA 261
CONSTRUCTION
    CONSTRUCTION COSTS 251
    CONSTRUCTION EQUIPMENT
       253
    CONSTRUCTION INDUSTRY
       150
    CONSTRUCTION PRACTICES
       253
    CONSTRUCTION
       PROCEDURES 253
    CONSTRUCTION
       PROGRAMMES 253
    CONSTRUCTION WORKERS
       451
    TEST CONSTRUCTION 392
CONSULTANTS
    CONSULTANTS 430
    INTERNATIONAL EDUCATION
       CONSULTANTS 430
    MEDICAL CONSULTANTS 433
    READING CONSULTANTS 430
    SCIENCE CONSULTANTS 430
CONSUMER
    CONSUMER EDUCATION 186
CONTENT
    CONTENT ANALYSIS 331
    PROGRAMME CONTENT 361
    TEXTBOOK CONTENT 331
CONTINUATION
    CONTINUATION EDUCATION
       184
    CONTINUATION STUDENTS
       412

CONTINUOUS
    CONTINUOUS ASSESSMENT 391
    CONTINUOUS PROGRESS PLAN 331
CONTRACTS
    CONTRACTS 241
CONTRASTIVE
    CONTRASTIVE LINGUISTICS 621
CONTROL
    COMMUNITY CONTROL 102
    CONTROL GROUPS 283
    DISEASE CONTROL 161
    SELF CONTROL 560
CONVENTIONAL
    CONVENTIONAL INSTRUCTION 352
CONVENTIONS
    INTERNATIONAL CONVENTIONS 170
CONVERSATIONAL
    CONVERSATIONAL LANGUAGE COURSES 663
COOK
    COOK ISLANDS 806
COOPERATION
    ADULT EDUCATION SCHOOL COOPERATION 263
    ADULT EDUCATION–INDUSTRY COOPERATION 263
    COLLEGE SCHOOL COOPERATION 265
    INTERINSTITUTIONAL COOPERATION 262
    INTERNATIONAL COOPERATION 105
    INTERORGANIZATIONAL COOPERATION 262
    NATIONAL REGIONAL COOPERATION 105
    PARENT TEACHER COOPERATION 380
    REGIONAL COOPERATION 105
    SCHOOL COMMUNITY COOPERATION 263
COOPERATIVES
    COOPERATIVES 150
COORDINATING
    COORDINATING AGENCIES 103
    COORDINATING ORGANIZATIONS 110
    RESEARCH COORDINATING UNITS 261
COORDINATION
    COORDINATION 102
    EDUCATIONAL COORDINATION 200
    NATIONAL INTERAGENCY COORDINATION 105
    PERCEPTUAL MOTOR COORDINATION 510
    PROGRAMME COORDINATION 205
COPYRIGHTS
    COPYRIGHTS 170
CORE
    COMMON CORE 342
    CORE COURSES 333
    CORE CURRICULUM 330
CORRECTIONAL
    CORRECTIONAL EDUCATION 186
    CORRECTIONAL INSTITUTIONS 170
    CORRECTIONAL SCHOOLS 304
CORRECTIVE
    CORRECTIVE READING 660
CORRELATION
    CORRELATION 283
CORRESPONDENCE
    CORRESPONDENCE COURSES 333
    CORRESPONDENCE SCHOOLS 303
    CORRESPONDENCE TUITION 335
    LETTERS (CORRESPONDENCE) 721
COST
    COST EFFECTIVENESS 243
    COST REDUCTION 243
COSTA
    COSTA RICA 803
COSTS
    CONSTRUCTION COSTS 251
    COSTS 241
    ESTIMATED COSTS 243
    PROGRAMME COSTS 243
    UNIT COSTS 243

COUNCIL
    COUNCIL OF EUROPE 852
    SECURITY COUNCIL 850
    TRUSTEESHIP COUNCIL 850
COUNSELLING
    ADULT COUNSELLING 371
    BEHAVIOURAL COUNSELLING 370
    CAREER COUNSELLING 370
    COUNSELLING 370
    COUNSELLING CENTRES 311
    COUNSELLING OBJECTIVES 370
    EDUCATIONAL COUNSELLING 370
    FAMILY COUNSELLING 371
    GROUP COUNSELLING 371
    INDIVIDUAL COUNSELLING 371
    MARRIAGE COUNSELLING 371
    REHABILITATION COUNSELLING 370
    TEACHER COUNSELLING 371
COUNSELLOR
    COUNSELLOR FUNCTIONS 370
    COUNSELLOR QUALIFICATIONS 223
    COUNSELLOR TRAINING 681
COUNSELLORS
    ADULT COUNSELLORS 431
    COUNSELLORS 431
    EMPLOYMENT COUNSELLORS 431
    PRIMARY SCHOOL COUNSELLORS 431
    SECONDARY SCHOOL COUNSELLORS 431
COUNTRIES
    ARAB COUNTRIES 801
    DEVELOPED COUNTRIES 101
    DEVELOPING COUNTRIES 101
    MEDITERRANEAN COUNTRIES 801
COURSE
    COURSE COMPLETION 266
    COURSE DURATION 333
    COURSE EVALUATION 333
    COURSE OBJECTIVES 300
    COURSE ORGANIZATION 333
COURSES
    ACCELERATED COURSES 333
    COMPULSORY COURSES 331

COURSES
    CONVERSATIONAL LANGUAGE COURSES 663
    CORE COURSES 333
    CORRESPONDENCE COURSES 333
    COURSES 333
    CREDIT COURSES 333
    EDUCATION COURSES 691
    ELECTIVE COURSES 333
    EVENING COURSES 307
    INSERVICE COURSES 334
    INSTITUTE TYPE COURSES 334
    INTENSIVE LANGUAGE COURSES 663
    LONG COURSES 333
    METHODS COURSES 691
    NON VOCATIONAL COURSES 333
    NONCREDIT COURSES 333
    OPTIONAL COURSES 333
    ORIENTATION COURSES 333
    REMEDIAL COURSES 333
    SANDWICH COURSES 333
    SHORT COURSES 334
    VACATION COURSES 334
COURT
    COURT LITIGATION 170
COURTS
    COURTS 170
CREATIVE
    CREATIVE ABILITY 520
    CREATIVE DEVELOPMENT 530
    CREATIVE TEACHING 350
    CREATIVE THINKING 521
CREATIVITY
    CREATIVITY 522
CREDENTIALS
    CREDENTIALS 232
CREDIT
    CREDIT COURSES 333
    CREDIT SYSTEM 390
CREFAL
    CREFAL 852
CREOLES
    CREOLES 625
CRIPPLES
    CRIPPLES 403
CRITERIA
    CRITERIA 283
    EVALUATION CRITERIA 210

CRITERIA
   LESSON OBSERVATION CRITERIA 691
   PERFORMANCE CRITERIA 232
   RESEARCH CRITERIA 283
CRITERION
   CRITERION REFERENCED TESTS 392
CRITICAL
   CRITICAL THINKING 521
CRITICISM
   LITERARY CRITICISM 615
CROSS
   CROSS AGE TEACHING 350
   CROSS CULTURAL STUDIES 282
CRUZ
   SANTA CRUZ ISLANDS 806
CSME
   CSME 853
CUBA
   CUBA 803
CULTURAL
   CROSS CULTURAL STUDIES 282
   CULTURAL ACTIVITIES 537
   CULTURAL BACKGROUND 130
   CULTURAL CENTRES 310
   CULTURAL DEVELOPMENT 151
   CULTURAL DISADVANTAGEMENT 130
   CULTURAL ENVIRONMENT 550
   CULTURAL EXCHANGE 130
   CULTURAL FACTORS 285
   CULTURAL INTERRELATIONSHIPS 130
   CULTURAL ISOLATION 130
   CULTURAL POLICIES 130
   CULTURAL TRAITS 561
   RELIGIOUS CULTURAL GROUPS 443
CULTURALLY
   CULTURALLY DISADVANTAGED 402
CULTURE
   CULTURE 130
   URBAN CULTURE 130
CULTURES
   CULTURES 600

CURIOSITY
   CURIOSITY 561
CURRICULUM
   COLLEGE CURRICULUM 330
   CORE CURRICULUM 330
   CURRICULUM 330
   CURRICULUM DEVELOPMENT 331
   CURRICULUM EVALUATION 213
   CURRICULUM GUIDES 724
   CURRICULUM PLANNING 213
   CURRICULUM PROBLEMS 281
   CURRICULUM RESEARCH 280
   CURRICULUM STUDY CENTRES 312
   EXPERIMENTAL CURRICULUM 332
   INDIVIDUALIZED CURRICULUM 332
   INTEGRATED CURRICULUM 332
   NONGRADED CURRICULUM 332
   PREPRIMARY CURRICULUM 330
   PRIMARY SCHOOL CURRICULUM 330
   SECONDARY SCHOOL CURRICULUM 330
   SHOP CURRICULUM 672
   TEACHER EDUCATION CURRICULUM 330
   VOCATIONAL SCHOOL CURRICULUM 330
CYBERNETICS
   CYBERNETICS 650
CYPRUS
   CYPRUS 805
CZECHOSLOVAKIA
   CZECHOSLOVAKIA 805
DANCE
   DANCE 610
DATA
   CENSUS DATA 124
   DATA ANALYSIS 284
   DATA BASE 283
   DATA COLLECTION 203
   DATA PROCESSING 284
   PERSONNEL DATA 220
   STATISTICAL DATA 284

DAY
    DAY CARE SERVICES 270
    DAY RELEASE 222
    DAY SCHOOLS 303
    DAY STUDENTS 410
    DAY TIME PROGRAMMES 321
    EXTENDED DAY SCHOOLS 303
DEAF
    DEAF 403
    DEAF EDUCATION 322
DEANS
    COLLEGE DEANS 422
DEATH
    DEATH 500
DECENTRALIZATION
    DECENTRALIZATION 200
DECISION
    DECISION MAKING 201
DEDUCTIVE
    DEDUCTIVE METHODS 355
DEFICIT
    DEFICIT (FACILITIES) 250
    DEFICIT FINANCING 243
DEGREE
    DEGREE REQUIREMENTS 390
    SPECIAL DEGREE PROGRAMMES 320
DEGREES
    BACHELORS DEGREES 390
    DEGREES (TITLES) 390
    DOCTORAL DEGREES 390
    MASTERS DEGREES 390
    SPECIALIST IN EDUCATION DEGREES 390
DELINQUENCY
    DELINQUENCY 572
    DELINQUENCY CAUSES 285
    DELINQUENCY PREVENTION 281
DELINQUENTS
    DELINQUENTS 403
DEMAND
    EDUCATIONAL DEMAND 181
    TEACHER SUPPLY AND DEMAND 207
DEMANDS
    LABOUR DEMANDS 153
DEMOCRACY
    DEMOCRACY 101
DEMOCRATIC

DEMOCRATIC
    DEMOCRATIC KAMPUCHEA 804
    DEMOCRATIC YEMEN 807
DEMOCRATIZATION
    DEMOCRATIZATION OF EDUCATION 180
DEMOGRAPHY
    DEMOGRAPHY 640
    NATIONAL DEMOGRAPHY 124
DEMONSTRATION
    DEMONSTRATION PROJECTS 272
DEMONSTRATIONS
    DEMONSTRATIONS (EDUCATIONAL) 671
DENMARK
    DENMARK 805
DENTAL
    DENTAL HEALTH 502
DENTISTRY
    DENTISTRY 651
DENTISTS
    DENTISTS 433
DEPARTMENT
    HEADS OF DEPARTMENT (SCHOOL) 423
DEPARTMENTAL
    DEPARTMENTAL TEACHING PLANS 340
DEPARTMENTS
    DEPARTMENTS (SCHOOL) 340
    PROVINCIAL DEPARTMENTS OF EDUCATION 261
    UNIVERSITY EXTENSION DEPARTMENTS 307
DEPRESSED
    DEPRESSED AREAS (ECONOMIC) 151
DEPRIVATION
    SENSORY DEPRIVATION 570
DESCRIPTIONS
    PROGRAMME DESCRIPTIONS 203
DESCRIPTIVE
    DESCRIPTIVE LINGUISTICS 621
DESIGN
    BUILDING DESIGN 252
    DESIGN PROCEDURE 252
    FACILITIES DESIGN 252
    FURNITURE DESIGN 252

DESIGN
  PROGRAMME DESIGN 205
  RESEARCH DESIGN 283
DETECTION
  HANDICAP DETECTION 372
DETERIORATION
  INTELLECTUAL
    DETERIORATION 520
DETERRENTS
  PARTICIPATION DETERRENTS 285
DEVELOPED
  DEVELOPED COUNTRIES 101
  STUDENT DEVELOPED
    MATERIALS 725
  TEACHER DEVELOPED
    MATERIALS 725
DEVELOPING
  DEVELOPING COUNTRIES 101
DEVELOPMENT
  ADULT DEVELOPMENT 530
  AGRICULTURAL
    DEVELOPMENT 151
  BEHAVIOUR DEVELOPMENT 530
  CHILD DEVELOPMENT 530
  CHILD DEVELOPMENT
    SPECIALISTS 430
  COGNITIVE DEVELOPMENT 530
  COMMUNITY DEVELOPMENT 151
  CREATIVE DEVELOPMENT 530
  CULTURAL DEVELOPMENT 151
  CURRICULUM DEVELOPMENT 331
  DEVELOPMENT 151
  DEVELOPMENT EDUCATION 682
  DEVELOPMENT STUDIES 640
  ECONOMIC DEVELOPMENT 151
  EDUCATIONAL
    DEVELOPMENT 182
  EDUCATIONAL
    DEVELOPMENT TRENDS 182
  EMOTIONAL DEVELOPMENT 530
  HANDWRITING
    DEVELOPMENT 534

DEVELOPMENT
  HUMAN RESOURCES
    DEVELOPMENT 151
  INDIVIDUAL DEVELOPMENT 530
  INDIVIDUAL DEVELOPMENT
    EDUCATION 183
  INDIVIDUAL DEVELOPMENT
    PROGRAMMES 321
  INTEGRATED RURAL
    DEVELOPMENT 151
  INTELLECTUAL
    DEVELOPMENT 530
  LANGUAGE DEVELOPMENT 530
  MANPOWER DEVELOPMENT 151
  MENTAL DEVELOPMENT 530
  MOTOR DEVELOPMENT 530
  PERSONALITY DEVELOPMENT 530
  PHYSICAL DEVELOPMENT 530
  READING DEVELOPMENT 534
  RESEARCH AND
    DEVELOPMENT 282
  RURAL DEVELOPMENT 151
  SKILL DEVELOPMENT 534
  SOCIAL DEVELOPMENT 151
  VOCABULARY DEVELOPMENT 534
  VOCATIONAL DEVELOPMENT 534
DEVELOPMENTAL
  DEVELOPMENTAL
    PSYCHOLOGY 642
DEVICES
  STIMULUS DEVICES 734
DIAGNOSIS
  CLINICAL DIAGNOSIS 372
  EDUCATIONAL DIAGNOSIS 391
DIAGNOSTIC
  DIAGNOSTIC TEACHING 350
  DIAGNOSTIC TESTS 392
DIAGRAMS
  DIAGRAMS 733
DIALECTS
  DIALECTS 625
DICTION
  DICTION 532
DICTIONARY
  DICTIONARY 880

DIFFERENCES
  AGE DIFFERENCES 500
  INDIVIDUAL DIFFERENCES 530
  RURAL URBAN DIFFERENCES 122
  SEX DIFFERENCES 501
DIFFERENTIATED
  DIFFERENTIATED STAFFS 424
DIFFICULTIES
  LEARNING DIFFICULTIES 513
DIFFICULTY
  READING DIFFICULTY 660
DIFFUSION
  DIFFUSION 204
DIGNITY
  HUMAN DIGNITY 100
DIPLOMAS
  DIPLOMAS 390
DIRECT
  DIRECT TEACHING 352
DIRECTED
  DIRECTED STUDY 335
  SELF DIRECTED GROUPS 443
DIRECTORS
  RESEARCH DIRECTORS 430
DIRECTORY
  DIRECTORY 880
DISABILITIES
  LEARNING DISABILITIES 513
DISADVANTAGED
  CULTURALLY DISADVANTAGED 402
  DISADVANTAGED GROUPS 443
  DISADVANTAGED SCHOOLS 304
  ECONOMICALLY DISADVANTAGED 402
  EDUCATIONALLY DISADVANTAGED 402
  SOCIALLY DISADVANTAGED 402
DISADVANTAGEMENT
  CULTURAL DISADVANTAGEMENT 130
  EDUCATIONAL DISADVANTAGEMENT 181
  SOCIAL DISADVANTAGEMENT 121
DISARMAMENT
  DISARMAMENT EDUCATION 682
DISASTER
  NATURAL DISASTER 250
DISCIPLINE
  DISCIPLINE 267
  DISCIPLINE POLICY 231
  DISCIPLINE PROBLEMS 281
DISCOURSE
  CONNECTED DISCOURSE 620
DISCOVERY
  DISCOVERY LEARNING 512
DISCRIMINATION
  EDUCATIONAL DISCRIMINATION 181
  RACIAL DISCRIMINATION 123
  SOCIAL DISCRIMINATION 121
DISCUSSION
  DISCUSSION GROUPS 343
  DISCUSSION (TEACHING TECHNIQUE) 356
  GROUP DISCUSSION 356
DISEASE
  DISEASE CONTROL 161
  DISEASE RATE 161
DISEASES
  COMMUNICABLE DISEASES 161
  DISEASES 161
  PSYCHOSOMATIC DISEASES 570
DISENGAGEMENT
  SOCIAL DISENGAGEMENT 531
DISORDERS
  PERCEPTUAL DISORDERS 571
DISPARITIES
  NATIONAL REGIONAL DISPARITIES 151
DISPLAY
  DISPLAY BOARDS 741
DISPUTE
  DISPUTE SETTLEMENT 233
DISQUALIFICATION
  DISQUALIFICATION 233
DISSEMINATION
  INFORMATION DISSEMINATION 204
DISTANCE
  DISTANCE 264
  DISTANCE EDUCATION 355
  DISTANCE STUDY 335

DISTANCE
    DISTANCE TEACHING 352
    DISTANCE TEACHING
      INSTITUTIONS 311
DISTRIBUTION
    ETHNIC DISTRIBUTION 123
    GEOGRAPHIC DISTRIBUTION 124
    POPULATION DISTRIBUTION 124
    SCHOOL DISTRIBUTION 208
    TEACHER DISTRIBUTION 207
DISTRIBUTIVE
    DISTRIBUTIVE EDUCATION 672
    DISTRIBUTIVE WORKERS 451
DISTRICT
    SCHOOL DISTRICT AUTONOMY 263
DISTRICTS
    SCHOOL DISTRICTS 264
DISTURBANCE
    EMOTIONAL DISTURBANCE 572
DISTURBED
    EMOTIONALLY DISTURBED 403
DIVISIONS
    GRADES (PROGRAMME DIVISIONS) 342
    SEMESTER DIVISIONS 344
DJIBOUTI
    DJIBOUTI 802
DOCTORAL
    DOCTORAL DEGREES 390
    DOCTORAL PROGRAMMES 320
    DOCTORAL THESES 721
DOCUMENTALISTS
    DOCUMENTALISTS 462
DOCUMENTATION
    DOCUMENTATION 202
    DOCUMENTATION CENTRES 310
    EDUCATIONAL DOCUMENTATION 202
DOCUMENTS
    DOCUMENTS 721
DOMINANCE
    LATERAL DOMINANCE 503
DOMINICA
    DOMINICA 803

DOMINICAN
    DOMINICAN REPUBLIC 803
DOUBLE
    DOUBLE SHIFT SCHOOLS 303
DOWNS
    DOWNS SYNDROME 570
DRAFTSMEN
    DRAFTSMEN 452
DRAIN
    BRAIN DRAIN 124
DRAMA
    DRAMA 616
    DRAMA WORKSHOPS 381
DRAVIDIAN
    DRAVIDIAN LANGUAGES 625
DRAWING
    TECHNICAL DRAWING 647
DRAWINGS
    ARCHITECTURAL DRAWINGS 252
DRILLS
    PATTERN DRILLS (LANGUAGE) 663
DROPOUT
    DROPOUT PROGRAMMES 320
    DROPOUT RATE 206
DROPOUTS
    DROPOUTS 411
DROPPING
    DROPPING OUT 266
DRUG
    DRUG ABUSE 572
    DRUG EDUCATION 683
DUAL
    DUAL ENROLMENT 206
DURATION
    COURSE DURATION 333
DYNAMICS
    GROUP DYNAMICS 355
DYSLEXIA
    DYSLEXIA 570
EARLY
    EARLY ADULTHOOD 500
    EARLY CHILDHOOD 500
    EARLY CHILDHOOD EDUCATION 186
EARNINGS
    LOSS OF EARNINGS PAYMENTS 242
EARTH
    EARTH SCIENCES 633

EAST
    EAST AFRICA 801
    FAR EAST 801
    MIDDLE EAST 801
    SOUTH EAST ASIA 801
EASTER
    EASTER ISLAND 806
EASTERN
    EASTERN EUROPE 801
    EASTERN HEMISPHERE 801
ECA
    ECA 850
ECE
    ECE 850
ECLA
    ECLA 850
ECOLOGY
    ECOLOGY 632
ECONOMIC
    DEPRESSED AREAS (ECONOMIC) 151
    ECONOMIC CLIMATE 150
    ECONOMIC DEVELOPMENT 151
    ECONOMIC FACTORS 285
    ECONOMIC POLICIES 150
    ECONOMIC PROGRESS 150
    ECONOMIC RESEARCH 280
    ECONOMIC STATUS 121
ECONOMICALLY
    ECONOMICALLY DISADVANTAGED 402
ECONOMICS
    ECONOMICS 640
    EDUCATIONAL ECONOMICS 640
    HOME ECONOMICS 640
    HOME ECONOMICS EDUCATION 683
    HOME ECONOMICS TEACHERS 425
ECOSOC
    ECOSOC 850
ECUADOR
    ECUADOR 803
ECWA
    ECWA 852
EDUCATED
    EDUCATED UNEMPLOYMENT 154
EDUCATION
    ACCESS TO EDUCATION 181

EDUCATION
    ADMINISTRATOR EDUCATION 672
    ADULT EDUCATION 186
    ADULT EDUCATION ACCOMMODATION 711
    ADULT EDUCATION AGENCIES 103
    ADULT EDUCATION ASSOCIATIONS 110
    ADULT EDUCATION CENTRES 311
    ADULT EDUCATION PROGRAMMES 321
    ADULT EDUCATION REGULATIONS 230
    ADULT EDUCATION SCHOOL COOPERATION 263
    ADULT EDUCATION SYSTEMS 260
    ADULT EDUCATION TAXES 240
    ADULT EDUCATION–COMMUNITY RELATIONS 263
    ADULT EDUCATION–INDUSTRY COOPERATION 263
    AESTHETIC EDUCATION 684
    AGRICULTURAL EDUCATION 672
    ALCOHOL EDUCATION 683
    ALTERNATIVE EDUCATION 184
    ARMED FORCES EDUCATION 186
    ART EDUCATION 684
    ATHEISTIC EDUCATION 188
    BASIC EDUCATION 183
    BILINGUAL EDUCATION 183
    BLIND EDUCATION 322
    CAREER EDUCATION 183
    CHRISTIAN EDUCATION 188
    COMMERCIAL EDUCATION 672
    COMMUNIST EDUCATION 188
    COMMUNITY EDUCATION 186
    COMPARATIVE EDUCATION 640
    COMPENSATORY EDUCATION 186

EDUCATION
- COMPENSATORY EDUCATION PROGRAMMES 271
- COMPETENCY-BASED EDUCATION 352
- COMPLEMENTARY EDUCATION 184
- COMPULSORY EDUCATION 180
- CONSUMER EDUCATION 186
- CONTINUATION EDUCATION 184
- CORRECTIONAL EDUCATION 186
- DEAF EDUCATION 322
- DEMOCRATIZATION OF EDUCATION 180
- DEVELOPMENT EDUCATION 682
- DISARMAMENT EDUCATION 682
- DISTANCE EDUCATION 355
- DISTRIBUTIVE EDUCATION 672
- DRUG EDUCATION 683
- EARLY CHILDHOOD EDUCATION 186
- EDUCATION 180
- EDUCATION COURSES 691
- EDUCATION WORK RELATIONSHIP 182
- ELITIST EDUCATION 180
- ENGINEERING EDUCATION 681
- ENVIRONMENTAL EDUCATION 683
- EQUAL EDUCATION 180
- EXCEPTIONAL CHILD EDUCATION 322
- EXPERIMENTAL EDUCATION 280
- EXTENSION EDUCATION 382
- FAMILY EDUCATION 186
- FOREIGN WORKER EDUCATION 186
- FREE EDUCATION 180
- FULL TIME EDUCATION 184
- GENERAL EDUCATION 183
- HANDICAPPED EDUCATION 322
- HEALTH EDUCATION 683
- HIGHER EDUCATION 185

EDUCATION
- HOME ECONOMICS EDUCATION 683
- INDIVIDUAL DEVELOPMENT EDUCATION 183
- INDUSTRIAL EDUCATION 672
- INFORMAL EDUCATION 184
- INSERVICE EDUCATION 321
- INSERVICE TEACHER EDUCATION 690
- INTERNATIONAL EDUCATION 640
- INTERNATIONAL EDUCATION CONSULTANTS 430
- ISLAMIC EDUCATION 188
- LEGAL EDUCATION 681
- LEVELS OF EDUCATION 185
- LIFELONG EDUCATION 180
- LOCAL EDUCATION AUTHORITIES 263
- LOWER SECONDARY EDUCATION 185
- MANAGEMENT EDUCATION 672
- MASS EDUCATION 352
- MEDICAL EDUCATION 681
- MIGRANT EDUCATION 186
- MINISTRY OF EDUCATION 860
- MINISTRY OF EDUCATION REPORT 880
- MORAL EDUCATION 682
- MUSIC EDUCATION 684
- NONFORMAL EDUCATION 184
- OUT OF SCHOOL EDUCATION 184
- PARENT EDUCATION 186
- PARENT EDUCATION PROGRAMMES 321
- PART TIME EDUCATION 184
- PEACE EDUCATION 682
- PHYSICAL EDUCATION 683
- POLITICAL EDUCATION 680
- POLYTECHNICAL EDUCATION 183
- POPULATION EDUCATION 683
- PRE RETIREMENT EDUCATION 183
- PREPRIMARY EDUCATION 185
- PRESERVICE TEACHER EDUCATION 690

EDUCATION
- PREVOCATIONAL EDUCATION 670
- PRIMARY EDUCATION 185
- PRIVATE ADULT EDUCATION 187
- PRIVATE EDUCATION 187
- PRIVATE EDUCATION SYSTEMS 260
- PROFESSIONAL EDUCATION 183
- PROVINCIAL DEPARTMENTS OF EDUCATION 261
- PUBLIC EDUCATION 187
- PUBLIC EDUCATION SYSTEMS 260
- RECURRENT EDUCATION 184
- RELIGIOUS EDUCATION 682
- RESIDENTIAL ADULT EDUCATION 184
- RIGHT TO EDUCATION 180
- ROLE EDUCATION 183
- RURAL EDUCATION 186
- SAFETY EDUCATION 683
- SCIENCE EDUCATION 670
- SEAFARER EDUCATION 186
- SECONDARY EDUCATION 185
- SECULAR EDUCATION 180
- SEX EDUCATION 683
- SPECIAL EDUCATION 186
- SPECIAL EDUCATION TEACHERS 421
- SPECIALIST IN EDUCATION DEGREES 390
- TEACHER EDUCATION 690
- TEACHER EDUCATION CURRICULUM 330
- TEACHER EDUCATOR EDUCATION 690
- TECHNICAL EDUCATION 183
- TERMINAL EDUCATION 184
- THEOLOGICAL EDUCATION 681
- TRADITIONAL EDUCATION 180
- UNEMPLOYED EDUCATION PROGRAMMES 321
- UNESCO EDUCATION SECTOR 851
- UNIVERSAL EDUCATION 180
- UPPER SECONDARY EDUCATION 185

EDUCATION
- URBAN EDUCATION 186
- VOCATIONAL EDUCATION 183
- VOCATIONAL EDUCATION TEACHERS 425
- VOLUNTARILY PROVIDED ADULT EDUCATION 187
- VOLUNTARY EDUCATION 180
- WOMENS EDUCATION 180
- WORK EDUCATION 682
- WORKERS EDUCATION 186

EDUCATIONAL
- CENTRAL EDUCATIONAL AGENCIES 261
- DEMONSTRATIONS (EDUCATIONAL) 671
- EDUCATIONAL ADMINISTRATION 200
- EDUCATIONAL ADMINISTRATORS 420
- EDUCATIONAL AIMS 200
- EDUCATIONAL ALLOWANCES 242
- EDUCATIONAL ANTHROPOLOGY 642
- EDUCATIONAL ATTITUDES 181
- EDUCATIONAL BACKGROUND 221
- EDUCATIONAL BENEFITS 181
- EDUCATIONAL CERTIFICATES 390
- EDUCATIONAL CHOICE 181
- EDUCATIONAL COMPLEXES 187
- EDUCATIONAL COORDINATION 200
- EDUCATIONAL COUNSELLING 370
- EDUCATIONAL DEMAND 181
- EDUCATIONAL DEVELOPMENT 182
- EDUCATIONAL DEVELOPMENT TRENDS 182
- EDUCATIONAL DIAGNOSIS 391
- EDUCATIONAL DISADVANTAGEMENT 181
- EDUCATIONAL DISCRIMINATION 181
- EDUCATIONAL DOCUMENTATION 202

EDUCATIONAL
- EDUCATIONAL ECONOMICS 640
- EDUCATIONAL ENVIRONMENT 380
- EDUCATIONAL EQUIPMENT 740
- EDUCATIONAL EXPECTATIONS 541
- EDUCATIONAL EXPERIENCE 562
- EDUCATIONAL EXPERIMENTS 282
- EDUCATIONAL FACILITIES 710
- EDUCATIONAL FINANCE 243
- EDUCATIONAL FUTUROLOGY 100
- EDUCATIONAL GAMES 356
- EDUCATIONAL GOALS 180
- EDUCATIONAL GUIDANCE 211
- EDUCATIONAL HISTORY 641
- EDUCATIONAL IMPROVEMENT 182
- EDUCATIONAL INFORMATION 200
- EDUCATIONAL INFRASTRUCTURE 181
- EDUCATIONAL INNOVATIONS 200
- EDUCATIONAL INSTITUTIONS 125
- EDUCATIONAL INTEREST 541
- EDUCATIONAL LEAVE 222
- EDUCATIONAL LEGISLATION 230
- EDUCATIONAL LEISURE 357
- EDUCATIONAL MEDIA 360
- EDUCATIONAL METHODS 355
- EDUCATIONAL MISSIONS 205
- EDUCATIONAL NEEDS 181
- EDUCATIONAL OBJECTIVES 300
- EDUCATIONAL OPPORTUNITIES 180
- EDUCATIONAL ORGANIZATION 260
- EDUCATIONAL OUTPUT 181
- EDUCATIONAL PERSONNEL 420

EDUCATIONAL
- EDUCATIONAL PHILOSOPHY 180
- EDUCATIONAL PLANNING 205
- EDUCATIONAL POLICIES 182
- EDUCATIONAL POLICY TRENDS 182
- EDUCATIONAL PRACTICE 182
- EDUCATIONAL PRIORITIES 182
- EDUCATIONAL PROBLEMS 182
- EDUCATIONAL PROGRAMMES 271
- EDUCATIONAL PSYCHOLOGY 642
- EDUCATIONAL PUBLICITY 182
- EDUCATIONAL QUALITY 181
- EDUCATIONAL RADIO 360
- EDUCATIONAL READINGS 690
- EDUCATIONAL RECREATION 357
- EDUCATIONAL REFORM 200
- EDUCATIONAL RESEARCH 280
- EDUCATIONAL RESEARCHERS 430
- EDUCATIONAL RESOURCES 700
- EDUCATIONAL SCIENCES 640
- EDUCATIONAL SEMINARS 204
- EDUCATIONAL SOCIOLOGY 642
- EDUCATIONAL SPACES 711
- EDUCATIONAL SPECIFICATIONS 232
- EDUCATIONAL STATISTICS 284
- EDUCATIONAL STRATEGIES 182
- EDUCATIONAL TECHNOLOGY 360
- EDUCATIONAL TELEVISION 360
- EDUCATIONAL TESTING 391
- EDUCATIONAL TESTS 392
- EDUCATIONAL THEORIES 180
- EDUCATIONAL VOUCHERS 242
- EDUCATIONAL WASTAGE 205
- MOBILE EDUCATIONAL SERVICES 270
- PAID EDUCATIONAL LEAVE 222

EDUCATIONALLY
    EDUCATIONALLY
      DISADVANTAGED 402
EDUCATOR
    TEACHER EDUCATOR
      EDUCATION 690
EDUCATORS
    ADULT EDUCATORS 421
    FULL TIME EDUCATORS 424
    PART TIME EDUCATORS 424
    TEACHER EDUCATORS 422
EEC
    EEC 852
EFFECTIVENESS
    COST EFFECTIVENESS 243
EFFORT
    TAX EFFORT 152
EGYPT
    EGYPT 807
EIDETIC
    EIDETIC IMAGES 511
EIGHTEENTH
    EIGHTEENTH CENTURY 840
ELDERLY
    ELDERLY PEOPLE 400
ELECTIVE
    ELECTIVE COURSES 333
ELECTRICAL
    ELECTRICAL ENGINEERS 463
    ELECTRICAL INDUSTRY 150
ELECTRICIANS
    ELECTRICIANS 452
ELECTRICITY
    ELECTRICITY 633
ELECTROMECHANICAL
    ELECTROMECHANICAL
      TECHNOLOGY 645
ELECTRONIC
    ELECTRONIC TECHNICIANS
      452
ELECTRONICS
    ELECTRONICS 633
    ELECTRONICS INDUSTRY 150
ELEMENTARY
    ELEMENTARY SCIENCE 670
ELEMENTS
    BUILDING ELEMENTS 253
ELITIST
    ELITIST EDUCATION 180
EMERGENCY
    EMERGENCY PROGRAMMES
      271

EMIGRATION
    EMIGRATION 124
EMIRATES
    UNITED ARAB EMIRATES 807
EMOTIONAL
    EMOTIONAL ADJUSTMENT
      551
    EMOTIONAL DEVELOPMENT
      530
    EMOTIONAL DISTURBANCE
      572
    EMOTIONAL EXPERIENCE 562
    EMOTIONAL PROBLEMS 540
EMOTIONALLY
    EMOTIONALLY DISTURBED
      403
EMPIRICAL
    EMPIRICAL RESEARCH 282
EMPLOYED
    SELF EMPLOYED 450
EMPLOYEES
    EMPLOYEES 450
EMPLOYERS
    EMPLOYERS 450
EMPLOYMENT
    EMPLOYMENT 154
    EMPLOYMENT COUNSELLORS
      431
    EMPLOYMENT EXPERIENCE
      221
    EMPLOYMENT
      OPPORTUNITIES 154
    EMPLOYMENT PROGRAMMES
      154
    EMPLOYMENT
      QUALIFICATIONS 390
    EMPLOYMENT SERVICES 154
    EMPLOYMENT STATISTICS 154
    EMPLOYMENT STRATEGIES
      154
    FULL TIME EMPLOYMENT 222
    INITIAL EMPLOYMENT 154
    PART TIME EMPLOYMENT 222
    SEASONAL EMPLOYMENT 154
    SHELTERED EMPLOYMENT
      374
    STUDENT EMPLOYMENT 266
    TEACHER EMPLOYMENT 223
ENCYCLOPAEDIA
    ENCYCLOPAEDIA 880
ENDERBY

ENDERBY
- CANTON AND ENDERBY ISLANDS 806

ENFORCEMENT
- LAW ENFORCEMENT 170

ENGINEERING
- AGRICULTURAL ENGINEERING 646
- BUILDING ENGINEERING 252
- CIVIL ENGINEERING 647
- ENGINEERING 647
- ENGINEERING EDUCATION 681
- ENGINEERING TECHNICIANS 452
- ENGINEERING TECHNOLOGY 645
- HUMAN ENGINEERING 140
- MECHANICAL ENGINEERING 647

ENGINEERS
- CHEMICAL ENGINEERS 463
- ELECTRICAL ENGINEERS 463
- ENGINEERS 463
- MECHANICAL ENGINEERS 463
- MINING ENGINEERS 463

ENGINES
- ENGINES 742

ENGLISH
- ENGLISH 626
- ENGLISH SPEAKING AFRICA 801

ENRICHMENT
- ENRICHMENT PROGRAMMES 320
- LANGUAGE ENRICHMENT 662

ENROLMENT
- DUAL ENROLMENT 206
- ENROLMENT 266
- ENROLMENT INFLUENCES 285
- ENROLMENT PROJECTIONS 206
- ENROLMENT RATIO 206
- ENROLMENT TRENDS 206
- GIRLS ENROLMENT 186
- OPEN ENROLMENT 266

ENTERPRISES
- ENTERPRISES 110
- PRIVATE ENTERPRISES 150
- PUBLIC ENTERPRISES 150

ENTRANCE
- COLLEGE ENTRANCE EXAMINATIONS 392
- ENTRANCE EXAMINATIONS 392

ENVIRONMENT
- CLASSROOM ENVIRONMENT 380
- CULTURAL ENVIRONMENT 550
- EDUCATIONAL ENVIRONMENT 380
- ENVIRONMENT 140
- HOME ENVIRONMENT 550
- PHYSICAL ENVIRONMENT 550
- SOCIAL ENVIRONMENT 550
- WORK ENVIRONMENT 550

ENVIRONMENTAL
- ENVIRONMENTAL EDUCATION 683
- ENVIRONMENTAL INFLUENCES 550

EQUAL
- EQUAL EDUCATION 180
- EQUAL OPPORTUNITIES (JOBS) 153

EQUALITY
- INTERGENERATIONAL EQUALITY 181

EQUALIZATION
- EQUALIZATION AID 152

EQUATORIAL
- EQUATORIAL GUINEA 802

EQUIPMENT
- ATHLETIC EQUIPMENT 740
- AUDIOVISUAL EQUIPMENT 731
- CONSTRUCTION EQUIPMENT 253
- EDUCATIONAL EQUIPMENT 740
- EQUIPMENT 740
- EQUIPMENT STANDARDS 232
- LABORATORY EQUIPMENT 740
- LIBRARY EQUIPMENT 740
- MECHANICAL EQUIPMENT 742
- PROJECTION EQUIPMENT 731
- SCIENCE EQUIPMENT 740

EQUIVALENCES
- EQUIVALENCES 232

ERGONOMICS
> ERGONOMICS 252

ESCAP
> ESCAP 850

ESSAY
> ESSAY TESTS 392

ESSAYS
> ESSAYS 616

ESTIMATED
> ESTIMATED COSTS 243

ESTONIAN
> ESTONIAN SSR 805

ETHICAL
> ETHICAL INSTRUCTION 682

ETHICS
> ETHICS 600

ETHIOPIA
> ETHIOPIA 802

ETHNIC
> ETHNIC CONFLICT 123
> ETHNIC DISTRIBUTION 123
> ETHNIC GROUPS 443
> ETHNIC ORIGINS 550

ETIOLOGY
> ETIOLOGY 285

ETYMOLOGY
> ETYMOLOGY 622

EUROPE
> COUNCIL OF EUROPE 852
> EASTERN EUROPE 801
> EUROPE 800
> WESTERN EUROPE 801

EUROPEAN
> EUROPEAN COMMUNITIES 852
> INDO EUROPEAN LANGUAGES 625

EVALUATION
> BUILDING EVALUATION 251
> COURSE EVALUATION 333
> CURRICULUM EVALUATION 213
> EVALUATION 210
> EVALUATION CRITERIA 210
> EVALUATION METHODS 210
> FORMATIVE EVALUATION 205
> MATERIALS EVALUATION 213
> MEDICAL EVALUATION 391
> PERSONNEL EVALUATION 210
> PROGRAMME EVALUATION 205

EVALUATION
> PSYCHOLOGICAL EVALUATION 391
> SELF EVALUATION 555
> STUDENT EVALUATION 391
> SUMMATIVE EVALUATION 205
> TEACHER EVALUATION 212

EVENING
> EVENING COURSES 307
> EVENING SCHOOLS 303
> EVENING STUDENTS 410

EXAMINATIONS
> COLLEGE ENTRANCE EXAMINATIONS 392
> ENTRANCE EXAMINATIONS 392
> EXAMINATIONS 392
> PHYSICAL EXAMINATIONS 392

EXAMINERS
> EXAMINERS 420

EXCEPTIONAL
> EXCEPTIONAL CHILD EDUCATION 322
> EXCEPTIONAL CHILD RESEARCH 280
> EXCEPTIONAL STUDENTS 416

EXCHANGE
> CULTURAL EXCHANGE 130
> EXCHANGE PROGRAMMES 271
> INFORMATION EXCHANGE 204

EXECUTIVE
> UNESCO EXECUTIVE BOARD 851

EXERCISE
> EXERCISE (PHYSIOLOGY) 503

EXHIBITION
> EXHIBITION AREAS 711

EXHIBITS
> EXHIBITS 733

EXPECTATIONS
> EDUCATIONAL EXPECTATIONS 541

EXPENDITURE
> EXPENDITURE PER STUDENT 243

EXPENDITURES
> EXPENDITURES 241

EXPENSES
> OPERATING EXPENSES 241

EXPERIENCE
    EDUCATIONAL EXPERIENCE 562
    EMOTIONAL EXPERIENCE 562
    EMPLOYMENT EXPERIENCE 221
    EXPERIENCE 562
    FIELD EXPERIENCE PROGRAMMES 671
    SENSORY EXPERIENCE 562
    SOCIAL EXPERIENCE 562
    TEACHING EXPERIENCE 690
    WORK EXPERIENCE 562
    WORK EXPERIENCE PROGRAMMES 673

EXPERIMENTAL
    EXPERIMENTAL CURRICULUM 332
    EXPERIMENTAL EDUCATION 280
    EXPERIMENTAL GROUPS 283
    EXPERIMENTAL PSYCHOLOGY 642
    EXPERIMENTAL RESEARCH 282
    EXPERIMENTAL SCHOOLS 305
    EXPERIMENTAL TEACHING 282

EXPERIMENTS
    EDUCATIONAL EXPERIMENTS 282
    EXPERIMENTS 671
    LABORATORY EXPERIMENTS 671
    SCIENCE EXPERIMENTS 671

EXPERTS
    INTERNATIONAL EXPERTS 430

EXPRESSION
    SELF EXPRESSION 555

EXPULSION
    EXPULSION 267

EXTENDED
    EXTENDED DAY SCHOOLS 303
    EXTENDED SCHOOL YEAR 344

EXTENSION
    EXTENSION AGENTS 440
    EXTENSION EDUCATION 382
    EXTENSION PROGRAMMES 321

EXTENSION
    EXTENSION TEACHERS 422
    LIBRARY EXTENSION 382
    RURAL EXTENSION 382
    RURAL EXTENSION PROGRAMMES 321
    UNIVERSITY EXTENSION 382
    UNIVERSITY EXTENSION DEPARTMENTS 307
    UNIVERSITY EXTENSION PROGRAMMES 321
    UNIVERSITY EXTENSION TEACHERS 422
    URBAN EXTENSION 382

EXTERNAL
    EXTERNAL CANDIDATES 412

EXTINCTION
    EXTINCTION (PSYCHOLOGY) 511

EXTRACURRICULAR
    EXTRACURRICULAR ACTIVITIES 357

EYE
    EYE MOVEMENTS 503

FABLES
    FABLES 616

FACILITIES
    BOARDING FACILITIES 712
    DEFICIT (FACILITIES) 250
    EDUCATIONAL FACILITIES 710
    FACILITIES DESIGN 252
    FACILITIES MANAGEMENT 251
    FACILITIES PLANNING 650
    PROGRAMMING (FACILITIES) 250
    RECREATIONAL FACILITIES 712
    RELOCATABLE FACILITIES 710
    SOCIOCULTURAL FACILITIES 710
    SPORTS FACILITIES 712

FACILITY
    FACILITY GUIDELINES 232
    FACILITY REQUIREMENTS 250

FACTORS
    CLIMATIC FACTORS 285
    CULTURAL FACTORS 285
    ECONOMIC FACTORS 285
    FAILURE FACTORS 285
    INTELLIGENCE FACTORS 285

FACTORS
    PERFORMANCE FACTORS 535
    POLITICAL FACTORS 285
    RELIGIOUS FACTORS 285
    SOCIAL FACTORS 285
    SUCCESS FACTORS 285
    TIME FACTORS (LEARNING) 511
FAEROE
    FAEROE ISLANDS 805
FAILURE
    FAILURE 267
    FAILURE FACTORS 285
    FAILURE RATE 266
FALKLAND
    FALKLAND ISLANDS 808
FAMILY
    FAMILY ATTITUDES 552
    FAMILY BACKGROUND 126
    FAMILY COUNSELLING 371
    FAMILY EDUCATION 186
    FAMILY INFLUENCE 550
    FAMILY MOBILITY 124
    FAMILY PLANNING 126
    FAMILY PROBLEMS 281
    FAMILY PROJECTS 272
    FAMILY RELATIONSHIP 553
    FAMILY ROLE 126
    FAMILY SCHOOL RELATIONSHIP 380
    FAMILY (SOCIOLOGICAL UNIT) 126
    FAMILY STRUCTURE 126
    FOSTER FAMILY 126
    RURAL FAMILY 126
FAO
    FAO 850
FAR
    FAR EAST 801
FARM
    SUPERVISED FARM PRACTICE 673
FARMERS
    FARMERS 451
FATHERS
    FATHERS 401
FATIGUE
    FATIGUE 503
FEAR
    FEAR 540
FEASIBILITY
    FEASIBILITY STUDIES 282

FED
    FED 852
FEDERATIVE
    FEDERATIVE STRUCTURE 102
FEEDBACK
    FEEDBACK 204
FEES
    FEES 240
FELLOWSHIPS
    FELLOWSHIPS 242
FEMALE
    FEMALE 501
FEMINISM
    FEMINISM 101
FICTION
    FICTION 616
FID
    FID 853
FIELD
    FIELD EXPERIENCE PROGRAMMES 671
    FIELD RESEARCH 282
    FIELD STUDIES 282
FIELDS
    UNITS OF STUDY (SUBJECT FIELDS) 331
FIGURATIVE
    FIGURATIVE LANGUAGE 620
FIJI
    FIJI ISLANDS 806
FILING
    FILING 202
FILM
    FILM PROJECTORS 731
FILMS
    FILMS 730
    INSTRUCTIONAL FILMS 730
    SINGLE CONCEPT FILMS 730
    SOUND FILMS 730
FILMSTRIPS
    FILMSTRIPS 730
FINANCE
    BUILDING FINANCE 251
    EDUCATIONAL FINANCE 243
    PUBLIC FINANCE 240
FINANCIAL
    FINANCIAL NEEDS 152
    FINANCIAL POLICY 152
    FINANCIAL RESOURCES 240
    FINANCIAL SERVICES 150
    FINANCIAL SUPPORT 240

FINANCIAL
    PRIVATE FINANCIAL SUPPORT 240
FINANCING
    DEFICIT FINANCING 243
FINDINGS
    RESEARCH FINDINGS 283
FINE
    FINE ARTS 610
FINES
    FINES (PENALTIES) 233
FINISHES
    FINISHES 253
FINLAND
    FINLAND 805
FIREFIGHTERS
    FIREFIGHTERS 460
FIRST
    FIRST AID 683
    TWENTY FIRST CENTURY 840
FISCAL
    FISCAL MANAGEMENT 152
FISE
    FISE 853
FISHERIES
    FISHERIES 750
FIXED
    CAPITAL OUTLAY (FOR FIXED ASSETS) 241
FLEXIBLE
    FLEXIBLE TIMETABLING 340
FOLLOWUP
    FOLLOWUP STUDIES 282
FOOD
    FOOD 160
    FOOD INDUSTRY 150
    FOOD INDUSTRY WORKERS 451
    FOOD SERVICES 160
FORCE
    LABOUR FORCE 153
    LABOUR FORCE NONPARTICIPANTS 450
FORCES
    ARMED FORCES EDUCATION 186
FOREIGN
    FOREIGN POLICY 102
    FOREIGN STUDENT ADVISERS 431
    FOREIGN STUDENTS 413

FOREIGN
    FOREIGN WORKER EDUCATION 186
    FOREIGN WORKERS 470
FOREMEN
    FOREMEN 451
FORESTRY
    FORESTRY 646
    FORESTRY WORKERS 451
FORM
    FORM CLASSES (LANGUAGES) 622
FORMATION
    CONCEPT FORMATION 513
    HABIT FORMATION 542
FORMATIVE
    FORMATIVE EVALUATION 205
FORMER
    FORMER TEACHERS 424
FORMS
    RECORDS (FORMS) 723
FOSTER
    FOSTER FAMILY 126
    FOSTER HOMES 126
FOUNDATION
    FOUNDATION PROGRAMMES 109
FRAMEWORK
    INSTITUTIONAL FRAMEWORK 260
FRANCE
    FRANCE 805
FREE
    FREE EDUCATION 180
FREEDOM
    ACADEMIC FREEDOM 180
    FREEDOM OF ASSOCIATION 100
    FREEDOM OF SPEECH 100
FRENCH
    FRENCH 626
    FRENCH GUIANA 803
    FRENCH POLYNESIA 806
    FRENCH SPEAKING AFRICA 801
FREQUENCY
    WORD FREQUENCY 620
FULL
    FULL TIME EDUCATION 184
    FULL TIME EDUCATORS 424
    FULL TIME EMPLOYMENT 222
    FULL TIME STUDENTS 410

FULL
    FULL TIME TRAINING 351
FUNCTIONAL
    FUNCTIONAL LITERACY 180
    FUNCTIONAL LITERACY PROGRAMMES 321
    FUNCTIONAL LITERACY PROJECTS 321
    FUNCTIONAL READING 521
FUNCTIONS
    COUNSELLOR FUNCTIONS 370
    GUIDANCE FUNCTIONS 211
FUNDAMENTAL
    FUNDAMENTAL CONCEPTS 522
    FUNDAMENTAL RESEARCH 282
FUNDS
    FUNDS IN TRUST 240
    SCHOOL FUNDS 240
FURNITURE
    FURNITURE 741
    FURNITURE DESIGN 252
    FURNITURE INDUSTRY 150
FURTHER
    FURTHER TRAINING 351
FUTUNA
    WALLIS AND FUTUNA ISLANDS 806
FUTURE
    FUTURE 840
FUTUROLOGY
    EDUCATIONAL FUTUROLOGY 100
GABON
    GABON 802
GALAPAGOS
    GALAPAGOS ISLANDS 803
GAMBIA
    GAMBIA 802
GAMES
    CHILDRENS GAMES 537
    EDUCATIONAL GAMES 356
    MANAGEMENT GAMES 355
GATHERING
    INFORMATION GATHERING 204
GENERAL
    GENERAL ASSEMBLY 850
    GENERAL EDUCATION 183
    GENERAL SCIENCE 670

GENERAL
    GENERAL SECONDARY SCHOOLS 306
    UNESCO GENERAL CONFERENCE 851
GENERALIZATION
    GENERALIZATION 522
GENERATIVE
    GENERATIVE GRAMMAR 622
GENETICS
    GENETICS 632
GENRES
    LITERARY GENRES 616
GEOGRAPHIC
    GEOGRAPHIC CONCEPTS 640
    GEOGRAPHIC DISTRIBUTION 124
    GEOGRAPHIC REGIONS 102
GEOGRAPHY
    GEOGRAPHY 640
    GEOGRAPHY INSTRUCTION 680
    GEOGRAPHY TEACHERS 425
GEOLOGY
    GEOLOGY 633
GEOMETRIC
    GEOMETRIC CONCEPTS 631
GEOMETRY
    GEOMETRY 631
GEORGIAN
    GEORGIAN SSR 805
GERIATRICS
    GERIATRICS 651
GERMAN
    GERMAN 626
    GERMAN DR 805
GERMANIC
    GERMANIC LANGUAGES 625
GERMANY
    GERMANY FR 805
GHANA
    GHANA 802
GIBRALTAR
    GIBRALTAR 805
GIFTED
    GIFTED STUDENTS 416
    GIFTED TEACHERS 424
GIRLS
    GIRLS ENROLMENT 186
GLOBAL
    GLOBAL METHOD 661

GLOSSARY
   GLOSSARY 880
GOAL
   GOAL ORIENTATION 541
GOALS
   EDUCATIONAL GOALS 180
GOVERNANCE
   SCHOOL GOVERNANCE 230
GOVERNING
   GOVERNING BOARDS 261
GOVERNMENT
   CENTRAL GOVERNMENT 103
   CENTRAL GOVERNMENT AID 106
   CENTRAL GOVERNMENT LAWS 170
   CITY GOVERNMENT 104
   GOVERNMENT 102
   GOVERNMENT PROGRAMMES 109
   GOVERNMENT PUBLICATIONS 720
   GOVERNMENT ROLE 105
   GOVERNMENT SUPERVISION 105
   LOCAL GOVERNMENT 104
   LOCAL GOVERNMENT AID 106
   PROVINCIAL GOVERNMENT 104
   PROVINCIAL GOVERNMENT AID 106
GOVERNMENTAL
   GOVERNMENTAL STRUCTURE 103
GRADE
   GRADE ORGANIZATION 342
   GRADE REPETITION 267
GRADES
   GRADES (PROGRAMME DIVISIONS) 342
   INTERMEDIATE GRADES 342
   PRIMARY GRADES 342
   SECONDARY GRADES 342
GRADING
   GRADING 391
GRADUATE
   GRADUATE STUDY 330
GRADUATES
   COLLEGE GRADUATES 413
   GRADUATES 410

GRADUATES
   SECONDARY SCHOOL GRADUATES 411
GRADUATION
   GRADUATION 390
GRAMMAR
   GENERATIVE GRAMMAR 622
   GRAMMAR 622
   STRUCTURAL GRAMMAR 622
   TRADITIONAL GRAMMAR 622
GRANT
   CONDITIONS OF GRANT 232
GRANTS
   GRANTS 241
GRAPHIC
   GRAPHIC ARTS 610
GRATIFICATION
   NEED GRATIFICATION 536
GREECE
   GREECE 805
GREENLAND
   GREENLAND 805
GRENADA
   GRENADA 803
GROUP
   GROUP ACTIVITIES 357
   GROUP BEHAVIOUR 560
   GROUP COUNSELLING 371
   GROUP DISCUSSION 356
   GROUP DYNAMICS 355
   GROUP INSTRUCTION 352
   GROUP LEADERSHIP 554
   GROUP MEMBERSHIP 554
   GROUP NORMS 284
   GROUP STRUCTURE 122
   GROUP TRAINING CENTRES 311
   GROUP UNITY 122
   LARGE GROUP INSTRUCTION 352
   MINORITY GROUP CHILDREN 402
   MINORITY GROUP TEACHERS 424
GROUPING
   ABILITY GROUPING 341
   GROUPING (INSTRUCTIONAL PURPOSES) 341
   GROUPING PROCEDURES 341
   HETEROGENEOUS GROUPING 341

GROUPING
    HOMOGENEOUS GROUPING 341
GROUPS
    AGE GROUPS 443
    CONTROL GROUPS 283
    DISADVANTAGED GROUPS 443
    DISCUSSION GROUPS 343
    ETHNIC GROUPS 443
    EXPERIMENTAL GROUPS 283
    GROUPS 443
    LISTENING GROUPS 343
    LOW INCOME GROUPS 443
    MINORITY GROUPS 443
    PEER GROUPS 443
    RELIGIOUS CULTURAL GROUPS 443
    SELF DIRECTED GROUPS 443
    TARGET GROUPS 443
    USER GROUPS 443
GROWTH
    GROWTH PATTERNS 502
    PERSONAL GROWTH 531
GUADELOUPE
    GUADELOUPE 803
GUAM
    GUAM 806
GUATEMALA
    GUATEMALA 803
GUIANA
    FRENCH GUIANA 803
GUIDANCE
    EDUCATIONAL GUIDANCE 211
    GUIDANCE 211
    GUIDANCE AIMS 211
    GUIDANCE FUNCTIONS 211
    GUIDANCE PERSONNEL 431
    GUIDANCE PROGRAMMES 271
    GUIDANCE SERVICES 270
    GUIDANCE THEORIES 211
    VOCATIONAL GUIDANCE 211
GUIDE
    STUDY GUIDE 880
    TEACHING GUIDE 880
GUIDELINES
    FACILITY GUIDELINES 232
GUIDES
    CURRICULUM GUIDES 724
    GUIDES 724

GUINEA
    EQUATORIAL GUINEA 802
    GUINEA 802
    GUINEA–BISSAU 802
    PAPUA NEW GUINEA 804
GULF
    GULF STATES 807
GUYANA
    GUYANA 803
HABIT
    HABIT FORMATION 542
HABITS
    LISTENING HABITS 542
    READING HABITS 542
    SPEECH HABITS 542
    STUDY HABITS 542
HAITI
    HAITI 803
HALLS
    LECTURE HALLS 711
HAND
    HAND TOOLS 742
HANDICAP
    HANDICAP DETECTION 372
HANDICAPPED
    HANDICAPPED 403
    HANDICAPPED EDUCATION 322
    HANDICAPPED STUDENTS 411
    MENTALLY HANDICAPPED 403
    PHYSICALLY HANDICAPPED 403
HANDICAPS
    HANDICAPS 571
    LANGUAGE HANDICAPS 571
    MENTAL HANDICAPS 571
    MULTIPLE HANDICAPS 571
    NEUROLOGICAL HANDICAPS 571
    PHYSICAL HANDICAPS 571
    SPEECH HANDICAPS 571
    VISUAL HANDICAPS 571
HANDICRAFTS
    HANDICRAFTS 610
HANDWRITING
    HANDWRITING 620
    HANDWRITING DEVELOPMENT 534
    HANDWRITING INSTRUCTION 663

HARD
    HARD OF HEARING 403
HAWAII
    HAWAII 806
HEADS
    HEADS OF DEPARTMENT (SCHOOL) 423
    HEADS OF HOUSEHOLDS 401
HEALTH
    DENTAL HEALTH 502
    HEALTH 160
    HEALTH ACTIVITIES 357
    HEALTH EDUCATION 683
    HEALTH NEEDS 160
    HEALTH PERSONNEL 433
    HEALTH PROGRAMMES 160
    HEALTH SERVICES 107
    MENTAL HEALTH 502
    MENTAL HEALTH PROGRAMMES 320
    PHYSICAL HEALTH 502
    PUBLIC HEALTH 160
    PUBLIC HEALTH LAWS 170
    SCHOOL HEALTH SERVICES 270
HEARING
    HARD OF HEARING 403
    HEARING AIDS 734
    HEARING THERAPISTS 432
    HEARING THERAPY 373
HEIGHT
    BODY HEIGHT 502
HELENA
    SAINT HELENA 808
HEMISPHERE
    EASTERN HEMISPHERE 801
    NORTHERN HEMISPHERE 801
    SOUTHERN HEMISPHERE 801
    WESTERN HEMISPHERE 801
HEREDITY
    HEREDITY 502
HETEROGENEOUS
    HETEROGENEOUS GROUPING 341
HIGH
    HIGH ACHIEVERS 415
HIGHER
    HIGHER EDUCATION 185
HIMALAYAN
    HIMALAYAN STATES 804
HISTORY
    EDUCATIONAL HISTORY 641

HISTORY
    HISTORY 641
    HISTORY INSTRUCTION 680
    HISTORY TEACHERS 425
    LITERARY HISTORY 615
    MODERN HISTORY 641
    NATIONAL HISTORY 641
    WORLD HISTORY 641
HOLDING
    SCHOOL HOLDING POWER 208
HOLY
    HOLY SEE 805
HOME
    HOME ECONOMICS 640
    HOME ECONOMICS EDUCATION 683
    HOME ECONOMICS TEACHERS 425
    HOME ENVIRONMENT 550
    HOME INSTRUCTION 352
    HOME STUDY 335
HOMEBOUND
    HOMEBOUND PERSONS 403
HOMES
    FOSTER HOMES 126
HOMEWORK
    HOMEWORK 356
HOMOGENEOUS
    HOMOGENEOUS GROUPING 341
HONDURAS
    HONDURAS 803
HORIZONTAL
    HORIZONTAL INTEGRATION (LEARNING) 514
HORTICULTURE
    HORTICULTURE 646
HOSPITAL
    HOSPITAL SCHOOLS 304
HOSPITALIZED
    HOSPITALIZED PERSONS 403
HOSPITALS
    HOSPITALS 313
HOTEL
    HOTEL WORKERS 451
HOURS
    WORKING HOURS 153
HOUSEHOLDS
    HEADS OF HOUSEHOLDS 401
HOUSEWIVES
    HOUSEWIVES 451

HOUSING
  HOUSING 126
  STAFF HOUSING 712
  STUDENT HOUSING 712
HOWE
  LORD HOWE ISLAND 806
HUMAN
  HUMAN BODY 502
  HUMAN DIGNITY 100
  HUMAN ENGINEERING 140
  HUMAN RELATIONS 122
  HUMAN RESOURCES 153
  HUMAN RESOURCES
    DEVELOPMENT 151
  HUMAN RIGHTS 100
HUMANISM
  HUMANISM 600
HUMANITIES
  HUMANITIES 600
HUNGARY
  HUNGARY 805
HUNGER
  HUNGER 503
HYDRAULICS
  HYDRAULICS 647
HYGIENE
  HYGIENE 502
IAMCR
  IAMCR 853
IAU
  IAU 853
IBE
  IBE 851
IBRD
  IBRD 850
ICE
  ICE 851
ICELAND
  ICELAND 805
ICET
  ICET 853
ICSSD
  ICSSD 853
ICSUAB
  ICSUAB 853
ICVA
  ICVA 853
IDA
  IDA 850
IDB
  IDB 852

IDENTIFICATION
  IDENTIFICATION 372
  IDENTIFICATION
    (PSYCHOLOGICAL) 555
  TALENT IDENTIFICATION 211
IFFTU
  IFFTU 853
IFLA
  IFLA 853
IIALM
  IIALM 851
IIEP
  IIEP 851
ILCE
  ILCE 852
ILLITERACY
  ILLITERACY 180
ILLITERATE
  ILLITERATE ADULTS 402
ILLNESS
  MENTAL ILLNESS 570
ILLUSTRATIONS
  ILLUSTRATIONS 733
ILO
  ILO 850
IMAGES
  EIDETIC IMAGES 511
IMAGINATION
  IMAGINATION 522
IMMATURITY
  IMMATURITY 531
IMMIGRANTS
  IMMIGRANTS 470
IMMIGRATION
  IMMIGRATION 124
  URBAN IMMIGRATION 124
IMMUNIZATION
  IMMUNIZATION
    PROGRAMMES 161
IMPROVEMENT
  BUILDING IMPROVEMENT 253
  EDUCATIONAL
    IMPROVEMENT 182
  INSTRUCTIONAL
    IMPROVEMENT 352
  TEACHER IMPROVEMENT 212
INCENTIVE
  INCENTIVE SYSTEMS 233
INCENTIVES
  PARTICIPATION INCENTIVES
    285

INCENTIVES
   PERFORMANCE INCENTIVES 266
INCOME
   INCOME 153
   LOW INCOME GROUPS 443
INDEPENDANT
   INDEPENDANT LEARNERS 412
INDEPENDENT
   INDEPENDENT READING 661
   INDEPENDENT STUDY 335
INDEXES
   INDEXES (LOCATERS) 721
INDEXING
   INDEXING 202
INDIA
   INDIA 804
INDIAN
   AMERICAN INDIAN LANGUAGES 625
   INDIAN OCEAN TERRITORIES 801
INDIVIDUAL
   INDIVIDUAL CHARACTERISTICS 561
   INDIVIDUAL COUNSELLING 371
   INDIVIDUAL DEVELOPMENT 530
   INDIVIDUAL DEVELOPMENT EDUCATION 183
   INDIVIDUAL DEVELOPMENT PROGRAMMES 321
   INDIVIDUAL DIFFERENCES 530
   INDIVIDUAL LEARNING AREAS 711
   INDIVIDUAL NEEDS 536
   INDIVIDUAL PSYCHOLOGY 642
   INDIVIDUAL STUDY 335
INDIVIDUALIZED
   INDIVIDUALIZED CURRICULUM 332
   INDIVIDUALIZED INSTRUCTION 352
INDO
   INDO EUROPEAN LANGUAGES 625
INDONESIA
   INDONESIA 804

INDUCTION
   INDUCTION TRAINING 351
INDUCTIVE
   INDUCTIVE METHODS 355
INDUSTRIAL
   INDUSTRIAL ARTS 647
   INDUSTRIAL EDUCATION 672
   INDUSTRIAL OCCUPATIONS 155
   INDUSTRIAL PERSONNEL 441
   INDUSTRIAL TECHNOLOGY 645
   POST INDUSTRIAL SOCIETY 150
   PRE INDUSTRIAL SOCIETY 150
INDUSTRIALIZATION
   INDUSTRIALIZATION 150
INDUSTRIALIZED
   INDUSTRIALIZED BUILDINGS 253
INDUSTRIES
   SERVICE INDUSTRIES 150
INDUSTRY
   ADULT EDUCATION-INDUSTRY COOPERATION 263
   AEROSPACE INDUSTRY 150
   CHEMICAL INDUSTRY 150
   CLOTHING INDUSTRY 150
   CONSTRUCTION INDUSTRY 150
   ELECTRICAL INDUSTRY 150
   ELECTRONICS INDUSTRY 150
   FOOD INDUSTRY 150
   FOOD INDUSTRY WORKERS 451
   FURNITURE INDUSTRY 150
   INDUSTRY 150
   MANUFACTURED INDUSTRY 150
   METAL INDUSTRY 150
   MINING INDUSTRY 150
   MOTOR VEHICLE INDUSTRY 150
   PETROLEUM INDUSTRY 150
   PRINTING INDUSTRY 150
   PUBLISHING INDUSTRY 150
   SCHOOL INDUSTRY RELATIONSHIP 263
   SMALL SCALE INDUSTRY 150
   TEXTILE INDUSTRY 150

INFANCY
   INFANCY 500
INFANT
   INFANT BEHAVIOUR 560
INFANTS
   INFANTS 400
INFLUENCE
   COMMUNITY INFLUENCE 122
   FAMILY INFLUENCE 550
   TEACHER INFLUENCE 350
INFLUENCES
   ENROLMENT INFLUENCES 285
   ENVIRONMENTAL INFLUENCES 550
   LITERARY INFLUENCES 615
   PRENATAL INFLUENCES 550
INFORMAL
   INFORMAL EDUCATION 184
INFORMATION
   EDUCATIONAL INFORMATION 200
   INFORMATION CENTRES 310
   INFORMATION DISSEMINATION 204
   INFORMATION EXCHANGE 204
   INFORMATION GATHERING 204
   INFORMATION NETWORKS 202
   INFORMATION PROCESSING 202
   INFORMATION SCIENCE 630
   INFORMATION SEEKING 541
   INFORMATION SERVICES 107
   INFORMATION SPECIALISTS 462
   INFORMATION SYSTEMS 201
   INFORMATION THEORY 204
   INFORMATION UTILIZATION 204
   OCCUPATIONAL INFORMATION 371
INFRASTRUCTURE
   EDUCATIONAL INFRASTRUCTURE 181
INITIAL
   INITIAL EMPLOYMENT 154
   INITIAL TEACHING ALPHABET 661

INJURY
   MINIMAL BRAIN INJURY 570
INNOVATION
   INNOVATION 200
   INSTRUCTIONAL INNOVATION 352
INNOVATIONS
   ADOPTION OF INNOVATIONS 200
   EDUCATIONAL INNOVATIONS 200
   REPLICATION OF INNOVATIONS 204
INPLANT
   INPLANT PROGRAMMES 673
INSECURITY
   INSECURITY 540
INSERVICE
   INSERVICE COURSES 334
   INSERVICE EDUCATION 321
   INSERVICE TEACHER EDUCATION 690
INSPECTORS
   INSPECTORS 420
   PRIMARY SCHOOL INSPECTORS 420
   SECONDARY SCHOOL INSPECTORS 420
INSTITUTE
   INSTITUTE TYPE COURSES 334
INSTITUTION
   ADULT STUDENT-INSTITUTION RELATIONSHIP 380
   RELIGIOUS INSTITUTION ROLE 125
INSTITUTIONAL
   INSTITUTIONAL FRAMEWORK 260
   INSTITUTIONAL SELF MANAGEMENT 261
INSTITUTIONS
   ACCREDITATION (INSTITUTIONS) 210
   CORRECTIONAL INSTITUTIONS 170
   DISTANCE TEACHING INSTITUTIONS 311
   EDUCATIONAL INSTITUTIONS 125
   INSTITUTIONS 125

INSTITUTIONS
    RELIGIOUS INSTITUTIONS 125
INSTRUCTION
    AUDIOVISUAL INSTRUCTION 360
    COLLEGE INSTRUCTION 352
    COMPUTER ASSISTED INSTRUCTION 361
    CONVENTIONAL INSTRUCTION 352
    ETHICAL INSTRUCTION 682
    GEOGRAPHY INSTRUCTION 680
    GROUP INSTRUCTION 352
    HANDWRITING INSTRUCTION 663
    HISTORY INSTRUCTION 680
    HOME INSTRUCTION 352
    INDIVIDUALIZED INSTRUCTION 352
    INSTRUCTION 352
    LANGUAGE INSTRUCTION 662
    LARGE GROUP INSTRUCTION 352
    MATHEMATICS INSTRUCTION 670
    MODERN LANGUAGE INSTRUCTION 662
    MOTHER TONGUE INSTRUCTION 662
    MULTIMEDIA INSTRUCTION 360
    PROGRAMMED INSTRUCTION 361
    READING INSTRUCTION 660
    REMEDIAL INSTRUCTION 352
    RESEARCH AND INSTRUCTION UNITS 340
    SCIENCE INSTRUCTION 670
    SECOND LANGUAGE INSTRUCTION 662
    SELF INSTRUCTION 352
    SPEECH INSTRUCTION 662
    SPELLING INSTRUCTION 663
    TELEPHONE INSTRUCTION 360
INSTRUCTIONAL
    GROUPING (INSTRUCTIONAL PURPOSES) 341
    INSTRUCTIONAL FILMS 730
    INSTRUCTIONAL IMPROVEMENT 352
    INSTRUCTIONAL INNOVATION 352
    INSTRUCTIONAL LEVEL 352
    INSTRUCTIONAL MATERIALS 725
    INSTRUCTIONAL PROGRAMMES 320
    INSTRUCTIONAL PROGRAMMING 361
    INSTRUCTIONAL TELEVISION 360
    INSTRUCTIONAL TRIPS 381
    SELF INSTRUCTIONAL AIDS 730
    SELF INSTRUCTIONAL METHODS 355
    SELF INSTRUCTIONAL PROGRAMMES 320
INSTRUMENTS
    MEASUREMENT INSTRUMENTS 742
    MUSICAL INSTRUMENTS 741
INSURANCE
    INSURANCE PROGRAMMES 241
INTEGRATED
    INTEGRATED ACTIVITIES 357
    INTEGRATED CURRICULUM 332
    INTEGRATED RURAL DEVELOPMENT 151
INTEGRATION
    HORIZONTAL INTEGRATION (LEARNING) 514
    LEARNING INTEGRATION 514
    NATIONAL INTEGRATION 101
    RACIAL INTEGRATION 123
    SCHOOL INTEGRATION 230
    SOCIAL INTEGRATION 121
    VERTICAL INTEGRATION (LEARNING) 514
INTELLECTUAL
    INTELLECTUAL DETERIORATION 520
    INTELLECTUAL DEVELOPMENT 530
INTELLIGENCE
    INTELLIGENCE 520
    INTELLIGENCE FACTORS 285
    INTELLIGENCE QUOTIENT 520
    INTELLIGENCE TESTS 394

INTENSIVE
    INTENSIVE LANGUAGE
        COURSES 663
INTERACTION
    INTERACTION 285
    INTERACTION PROCESS 352
INTERAGENCY
    NATIONAL INTERAGENCY
        COORDINATION 105
INTERCULTURAL
    INTERCULTURAL
        PROGRAMMES 680
INTERDISCIPLINARITY
    INTERDISCIPLINARITY 331
INTERDISCIPLINARY
    INTERDISCIPLINARY
        APPROACH 331
INTEREST
    CENTRES OF INTEREST 331
    EDUCATIONAL INTEREST 541
    INTEREST 241
    INTEREST TESTS 393
INTERESTS
    INTERESTS 541
    VOCATIONAL INTERESTS 541
INTERGENERATIONAL
    INTERGENERATIONAL
        EQUALITY 181
INTERGROUP
    INTERGROUP RELATIONS 122
INTERINSTITUTIONAL
    INTERINSTITUTIONAL
        COOPERATION 262
INTERMEDIATE
    INTERMEDIATE
        ADMINISTRATIVE UNITS 261
    INTERMEDIATE GRADES 342
    INTERMEDIATE
        TECHNOLOGIES 360
INTERNAL
    INTERNAL ASSESSMENT 391
INTERNATIONAL
    INTERNATIONAL AGENCIES
        103
    INTERNATIONAL
        CONVENTIONS 170
    INTERNATIONAL
        COOPERATION 105
    INTERNATIONAL EDUCATION
        640
    INTERNATIONAL EDUCATION
        CONSULTANTS 430

INTERNATIONAL
    INTERNATIONAL EXPERTS
        430
    INTERNATIONAL
        ORGANIZATIONS 110
    INTERNATIONAL
        PROGRAMMES 109
    INTERNATIONAL
        RECOMMENDATIONS 170
    INTERNATIONAL RELATIONS
        640
    INTERNATIONAL SCHOOLS
        302
    INTERNATIONAL SURVEYS
        203
    INTERNATIONAL
        UNDERSTANDING 101
INTERNS
    TEACHER INTERNS 424
INTERNSHIP
    INTERNSHIP PROGRAMMES
        222
INTERORGANIZATIONAL
    INTERORGANIZATIONAL
        COOPERATION 262
INTERPERSONAL
    INTERPERSONAL PROBLEMS
        554
    INTERPERSONAL
        RELATIONSHIP 553
INTERPRETERS
    INTERPRETERS 462
INTERRELATIONSHIPS
    CULTURAL
        INTERRELATIONSHIPS 130
INTERVENTION
    INTERVENTION 355
INTERVIEWS
    INTERVIEWS 221
INTONATION
    INTONATION 622
INVESTMENT
    INVESTMENT 152
INVOLVEMENT
    PARTICIPANT INVOLVEMENT
        554
IPPF
    IPPF 853
IRAN
    IRAN (ISLAMIC REPUBLIC)
        804

IRAQ
    IRAQ 807
IRELAND
    IRELAND 805
ISLAMIC
    IRAN (ISLAMIC REPUBLIC) 804
    ISLAMIC EDUCATION 188
ISLAND
    ASCENSION ISLAND 808
    BOUVET ISLAND 808
    CHRISTMAS ISLAND 809
    EASTER ISLAND 806
    JOHNSTON ISLAND 806
    LORD HOWE ISLAND 806
    NAURU ISLAND 806
    NIUE ISLAND 806
    NORFOLK ISLAND 806
    REUNION ISLAND 809
ISLANDS
    BANKS ISLANDS 806
    CANARY ISLANDS 808
    CANTON AND ENDERBY ISLANDS 806
    CAROLINE ISLANDS 806
    CAYMAN ISLANDS 803
    CHANNEL ISLANDS 805
    COOK ISLANDS 806
    FAEROE ISLANDS 805
    FALKLAND ISLANDS 808
    FIJI ISLANDS 806
    GALAPAGOS ISLANDS 803
    KERMADEC ISLANDS 806
    LINE ISLANDS 806
    MANIHIKI ISLANDS 806
    MARIANA ISLANDS 806
    MARSHALL ISLANDS 806
    MIDWAY ISLANDS 806
    PITCAIRN ISLANDS 806
    RYUKU ISLANDS 804
    SAINT PIERRE AND MIQUELON ISLANDS 803
    SANTA CRUZ ISLANDS 806
    SOCIETY ISLANDS 806
    SOLOMON ISLANDS 806
    TOKELAU ISLANDS 806
    TUAMOTU ISLANDS 806
    TUBUAI ISLANDS 806
    TURKS AND CAICOS ISLANDS 803
    VIRGIN ISLANDS (UK) 803
    VIRGIN ISLANDS (USA) 803

ISLANDS
    WAKE ISLANDS 806
    WALLIS AND FUTUNA ISLANDS 806
ISO
    ISO 853
ISOLATION
    CULTURAL ISOLATION 130
ISRAEL
    ISRAEL 804
ISSUES
    BOND ISSUES 240
    MORAL ISSUES 100
    POLITICAL ISSUES 100
ITALY
    ITALY 805
ITINERANT
    ITINERANT TEACHERS 424
ITU
    ITU 850
IVORY
    IVORY COAST 802
JAMAHIRIYA
    LIBYAN ARAB JAMAHIRIYA 807
JAMAICA
    JAMAICA 803
JAPAN
    JAPAN 804
JEWS
    JEWS 475
JOB
    JOB ANALYSIS 221
    JOB APPLICANTS 451
    JOB APPLICATION 221
    JOB SATISFACTION 563
    JOB TENURE 153
    OFF THE JOB TRAINING 351
    ON THE JOB TRAINING 351
JOBS
    EQUAL OPPORTUNITIES (JOBS) 153
JOHNSTON
    JOHNSTON ISLAND 806
JORDAN
    JORDAN 807
JOURNALISM
    JOURNALISM 650
JUNIOR
    JUNIOR COLLEGES 307
KAMPUCHEA

KAMPUCHEA
  DEMOCRATIC KAMPUCHEA 804
KAZAKH
  KAZAKH SSR 805
KENYA
  KENYA 802
KERMADEC
  KERMADEC ISLANDS 806
KINDERGARTEN
  KINDERGARTEN 342
  KINDERGARTEN CHILDREN 411
KIRIBATI
  KIRIBATI 806
KITTS
  SAINT KITTS-NEVIS-ANGUILLA 803
KNOWLEDGE
  KNOWLEDGE LEVEL 535
  KNOWLEDGE OBSOLESCENCE 181
  KNOWLEDGE TRANSMISSION 512
  PRIOR KNOWLEDGE LEVEL 391
KONG
  HONG KONG 804
KOREA
  KOREA DPR 804
  KOREA R 804
KUWAIT
  KUWAIT 807
LABORATORIES
  LABORATORIES 711
  LANGUAGE LABORATORIES 731
LABORATORY
  LABORATORY EQUIPMENT 740
  LABORATORY EXPERIMENTS 671
  LABORATORY PROCEDURES 671
  LABORATORY SCHOOLS 305
  LABORATORY TECHNIQUES 671
  LABORATORY TRAINING 352
LABOUR
  CHILD LABOUR 153
  LABOUR 153
  LABOUR DEMANDS 153

LABOUR
  LABOUR FORCE 153
  LABOUR FORCE NONPARTICIPANTS 450
  LABOUR LAWS 170
  LABOUR MARKET 154
  LABOUR RELATIONS 153
LAITY
  LAITY 475
LANGUAGE
  CHILD LANGUAGE 532
  CONVERSATIONAL LANGUAGE COURSES 663
  FIGURATIVE LANGUAGE 620
  INTENSIVE LANGUAGE COURSES 663
  LANGUAGE 131
  LANGUAGE ABILITY 520
  LANGUAGE ARTS 620
  LANGUAGE DEVELOPMENT 530
  LANGUAGE ENRICHMENT 662
  LANGUAGE HANDICAPS 571
  LANGUAGE INSTRUCTION 662
  LANGUAGE LABORATORIES 731
  LANGUAGE PATTERNS 621
  LANGUAGE POLICY 131
  LANGUAGE PROFICIENCY 535
  LANGUAGE PROGRAMMES 662
  LANGUAGE RESEARCH 280
  LANGUAGE ROLE 285
  LANGUAGE SKILLS 533
  LANGUAGE TEACHERS 425
  LANGUAGE TESTS 393
  LANGUAGE TYPOLOGY 621
  LANGUAGE USAGE 131
  MODERN LANGUAGE INSTRUCTION 662
  MODERN LANGUAGE PRIMARY PROGRAMMES 662
  NATIONAL LANGUAGE 626
  PATTERN DRILLS (LANGUAGE) 663
  SECOND LANGUAGE INSTRUCTION 662
  TRANSFORMATION THEORY (LANGUAGE) 622
LANGUAGES
  AFRICAN LANGUAGES 625

LANGUAGES
  AFRO ASIATIC LANGUAGES 625
  AMERICAN INDIAN LANGUAGES 625
  CAUCASIAN LANGUAGES 625
  CLASSICAL LANGUAGES 627
  COMPUTER LANGUAGES 760
  DRAVIDIAN LANGUAGES 625
  FORM CLASSES (LANGUAGES) 622
  GERMANIC LANGUAGES 625
  INDO EUROPEAN LANGUAGES 625
  LANGUAGES 625
  MALAYO POLYNESIAN LANGUAGES 625
  MODERN LANGUAGES 627
  MORPHOLOGY (LANGUAGES) 622
  OFFICIAL LANGUAGES 131
  PROGRAMMING LANGUAGES 621
  ROMANCE LANGUAGES 625
  SECOND LANGUAGES 131
  SINO TIBETAN LANGUAGES 625
  SLAVIC LANGUAGES 625
  UNWRITTEN LANGUAGES 621
  URALIC ALTAIC LANGUAGES 625
LANKA
  SRI LANKA 804
LAO
  LAO PDR 804
LAPLAND
  LAPLAND 805
LARGE
  LARGE GROUP INSTRUCTION 352
  LARGE TYPE MATERIALS 734
LATERAL
  LATERAL DOMINANCE 503
LATIN
  LATIN AMERICA 801
LATVIAN
  LATVIAN SSR 805
LAW
  LAW ENFORCEMENT 170
LAWS
  CENTRAL GOVERNMENT LAWS 170

LAWS
  LABOUR LAWS 170
  LAWS 170
  PROVINCIAL LAWS 170
  PUBLIC HEALTH LAWS 170
  SCHOOL ATTENDANCE LAWS 230
LAWYERS
  LAWYERS 460
LEADER
  TEAM LEADER (TEACHING) 426
LEADERS
  ADULT LEADERS 440
  COMMUNITY LEADERS 440
  YOUTH LEADERS 440
LEADERSHIP
  GROUP LEADERSHIP 554
  LEADERSHIP 554
  LEADERSHIP TRAINING 681
LEAGUE
  LEAGUE OF ARAB STATES 852
LEARNERS
  INDEPENDANT LEARNERS 412
  SLOW LEARNERS 415
LEARNING
  ACTIVITY LEARNING 512
  ADULT LEARNING 514
  ASSOCIATIVE LEARNING 512
  DISCOVERY LEARNING 512
  HORIZONTAL INTEGRATION (LEARNING) 514
  INDIVIDUAL LEARNING AREAS 711
  LEARNING 512
  LEARNING ACTIVITIES 537
  LEARNING DIFFICULTIES 513
  LEARNING DISABILITIES 513
  LEARNING INTEGRATION 514
  LEARNING NEEDS 536
  LEARNING PROCESSES 513
  LEARNING READINESS 531
  LEARNING SPECIALISTS 430
  LEARNING SPEED 513
  LEARNING THEORIES 513
  MULTISENSORY LEARNING 512
  OPEN LEARNING SYSTEMS 355
  PRESCHOOL LEARNING 514
  ROTE LEARNING 512
  SEQUENTIAL LEARNING 512

LEARNING
    SYMBOLIC LEARNING 512
    TIME FACTORS (LEARNING) 511
    VERBAL LEARNING 512
    VERTICAL INTEGRATION (LEARNING) 514
    VISUAL LEARNING 512
LEATHERWORKERS
    LEATHERWORKERS 451
LEAVE
    EDUCATIONAL LEAVE 222
    LEAVE OF ABSENCE 222
    PAID EDUCATIONAL LEAVE 222
LEAVERS
    SCHOOL LEAVERS 411
LEAVING
    SCHOOL LEAVING 266
LEBANON
    LEBANON 807
LECTURE
    LECTURE HALLS 711
LECTURERS
    LECTURERS 422
LECTURES
    LECTURES 355
LEGAL
    LEGAL AID 170
    LEGAL EDUCATION 681
    LEGAL RESPONSIBILITY 170
LEGISLATION
    EDUCATIONAL LEGISLATION 230
    RECREATION LEGISLATION 230
LEGISLATORS
    LEGISLATORS 460
LEISURE
    EDUCATIONAL LEISURE 357
    LEISURE 126
LENGTH
    PROGRAMME LENGTH 361
LEONE
    SIERRA LEONE 802
LESOTHO
    LESOTHO 802
LESSON
    LESSON OBSERVATION CRITERIA 691
    LESSON PLANS 356

LETTERS
    LETTERS (CORRESPONDENCE) 721
LEVEL
    COMPLEXITY LEVEL 522
    INSTRUCTIONAL LEVEL 352
    KNOWLEDGE LEVEL 535
    PRIOR KNOWLEDGE LEVEL 391
    READING LEVEL 660
LEVELS
    LEVELS OF EDUCATION 185
LEXICOLOGY
    LEXICOLOGY 650
LIBERIA
    LIBERIA 802
LIBRARIANS
    LIBRARIANS 462
    SCHOOL LIBRARIANS 462
LIBRARIES
    COLLEGE LIBRARIES 310
    LIBRARIES 310
    NATIONAL LIBRARIES 310
    PUBLIC LIBRARIES 310
    SCHOOL LIBRARIES 310
LIBRARY
    LIBRARY COLLECTIONS 722
    LIBRARY EQUIPMENT 740
    LIBRARY EXTENSION 382
    LIBRARY SCIENCE 650
    LIBRARY SCIENCE TRAINING 681
    LIBRARY SERVICES 270
LIBYAN
    LIBYAN ARAB JAMAHIRIYA 807
LIECHTENSTEIN
    LIECHTENSTEIN 805
LIFE
    WORKING LIFE 154
LIFELONG
    LIFELONG EDUCATION 180
LIGHTING
    LIGHTING 252
LINE
    LINE ISLANDS 806
LINEAR
    LINEAR PROGRAMMES 361
LINGUISTIC
    LINGUISTIC THEORY 621
LINGUISTICS

LINGUISTICS
    CONTRASTIVE LINGUISTICS 621
    DESCRIPTIVE LINGUISTICS 621
    LINGUISTICS 621
LIPREADING
    LIPREADING 374
LISTENING
    LISTENING 620
    LISTENING GROUPS 343
    LISTENING HABITS 542
LISTS
    WORD LISTS 721
LITERACY
    FUNCTIONAL LITERACY 180
    FUNCTIONAL LITERACY PROGRAMMES 321
    FUNCTIONAL LITERACY PROJECTS 321
    LITERACY 180
    LITERACY ACHIEVEMENT 535
    LITERACY CAMPAIGNS 271
    LITERACY CENTRES 311
    LITERACY CLASSES 343
    LITERACY METHODS 661
    LITERACY ORGANIZATIONS 110
    LITERACY PRIMERS 725
    LITERACY PROGRAMMES 321
    LITERACY RETENTION 535
    LITERACY STATISTICS 284
    LITERACY TESTS 393
    LITERACY WORKERS 424
LITERARY
    COMPOSITION (LITERARY) 620
    LITERARY ANALYSIS 615
    LITERARY CRITICISM 615
    LITERARY GENRES 616
    LITERARY HISTORY 615
    LITERARY INFLUENCES 615
    SYMBOLS (LITERARY) 615
LITERATES
    NEW LITERATES 412
LITERATURE
    LITERATURE 615
    LITERATURE APPRECIATION 684
    LITERATURE REVIEW 880
    NATIONAL LITERATURE 615
    WORLD LITERATURE 615

LITHUANIAN
    LITHUANIAN SSR 805
LITIGATION
    COURT LITIGATION 170
LIVESTOCK
    LIVESTOCK 750
LIVING
    LIVING STANDARDS 150
    PRODUCTIVE LIVING 100
LOAD
    TEACHING LOAD 265
LOANS
    STUDENT LOANS 242
LOCAL
    LOCAL AUTONOMY 263
    LOCAL EDUCATION AUTHORITIES 263
    LOCAL GOVERNMENT 104
    LOCAL GOVERNMENT AID 106
    LOCAL MATERIALS 253
    LOCAL PROGRAMMING 271
    PROVINCIAL LOCAL RELATIONSHIP 262
LOCATERS
    INDEXES (LOCATERS) 721
LOCATION
    COLLEGE LOCATION 208
LOGIC
    LOGIC 600
LOGICAL
    LOGICAL THINKING 521
LONG
    LONG COURSES 333
LONGITUDINAL
    LONGITUDINAL STUDIES 282
LORD
    LORD HOWE ISLAND 806
LOSS
    LOSS OF EARNINGS PAYMENTS 242
LOW
    LOW ACHIEVERS 415
    LOW INCOME GROUPS 443
LOWER
    LOWER SECONDARY EDUCATION 185
    LOWER SECONDARY SCHOOLS 301
LUCIA
    SAINT LUCIA 803

LUXEMBOURG
  LUXEMBOURG 805
MACAO
  MACAO 804
MACHINE
  MACHINE TOOLS 742
MACHINES
  OFFICE MACHINES 742
  TEACHING MACHINES 731
MADAGASCAR
  MADAGASCAR 802
MADEIRA
  MADEIRA 808
MAINTENANCE
  MAINTENANCE 251
  SCHOOL MAINTENANCE 265
MAJORS
  COLLEGE MAJORS 333
MAKING
  DECISION MAKING 201
  POLICY MAKING 102
MALADJUSTED
  SOCIALLY MALADJUSTED 403
MALADJUSTMENT
  MALADJUSTMENT 551
MALAWI
  MALAWI 802
MALAYA
  MALAYA 804
MALAYO
  MALAYO POLYNESIAN
    LANGUAGES 625
MALAYSIA
  MALAYSIA 804
MALDIVES
  MALDIVES 804
MALE
  MALE 501
MALI
  MALI 802
MALTA
  MALTA 805
MANAGEMENT
  CLASS MANAGEMENT 691
  FACILITIES MANAGEMENT
    251
  FISCAL MANAGEMENT 152
  INSTITUTIONAL SELF
    MANAGEMENT 261
  MANAGEMENT 201
  MANAGEMENT EDUCATION
    672

MANAGEMENT
  MANAGEMENT GAMES 355
  MANAGEMENT SYSTEMS 201
  PERSONNEL MANAGEMENT
    220
MANAGERS
  MANAGERS 450
MANIHIKI
  MANIHIKI ISLANDS 806
MANIPULATIVE
  MANIPULATIVE MATERIALS
    725
MANPOWER
  MANPOWER DEVELOPMENT
    151
  MANPOWER NEEDS 154
  MANPOWER PLANNING 154
  MANPOWER POLICY 154
  SCIENTIFIC MANPOWER 154
MANUAL
  MANUAL 880
  MANUAL COMMUNICATION
    374
  MANUAL WORKERS 451
MANUFACTURED
  MANUFACTURED INDUSTRY
    150
MAPPING
  SCHOOL MAPPING 208
MARIANA
  MARIANA ISLANDS 806
MARINO
  SAN MARINO 805
MARITAL
  MARITAL STATUS 126
MARKET
  LABOUR MARKET 154
MARKETING
  MARKETING 150
MARKING
  MARKING 391
MARRIAGE
  MARRIAGE COUNSELLING 371
MARRIED
  MARRIED STUDENTS 413
  MARRIED WOMEN
    RETURNERS 451
MARSHALL
  MARSHALL ISLANDS 806
MARTIN
  SAINT MARTIN 803

MARTINIQUE
  MARTINIQUE 803
MASS
  MASS EDUCATION 352
  MASS MEDIA 145
MASTER
  MASTER TEACHERS 426
  MASTER THESES 721
MASTERS
  MASTERS DEGREES 390
MATERIALS
  BUILDING MATERIALS 253
  CLASSROOM MATERIALS 741
  INSTRUCTIONAL MATERIALS 725
  LARGE TYPE MATERIALS 734
  LOCAL MATERIALS 253
  MANIPULATIVE MATERIALS 725
  MATERIALS EVALUATION 213
  MATERIALS PREPARATION 213
  MATERIALS SELECTION 265
  PROGRAMMED MATERIALS 725
  PROTOCOL MATERIALS 732
  READING MATERIALS 725
  REFERENCE MATERIALS 720
  RESOURCE MATERIALS 700
  STUDENT DEVELOPED MATERIALS 725
  SUPPLEMENTARY READING MATERIALS 725
  TEACHER DEVELOPED MATERIALS 725
  TELEGRAPHIC MATERIALS 725
MATHEMATICAL
  MATHEMATICAL CONCEPTS 631
MATHEMATICS
  APPLIED MATHEMATICS 631
  MATHEMATICS 631
  MATHEMATICS INSTRUCTION 670
  MATHEMATICS TEACHERS 425
  MODERN MATHEMATICS 631
  PRIMARY SCHOOL MATHEMATICS 670
  SECONDARY SCHOOL MATHEMATICS 670

MATURATION
  MATURATION 531
MATURITY
  SOCIAL MATURITY 531
  VOCATIONAL MATURITY 531
MAURITANIA
  MAURITANIA 802
MAURITIUS
  MAURITIUS 809
MEAL
  SCHOOL MEAL PROGRAMMES 272
MEASUREMENT
  MEASUREMENT 391
  MEASUREMENT AIMS 391
  MEASUREMENT INSTRUMENTS 742
  MEASUREMENT TECHNIQUES 391
MECHANICAL
  MECHANICAL ENGINEERING 647
  MECHANICAL ENGINEERS 463
  MECHANICAL EQUIPMENT 742
  MECHANICAL SKILLS 533
MECHANICS
  MECHANICS (PROCESS) 647
MEDIA
  EDUCATIONAL MEDIA 360
  MASS MEDIA 145
  MEDIA RESEARCH 280
  MEDIA RESOURCES CENTRES 312
  MEDIA SPECIALISTS 430
  MEDIA TECHNOLOGY 140
MEDIATION
  MEDIATION THEORY 511
MEDICAL
  MEDICAL CONSULTANTS 433
  MEDICAL EDUCATION 681
  MEDICAL EVALUATION 391
  MEDICAL SERVICES 160
  MEDICAL SUPPLIES 751
  MEDICAL TREATMENT 373
MEDICINE
  MEDICINE 651
MEDITERRANEAN
  MEDITERRANEAN COUNTRIES 801
MEETINGS
  MEETINGS 204

MELANESIA
   MELANESIA 801
MEMBERS
   UNION MEMBERS 450
MEMBERSHIP
   GROUP MEMBERSHIP 554
MEMORIZING
   MEMORIZING 521
MEMORY
   SHORT TERM MEMORY 521
MEN
   MEN 443
MENTAL
   MENTAL DEVELOPMENT 530
   MENTAL HANDICAPS 571
   MENTAL HEALTH 502
   MENTAL HEALTH
     PROGRAMMES 320
   MENTAL ILLNESS 570
   MENTAL RETARDATION 570
   MENTAL SET 513
   MENTAL TESTS 394
MENTALLY
   MENTALLY HANDICAPPED 403
METAL
   METAL INDUSTRY 150
METALLURGISTS
   METALLURGISTS 463
METALWORKERS
   METALWORKERS 451
METALWORKING
   METALWORKING 647
METEOROLOGY
   METEOROLOGY 633
METHOD
   GLOBAL METHOD 661
   SIGHT METHOD 661
METHODOLOGICAL
   METHODOLOGICAL
     PROBLEMS 281
METHODOLOGY
   RESEARCH METHODOLOGY 283
METHODS
   ACTIVITY METHODS 355
   ANIMATION METHODS 355
   CASE STUDY METHODS 355
   DEDUCTIVE METHODS 355
   EDUCATIONAL METHODS 355
   EVALUATION METHODS 210
   INDUCTIVE METHODS 355

METHODS
   LITERACY METHODS 661
   METHODS COURSES 691
   METHODS TEACHERS 426
   PROJECT TRAINING
     METHODS 673
   SELF INSTRUCTIONAL
     METHODS 355
   SUPERVISORY METHODS 210
   TEACHING METHODS 355
METRIC
   METRIC SYSTEM 631
MEXICO
   MEXICO 803
MICROFORM
   MICROFORM READERS 731
MICROFORMS
   MICROFORMS 721
MICRONESIA
   MICRONESIA 801
MICROTEACHING
   MICROTEACHING 691
MIDDLE
   MIDDLE AGE 500
   MIDDLE AGE PEOPLE 400
   MIDDLE AGES 840
   MIDDLE CLASS 121
   MIDDLE CLASS PARENTS 401
   MIDDLE EAST 801
   MIDDLE SCHOOLS 301
MIDWAY
   MIDWAY ISLANDS 806
MIGRANT
   MIGRANT EDUCATION 186
   MIGRANT PROBLEMS 124
MIGRANTS
   MIGRANTS 470
MIGRATION
   MIGRATION 124
MILITARY
   MILITARY PERSONNEL 441
   MILITARY SCIENCE 630
   MILITARY TRAINING 351
MINERS
   MINERS 451
MINIMAL
   MINIMAL BRAIN INJURY 570
MINIMUM
   MINIMUM AGE 500
MINING
   MINING ENGINEERS 463
   MINING INDUSTRY 150

MINISTRY
MINISTRY OF EDUCATION 860
MINISTRY OF EDUCATION REPORT 880
MINORITY
MINORITY GROUP CHILDREN 402
MINORITY GROUP TEACHERS 424
MINORITY GROUPS 443
MINORITY ROLE 123
MINORS
COLLEGE MINORS 333
MIQUELON
SAINT PIERRE AND MIQUELON ISLANDS 803
MISSIONS
EDUCATIONAL MISSIONS 205
MIXED
MIXED SYSTEMS 260
MOBILE
MOBILE EDUCATIONAL SERVICES 270
MOBILE SCHOOLS 303
MOBILITY
FAMILY MOBILITY 124
MOBILITY 124
MOBILITY AIDS 734
OCCUPATIONAL MOBILITY 563
SOCIAL MOBILITY 121
STUDENT MOBILITY 206
TEACHER MOBILITY 207
MODE
RESPONSE MODE 511
MODELS
MODELS 733
MODERN
MODERN HISTORY 641
MODERN LANGUAGE INSTRUCTION 662
MODERN LANGUAGE PRIMARY PROGRAMMES 662
MODERN LANGUAGES 627
MODERN MATHEMATICS 631
MODERN TIMES 840
MODULAR
MODULAR APPROACH 331
MODULAR TRAINING 351
MOLDAVIAN
MOLDAVIAN SSR 805

MOMENTS
TEACHABLE MOMENTS 531
MONACO
MONACO 805
MONGOLIA
MONGOLIA 804
MONTSERRAT
MONTSERRAT 803
MORAL
MORAL EDUCATION 682
MORAL ISSUES 100
MORAL VALUES 555
MOROCCO
MOROCCO 807
MORPHEMES
MORPHEMES 622
MORPHOLOGY
MORPHOLOGY (LANGUAGES) 622
MOSLEMS
MOSLEMS 475
MOTHER
MOTHER TONGUE 131
MOTHER TONGUE INSTRUCTION 662
MOTHERS
MOTHERS 401
MOTIVATION
MOTIVATION 541
STUDENT MOTIVATION 541
TEACHER MOTIVATION 350
MOTOR
MOTOR DEVELOPMENT 530
MOTOR REACTIONS 511
MOTOR VEHICLE INDUSTRY 150
MOTOR VEHICLES 743
PERCEPTUAL MOTOR COORDINATION 510
MOVEMENTS
EYE MOVEMENTS 503
MOZAMBIQUE
MOZAMBIQUE 802
MULTI
MULTI PURPOSE CENTRES 311
MULTILATERAL
MULTILATERAL AID 106
MULTIMEDIA
MULTIMEDIA INSTRUCTION 360
MULTIMEDIA ORGANIZATIONS 187

307

MULTIPLE
MULTIPLE CHOICE TESTS 392
MULTIPLE CLASS TEACHING 340
MULTIPLE HANDICAPS 571
MULTISENSORY
MULTISENSORY LEARNING 512
MUNICIPALITIES
MUNICIPALITIES 102
MUSEUMS
MUSEUMS 310
MUSIC
MUSIC 610
MUSIC APPRECIATION 684
MUSIC EDUCATION 684
MUSIC TEACHERS 425
MUSICAL
MUSICAL INSTRUMENTS 741
MUSICIANS
MUSICIANS 461
MYTHOLOGY
MYTHOLOGY 616
NAM
VIET NAM SR 804
NAMIBIA
NAMIBIA 802
NATIONAL
NATIONAL CADRES 441
NATIONAL COMMISSION FOR UNESCO 860
NATIONAL DEMOGRAPHY 124
NATIONAL HISTORY 641
NATIONAL INTEGRATION 101
NATIONAL INTERAGENCY COORDINATION 105
NATIONAL LANGUAGE 626
NATIONAL LIBRARIES 310
NATIONAL LITERATURE 615
NATIONAL NORMS 284
NATIONAL ORGANIZATIONS 110
NATIONAL PLANNING 108
NATIONAL PROGRAMMES 109
NATIONAL REGIONAL COOPERATION 105
NATIONAL REGIONAL DISPARITIES 151
NATIONAL REGIONAL PLANNING 108
NATIONAL REGIONAL PROGRAMMES 109

NATIONAL
NATIONAL SERVICE 125
NATIONAL SURVEYS 203
NATIONALISM
NATIONALISM 101
NATURAL
NATURAL DISASTER 250
NATURAL RESOURCES 700
NAURU
NAURU ISLAND 806
NEED
ACHIEVEMENT NEED 536
NEED GRATIFICATION 536
STATUS NEED 536
NEEDS
CHILDHOOD NEEDS 536
EDUCATIONAL NEEDS 181
FINANCIAL NEEDS 152
HEALTH NEEDS 160
INDIVIDUAL NEEDS 536
LEARNING NEEDS 536
MANPOWER NEEDS 154
NEEDS 100
NEEDS ASSESSMENT 151
PSYCHOLOGICAL NEEDS 536
STUDENT NEEDS 350
NEPAL
NEPAL 804
NERVOUS
NERVOUS SYSTEM 502
NETHERLANDS
NETHERLANDS 805
NETHERLANDS ANTILLES 803
NETWORK
NETWORK ANALYSIS 201
NETWORKS
INFORMATION NETWORKS 202
NETWORKS 760
NEUROLOGICAL
NEUROLOGICAL HANDICAPS 571
NEUROTICS
NEUROTICS 403
NEVIS
SAINT KITTS–NEVIS–ANGUILLA 803
NEW
NEW CALEDONIA 806
NEW LITERATES 412
NEW ZEALAND 806
PAPUA NEW GUINEA 804

NEWSPAPERS
  NEWSPAPERS 720
NGO
  NGO 853
NICARAGUA
  NICARAGUA 803
NIGER
  NIGER 802
NIGERIA
  NIGERIA 802
NINETEENTH
  NINETEENTH CENTURY 840
NIUE
  NIUE ISLAND 806
NOMADISM
  NOMADISM 124
NOMADS
  NOMADS 470
NON
  NON PARTICIPATION 554
  NON SUBSIDIZED ORGANIZATIONS 110
  NON VOCATIONAL COURSES 333
  NON-PARTICIPANTS 410
NONCREDIT
  NONCREDIT COURSES 333
NONFORMAL
  NONFORMAL EDUCATION 184
NONGRADED
  NONGRADED CLASSES 340
  NONGRADED CURRICULUM 332
  NONGRADED SCHOOLS 303
  NONGRADED SYSTEM 340
NONINSTRUCTIONAL
  NONINSTRUCTIONAL RESPONSIBILITY 231
NONMANUAL
  NONMANUAL WORKERS 451
NONPARTICIPANTS
  LABOUR FORCE NONPARTICIPANTS 450
NONPROFESSIONAL
  NONPROFESSIONAL PERSONNEL 441
NORFOLK
  NORFOLK ISLAND 806
NORMS
  GROUP NORMS 284
  NATIONAL NORMS 284

NORTH
  NORTH AFRICA 801
  NORTH AMERICA 801
  NORTH POLE 801
NORTHERN
  NORTHERN HEMISPHERE 801
NORWAY
  NORWAY 805
NOVELS
  NOVELS 616
NUCLEAR
  NUCLEAR PHYSICS 633
  NUCLEAR PLANNING 250
NUMBER
  NUMBER CONCEPTS 631
NUMBERS
  NUMBERS 631
NUMERUS
  NUMERUS CLAUSUS 266
NURSERY
  NURSERY SCHOOLS 301
NURSES
  NURSES 433
  SCHOOL NURSES 433
NURSING
  NURSING 155
NUTRITION
  NUTRITION 160
OAS
  OAS 852
OAU
  OAU 852
OBJECTIVE
  OBJECTIVE TESTS 392
OBJECTIVES
  AFFECTIVE OBJECTIVES 300
  BEHAVIOURAL OBJECTIVES 300
  COGNITIVE OBJECTIVES 300
  COUNSELLING OBJECTIVES 370
  COURSE OBJECTIVES 300
  EDUCATIONAL OBJECTIVES 300
  PSYCHOMOTOR OBJECTIVES 300
  TRAINING OBJECTIVES 300
OBSERVATION
  LESSON OBSERVATION CRITERIA 691
  OBSERVATION 671

OBSERVATIONAL
    OBSERVATIONAL STUDIES 282
OBSOLESCENCE
    KNOWLEDGE OBSOLESCENCE 181
    SKILL OBSOLESCENCE 181
OCAM
    OCAM 852
OCAS
    OCAS 852
OCCUPATIONAL
    OCCUPATIONAL ADVANCEMENT 154
    OCCUPATIONAL CHANGE 155
    OCCUPATIONAL CLUSTERS 155
    OCCUPATIONAL INFORMATION 371
    OCCUPATIONAL MOBILITY 563
    OCCUPATIONAL SURVEYS 282
    OCCUPATIONAL THERAPISTS 432
OCCUPATIONS
    AGRICULTURAL OCCUPATIONS 155
    CLERICAL OCCUPATIONS 155
    INDUSTRIAL OCCUPATIONS 155
    OCCUPATIONS 155
    SEMISKILLED OCCUPATIONS 155
    SERVICE OCCUPATIONS 155
    SKILLED OCCUPATIONS 155
    UNSKILLED OCCUPATIONS 155
OCEAN
    ATLANTIC OCEAN TERRITORIES 801
    INDIAN OCEAN TERRITORIES 801
OCEANIA
    OCEANIA 800
OECD
    OECD 852
OEI
    OEI 852
OFF
    OFF THE JOB TRAINING 351
OFFICE
    OFFICE MACHINES 742

OFFICERS
    ATTENDANCE OFFICERS 420
OFFICIAL
    OFFICIAL LANGUAGES 131
    OFFICIAL REPORTS 720
OLD
    OLD AGE 500
OMAN
    OMAN 804
OMBUDSMEN
    OMBUDSMEN 460
ONE
    ONE TEACHER SCHOOLS 303
OPEN
    OPEN COLLEGES 307
    OPEN ENROLMENT 266
    OPEN LEARNING SYSTEMS 355
    OPEN PLAN SCHOOLS 340
OPERATING
    OPERATING EXPENSES 241
OPERATIONS
    OPERATIONS RESEARCH 282
OPINIONS
    OPINIONS 552
OPPORTUNITIES
    EDUCATIONAL OPPORTUNITIES 180
    EMPLOYMENT OPPORTUNITIES 154
    EQUAL OPPORTUNITIES (JOBS) 153
    OPPORTUNITIES 100
    RESEARCH OPPORTUNITIES 223
    YOUTH OPPORTUNITIES 100
OPPORTUNITY
    OPPORTUNITY CLASSES 343
OPTICIANS
    OPTICIANS 433
OPTICS
    OPTICS 633
OPTIONAL
    OPTIONAL COURSES 333
ORAL
    ORAL READING 620
ORDER
    BIRTH ORDER 500
OREALC
    OREALC 851
ORGANIZATION

ORGANIZATION
- ADMINISTRATIVE ORGANIZATION 261
- COURSE ORGANIZATION 333
- EDUCATIONAL ORGANIZATION 260
- GRADE ORGANIZATION 342
- SCHOOL ORGANIZATION 340

ORGANIZATIONS
- COMMUNITY ORGANIZATIONS 110
- COORDINATING ORGANIZATIONS 110
- INTERNATIONAL ORGANIZATIONS 110
- LITERACY ORGANIZATIONS 110
- MULTIMEDIA ORGANIZATIONS 187
- NATIONAL ORGANIZATIONS 110
- NON SUBSIDIZED ORGANIZATIONS 110
- ORGANIZATIONS 110
- POLITICAL ORGANIZATIONS 110
- RELIGIOUS ORGANIZATIONS 110
- STUDENT ORGANIZATIONS 110
- VOLUNTARY ORGANIZATIONS 110
- YOUTH ORGANIZATIONS 110

ORIENTATION
- GOAL ORIENTATION 541
- ORIENTATION COURSES 333
- TEACHER ORIENTATION 690

ORIGINALITY
- ORIGINALITY 522

ORIGINS
- ETHNIC ORIGINS 550

ORTHOGRAPHIC
- ORTHOGRAPHIC SYMBOLS 620

OUTDOOR
- OUTDOOR ACTIVITIES 357
- OUTDOOR TEACHING AREAS 711

OUTLAY
- CAPITAL OUTLAY (FOR FIXED ASSETS) 241

OUTPUT
- EDUCATIONAL OUTPUT 181

OVERACHIEVERS
- OVERACHIEVERS 415

OVERCROWDED
- OVERCROWDED CLASSES 265

OVERHEAD
- OVERHEAD PROJECTORS 731

OVERTIME
- OVERTIME 222

PAID
- PAID EDUCATIONAL LEAVE 222

PAINTING
- PAINTING 610

PAKISTAN
- PAKISTAN 804

PANAMA
- PANAMA 803
- PANAMA CANAL ZONE 803

PAPUA
- PAPUA NEW GUINEA 804

PARAGUAY
- PARAGUAY 803

PARAPROFESSIONAL
- PARAPROFESSIONAL SCHOOL PERSONNEL 423

PARENT
- PARENT ASSOCIATIONS 110
- PARENT CHILD RELATIONSHIP 553
- PARENT EDUCATION 186
- PARENT EDUCATION PROGRAMMES 321
- PARENT PARTICIPATION 380
- PARENT RESPONSIBILITY 231
- PARENT ROLE 553
- PARENT STUDENT RELATIONSHIP 380
- PARENT TEACHER ASSOCIATIONS 110
- PARENT TEACHER COOPERATION 380

PARENTS
- MIDDLE CLASS PARENTS 401
- PARENTS 401
- WORKING CLASS PARENTS 401
- WORKING PARENTS 401

PART
- PART TIME EDUCATION 184
- PART TIME EDUCATORS 424
- PART TIME EMPLOYMENT 222
- PART TIME STUDENTS 410

PART
    PART TIME TEACHERS 424
    PART TIME TRAINING 351
PARTIALLY
    PARTIALLY SIGHTED 403
PARTICIPANT
    PARTICIPANT INVOLVEMENT 554
    PARTICIPANT SATISFACTION 554
PARTICIPANTS
    NON-PARTICIPANTS 410
PARTICIPATION
    CITIZEN PARTICIPATION 105
    CLASSROOM PARTICIPATION 356
    COMMUNITY PARTICIPATION 122
    NON PARTICIPATION 554
    PARENT PARTICIPATION 380
    PARTICIPATION 554
    PARTICIPATION DETERRENTS 285
    PARTICIPATION INCENTIVES 285
    PARTICIPATION PROBLEMS 281
    PARTICIPATION RATE 206
    STUDENT PARTICIPATION 380
    TEACHER PARTICIPATION 380
PAST
    PAST STUDENTS 410
PATHOLOGY
    SPEECH PATHOLOGY 372
PATIENTS
    PATIENTS (PERSONS) 433
PATRIOTISM
    PATRIOTISM 101
PATTERN
    PATTERN DRILLS (LANGUAGE) 663
    PATTERN RECOGNITION 511
PATTERNS
    GROWTH PATTERNS 502
    LANGUAGE PATTERNS 621
    PSYCHOLOGICAL PATTERNS 551
    SOCIOCULTURAL PATTERNS 120
PAY
    PREMIUM PAY 242

PAYMENTS
    LOSS OF EARNINGS PAYMENTS 242
PAYROLL
    PAYROLL RECORDS 723
PEACE
    PEACE EDUCATION 682
PEDAGOGY
    PEDAGOGY 350
PEDIATRY
    PEDIATRY 651
PEER
    PEER ACCEPTANCE 554
    PEER GROUPS 443
    PEER RELATIONSHIP 554
    PEER TEACHING 350
PENALTIES
    FINES (PENALTIES) 233
PEOPLE
    ELDERLY PEOPLE 400
    MIDDLE AGE PEOPLE 400
PERCEPTION
    AUDITORY PERCEPTION 510
    PERCEPTION 510
    ROLE PERCEPTION 553
    VISUAL PERCEPTION 510
PERCEPTUAL
    PERCEPTUAL DISORDERS 571
    PERCEPTUAL MOTOR COORDINATION 510
PERFORMANCE
    PERFORMANCE 535
    PERFORMANCE CRITERIA 232
    PERFORMANCE FACTORS 535
    PERFORMANCE INCENTIVES 266
    PERFORMANCE SPECIFICATIONS 232
    PERFORMANCE TESTS 393
PERIOD
    PROBATIONARY PERIOD 222
PERIODICALS
    PERIODICALS 720
PERIODS
    PRACTICE PERIODS 673
PERSISTENCE
    PERSISTENCE 535
PERSONAL
    PERSONAL GROWTH 531
PERSONALITY
    PERSONALITY 555

PERSONALITY
    PERSONALITY ASSESSMENT 221
    PERSONALITY DEVELOPMENT 530
    PERSONALITY PROBLEMS 572
    PERSONALITY STUDIES 282
    PERSONALITY TESTS 394
    PERSONALITY THEORIES 555

PERSONNEL
    EDUCATIONAL PERSONNEL 420
    GUIDANCE PERSONNEL 431
    HEALTH PERSONNEL 433
    INDUSTRIAL PERSONNEL 441
    MILITARY PERSONNEL 441
    NONPROFESSIONAL PERSONNEL 441
    PARAPROFESSIONAL SCHOOL PERSONNEL 423
    PERSONNEL 441
    PERSONNEL DATA 220
    PERSONNEL EVALUATION 210
    PERSONNEL MANAGEMENT 220
    PROFESSIONAL PERSONNEL 441
    SCHOOL PERSONNEL 423
    SCIENTIFIC PERSONNEL 441
    STUDENT PERSONNEL SERVICES 270
    TEACHING PERSONNEL 424

PERSONS
    HOMEBOUND PERSONS 403
    HOSPITALIZED PERSONS 403
    PATIENTS (PERSONS) 433
    RESOURCE PERSONS 421
    RETIRED PERSONS 400

PERU
    PERU 803

PETROLEUM
    PETROLEUM INDUSTRY 150
    PETROLEUM WORKERS 451

PHARMACISTS
    PHARMACISTS 433

PHILIPPINES
    PHILIPPINES 804

PHILOSOPHY
    EDUCATIONAL PHILOSOPHY 180
    PHILOSOPHY 600

PHONETICS
    PHONETICS 622

PHONICS
    PHONICS 661

PHONOGRAPH
    PHONOGRAPH RECORDS 730

PHONOLOGY
    PHONOLOGY 622

PHOTOGRAPHY
    PHOTOGRAPHY 647

PHYSICAL
    PHYSICAL ACTIVITIES 537
    PHYSICAL CHARACTERISTICS 561
    PHYSICAL DEVELOPMENT 530
    PHYSICAL EDUCATION 683
    PHYSICAL ENVIRONMENT 550
    PHYSICAL EXAMINATIONS 392
    PHYSICAL HANDICAPS 571
    PHYSICAL HEALTH 502
    PHYSICAL PLANNING 108
    PHYSICAL PLANS 250
    PHYSICAL THERAPISTS 432

PHYSICALLY
    PHYSICALLY HANDICAPPED 403

PHYSICIANS
    PHYSICIANS 433

PHYSICISTS
    PHYSICISTS 463

PHYSICS
    NUCLEAR PHYSICS 633
    PHYSICS 633

PHYSIOLOGY
    AUDITION (PHYSIOLOGY) 503
    EXERCISE (PHYSIOLOGY) 503
    PHYSIOLOGY 632

PIERRE
    SAINT PIERRE AND MIQUELON ISLANDS 803

PILOT
    PILOT PROJECTS 272

PITCAIRN
    PITCAIRN ISLANDS 806

PLACEMENT
    COLLEGE PLACEMENT 266
    PLACEMENT 154
    REGULAR CLASS PLACEMENT 341
    TEACHER PLACEMENT 223

PLAN
  COLOMBO PLAN 852
  CONTINUOUS PROGRESS
    PLAN 331
  OPEN PLAN SCHOOLS 340
PLANNING
  CAREER PLANNING 563
  COLLEGE PLANNING 205
  COMMUNITY PLANNING 108
  CURRICULUM PLANNING 213
  EDUCATIONAL PLANNING 205
  FACILITIES PLANNING 650
  FAMILY PLANNING 126
  MANPOWER PLANNING 154
  NATIONAL PLANNING 108
  NATIONAL REGIONAL
    PLANNING 108
  NUCLEAR PLANNING 250
  PHYSICAL PLANNING 108
  PLANNING 108
  PLANNING BODIES 261
  PROGRAMME PLANNING 205
  REGIONAL PLANNING 108
  SCHOOL PLANNING 205
  SITE PLANNING 250
  SOCIAL PLANNING 120
PLANS
  DEPARTMENTAL TEACHING
    PLANS 340
  LESSON PLANS 356
  PHYSICAL PLANS 250
PLANTATION
  PLANTATION WORKERS 451
PLAY
  PLAY 536
PLAYING
  ROLE PLAYING 553
PLURICULTURALISM
  PLURICULTURALISM 130
PLURILINGUALISM
  PLURILINGUALISM 131
POETRY
  POETRY 616
POLAND
  POLAND 805
POLAR
  POLAR REGIONS 801
POLE
  NORTH POLE 801
  SOUTH POLE 801
POLICE
  POLICE 460

POLICE
  POLICE SCHOOL
    RELATIONSHIP 263
POLICIES
  ADMINISTRATIVE POLICIES
    200
  CULTURAL POLICIES 130
  ECONOMIC POLICIES 150
  EDUCATIONAL POLICIES 182
  POLICIES 101
  PROMOTION POLICIES 200
  SOCIAL POLICIES 120
POLICY
  DISCIPLINE POLICY 231
  EDUCATIONAL POLICY
    TRENDS 182
  FINANCIAL POLICY 152
  FOREIGN POLICY 102
  LANGUAGE POLICY 131
  MANPOWER POLICY 154
  POLICY MAKING 102
  RESEARCH POLICY 140
  TRANSFER POLICY 200
POLITICAL
  POLITICAL EDUCATION 680
  POLITICAL FACTORS 285
  POLITICAL ISSUES 100
  POLITICAL ORGANIZATIONS
    110
  POLITICAL SCIENCE 640
  POLITICAL SOCIALIZATION
    553
  POLITICAL THEORIES 101
POLYNESIA
  FRENCH POLYNESIA 806
  POLYNESIA 801
POLYNESIAN
  MALAYO POLYNESIAN
    LANGUAGES 625
POLYTECHNICAL
  POLYTECHNICAL EDUCATION
    183
POPULATION
  ADULT POPULATION 124
  POPULATION DISTRIBUTION
    124
  POPULATION EDUCATION 683
  POPULATION PROBLEMS 124
  POPULATION TRENDS 124
  RURAL POPULATION 124
  SCHOOL AGE POPULATION
    206

POPULATION
   URBAN POPULATION 124
PORTUGAL
   PORTUGAL 805
PORTUGUESE
   PORTUGUESE TIMOR 804
POST
   POST INDUSTRIAL SOCIETY 150
POSTGRADUATE
   POSTGRADUATE STUDENTS 413
POVERTY
   POVERTY 151
POWER
   SCHOOL HOLDING POWER 208
POWERS
   PROVINCIAL POWERS 102
PRACTICE
   EDUCATIONAL PRACTICE 182
   PRACTICE PERIODS 673
   PRACTICE TEACHING 690
   SUPERVISED FARM PRACTICE 673
PRACTICES
   CONSTRUCTION PRACTICES 253
PRACTICUMS
   PRACTICUMS 671
PRE
   PRE INDUSTRIAL SOCIETY 150
   PRE RETIREMENT EDUCATION 183
   PRE RETIREMENT PROGRAMMES 321
PREDICTION
   PREDICTION 283
PREGNANCY
   PREGNANCY 502
PREMIUM
   PREMIUM PAY 242
PRENATAL
   PRENATAL INFLUENCES 550
PREPARATION
   COLLEGE PREPARATION 330
   MATERIALS PREPARATION 213
PREPRIMARY
   PREPRIMARY CHILDREN 411

PREPRIMARY
   PREPRIMARY CURRICULUM 330
   PREPRIMARY EDUCATION 185
   PREPRIMARY PROGRAMMES 320
   PREPRIMARY TEACHERS 421
PRESCHOOL
   PRESCHOOL CENTRES 311
   PRESCHOOL LEARNING 514
PRESENTATIONS
   SOUND SLIDE PRESENTATIONS 732
PRESERVICE
   PRESERVICE TEACHER EDUCATION 690
PRESIDENTS
   PRESIDENTS 422
PRESS
   PRESS 145
PRETECHNOLOGY
   PRETECHNOLOGY PROGRAMMES 670
PREVENTION
   ACCIDENT PREVENTION 673
   DELINQUENCY PREVENTION 281
PREVOCATIONAL
   PREVOCATIONAL EDUCATION 670
PRIESTS
   PRIESTS 462
PRIMARY
   MODERN LANGUAGE PRIMARY PROGRAMMES 662
   PRIMARY EDUCATION 185
   PRIMARY GRADES 342
   PRIMARY SCHOOL CERTIFICATES 390
   PRIMARY SCHOOL COUNSELLORS 431
   PRIMARY SCHOOL CURRICULUM 330
   PRIMARY SCHOOL INSPECTORS 420
   PRIMARY SCHOOL MATHEMATICS 670
   PRIMARY SCHOOL SCIENCE 670
   PRIMARY SCHOOL STUDENTS 411

PRIMARY
    PRIMARY SCHOOL TEACHERS 421
    PRIMARY SCHOOLS 301
PRIMERS
    LITERACY PRIMERS 725
PRINCIPALS
    PRINCIPALS 423
PRINCIPE
    SAO TOME AND PRINCIPE 802
PRINCIPLES
    ADMINISTRATIVE PRINCIPLES 200
    PRINCIPLES OF TEACHING 690
    SCIENTIFIC PRINCIPLES 140
PRINTING
    PRINTING 647
    PRINTING INDUSTRY 150
    PRINTING WORKERS 451
PRIOR
    PRIOR KNOWLEDGE LEVEL 391
PRIORITIES
    EDUCATIONAL PRIORITIES 182
PRISONERS
    PRISONERS 403
PRIVATE
    PRIVATE ADULT EDUCATION 187
    PRIVATE COLLEGES 307
    PRIVATE EDUCATION 187
    PRIVATE EDUCATION SYSTEMS 260
    PRIVATE ENTERPRISES 150
    PRIVATE FINANCIAL SUPPORT 240
    PRIVATE SCHOOL TEACHERS 423
    PRIVATE SCHOOLS 302
PROBABILITY
    PROBABILITY 631
PROBATIONARY
    PROBATIONARY PERIOD 222
PROBLEM
    PROBLEM SOLVING 522
PROBLEMS
    ADJUSTMENT PROBLEMS 551
    ADMINISTRATIVE PROBLEMS 281
    BEHAVIOUR PROBLEMS 281

PROBLEMS
    COMMUNICATION PROBLEMS 204
    COMMUNITY PROBLEMS 122
    CURRICULUM PROBLEMS 281
    DISCIPLINE PROBLEMS 281
    EDUCATIONAL PROBLEMS 182
    EMOTIONAL PROBLEMS 540
    FAMILY PROBLEMS 281
    INTERPERSONAL PROBLEMS 554
    METHODOLOGICAL PROBLEMS 281
    MIGRANT PROBLEMS 124
    PARTICIPATION PROBLEMS 281
    PERSONALITY PROBLEMS 572
    POPULATION PROBLEMS 124
    RESEARCH PROBLEMS 281
    SOCIAL PROBLEMS 121
    WELFARE PROBLEMS 281
    WORLD PROBLEMS 101
    YOUTH PROBLEMS 572
PROCEDURE
    DESIGN PROCEDURE 252
PROCEDURES
    CONSTRUCTION PROCEDURES 253
    GROUPING PROCEDURES 341
    LABORATORY PROCEDURES 671
    SELECTION PROCEDURES 266
    TEACHING PROCEDURES 356
PROCESS
    INTERACTION PROCESS 352
    MECHANICS (PROCESS) 647
PROCESSES
    COGNITIVE PROCESSES 521
    LEARNING PROCESSES 513
    PSYCHOEDUCATIONAL PROCESSES 350
    READING PROCESSES 521
    THOUGHT PROCESSES 521
PROCESSING
    DATA PROCESSING 284
    INFORMATION PROCESSING 202
PRODUCTION
    AGRICULTURAL PRODUCTION 150
    PRODUCTION WORKERS 451

PRODUCTIVE
    PRODUCTIVE LIVING 100
    PRODUCTIVE THINKING 521
PRODUCTIVITY
    PRODUCTIVITY 150
PROFESSIONAL
    PROFESSIONAL ASSOCIATIONS 110
    PROFESSIONAL EDUCATION 183
    PROFESSIONAL PERSONNEL 441
    PROFESSIONAL RECOGNITION 121
    PROFESSIONAL SERVICES 270
PROFESSIONS
    PROFESSIONS 155
PROFESSORS
    PROFESSORS 422
    WOMEN PROFESSORS 422
PROFICIENCY
    LANGUAGE PROFICIENCY 535
PROFILE
    TEACHER PROFILE 223
PROGNOSTIC
    PROGNOSTIC TESTS 392
PROGRAMME
    ADULT PROGRAMME COMMITTEES 442
    GRADES (PROGRAMME DIVISIONS) 342
    PROGRAMME ADMINISTRATION 262
    PROGRAMME CONTENT 361
    PROGRAMME COORDINATION 205
    PROGRAMME COSTS 243
    PROGRAMME DESCRIPTIONS 203
    PROGRAMME DESIGN 205
    PROGRAMME EVALUATION 205
    PROGRAMME LENGTH 361
    PROGRAMME PLANNING 205
    RESEARCH PROGRAMME 140
PROGRAMMED
    PROGRAMMED INSTRUCTION 361
    PROGRAMMED MATERIALS 725
PROGRAMMES

PROGRAMMES
    ACCELERATED PROGRAMMES 320
    ACTION PROGRAMMES (COMMUNITY) 282
    ADULT EDUCATION PROGRAMMES 321
    ADULT READING PROGRAMMES 660
    AUDIOVISUAL PROGRAMMES 732
    BRANCHING PROGRAMMES 361
    COLLEGE PROGRAMMES 320
    COMMUNITY PROGRAMMES 109
    COMPENSATORY EDUCATION PROGRAMMES 271
    COMPUTER PROGRAMMES 760
    CONSTRUCTION PROGRAMMES 253
    DAY TIME PROGRAMMES 321
    DOCTORAL PROGRAMMES 320
    DROPOUT PROGRAMMES 320
    EDUCATIONAL PROGRAMMES 271
    EMERGENCY PROGRAMMES 271
    EMPLOYMENT PROGRAMMES 154
    ENRICHMENT PROGRAMMES 320
    EXCHANGE PROGRAMMES 271
    EXTENSION PROGRAMMES 321
    FIELD EXPERIENCE PROGRAMMES 671
    FOUNDATION PROGRAMMES 109
    FUNCTIONAL LITERACY PROGRAMMES 321
    GOVERNMENT PROGRAMMES 109
    GUIDANCE PROGRAMMES 271
    HEALTH PROGRAMMES 160
    IMMUNIZATION PROGRAMMES 161
    INDIVIDUAL DEVELOPMENT PROGRAMMES 321
    INPLANT PROGRAMMES 673

PROGRAMMES
  INSTRUCTIONAL
    PROGRAMMES 320
  INSURANCE PROGRAMMES
    241
  INTERCULTURAL
    PROGRAMMES 680
  INTERNATIONAL
    PROGRAMMES 109
  INTERNSHIP PROGRAMMES
    222
  LANGUAGE PROGRAMMES
    662
  LINEAR PROGRAMMES 361
  LITERACY PROGRAMMES 321
  MENTAL HEALTH
    PROGRAMMES 320
  MODERN LANGUAGE
    PRIMARY PROGRAMMES 662
  NATIONAL PROGRAMMES 109
  NATIONAL REGIONAL
    PROGRAMMES 109
  PARENT EDUCATION
    PROGRAMMES 321
  PRE RETIREMENT
    PROGRAMMES 321
  PREPRIMARY PROGRAMMES
    320
  PRETECHNOLOGY
    PROGRAMMES 670
  PROGRAMMES 109
  PROVINCIAL PROGRAMMES
    271
  READING PROGRAMMES 660
  RECREATIONAL
    PROGRAMMES 271
  REGIONAL PROGRAMMES 109
  REHABILITATION
    PROGRAMMES 271
  REMEDIAL READING
    PROGRAMMES 660
  RESIDENTIAL PROGRAMMES
    321
  RURAL EXTENSION
    PROGRAMMES 321
  SCHOOL COMMUNITY
    PROGRAMMES 272
  SCHOOL MEAL PROGRAMMES
    272
  SCHOOL RECREATIONAL
    PROGRAMMES 272
  SCIENCE PROGRAMMES 670

PROGRAMMES
  SELF INSTRUCTIONAL
    PROGRAMMES 320
  SPECIAL DEGREE
    PROGRAMMES 320
  SPECIAL PROGRAMMES 320
  TRAINING PROGRAMMES 351
  UNEMPLOYED EDUCATION
    PROGRAMMES 321
  UNIVERSITY EXTENSION
    PROGRAMMES 321
  VOCATIONAL TRAINING
    PROGRAMMES 321
  WORK EXPERIENCE
    PROGRAMMES 673
  YOUTH PROGRAMMES 381
PROGRAMMING
  INSTRUCTIONAL
    PROGRAMMING 361
  LOCAL PROGRAMMING 271
  PROGRAMMING (FACILITIES)
    250
  PROGRAMMING LANGUAGES
    621
PROGRESS
  CONTINUOUS PROGRESS
    PLAN 331
  ECONOMIC PROGRESS 150
  STUDENT PROGRESS 266
PROJECT
  PROJECT TRAINING
    METHODS 673
PROJECTION
  PROJECTION EQUIPMENT 731
PROJECTIONS
  ENROLMENT PROJECTIONS
    206
PROJECTIVE
  PROJECTIVE TESTS 394
PROJECTORS
  FILM PROJECTORS 731
  OVERHEAD PROJECTORS 731
PROJECTS
  DEMONSTRATION PROJECTS
    272
  FAMILY PROJECTS 272
  FUNCTIONAL LITERACY
    PROJECTS 321
  PILOT PROJECTS 272
  PROJECTS 272
  RESEARCH PROJECTS 272
  STUDENT PROJECTS 357

PROMOTION
    PROMOTION POLICIES 200
    STUDENT PROMOTION 266
    TEACHER PROMOTION 223
PROMPTING
    PROMPTING 361
PRONUNCIATION
    PRONUNCIATION 532
PROPRIETARY
    PROPRIETARY SCHOOLS 302
PROSE
    PROSE 616
PROSTHESES
    PROSTHESES 734
PROTESTANTS
    PROTESTANTS 475
PROTOCOL
    PROTOCOL MATERIALS 732
PROVIDED
    VOLUNTARILY PROVIDED ADULT EDUCATION 187
PROVINCES
    STATE AID TO PROVINCES 106
PROVINCIAL
    CENTRAL PROVINCIAL RELATIONSHIP 105
    PROVINCIAL AGENCIES 104
    PROVINCIAL DEPARTMENTS OF EDUCATION 261
    PROVINCIAL GOVERNMENT 104
    PROVINCIAL GOVERNMENT AID 106
    PROVINCIAL LAWS 170
    PROVINCIAL LOCAL RELATIONSHIP 262
    PROVINCIAL POWERS 102
    PROVINCIAL PROGRAMMES 271
    PROVINCIAL SURVEYS 203
PSYCHIATRISTS
    PSYCHIATRISTS 462
PSYCHIATRY
    PSYCHIATRY 651
PSYCHOEDUCATIONAL
    PSYCHOEDUCATIONAL CLINICS 313
    PSYCHOEDUCATIONAL PROCESSES 350
PSYCHOLOGICAL

PSYCHOLOGICAL
    IDENTIFICATION (PSYCHOLOGICAL) 555
    PSYCHOLOGICAL CHARACTERISTICS 561
    PSYCHOLOGICAL EVALUATION 391
    PSYCHOLOGICAL NEEDS 536
    PSYCHOLOGICAL PATTERNS 551
    PSYCHOLOGICAL STUDIES 282
    PSYCHOLOGICAL TESTING 391
    PSYCHOLOGICAL TESTS 392
    RECALL (PSYCHOLOGICAL) 511
PSYCHOLOGISTS
    PSYCHOLOGISTS 462
    SCHOOL PSYCHOLOGISTS 430
PSYCHOLOGY
    CHILD PSYCHOLOGY 642
    DEVELOPMENTAL PSYCHOLOGY 642
    EDUCATIONAL PSYCHOLOGY 642
    EXPERIMENTAL PSYCHOLOGY 642
    EXTINCTION (PSYCHOLOGY) 511
    INDIVIDUAL PSYCHOLOGY 642
    PSYCHOLOGY 642
    SOCIAL PSYCHOLOGY 642
PSYCHOMETRICS
    PSYCHOMETRICS 391
PSYCHOMOTOR
    PSYCHOMOTOR OBJECTIVES 300
    PSYCHOMOTOR SKILLS 533
PSYCHOPATHOLOGY
    PSYCHOPATHOLOGY 642
PSYCHOSOMATIC
    PSYCHOSOMATIC DISEASES 570
PSYCHOTHERAPY
    PSYCHOTHERAPY 373
PSYCHOTICS
    PSYCHOTICS 403
PUBLIC
    COMMUNITY AGENCIES (PUBLIC) 104
    PUBLIC COLLEGES 307
    PUBLIC EDUCATION 187

PUBLIC
  PUBLIC EDUCATION SYSTEMS 260
  PUBLIC ENTERPRISES 150
  PUBLIC FINANCE 240
  PUBLIC HEALTH 160
  PUBLIC HEALTH LAWS 170
  PUBLIC LIBRARIES 310
  PUBLIC RELATIONS 145
  PUBLIC SCHOOL SYSTEMS 260
  PUBLIC SCHOOL TEACHERS 423
  PUBLIC SCHOOLS 302
  PUBLIC SUPPORT 100
PUBLICATION
  PUBLICATION 204
PUBLICATIONS
  GOVERNMENT PUBLICATIONS 720
  PUBLICATIONS 720
  SCHOOL PUBLICATIONS 720
PUBLICITY
  EDUCATIONAL PUBLICITY 182
PUBLISHING
  PUBLISHING INDUSTRY 150
PUNISHMENT
  PUNISHMENT 267
PURCHASING
  PURCHASING 241
PURPOSE
  MULTI PURPOSE CENTRES 311
PURPOSES
  GROUPING (INSTRUCTIONAL PURPOSES) 341
QATAR
  QATAR 807
QUALIFICATIONS
  COUNSELLOR QUALIFICATIONS 223
  EMPLOYMENT QUALIFICATIONS 390
  QUALIFICATIONS 221
  SUPERVISOR QUALIFICATIONS 223
  TEACHER QUALIFICATIONS 223
QUALITY
  EDUCATIONAL QUALITY 181
  TEACHING QUALITY 212
QUANTITY
  QUANTITY SURVEYING 650

QUARTER
  QUARTER SYSTEM 344
QUESTIONING
  QUESTIONING TECHNIQUES 356
QUESTIONNAIRES
  QUESTIONNAIRES 203
QUOTA
  QUOTA SYSTEM 205
QUOTIENT
  INTELLIGENCE QUOTIENT 520
R
  KOREA R 804
RACE
  RACE 123
  RACE RELATIONS 123
RACIAL
  RACIAL DISCRIMINATION 123
  RACIAL INTEGRATION 123
  RACIAL SEGREGATION 123
RACISM
  RACISM 101
RADIO
  EDUCATIONAL RADIO 360
  RADIO 145
  RADIO TECHNOLOGY 645
RAILWAY
  RAILWAY WORKERS 451
RAPID
  RAPID READING 660
RATE
  ATTENDANCE RATE 206
  DISEASE RATE 161
  DROPOUT RATE 206
  FAILURE RATE 266
  PARTICIPATION RATE 206
  REPETITION RATE 206
RATING
  ACHIEVEMENT RATING 391
  RATING SCALES 392
RATIO
  ENROLMENT RATIO 206
  STUDENT TEACHER RATIO 207
REACTION
  REACTION TIME 511
REACTIONS
  MOTOR REACTIONS 511
READABILITY
  READABILITY 660
READERS
  MICROFORM READERS 731

READINESS
    LEARNING READINESS 531
    READINESS 531
    READING READINESS 531
    SCHOOL READINESS 531
READING
    ADULT READING PROGRAMMES 660
    BEGINNING READING 660
    CORRECTIVE READING 660
    FUNCTIONAL READING 521
    INDEPENDENT READING 661
    ORAL READING 620
    RAPID READING 660
    READING 620
    READING ABILITY 520
    READING CONSULTANTS 430
    READING DEVELOPMENT 534
    READING DIFFICULTY 660
    READING HABITS 542
    READING INSTRUCTION 660
    READING LEVEL 660
    READING MATERIALS 725
    READING PROCESSES 521
    READING PROGRAMMES 660
    READING READINESS 531
    READING RESEARCH 280
    READING TESTS 393
    REMEDIAL READING PROGRAMMES 660
    SILENT READING 661
    SUPPLEMENTARY READING MATERIALS 725
READINGS
    EDUCATIONAL READINGS 690
REALISM
    REALISM 615
REASONING
    ABSTRACT REASONING 522
RECALL
    RECALL (PSYCHOLOGICAL) 511
RECOGNITION
    PATTERN RECOGNITION 511
    PROFESSIONAL RECOGNITION 121
    RECOGNITION 511
RECOMMENDATIONS
    INTERNATIONAL RECOMMENDATIONS 170
RECORDERS
    TAPE RECORDERS 731

RECORDINGS
    TAPE RECORDINGS 732
    VIDEO TAPE RECORDINGS 732
RECORDKEEPING
    RECORDKEEPING 202
RECORDS
    ATTENDANCE RECORDS 723
    PAYROLL RECORDS 723
    PHONOGRAPH RECORDS 730
    RECORDS (FORMS) 723
    STUDENT RECORDS 723
RECREATION
    EDUCATIONAL RECREATION 357
    RECREATION 126
    RECREATION LEGISLATION 230
RECREATIONAL
    RECREATIONAL ACTIVITIES 357
    RECREATIONAL FACILITIES 712
    RECREATIONAL PROGRAMMES 271
    SCHOOL RECREATIONAL PROGRAMMES 272
RECRUITMENT
    RECRUITMENT 221
    STUDENT RECRUITMENT 266
RECURRENT
    RECURRENT EDUCATION 184
REDISTRICTING
    SCHOOL REDISTRICTING 264
REDUCTION
    COST REDUCTION 243
REDUNDANCY
    REDUNDANCY 222
REFERENCE
    REFERENCE MATERIALS 720
REFERENCED
    CRITERION REFERENCED TESTS 392
REFERRAL
    REFERRAL 372
REFORM
    AGRARIAN REFORM 151
    EDUCATIONAL REFORM 200
REFRESHER
    REFRESHER TRAINING 333
REFUGEES
    REFUGEES 470

REGIONAL
    NATIONAL REGIONAL COOPERATION 105
    NATIONAL REGIONAL DISPARITIES 151
    NATIONAL REGIONAL PLANNING 108
    NATIONAL REGIONAL PROGRAMMES 109
    REGIONAL AGENCIES 103
    REGIONAL COOPERATION 105
    REGIONAL PLANNING 108
    REGIONAL PROGRAMMES 109
    REGIONAL SURVEYS 203

REGIONS
    ANTARCTIC REGIONS 801
    ARCTIC REGIONS 801
    GEOGRAPHIC REGIONS 102
    POLAR REGIONS 801

REGISTRATION
    SCHOOL REGISTRATION 264

REGULAR
    REGULAR CLASS PLACEMENT 341

REGULATIONS
    ADULT EDUCATION REGULATIONS 230
    SCHOOL REGULATIONS 230

REHABILITATION
    REHABILITATION 373
    REHABILITATION COUNSELLING 370
    REHABILITATION PROGRAMMES 271
    VOCATIONAL REHABILITATION 373

REINFORCEMENT
    REINFORCEMENT 511

REJECTION
    REJECTION 540

RELATIONS
    ADULT EDUCATION–COMMUNITY RELATIONS 263
    HUMAN RELATIONS 122
    INTERGROUP RELATIONS 122
    INTERNATIONAL RELATIONS 640
    LABOUR RELATIONS 153
    PUBLIC RELATIONS 145
    RACE RELATIONS 123
    SOCIAL RELATIONS 553

RELATIONSHIP
    ADULT STUDENT–INSTITUTION RELATIONSHIP 380
    CENTRAL PROVINCIAL RELATIONSHIP 105
    EDUCATION WORK RELATIONSHIP 182
    FAMILY RELATIONSHIP 553
    FAMILY SCHOOL RELATIONSHIP 380
    INTERPERSONAL RELATIONSHIP 553
    PARENT CHILD RELATIONSHIP 553
    PARENT STUDENT RELATIONSHIP 380
    PEER RELATIONSHIP 554
    POLICE SCHOOL RELATIONSHIP 263
    PROVINCIAL LOCAL RELATIONSHIP 262
    RELATIONSHIP 553
    SCHOOL COMMUNITY RELATIONSHIP 263
    SCHOOL INDUSTRY RELATIONSHIP 263
    STUDENT COLLEGE RELATIONSHIP 380
    STUDENT SCHOOL RELATIONSHIP 380
    STUDENT TEACHER RELATIONSHIP 380
    TEACHER ADMINISTRATION RELATIONSHIP 262

RELEASE
    BLOCK RELEASE 222
    DAY RELEASE 222

RELEASED
    RELEASED TIME 222

RELIABILITY
    RELIABILITY 283

RELIGION
    RELIGION 130

RELIGIOUS
    RELIGIOUS CULTURAL GROUPS 443
    RELIGIOUS EDUCATION 682
    RELIGIOUS FACTORS 285
    RELIGIOUS INSTITUTION ROLE 125
    RELIGIOUS INSTITUTIONS 125

RELIGIOUS
    RELIGIOUS ORGANIZATIONS 110
RELOCATABLE
    RELOCATABLE FACILITIES 710
REMEDIAL
    REMEDIAL COURSES 333
    REMEDIAL INSTRUCTION 352
    REMEDIAL READING PROGRAMMES 660
    REMEDIAL TEACHERS 426
RENAISSANCE
    RENAISSANCE 840
REPETITION
    GRADE REPETITION 267
    REPETITION RATE 206
REPLICATION
    REPLICATION OF INNOVATIONS 204
REPORT
    COMMISSION REPORT 880
    CONFERENCE REPORT 880
    MINISTRY OF EDUCATION REPORT 880
    REPORT CARDS 723
    RESEARCH REPORT 880
REPORTING
    REPORTING 201
REPORTS
    OFFICIAL REPORTS 720
REPUBLIC
    CENTRAL AFRICAN REPUBLIC 802
    DOMINICAN REPUBLIC 803
    IRAN (ISLAMIC REPUBLIC) 804
    SOUTH AFRICA (REPUBLIC) 802
REQUIREMENTS
    ADMISSION REQUIREMENTS 232
    DEGREE REQUIREMENTS 390
    FACILITY REQUIREMENTS 250
RESEARCH
    ACTION RESEARCH 282
    APPLIED RESEARCH 282
    BEHAVIOURAL SCIENCE RESEARCH 280
    CLASSROOM RESEARCH 280
    CURRICULUM RESEARCH 280
    ECONOMIC RESEARCH 280
    EDUCATIONAL RESEARCH 280

RESEARCH
    EMPIRICAL RESEARCH 282
    EXCEPTIONAL CHILD RESEARCH 280
    EXPERIMENTAL RESEARCH 282
    FIELD RESEARCH 282
    FUNDAMENTAL RESEARCH 282
    LANGUAGE RESEARCH 280
    MEDIA RESEARCH 280
    OPERATIONS RESEARCH 282
    READING RESEARCH 280
    RESEARCH 140
    RESEARCH AND DEVELOPMENT 282
    RESEARCH AND INSTRUCTION UNITS 340
    RESEARCH CENTRES 312
    RESEARCH COORDINATING UNITS 261
    RESEARCH CRITERIA 283
    RESEARCH DESIGN 283
    RESEARCH DIRECTORS 430
    RESEARCH FINDINGS 283
    RESEARCH METHODOLOGY 283
    RESEARCH OPPORTUNITIES 223
    RESEARCH POLICY 140
    RESEARCH PROBLEMS 281
    RESEARCH PROGRAMME 140
    RESEARCH PROJECTS 272
    RESEARCH REPORT 880
    RESEARCH REVIEWS 880
    RESEARCH UTILIZATION 204
    SCIENTIFIC RESEARCH 140
    STUDENT RESEARCH 357
RESEARCHERS
    EDUCATIONAL RESEARCHERS 430
    RESEARCHERS 430
RESIDENCE
    RESIDENCE CHARGES 240
RESIDENT
    RESIDENT STUDENTS 413
RESIDENTIAL
    RESIDENTIAL ADULT CENTRES 311
    RESIDENTIAL ADULT EDUCATION 184
    RESIDENTIAL CARE 374

RESIDENTIAL
    RESIDENTIAL COLLEGES 307
    RESIDENTIAL PROGRAMMES 321
RESOLUTION
    CONFLICT RESOLUTION 572
RESOURCE
    RESOURCE ALLOCATIONS 243
    RESOURCE MATERIALS 700
    RESOURCE PERSONS 421
    RESOURCE TEACHERS 426
RESOURCES
    COMMUNITY RESOURCES 700
    EDUCATIONAL RESOURCES 700
    FINANCIAL RESOURCES 240
    HUMAN RESOURCES 153
    HUMAN RESOURCES DEVELOPMENT 151
    MEDIA RESOURCES CENTRES 312
    NATURAL RESOURCES 700
    RESOURCES 700
RESPONSE
    CONDITIONED RESPONSE 511
    RESPONSE MODE 511
RESPONSIBILITY
    ADMINISTRATOR RESPONSIBILITY 231
    CHILD RESPONSIBILITY 231
    LEGAL RESPONSIBILITY 170
    NONINSTRUCTIONAL RESPONSIBILITY 231
    PARENT RESPONSIBILITY 231
    RESPONSIBILITY 231
    SCHOOL RESPONSIBILITY 231
    TEACHER RESPONSIBILITY 231
RESULTS
    TEST RESULTS 392
RETARDATION
    MENTAL RETARDATION 570
    RETARDATION 372
RETARDED
    RETARDED CHILDREN 403
RETENTION
    LITERACY RETENTION 535
    RETENTION 535
RETIRED
    RETIRED PERSONS 400
RETIREMENT
    PRE RETIREMENT EDUCATION 183
    PRE RETIREMENT PROGRAMMES 321
    RETIREMENT 222
RETRAINING
    RETRAINING 351
RETURNERS
    MARRIED WOMEN RETURNERS 451
REUNION
    REUNION ISLAND 809
REVENUE
    REVENUE 240
REVIEW
    LITERATURE REVIEW 880
REVIEWS
    RESEARCH REVIEWS 880
REWARDS
    REWARDS 511
RICA
    COSTA RICA 803
RICO
    PUERTO RICO 803
RIGHT
    RIGHT TO EDUCATION 180
RIGHTS
    CIVIL RIGHTS 170
    HUMAN RIGHTS 100
ROEAO
    ROEAO 851
ROLE
    ADMINISTRATOR ROLE 262
    AGENCY ROLE 105
    CITIZEN ROLE 105
    COLLEGE ROLE 187
    COMMUNITY ROLE 105
    FAMILY ROLE 126
    GOVERNMENT ROLE 105
    LANGUAGE ROLE 285
    MINORITY ROLE 123
    PARENT ROLE 553
    RELIGIOUS INSTITUTION ROLE 125
    ROLE CONFLICT 553
    ROLE EDUCATION 183
    ROLE PERCEPTION 553
    ROLE PLAYING 553
    ROLE THEORY 553
    SCHOOL ROLE 187
    STUDENT ROLE 187

ROLE
    SUPERINTENDENT ROLE 262
    TEACHER ROLE 187
ROMANCE
    ROMANCE LANGUAGES 625
ROMANIA
    ROMANIA 805
ROMANTICISM
    ROMANTICISM 615
ROTE
    ROTE LEARNING 512
ROUND
    YEAR ROUND SCHOOLS 303
RURAL
    INTEGRATED RURAL DEVELOPMENT 151
    RURAL AREAS 122
    RURAL DEVELOPMENT 151
    RURAL EDUCATION 186
    RURAL EXTENSION 382
    RURAL EXTENSION PROGRAMMES 321
    RURAL FAMILY 126
    RURAL POPULATION 124
    RURAL SCHOOL SYSTEMS 260
    RURAL SCHOOL TEACHERS 421
    RURAL SCHOOLS 303
    RURAL URBAN DIFFERENCES 122
    RURAL YOUTH 400
RUSSIAN
    RUSSIAN 626
    RUSSIAN SFSR 805
RWANDA
    RWANDA 802
RYUKU
    RYUKU ISLANDS 804
SABAH
    SABAH 804
SAFETY
    SAFETY 264
    SAFETY EDUCATION 683
    TRAFFIC SAFETY 264
SAHARA
    AFRICA SOUTH OF THE SAHARA 801
    WESTERN SAHARA 801
SAINT
    SAINT BARTHELEMY 803
    SAINT HELENA 808

SAINT
    SAINT KITTS–NEVIS–ANGUILLA 803
    SAINT LUCIA 803
    SAINT MARTIN 803
    SAINT PIERRE AND MIQUELON ISLANDS 803
    SAINT VINCENT 803
SALARIES
    SALARIES 242
    TEACHER SALARIES 242
SALESMEN
    SALESMEN 451
SALVADOR
    EL SALVADOR 803
SAMOA
    AMERICAN SAMOA 806
    SAMOA 806
SAMPLING
    SAMPLING 283
SANCTIONS
    SANCTIONS 233
SANDWICH
    SANDWICH COURSES 333
SANTA
    SANTA CRUZ ISLANDS 806
SARAWAK
    SARAWAK 804
SATELLITES
    COMMUNICATIONS SATELLITES 731
SATIRE
    SATIRE 616
SATISFACTION
    JOB SATISFACTION 563
    PARTICIPANT SATISFACTION 554
SAUDI
    SAUDI ARABIA 807
SCALE
    SMALL SCALE INDUSTRY 150
SCALES
    RATING SCALES 392
SCANDINAVIA
    SCANDINAVIA 801
SCHEDULING
    SCHEDULING 201
SCHEMES
    CONCEPTUAL SCHEMES 522
SCHOLARSHIPS
    SCHOLARSHIPS 242

SCHOOL
- ADULT EDUCATION SCHOOL COOPERATION 263
- COLLEGE SCHOOL COOPERATION 265
- DEPARTMENTS (SCHOOL) 340
- EXTENDED SCHOOL YEAR 344
- FAMILY SCHOOL RELATIONSHIP 380
- HEADS OF DEPARTMENT (SCHOOL) 423
- OUT OF SCHOOL ACTIVITIES 357
- OUT OF SCHOOL ACTIVITY CENTRES 311
- OUT OF SCHOOL EDUCATION 184
- OUT OF SCHOOL YOUTH 412
- PARAPROFESSIONAL SCHOOL PERSONNEL 423
- POLICE SCHOOL RELATIONSHIP 263
- PRIMARY SCHOOL CERTIFICATES 390
- PRIMARY SCHOOL COUNSELLORS 431
- PRIMARY SCHOOL CURRICULUM 330
- PRIMARY SCHOOL INSPECTORS 420
- PRIMARY SCHOOL MATHEMATICS 670
- PRIMARY SCHOOL SCIENCE 670
- PRIMARY SCHOOL STUDENTS 411
- PRIMARY SCHOOL TEACHERS 421
- PRIVATE SCHOOL TEACHERS 423
- PUBLIC SCHOOL SYSTEMS 260
- PUBLIC SCHOOL TEACHERS 423
- RURAL SCHOOL SYSTEMS 260
- RURAL SCHOOL TEACHERS 421
- SCHOOL ACCOUNTING 243
- SCHOOL ACTIVITIES 357
- SCHOOL ADMINISTRATION 265

SCHOOL
- SCHOOL AGE POPULATION 206
- SCHOOL ATTENDANCE LAWS 230
- SCHOOL ATTITUDES 552
- SCHOOL BUSES 743
- SCHOOL CALENDARS 344
- SCHOOL CLOSURE 263
- SCHOOL COMMUNITY COOPERATION 263
- SCHOOL COMMUNITY PROGRAMMES 272
- SCHOOL COMMUNITY RELATIONSHIP 263
- SCHOOL DISTRIBUTION 208
- SCHOOL DISTRICT AUTONOMY 263
- SCHOOL DISTRICTS 264
- SCHOOL FUNDS 240
- SCHOOL GOVERNANCE 230
- SCHOOL HEALTH SERVICES 270
- SCHOOL HOLDING POWER 208
- SCHOOL INDUSTRY RELATIONSHIP 263
- SCHOOL INTEGRATION 230
- SCHOOL LEAVERS 411
- SCHOOL LEAVING 266
- SCHOOL LIBRARIANS 462
- SCHOOL LIBRARIES 310
- SCHOOL MAINTENANCE 265
- SCHOOL MAPPING 208
- SCHOOL MEAL PROGRAMMES 272
- SCHOOL NURSES 433
- SCHOOL ORGANIZATION 340
- SCHOOL PERSONNEL 423
- SCHOOL PLANNING 205
- SCHOOL PSYCHOLOGISTS 430
- SCHOOL PUBLICATIONS 720
- SCHOOL READINESS 531
- SCHOOL RECREATIONAL PROGRAMMES 272
- SCHOOL REDISTRICTING 264
- SCHOOL REGISTRATION 264
- SCHOOL REGULATIONS 230
- SCHOOL RESPONSIBILITY 231
- SCHOOL ROLE 187
- SCHOOL SEGREGATION 180
- SCHOOL SERVICES 270

SCHOOL
- SCHOOL SHOPS 742
- SCHOOL SIZE 208
- SCHOOL STATISTICS 208
- SCHOOL SUPERVISION 210
- SCHOOL SURVEYS 203
- SCHOOL SYSTEMS 260
- SCHOOL TAXES 240
- SECONDARY SCHOOL CERTIFICATES 390
- SECONDARY SCHOOL COUNSELLORS 431
- SECONDARY SCHOOL CURRICULUM 330
- SECONDARY SCHOOL GRADUATES 411
- SECONDARY SCHOOL INSPECTORS 420
- SECONDARY SCHOOL MATHEMATICS 670
- SECONDARY SCHOOL SCIENCE 670
- SECONDARY SCHOOL STUDENTS 411
- SECONDARY SCHOOL TEACHERS 421
- STUDENT SCHOOL RELATIONSHIP 380
- VOCATIONAL SCHOOL CERTIFICATES 390
- VOCATIONAL SCHOOL CURRICULUM 330

SCHOOLS
- ACTIVE SCHOOLS 184
- ADULT SCHOOLS 187
- AFFILIATED SCHOOLS 305
- ASSOCIATED SCHOOLS (UNESCO) 305
- BASIC SCHOOLS 301
- BOARDING SCHOOLS 303
- COEDUCATIONAL SCHOOLS 303
- COMMUNITY SCHOOLS 302
- COMPREHENSIVE SCHOOLS 306
- COMPREHENSIVE SECONDARY SCHOOLS 306
- CONSOLIDATION OF SCHOOLS 264
- CORRECTIONAL SCHOOLS 304
- CORRESPONDENCE SCHOOLS 303

SCHOOLS
- DAY SCHOOLS 303
- DISADVANTAGED SCHOOLS 304
- DOUBLE SHIFT SCHOOLS 303
- EVENING SCHOOLS 303
- EXPERIMENTAL SCHOOLS 305
- EXTENDED DAY SCHOOLS 303
- GENERAL SECONDARY SCHOOLS 306
- HOSPITAL SCHOOLS 304
- INTERNATIONAL SCHOOLS 302
- LABORATORY SCHOOLS 305
- LOWER SECONDARY SCHOOLS 301
- MIDDLE SCHOOLS 301
- MOBILE SCHOOLS 303
- NONGRADED SCHOOLS 303
- NURSERY SCHOOLS 301
- ONE TEACHER SCHOOLS 303
- OPEN PLAN SCHOOLS 340
- PRIMARY SCHOOLS 301
- PRIVATE SCHOOLS 302
- PROPRIETARY SCHOOLS 302
- PUBLIC SCHOOLS 302
- RURAL SCHOOLS 303
- SCHOOLS 187
- SECONDARY SCHOOLS 301
- SMALL SCHOOLS 208
- SPECIAL SCHOOLS 304
- SUBURBAN SCHOOLS 303
- SUMMER SCHOOLS 303
- TEACHER TRAINING SCHOOLS 690
- TECHNICAL SECONDARY SCHOOLS 306
- UPPER SECONDARY SCHOOLS 301
- URBAN SCHOOLS 303
- VOCATIONAL SCHOOLS 306
- VOCATIONAL SECONDARY SCHOOLS 306
- WEEKEND SCHOOLS 303
- YEAR ROUND SCHOOLS 303

SCIENCE
- ANIMAL SCIENCE 646
- BEHAVIOURAL SCIENCE RESEARCH 280
- ELEMENTARY SCIENCE 670
- GENERAL SCIENCE 670

SCIENCE
- INFORMATION SCIENCE 630
- LIBRARY SCIENCE 650
- LIBRARY SCIENCE TRAINING 681
- MILITARY SCIENCE 630
- POLITICAL SCIENCE 640
- PRIMARY SCHOOL SCIENCE 670
- SCIENCE 140
- SCIENCE CONSULTANTS 430
- SCIENCE EDUCATION 670
- SCIENCE EQUIPMENT 740
- SCIENCE EXPERIMENTS 671
- SCIENCE INSTRUCTION 670
- SCIENCE PROGRAMMES 670
- SCIENCE TEACHERS 425
- SCIENCE TEACHING CENTRES 312
- SCIENCE TESTS 393
- SECONDARY SCHOOL SCIENCE 670

SCIENCES
- BEHAVIOURAL SCIENCES 642
- COMPUTER SCIENCES 630
- EARTH SCIENCES 633
- EDUCATIONAL SCIENCES 640
- SCIENCES 630
- SOCIAL SCIENCES 640

SCIENTIFIC
- SCIENTIFIC CONCEPTS 630
- SCIENTIFIC MANPOWER 154
- SCIENTIFIC PERSONNEL 441
- SCIENTIFIC PRINCIPLES 140
- SCIENTIFIC RESEARCH 140

SCIENTISTS
- SCIENTISTS 463
- SOCIAL SCIENTISTS 462

SCRIPTS
- SCRIPTS 721

SCULPTURE
- SCULPTURE 610

SEAFARER
- SEAFARER EDUCATION 186

SEAFARERS
- SEAFARERS 451

SEAMEO
- SEAMEO 852

SEASONAL
- SEASONAL EMPLOYMENT 154
- SEASONAL WORKERS 451

SECOND
- SECOND LANGUAGE INSTRUCTION 662
- SECOND LANGUAGES 131

SECONDARY
- COMPREHENSIVE SECONDARY SCHOOLS 306
- GENERAL SECONDARY SCHOOLS 306
- LOWER SECONDARY EDUCATION 185
- LOWER SECONDARY SCHOOLS 301
- SECONDARY EDUCATION 185
- SECONDARY GRADES 342
- SECONDARY SCHOOL CERTIFICATES 390
- SECONDARY SCHOOL COUNSELLORS 431
- SECONDARY SCHOOL CURRICULUM 330
- SECONDARY SCHOOL GRADUATES 411
- SECONDARY SCHOOL INSPECTORS 420
- SECONDARY SCHOOL MATHEMATICS 670
- SECONDARY SCHOOL SCIENCE 670
- SECONDARY SCHOOL STUDENTS 411
- SECONDARY SCHOOL TEACHERS 421
- SECONDARY SCHOOLS 301
- TECHNICAL SECONDARY SCHOOLS 306
- UPPER SECONDARY EDUCATION 185
- UPPER SECONDARY SCHOOLS 301
- VOCATIONAL SECONDARY SCHOOLS 306

SECRETARIAT
- COMMONWEALTH SECRETARIAT 852
- UNESCO SECRETARIAT 851

SECTOR
- UNESCO EDUCATION SECTOR 851

SECULAR
- SECULAR EDUCATION 180

SECURITY
  SECURITY 540
  SECURITY COUNCIL 850
SEE
  HOLY SEE 805
SEEKING
  INFORMATION SEEKING 541
SEGREGATION
  AGE SEGREGATION 341
  RACIAL SEGREGATION 123
  SCHOOL SEGREGATION 180
SELECTION
  ADMINISTRATOR SELECTION 223
  ANIMATEUR SELECTION 223
  COMPETITIVE SELECTION 266
  MATERIALS SELECTION 265
  SELECTION 266
  SELECTION PROCEDURES 266
  TEACHER SELECTION 223
SELF
  INSTITUTIONAL SELF MANAGEMENT 261
  SELF ACTUALIZATION 555
  SELF CONCEPT 555
  SELF CONTROL 560
  SELF DIRECTED GROUPS 443
  SELF EMPLOYED 450
  SELF EVALUATION 555
  SELF EXPRESSION 555
  SELF INSTRUCTION 352
  SELF INSTRUCTIONAL AIDS 730
  SELF INSTRUCTIONAL METHODS 355
  SELF INSTRUCTIONAL PROGRAMMES 320
SEMANTICS
  SEMANTICS 622
SEMESTER
  SEMESTER DIVISIONS 344
SEMINARS
  EDUCATIONAL SEMINARS 204
  SEMINARS 355
  TEACHER SEMINARS 691
SEMISKILLED
  SEMISKILLED OCCUPATIONS 155
  SEMISKILLED WORKERS 451
SENEGAL
  SENEGAL 802

SENESCENCE
  SENESCENCE 531
SENIOR
  SENIOR CIVIL SERVANTS 460
SENSORY
  SENSORY AIDS 734
  SENSORY DEPRIVATION 570
  SENSORY EXPERIENCE 562
  SENSORY TRAINING 351
SENTENCE
  SENTENCE STRUCTURE 622
SEPARATION
  STATE CHURCH SEPARATION 101
SEQUENTIAL
  SEQUENTIAL APPROACH 331
  SEQUENTIAL LEARNING 512
SERIALS
  SERIALS 720
SERVANTS
  CIVIL SERVANTS 460
  SENIOR CIVIL SERVANTS 460
SERVICE
  NATIONAL SERVICE 125
  SERVICE INDUSTRIES 150
  SERVICE OCCUPATIONS 155
  SERVICE WORKERS 451
SERVICES
  ADULT SERVICES 107
  ANCILLARY SERVICES 270
  COMMUNITY SERVICES 107
  DAY CARE SERVICES 270
  EMPLOYMENT SERVICES 154
  FINANCIAL SERVICES 150
  FOOD SERVICES 160
  GUIDANCE SERVICES 270
  HEALTH SERVICES 107
  INFORMATION SERVICES 107
  LIBRARY SERVICES 270
  MEDICAL SERVICES 160
  MOBILE EDUCATIONAL SERVICES 270
  PROFESSIONAL SERVICES 270
  SCHOOL HEALTH SERVICES 270
  SCHOOL SERVICES 270
  SERVICES 107
  SHARED SERVICES 270
  SOCIAL SERVICES 107
  SOCIOPSYCHOLOGICAL SERVICES 270

SERVICES
    STUDENT PERSONNEL SERVICES 270
    VOLUNTARY SERVICES 154
    WELFARE SERVICES 107
    YOUTH SERVICES 107
SET
    MENTAL SET 513
SETTLEMENT
    DISPUTE SETTLEMENT 233
SETTLEMENTS
    COLLECTIVE SETTLEMENTS 122
SEVENTEENTH
    SEVENTEENTH CENTURY 840
SEX
    SEX (CHARACTERISTICS) 501
    SEX DIFFERENCES 501
    SEX EDUCATION 683
SEXUALITY
    SEXUALITY 502
SEYCHELLES
    SEYCHELLES 809
SHARED
    SHARED SERVICES 270
SHARING
    TIME SHARING 284
SHELTERED
    SHELTERED EMPLOYMENT 374
SHIFT
    DOUBLE SHIFT SCHOOLS 303
SHOP
    SHOP CURRICULUM 672
SHOPS
    SCHOOL SHOPS 742
SHORT
    SHORT COURSES 334
    SHORT STORIES 616
    SHORT TERM MEMORY 521
SHORTAGE
    TEACHER SHORTAGE 207
    TEXTBOOK SHORTAGE 205
SIBERIA
    SIBERIA 805
SIBLINGS
    SIBLINGS 401
SIERRA
    SIERRA LEONE 802
SIGHT
    SIGHT 503
    SIGHT METHOD 661

SIGHT
    SIGHT VOCABULARY 620
SIGHTED
    PARTIALLY SIGHTED 403
SIGNIFICANCE
    TESTS OF SIGNIFICANCE 284
SIKKIM
    SIKKIM 804
SILENT
    SILENT READING 661
SIMULATION
    SIMULATION 355
SINGAPORE
    SINGAPORE 804
SINGING
    SINGING 610
SINGLE
    SINGLE CONCEPT FILMS 730
SINO
    SINO TIBETAN LANGUAGES 625
SITE
    SITE PLANNING 250
SITES
    SITES 710
SIZE
    CLASS SIZE 343
    SCHOOL SIZE 208
SKILL
    SKILL ANALYSIS 331
    SKILL DEVELOPMENT 534
    SKILL OBSOLESCENCE 181
SKILLED
    SKILLED OCCUPATIONS 155
    SKILLED WORKERS 451
SKILLS
    BASIC SKILLS 533
    COMMUNICATION SKILLS 533
    LANGUAGE SKILLS 533
    MECHANICAL SKILLS 533
    PSYCHOMOTOR SKILLS 533
    SKILLS 533
    STUDY SKILLS 533
    TEACHING SKILLS 533
SLAVIC
    SLAVIC LANGUAGES 625
SLEEP
    SLEEP 503
SLIDE
    SOUND SLIDE PRESENTATIONS 732

SLIDES
   SLIDES 730
SLOW
   SLOW LEARNERS 415
SMALL
   SMALL SCALE INDUSTRY 150
   SMALL SCHOOLS 208
SMOKING
   SMOKING 542
SOCIAL
   ANTI SOCIAL BEHAVIOUR 572
   SOCIAL ACTION 120
   SOCIAL ADJUSTMENT 551
   SOCIAL ADVANCEMENT 121
   SOCIAL AGENCIES 103
   SOCIAL ATTITUDES 552
   SOCIAL BACKGROUND 120
   SOCIAL CHANGE 120
   SOCIAL CLASS 121
   SOCIAL DEVELOPMENT 151
   SOCIAL DISADVANTAGEMENT 121
   SOCIAL DISCRIMINATION 121
   SOCIAL DISENGAGEMENT 531
   SOCIAL ENVIRONMENT 550
   SOCIAL EXPERIENCE 562
   SOCIAL FACTORS 285
   SOCIAL INTEGRATION 121
   SOCIAL MATURITY 531
   SOCIAL MOBILITY 121
   SOCIAL PLANNING 120
   SOCIAL POLICIES 120
   SOCIAL PROBLEMS 121
   SOCIAL PSYCHOLOGY 642
   SOCIAL RELATIONS 553
   SOCIAL SCIENCES 640
   SOCIAL SCIENTISTS 462
   SOCIAL SERVICES 107
   SOCIAL STATUS 121
   SOCIAL STUDIES 640
   SOCIAL SYSTEMS 120
   SOCIAL WELFARE 100
   SOCIAL WORK 120
   SOCIAL WORKERS 462
SOCIALIZATION
   POLITICAL SOCIALIZATION 553
   SOCIALIZATION 553
SOCIALLY
   SOCIALLY DISADVANTAGED 402
   SOCIALLY MALADJUSTED 403

SOCIETY
   POST INDUSTRIAL SOCIETY 150
   PRE INDUSTRIAL SOCIETY 150
   SOCIETY ISLANDS 806
SOCIOCULTURAL
   SOCIOCULTURAL FACILITIES 710
   SOCIOCULTURAL PATTERNS 120
SOCIOECONOMIC
   SOCIOECONOMIC BACKGROUND 120
   SOCIOECONOMIC STATUS 121
SOCIOLOGICAL
   FAMILY (SOCIOLOGICAL UNIT) 126
SOCIOLOGY
   EDUCATIONAL SOCIOLOGY 642
   SOCIOLOGY 642
SOCIOMETRIC
   SOCIOMETRIC TECHNIQUES 283
SOCIOPSYCHOLOGICAL
   SOCIOPSYCHOLOGICAL SERVICES 270
SOIL
   SOIL CONSERVATION 646
SOLOMON
   SOLOMON ISLANDS 806
SOLVING
   PROBLEM SOLVING 522
SOMALIA
   SOMALIA 802
SOUND
   SOUND FILMS 730
   SOUND SLIDE PRESENTATIONS 732
SOUTH
   AFRICA SOUTH OF THE SAHARA 801
   SOUTH AFRICA (REPUBLIC) 802
   SOUTH AMERICA 801
   SOUTH ASIA 804
   SOUTH EAST ASIA 801
   SOUTH POLE 801
SOUTHERN
   SOUTHERN AFRICA 801
   SOUTHERN HEMISPHERE 801

SPACE
    SPACE STANDARDS 250
SPACES
    ANCILLARY SPACES 712
    EDUCATIONAL SPACES 711
SPAIN
    SPAIN 805
SPAN
    ATTENTION SPAN 535
SPANISH
    SPANISH 626
SPEAKING
    ENGLISH SPEAKING AFRICA 801
    FRENCH SPEAKING AFRICA 801
    SPEAKING 620
    SPEAKING ACTIVITIES 537
SPECIAL
    SPECIAL CLASSES 343
    SPECIAL CLASSROOMS 711
    SPECIAL DEGREE PROGRAMMES 320
    SPECIAL EDUCATION 186
    SPECIAL EDUCATION TEACHERS 421
    SPECIAL PROGRAMMES 320
    SPECIAL SCHOOLS 304
SPECIALIST
    SPECIALIST IN EDUCATION DEGREES 390
SPECIALISTS
    CHILD DEVELOPMENT SPECIALISTS 430
    INFORMATION SPECIALISTS 462
    LEARNING SPECIALISTS 430
    MEDIA SPECIALISTS 430
    SPECIALISTS 430
SPECIFICATIONS
    EDUCATIONAL SPECIFICATIONS 232
    PERFORMANCE SPECIFICATIONS 232
    SPECIFICATIONS 232
SPEECH
    ARTICULATION (SPEECH) 532
    CODED SPEECH 374
    FREEDOM OF SPEECH 100
    SPEECH 532
    SPEECH HABITS 542
    SPEECH HANDICAPS 571

SPEECH
    SPEECH INSTRUCTION 662
    SPEECH PATHOLOGY 372
    SPEECH THERAPISTS 432
    SPEECH THERAPY 373
SPEED
    LEARNING SPEED 513
SPELLING
    SPELLING 620
    SPELLING INSTRUCTION 663
SPORTS
    SPORTS FACILITIES 712
STAFF
    STAFF HOUSING 712
STAFFS
    DIFFERENTIATED STAFFS 424
STAGES
    TRAINING BY STAGES 351
STANDARDIZED
    STANDARDIZED TESTS 392
STANDARDS
    ACADEMIC STANDARDS 391
    EQUIPMENT STANDARDS 232
    LIVING STANDARDS 150
    SPACE STANDARDS 250
    STANDARDS 232
STATE
    STATE AID TO PROVINCES 106
    STATE CHURCH SEPARATION 101
STATES
    GULF STATES 807
    HIMALAYAN STATES 804
    LEAGUE OF ARAB STATES 852
STATISTICAL
    STATISTICAL ANALYSIS 284
    STATISTICAL DATA 284
    STATISTICAL STUDIES 282
    STATISTICAL TABLES 880
STATISTICS
    EDUCATIONAL STATISTICS 284
    EMPLOYMENT STATISTICS 154
    LITERACY STATISTICS 284
    SCHOOL STATISTICS 208
STATUS
    ECONOMIC STATUS 121
    MARITAL STATUS 126
    SOCIAL STATUS 121
    SOCIOECONOMIC STATUS 121
    STATUS 121

STATUS
- STATUS NEED 536
- TEACHER STATUS 187

STEREOTYPES
- STEREOTYPES 552

STIMULANTS
- STIMULANTS 751

STIMULI
- AURAL STIMULI 510
- STIMULI 361
- VISUAL STIMULI 510

STIMULUS
- STIMULUS DEVICES 734

STORIES
- SHORT STORIES 616

STORY
- STORY TELLING 663

STRATEGIES
- EDUCATIONAL STRATEGIES 182
- EMPLOYMENT STRATEGIES 154

STRIKES
- TEACHER STRIKES 233

STRUCTURAL
- STRUCTURAL ANALYSIS 331
- STRUCTURAL GRAMMAR 622

STRUCTURE
- FAMILY STRUCTURE 126
- FEDERATIVE STRUCTURE 102
- GOVERNMENTAL STRUCTURE 103
- GROUP STRUCTURE 122
- SENTENCE STRUCTURE 622

STUDENT
- ADULT STUDENT–INSTITUTION RELATIONSHIP 380
- ALLOCATION PER STUDENT 243
- EXPENDITURE PER STUDENT 243
- FOREIGN STUDENT ADVISERS 431
- PARENT STUDENT RELATIONSHIP 380
- STUDENT ACHIEVEMENT 535
- STUDENT ADJUSTMENT 551
- STUDENT ATTITUDES 552
- STUDENT BEHAVIOUR 560
- STUDENT CHARACTERISTICS 561

STUDENT
- STUDENT COLLEGE RELATIONSHIP 380
- STUDENT DEVELOPED MATERIALS 725
- STUDENT EMPLOYMENT 266
- STUDENT EVALUATION 391
- STUDENT HOUSING 712
- STUDENT LOANS 242
- STUDENT MOBILITY 206
- STUDENT MOTIVATION 541
- STUDENT NEEDS 350
- STUDENT ORGANIZATIONS 110
- STUDENT PARTICIPATION 380
- STUDENT PERSONNEL SERVICES 270
- STUDENT PROGRESS 266
- STUDENT PROJECTS 357
- STUDENT PROMOTION 266
- STUDENT RECORDS 723
- STUDENT RECRUITMENT 266
- STUDENT RESEARCH 357
- STUDENT ROLE 187
- STUDENT SCHOOL RELATIONSHIP 380
- STUDENT TEACHER RATIO 207
- STUDENT TEACHER RELATIONSHIP 380
- STUDENT TEACHERS 424
- STUDENT TRANSFER 266
- STUDENT TURNOVER 206
- STUDENT UNREST 380
- STUDENT WELFARE 200

STUDENTS
- ABLE STUDENTS 416
- ADULT STUDENTS 412
- ADVANCED STUDENTS 416
- AVERAGE STUDENTS 416
- BILINGUAL STUDENTS 414
- COLLEGE STUDENTS 413
- CONTINUATION STUDENTS 412
- DAY STUDENTS 410
- EVENING STUDENTS 410
- EXCEPTIONAL STUDENTS 416
- FOREIGN STUDENTS 413
- FULL TIME STUDENTS 410
- GIFTED STUDENTS 416
- HANDICAPPED STUDENTS 411
- MARRIED STUDENTS 413

333

STUDENTS
   PART TIME STUDENTS 410
   PAST STUDENTS 410
   POSTGRADUATE STUDENTS 413
   PRIMARY SCHOOL STUDENTS 411
   RESIDENT STUDENTS 413
   SECONDARY SCHOOL STUDENTS 411
   STUDENTS 410
   TRANSFER STUDENTS 411
   UNILINGUAL STUDENTS 414
STUDIES
   AREA STUDIES 680
   CASE STUDIES 282
   CROSS CULTURAL STUDIES 282
   DEVELOPMENT STUDIES 640
   FEASIBILITY STUDIES 282
   FIELD STUDIES 282
   FOLLOWUP STUDIES 282
   LONGITUDINAL STUDIES 282
   OBSERVATIONAL STUDIES 282
   PERSONALITY STUDIES 282
   PSYCHOLOGICAL STUDIES 282
   SOCIAL STUDIES 640
   STATISTICAL STUDIES 282
STUDY
   CASE STUDY METHODS 355
   COMMUNITY STUDY 680
   CURRICULUM STUDY CENTRES 312
   DIRECTED STUDY 335
   DISTANCE STUDY 335
   GRADUATE STUDY 330
   HOME STUDY 335
   INDEPENDENT STUDY 335
   INDIVIDUAL STUDY 335
   STUDY 512
   STUDY ABROAD 335
   STUDY CENTRES 311
   STUDY GUIDE 880
   STUDY HABITS 542
   STUDY SKILLS 533
   STUDY TOURS 335
   SUBJECTS OF STUDY 331
   UNDERGRADUATE STUDY 330
   UNITS OF STUDY (SUBJECT FIELDS) 331
STYLES
   TEACHING STYLES 356

SUBJECT
   UNITS OF STUDY (SUBJECT FIELDS) 331
SUBJECTS
   BUSINESS SUBJECTS 673
   SUBJECTS OF STUDY 331
SUBSCRIPTIONS
   SUBSCRIPTIONS 240
SUBSIDIZED
   NON SUBSIDIZED ORGANIZATIONS 110
SUBSIDY
   CONDITIONS OF SUBSIDY 241
SUBSTITUTE
   SUBSTITUTE TEACHERS 424
SUBURBAN
   SUBURBAN SCHOOLS 303
SUBVENTIONS
   SUBVENTIONS 241
SUCCESS
   SUCCESS 535
   SUCCESS FACTORS 285
SUDAN
   SUDAN 807
SUMMATIVE
   SUMMATIVE EVALUATION 205
SUMMER
   SUMMER SCHOOLS 303
SUPERINTENDENT
   SUPERINTENDENT ROLE 262
SUPERINTENDENTS
   SUPERINTENDENTS 420
SUPERVISED
   SUPERVISED FARM PRACTICE 673
SUPERVISION
   GOVERNMENT SUPERVISION 105
   SCHOOL SUPERVISION 210
   SUPERVISION 210
   TEACHER SUPERVISION 210
SUPERVISOR
   SUPERVISOR QUALIFICATIONS 223
SUPERVISORS
   COLLEGE SUPERVISORS 426
   SUPERVISORS 420
SUPERVISORY
   SUPERVISORY METHODS 210
SUPPLEMENTARY
   SUPPLEMENTARY READING MATERIALS 725

SUPPLEMENTARY
    SUPPLEMENTARY TEXTBOOK 880
SUPPLIES
    AGRICULTURAL SUPPLIES 750
    MEDICAL SUPPLIES 751
    SUPPLIES 740
SUPPLY
    TEACHER SUPPLY AND DEMAND 207
SUPPORT
    FINANCIAL SUPPORT 240
    PRIVATE FINANCIAL SUPPORT 240
    PUBLIC SUPPORT 100
SURGEONS
    SURGEONS 433
SURINAME
    SURINAME 803
SURVEYING
    QUANTITY SURVEYING 650
SURVEYORS
    SURVEYORS 452
SURVEYS
    INTERNATIONAL SURVEYS 203
    NATIONAL SURVEYS 203
    OCCUPATIONAL SURVEYS 282
    PROVINCIAL SURVEYS 203
    REGIONAL SURVEYS 203
    SCHOOL SURVEYS 203
    SURVEYS 203
SWAZILAND
    SWAZILAND 802
SWEDEN
    SWEDEN 805
SWITZERLAND
    SWITZERLAND 805
SYLLABUSES
    SYLLABUSES 331
SYMBOLIC
    SYMBOLIC LEARNING 512
SYMBOLS
    ORTHOGRAPHIC SYMBOLS 620
    SYMBOLS (LITERARY) 615
SYMPOSIA
    SYMPOSIA 204
SYNDROME
    DOWNS SYNDROME 570
SYNTAX
    SYNTAX 622

SYRIAN
    SYRIAN AR 807
SYSTEM
    CARDIOVASCULAR SYSTEM 502
    CREDIT SYSTEM 390
    METRIC SYSTEM 631
    NERVOUS SYSTEM 502
    NONGRADED SYSTEM 340
    QUARTER SYSTEM 344
    QUOTA SYSTEM 205
SYSTEMS
    ADULT EDUCATION SYSTEMS 260
    INCENTIVE SYSTEMS 233
    INFORMATION SYSTEMS 201
    MANAGEMENT SYSTEMS 201
    MIXED SYSTEMS 260
    OPEN LEARNING SYSTEMS 355
    PRIVATE EDUCATION SYSTEMS 260
    PUBLIC EDUCATION SYSTEMS 260
    PUBLIC SCHOOL SYSTEMS 260
    RURAL SCHOOL SYSTEMS 260
    SCHOOL SYSTEMS 260
    SOCIAL SYSTEMS 120
    SYSTEMS ANALYSIS 201
TABLES
    STATISTICAL TABLES 880
TACTILE
    TACTILE ADAPTATION 374
TAIWAN
    TAIWAN 804
TALENT
    TALENT 520
    TALENT IDENTIFICATION 211
TANZANIA
    TANZANIA UR 802
TAPE
    TAPE RECORDERS 731
    TAPE RECORDINGS 732
    VIDEO TAPE RECORDINGS 732
TARGET
    TARGET GROUPS 443
TASMANIA
    TASMANIA 806
TAX
    TAX ALLOCATION 152
    TAX EFFORT 152

TAXES
    ADULT EDUCATION TAXES 240
    SCHOOL TAXES 240
    TAXES 152
    VOCATIONAL TRAINING TAXES 240

TAXONOMY
    TAXONOMY 283

TEACHABLE
    TEACHABLE MOMENTS 531

TEACHER
    INSERVICE TEACHER EDUCATION 690
    ONE TEACHER SCHOOLS 303
    PARENT TEACHER ASSOCIATIONS 110
    PARENT TEACHER COOPERATION 380
    PRESERVICE TEACHER EDUCATION 690
    STUDENT TEACHER RATIO 207
    STUDENT TEACHER RELATIONSHIP 380
    TEACHER ADMINISTRATION RELATIONSHIP 262
    TEACHER AIDES 424
    TEACHER ASSOCIATIONS 110
    TEACHER ATTITUDES 350
    TEACHER BACKGROUND 223
    TEACHER BEHAVIOUR 560
    TEACHER CENTRES 312
    TEACHER CERTIFICATION 390
    TEACHER CHARACTERISTICS 350
    TEACHER COUNSELLING 371
    TEACHER DEVELOPED MATERIALS 725
    TEACHER DISTRIBUTION 207
    TEACHER EDUCATION 690
    TEACHER EDUCATION CURRICULUM 330
    TEACHER EDUCATOR EDUCATION 690
    TEACHER EDUCATORS 422
    TEACHER EMPLOYMENT 223
    TEACHER EVALUATION 212
    TEACHER IMPROVEMENT 212
    TEACHER INFLUENCE 350
    TEACHER INTERNS 424
    TEACHER MOBILITY 207

TEACHER
    TEACHER MOTIVATION 350
    TEACHER ORIENTATION 690
    TEACHER PARTICIPATION 380
    TEACHER PLACEMENT 223
    TEACHER PROFILE 223
    TEACHER PROMOTION 223
    TEACHER QUALIFICATIONS 223
    TEACHER RESPONSIBILITY 231
    TEACHER ROLE 187
    TEACHER SALARIES 242
    TEACHER SELECTION 223
    TEACHER SEMINARS 691
    TEACHER SHORTAGE 207
    TEACHER STATUS 187
    TEACHER STRIKES 233
    TEACHER SUPERVISION 210
    TEACHER SUPPLY AND DEMAND 207
    TEACHER TRAINING SCHOOLS 690
    TEACHER TRANSFER 223
    TEACHER WELFARE 200

TEACHERS
    ART TEACHERS 425
    BEGINNING TEACHERS 424
    BILINGUAL TEACHERS 426
    COACHING TEACHERS 425
    COLLEGE TEACHERS 422
    EXTENSION TEACHERS 422
    FORMER TEACHERS 424
    GEOGRAPHY TEACHERS 425
    GIFTED TEACHERS 424
    HISTORY TEACHERS 425
    HOME ECONOMICS TEACHERS 425
    ITINERANT TEACHERS 424
    LANGUAGE TEACHERS 425
    MASTER TEACHERS 426
    MATHEMATICS TEACHERS 425
    METHODS TEACHERS 426
    MINORITY GROUP TEACHERS 424
    MUSIC TEACHERS 425
    PART TIME TEACHERS 424
    PREPRIMARY TEACHERS 421
    PRIMARY SCHOOL TEACHERS 421
    PRIVATE SCHOOL TEACHERS 423

TEACHERS
- PUBLIC SCHOOL TEACHERS 423
- REMEDIAL TEACHERS 426
- RESOURCE TEACHERS 426
- RURAL SCHOOL TEACHERS 421
- SCIENCE TEACHERS 425
- SECONDARY SCHOOL TEACHERS 421
- SPECIAL EDUCATION TEACHERS 421
- STUDENT TEACHERS 424
- SUBSTITUTE TEACHERS 424
- TEACHERS 421
- TEACHERS COLLEGES 307
- TELEVISION TEACHERS 426
- UNIVERSITY EXTENSION TEACHERS 422
- VOCATIONAL AGRICULTURE TEACHERS 425
- VOCATIONAL EDUCATION TEACHERS 425
- WOMEN TEACHERS 421

TEACHING
- ADULT TEACHING 352
- CONCEPT TEACHING 350
- CREATIVE TEACHING 350
- CROSS AGE TEACHING 350
- DEPARTMENTAL TEACHING PLANS 340
- DIAGNOSTIC TEACHING 350
- DIRECT TEACHING 352
- DISCUSSION (TEACHING TECHNIQUE) 356
- DISTANCE TEACHING 352
- DISTANCE TEACHING INSTITUTIONS 311
- EXPERIMENTAL TEACHING 282
- INITIAL TEACHING ALPHABET 661
- MULTIPLE CLASS TEACHING 340
- OUTDOOR TEACHING AREAS 711
- PEER TEACHING 350
- PRACTICE TEACHING 690
- PRINCIPLES OF TEACHING 690
- SCIENCE TEACHING CENTRES 312

TEACHING
- TEACHING 350
- TEACHING ASSIGNMENTS 356
- TEACHING ASSISTANTS 424
- TEACHING CONDITIONS 212
- TEACHING EXPERIENCE 690
- TEACHING GUIDE 880
- TEACHING LOAD 265
- TEACHING MACHINES 731
- TEACHING METHODS 355
- TEACHING PERSONNEL 424
- TEACHING PROCEDURES 356
- TEACHING QUALITY 212
- TEACHING SKILLS 533
- TEACHING STYLES 356
- TEACHING TECHNIQUES 356
- TEACHING UNITS 356
- TEAM LEADER (TEACHING) 426
- TEAM TEACHING 350

TEAM
- TEAM LEADER (TEACHING) 426
- TEAM TEACHING 350
- TEAM TRAINING 351

TEAMWORK
- TEAMWORK 554

TECHNICAL
- TECHNICAL ASSISTANCE 106
- TECHNICAL COLLEGES 307
- TECHNICAL DRAWING 647
- TECHNICAL EDUCATION 183
- TECHNICAL SECONDARY SCHOOLS 306

TECHNICIANS
- AGRICULTURAL TECHNICIANS 452
- ELECTRONIC TECHNICIANS 452
- ENGINEERING TECHNICIANS 452
- TECHNICIANS 452

TECHNIQUE
- DISCUSSION (TEACHING TECHNIQUE) 356

TECHNIQUES
- CLASSROOM TECHNIQUES 356
- LABORATORY TECHNIQUES 671
- MEASUREMENT TECHNIQUES 391

TECHNIQUES
  QUESTIONING TECHNIQUES 356
  SOCIOMETRIC TECHNIQUES 283
  TEACHING TECHNIQUES 356
  TRAINING TECHNIQUES 356
TECHNOLOGICAL
  TECHNOLOGICAL ADVANCEMENT 140
TECHNOLOGIES
  INTERMEDIATE TECHNOLOGIES 360
TECHNOLOGY
  AVIATION TECHNOLOGY 645
  EDUCATIONAL TECHNOLOGY 360
  ELECTROMECHANICAL TECHNOLOGY 645
  ENGINEERING TECHNOLOGY 645
  INDUSTRIAL TECHNOLOGY 645
  MEDIA TECHNOLOGY 140
  RADIO TECHNOLOGY 645
  TECHNOLOGY 140
TELECOMMUNICATION
  TELECOMMUNICATION 145
TELEGRAPHIC
  TELEGRAPHIC MATERIALS 725
TELEPHONE
  TELEPHONE INSTRUCTION 360
TELEVISION
  CLOSED CIRCUIT TELEVISION 360
  EDUCATIONAL TELEVISION 360
  INSTRUCTIONAL TELEVISION 360
  TELEVISION 145
  TELEVISION TEACHERS 426
  TELEVISION VIEWING 360
TELLING
  STORY TELLING 663
TENURE
  JOB TENURE 153
  TENURE 222
TERM
  SHORT TERM MEMORY 521

TERMINAL
  TERMINAL EDUCATION 184
TERRITORIES
  ATLANTIC OCEAN TERRITORIES 801
  INDIAN OCEAN TERRITORIES 801
TEST
  TEST CONSTRUCTION 392
  TEST RESULTS 392
TESTING
  EDUCATIONAL TESTING 391
  PSYCHOLOGICAL TESTING 391
  TESTING 391
TESTS
  ACHIEVEMENT TESTS 393
  APTITUDE TESTS 393
  AUDIOVISUAL TESTS 393
  CRITERION REFERENCED TESTS 392
  DIAGNOSTIC TESTS 392
  EDUCATIONAL TESTS 392
  ESSAY TESTS 392
  INTELLIGENCE TESTS 394
  INTEREST TESTS 393
  LANGUAGE TESTS 393
  LITERACY TESTS 393
  MENTAL TESTS 394
  MULTIPLE CHOICE TESTS 392
  OBJECTIVE TESTS 392
  PERFORMANCE TESTS 393
  PERSONALITY TESTS 394
  PROGNOSTIC TESTS 392
  PROJECTIVE TESTS 394
  PSYCHOLOGICAL TESTS 392
  READING TESTS 393
  SCIENCE TESTS 393
  STANDARDIZED TESTS 392
  TESTS OF SIGNIFICANCE 284
  VERBAL TESTS 393
TEXTBOOK
  SUPPLEMENTARY TEXTBOOK 880
  TEXTBOOK 880
  TEXTBOOK AUTHORIZATION 213
  TEXTBOOK CONTENT 331
  TEXTBOOK SHORTAGE 205
TEXTILE
  TEXTILE INDUSTRY 150
  TEXTILE WORKERS 451

THAILAND
    THAILAND 804
THEATRE
    THEATRE ARTS 610
THEATRES
    THEATRES 310
THEMATIC
    THEMATIC APPROACH 331
THEOLOGICAL
    THEOLOGICAL EDUCATION 681
THEORIES
    BEHAVIOUR THEORIES 560
    EDUCATIONAL THEORIES 180
    GUIDANCE THEORIES 211
    LEARNING THEORIES 513
    PERSONALITY THEORIES 555
    POLITICAL THEORIES 101
    THEORIES 522
THEORY
    INFORMATION THEORY 204
    LINGUISTIC THEORY 621
    MEDIATION THEORY 511
    ROLE THEORY 553
    TRANSFORMATION THEORY (LANGUAGE) 622
THERAPISTS
    HEARING THERAPISTS 432
    OCCUPATIONAL THERAPISTS 432
    PHYSICAL THERAPISTS 432
    SPEECH THERAPISTS 432
    THERAPISTS 432
THERAPY
    HEARING THERAPY 373
    SPEECH THERAPY 373
    THERAPY 373
THERMAL
    THERMAL COMFORT 252
THESES
    DOCTORAL THESES 721
    MASTER THESES 721
THINKING
    CREATIVE THINKING 521
    CRITICAL THINKING 521
    LOGICAL THINKING 521
    PRODUCTIVE THINKING 521
THOUGHT
    THOUGHT PROCESSES 521
TIBETAN
    SINO TIBETAN LANGUAGES 625

TIME
    ANCIENT TIME 840
    DAY TIME PROGRAMMES 321
    FULL TIME EDUCATION 184
    FULL TIME EDUCATORS 424
    FULL TIME EMPLOYMENT 222
    FULL TIME STUDENTS 410
    FULL TIME TRAINING 351
    PART TIME EDUCATION 184
    PART TIME EDUCATORS 424
    PART TIME EMPLOYMENT 222
    PART TIME STUDENTS 410
    PART TIME TEACHERS 424
    PART TIME TRAINING 351
    REACTION TIME 511
    RELEASED TIME 222
    TIME FACTORS (LEARNING) 511
    TIME SHARING 284
TIMES
    MODERN TIMES 840
TIMETABLES
    TIMETABLES 340
TIMETABLING
    FLEXIBLE TIMETABLING 340
TIMOR
    PORTUGUESE TIMOR 804
TITLES
    DEGREES (TITLES) 390
TOBAGO
    TRINIDAD AND TOBAGO 803
TOGO
    TOGO 802
TOKELAU
    TOKELAU ISLANDS 806
TOME
    SAO TOME AND PRINCIPE 802
TONGA
    TONGA 806
TONGUE
    MOTHER TONGUE 131
    MOTHER TONGUE INSTRUCTION 662
TOOLS
    HAND TOOLS 742
    MACHINE TOOLS 742
TOURISM
    TOURISM 145
TOURS
    STUDY TOURS 335
TOYS
    TOYS 741

TRADE
    TRADE UNIONS 125
TRADES
    BUILDING TRADES 155
TRADITIONAL
    TRADITIONAL EDUCATION 180
    TRADITIONAL GRAMMAR 622
TRAFFIC
    TRAFFIC SAFETY 264
TRAINEES
    TRAINEES 410
TRAINERS
    TRAINERS 421
TRAINING
    ACCELERATED VOCATIONAL TRAINING 351
    AGRICULTURAL TRAINING 673
    BASIC TRAINING 351
    COUNSELLOR TRAINING 681
    FULL TIME TRAINING 351
    FURTHER TRAINING 351
    GROUP TRAINING CENTRES 311
    INDUCTION TRAINING 351
    LABORATORY TRAINING 352
    LEADERSHIP TRAINING 681
    LIBRARY SCIENCE TRAINING 681
    MILITARY TRAINING 351
    MODULAR TRAINING 351
    OFF THE JOB TRAINING 351
    ON THE JOB TRAINING 351
    PART TIME TRAINING 351
    PROJECT TRAINING METHODS 673
    REFRESHER TRAINING 333
    SENSORY TRAINING 351
    TEACHER TRAINING SCHOOLS 690
    TEAM TRAINING 351
    TRAINING 351
    TRAINING ALLOWANCES 242
    TRAINING BY STAGES 351
    TRAINING OBJECTIVES 300
    TRAINING PROGRAMMES 351
    TRAINING TECHNIQUES 356
    TRANSFER OF TRAINING 511
    VOCATIONAL TRAINING 351
    VOCATIONAL TRAINING CENTRES 306

TRAINING
    VOCATIONAL TRAINING PROGRAMMES 321
    VOCATIONAL TRAINING TAXES 240
TRAITS
    CULTURAL TRAITS 561
    WORKER TRAITS 561
TRANSACTIONAL
    TRANSACTIONAL ANALYSIS 352
TRANSFER
    STUDENT TRANSFER 266
    TEACHER TRANSFER 223
    TRANSFER CLASSES 343
    TRANSFER OF TRAINING 511
    TRANSFER POLICY 200
    TRANSFER STUDENTS 411
TRANSFORMATION
    TRANSFORMATION THEORY (LANGUAGE) 622
TRANSLATION
    TRANSLATION 620
TRANSMISSION
    KNOWLEDGE TRANSMISSION 512
TRANSPARENCIES
    TRANSPARENCIES 730
TRANSPORT
    TRANSPORT WORKERS 451
TRANSPORTATION
    TRANSPORTATION 264
TRAVEL
    TRAVEL 145
TREATMENT
    MEDICAL TREATMENT 373
TRENDS
    EDUCATIONAL DEVELOPMENT TRENDS 182
    EDUCATIONAL POLICY TRENDS 182
    ENROLMENT TRENDS 206
    POPULATION TRENDS 124
TRIBES
    TRIBES 122
TRINIDAD
    TRINIDAD AND TOBAGO 803
TRIPS
    INSTRUCTIONAL TRIPS 381
TRUANCY
    TRUANCY 267

TRUST
    FUNDS IN TRUST 240
TRUSTEESHIP
    TRUSTEESHIP COUNCIL 850
TUAMOTU
    TUAMOTU ISLANDS 806
TUBUAI
    TUBUAI ISLANDS 806
TUITION
    CORRESPONDENCE TUITION 335
TUNISIA
    TUNISIA 807
TURKEY
    TURKEY 805
TURKS
    TURKS AND CAICOS ISLANDS 803
TURNOVER
    STUDENT TURNOVER 206
TUTORING
    TUTORING 355
TWENTIETH
    TWENTIETH CENTURY 840
TWENTY
    TWENTY FIRST CENTURY 840
TWINS
    TWINS 401
TYPE
    INSTITUTE TYPE COURSES 334
    LARGE TYPE MATERIALS 734
TYPOLOGY
    LANGUAGE TYPOLOGY 621
UGANDA
    UGANDA 802
UIEH
    UIEH 851
UK
    UK 805
    VIRGIN ISLANDS (UK) 803
UKRAINIAN
    UKRAINIAN SSR 805
UN
    UN 850
UNDERACHIEVERS
    UNDERACHIEVERS
UNDEREMPLOYED
    UNDEREMPLOYED 450
UNDEREMPLOYMENT
    UNDEREMPLOYMENT 154

UNDERGRADUATE
    UNDERGRADUATE STUDY 330
UNDERSTANDING
    INTERNATIONAL UNDERSTANDING 101
UNDP
    UNDP 850
UNEDBAS
    UNEDBAS 851
UNEMPLOYED
    UNEMPLOYED 450
    UNEMPLOYED EDUCATION PROGRAMMES 321
UNEMPLOYMENT
    EDUCATED UNEMPLOYMENT 154
    UNEMPLOYMENT 154
    YOUTH UNEMPLOYMENT 154
UNEP
    UNEP 850
UNESCO
    ASSOCIATED SCHOOLS (UNESCO) 305
    NATIONAL COMMISSION FOR UNESCO 860
    UNESCO 850
    UNESCO EDUCATION SECTOR 851
    UNESCO EXECUTIVE BOARD 851
    UNESCO GENERAL CONFERENCE 851
    UNESCO SECRETARIAT 851
UNFPA
    UNFPA 850
UNHCR
    UNHCR 850
UNICEF
    UNICEF 850
UNIDO
    UNIDO 850
UNILINGUAL
    UNILINGUAL STUDENTS 414
UNION
    UNION MEMBERS 450
UNIONS
    TRADE UNIONS 125
UNISIST
    UNISIST 851
UNIT
    FAMILY (SOCIOLOGICAL UNIT) 126

UNIT
    UNIT COSTS 243
UNITAR
    UNITAR 850
UNITED
    UNITED ARAB EMIRATES 807
UNITS
    INTERMEDIATE ADMINISTRATIVE UNITS 261
    RESEARCH AND INSTRUCTION UNITS 340
    RESEARCH COORDINATING UNITS 261
    TEACHING UNITS 356
    UNITS OF STUDY (SUBJECT FIELDS) 331
UNITY
    GROUP UNITY 122
UNIVERSAL
    UNIVERSAL EDUCATION 180
UNIVERSITIES
    UNIVERSITIES 187
UNIVERSITY
    UNIVERSITY EXTENSION 382
    UNIVERSITY EXTENSION DEPARTMENTS 307
    UNIVERSITY EXTENSION PROGRAMMES 321
    UNIVERSITY EXTENSION TEACHERS 422
UNREST
    STUDENT UNREST 380
UNRISD
    UNRISD 850
UNRWA
    UNRWA 850
UNSKILLED
    UNSKILLED OCCUPATIONS 155
    UNSKILLED WORKERS 451
UNU
    UNU 850
UNWRITTEN
    UNWRITTEN LANGUAGES 621
UPBRINGING
    UPBRINGING 180
UPPER
    UPPER CLASS 121
    UPPER SECONDARY EDUCATION 185
    UPPER SECONDARY SCHOOLS 301
    UPPER VOLTA 802
URALIC
    URALIC ALTAIC LANGUAGES 625
URBAN
    RURAL URBAN DIFFERENCES 122
    URBAN AREAS 122
    URBAN CULTURE 130
    URBAN EDUCATION 186
    URBAN EXTENSION 382
    URBAN IMMIGRATION 124
    URBAN POPULATION 124
    URBAN SCHOOLS 303
    URBAN YOUTH 400
URBANIZATION
    URBANIZATION 122
URUGUAY
    URUGUAY 803
USA
    USA 803
    VIRGIN ISLANDS (USA) 803
USAGE
    LANGUAGE USAGE 131
USE
    BUILDING USE 251
USER
    USER GROUPS 443
USSR
    USSR 805
UTILIZATION
    INFORMATION UTILIZATION 204
    RESEARCH UTILIZATION 204
VACATION
    VACATION COURSES 334
VACATIONS
    VACATIONS 344
VALIDITY
    VALIDITY 283
VALUES
    MORAL VALUES 555
    VALUES 555
VANUATU
    VANUATU 806
VEHICLE
    MOTOR VEHICLE INDUSTRY 150
VEHICLES
    MOTOR VEHICLES 743

VENEZUELA
   VENEZUELA 803
VERBAL
   VERBAL COMMUNICATION 662
   VERBAL LEARNING 512
   VERBAL TESTS 393
VERDE
   CAPE VERDE 808
VERTICAL
   VERTICAL INTEGRATION (LEARNING) 514
VETERINARIANS
   VETERINARIANS 433
VIDEO
   VIDEO TAPE RECORDINGS 732
VIET
   VIET NAM SR 804
VIEWING
   TELEVISION VIEWING 360
VINCENT
   SAINT VINCENT 803
VIRGIN
   VIRGIN ISLANDS (UK) 803
   VIRGIN ISLANDS (USA) 803
VISUAL
   VISUAL HANDICAPS 571
   VISUAL LEARNING 512
   VISUAL PERCEPTION 510
   VISUAL STIMULI 510
VISUALIZATION
   VISUALIZATION 521
VOCABULARY
   SIGHT VOCABULARY 620
   VOCABULARY 620
   VOCABULARY DEVELOPMENT 534
VOCATIONAL
   ACCELERATED VOCATIONAL TRAINING 351
   NON VOCATIONAL COURSES 333
   VOCATIONAL ADJUSTMENT 551
   VOCATIONAL AGRICULTURE TEACHERS 425
   VOCATIONAL APTITUDES 520
   VOCATIONAL DEVELOPMENT 534
   VOCATIONAL EDUCATION 183

VOCATIONAL
   VOCATIONAL EDUCATION TEACHERS 425
   VOCATIONAL GUIDANCE 211
   VOCATIONAL INTERESTS 541
   VOCATIONAL MATURITY 531
   VOCATIONAL REHABILITATION 373
   VOCATIONAL SCHOOL CERTIFICATES 390
   VOCATIONAL SCHOOL CURRICULUM 330
   VOCATIONAL SCHOOLS 306
   VOCATIONAL SECONDARY SCHOOLS 306
   VOCATIONAL TRAINING 351
   VOCATIONAL TRAINING CENTRES 306
   VOCATIONAL TRAINING PROGRAMMES 321
   VOCATIONAL TRAINING TAXES 240
VOLTA
   UPPER VOLTA 802
VOLUNTARILY
   VOLUNTARILY PROVIDED ADULT EDUCATION 187
VOLUNTARY
   VOLUNTARY EDUCATION 180
   VOLUNTARY ORGANIZATIONS 110
   VOLUNTARY SERVICES 154
VOLUNTEERS
   VOLUNTEERS 440
VOTING
   VOTING 102
VOUCHERS
   EDUCATIONAL VOUCHERS 242
WAKE
   WAKE ISLANDS 806
WALLIS
   WALLIS AND FUTUNA ISLANDS 806
WASTAGE
   EDUCATIONAL WASTAGE 205
WCC
   WCC 853
WCOTP
   WCOTP 853
WEEKEND
   WEEKEND SCHOOLS 303

WEIGHT
    BODY WEIGHT 502
WELFARE
    CHILD WELFARE 100
    SOCIAL WELFARE 100
    STUDENT WELFARE 200
    TEACHER WELFARE 200
    WELFARE 100
    WELFARE AGENCIES 103
    WELFARE PROBLEMS 281
    WELFARE SERVICES 107
    YOUTH WELFARE 100
WEST
    WEST AFRICA 801
WESTERN
    WESTERN EUROPE 801
    WESTERN HEMISPHERE 801
    WESTERN SAHARA 801
WFP
    WFP
WHO
    WHO 850
WOMEN
    MARRIED WOMEN
        RETURNERS 451
    WOMEN 443
    WOMEN PROFESSORS 422
    WOMEN TEACHERS 421
    WOMEN WORKERS 451
WOMENS
    WOMENS EDUCATION 180
WOODWORKERS
    WOODWORKERS 451
WOODWORKING
    WOODWORKING 647
WORD
    WORD FREQUENCY 620
    WORD LISTS 721
WORK
    EDUCATION WORK
        RELATIONSHIP 182
    SOCIAL WORK 120
    WORK ATTITUDES 552
    WORK EDUCATION 682
    WORK ENVIRONMENT 550
    WORK EXPERIENCE 562
    WORK EXPERIENCE
        PROGRAMMES 673
WORKER
    FOREIGN WORKER
        EDUCATION 186
    WORKER TRAITS 561

WORKERS
    ADMINISTRATIVE WORKERS
        451
    AGRICULTURAL WORKERS
        451
    CHEMICAL WORKERS 451
    CHILD CARE WORKERS 430
    CLERICAL WORKERS 451
    CLOTHING WORKERS 451
    COMMERCIAL WORKERS 451
    CONSTRUCTION WORKERS
        451
    DISTRIBUTIVE WORKERS 451
    FOOD INDUSTRY WORKERS
        451
    FOREIGN WORKERS 470
    FORESTRY WORKERS 451
    HOTEL WORKERS 451
    LITERACY WORKERS 424
    MANUAL WORKERS 451
    NONMANUAL WORKERS 451
    PETROLEUM WORKERS 451
    PLANTATION WORKERS 451
    PRINTING WORKERS 451
    PRODUCTION WORKERS 451
    RAILWAY WORKERS 451
    SEASONAL WORKERS 451
    SEMISKILLED WORKERS 451
    SERVICE WORKERS 451
    SKILLED WORKERS 451
    SOCIAL WORKERS 462
    TEXTILE WORKERS 451
    TRANSPORT WORKERS 451
    UNSKILLED WORKERS 451
    WOMEN WORKERS 451
    WORKERS 451
    WORKERS EDUCATION 186
WORKING
    WORKING CLASS 121
    WORKING CLASS PARENTS
        401
    WORKING CONDITIONS 153
    WORKING HOURS 153
    WORKING LIFE 154
    WORKING PARENTS 401
WORKSHOPS
    DRAMA WORKSHOPS 381
    WORKSHOPS 742
WORLD
    WORLD HISTORY 641
    WORLD LITERATURE 615
    WORLD PROBLEMS 101

WRITING
    WRITING 620
YEAR
    EXTENDED SCHOOL YEAR 344
    YEAR ROUND SCHOOLS 303
YEARBOOK
    YEARBOOK 880
YEMEN
    DEMOCRATIC YEMEN 807
    YEMEN 807
YOUNG
    YOUNG ADULTS 400
YOUTH
    OUT OF SCHOOL YOUTH 412
    RURAL YOUTH 400
    URBAN YOUTH 400
    YOUTH 400
    YOUTH AGENCIES 103
    YOUTH CLUBS 381
    YOUTH LEADERS 440
    YOUTH OPPORTUNITIES 100
    YOUTH ORGANIZATIONS 110
    YOUTH PROBLEMS 572
    YOUTH PROGRAMMES 381
    YOUTH SERVICES 107
    YOUTH UNEMPLOYMENT 154
    YOUTH WELFARE 100
YUGOSLAVIA
    YUGOSLAVIA 805
ZAIRE
    ZAIRE 802
ZAMBIA
    ZAMBIA 802
ZEALAND
    NEW ZEALAND 806
ZIMBABWE
    ZIMBABWE 802
ZONE
    PANAMA CANAL ZONE 803
ZOOLOGY
    ZOOLOGY 632